CISTERCIAN STUDIES SERIES : NUMBER EIGHTY-THREE

# SERVING GOD FIRST

*Insights on* The Rule of St Benedict

*by*

*Dom Sighard Kleiner*
*Abbot-General of the Order of Cîteaux*

*Translated from the French by*
*James Scharinger*

CISTERCIAN PUBLICATIONS
KALAMAZOO, MICHIGAN
1985

First published as *Dieu premier servi* by Éditions P. Tequi,
Paris, 1974

Available in Europe and Britain from
A. R. Mowbray & Co Ltd    St Thomas House
Becket Street    Oxford OX1 1SJ

Available elsewhere from the publisher
Cistercian Publications
WMU Station
Kalamazoo, Michigan 49008

*The work of Cistercian Publications is made possible in part
by support from Western Michigan University*

*Typeset by Gale Akins, Kalamazoo*
*Printed in the United States of America*

Library of Congress Number 84-21476
BX 3004.Z 5KS 313
ISBN: 0 87907 883 9

# TABLE OF CONTENTS

vi

*To my parents, who showed me the only way—Jesus Christ*

Saint Benedict, come back to help us rediscover our personal life, that personal life for which we thirst, that life which the development of modern life with its exasperated desire for being ourselves stifles at the same time it awakens it and frustrates at the same it makes us aware of it. And it is this thirst for a true personal life which preserves the full reality of the monastic ideal.

Pope Paul VI

Monte Cassino
24 October 1964

# TRANSLATOR'S NOTE

Translating Dom Sighard Kleiner's *Dieu premier servi* has been a pleasure and a privilege. When I first read the book, I was so impressed by it that I went to Father Blaise Fuez, Prior of the Abbey of Spring Bank, to tell him how much I thought of it. On this occasion, Fr Blaise mentioned that the book really should be translated into English. Somewhat later I mentioned the possibility of translating the book to Fr Odo Egres of Our Lady of Dallas Abbey. Surely, I thought, among the learned professors of that community, there must be someone who might undertake this work! Fr Odo, however, surprised me by saying, 'Why don't you do it?'

That was the beginning of this translation. After telling Fr Blaise about my conversation with Fr Odo, I was encouraged to go ahead with the work. Dom Sighard Kleiner himself also encouraged me in my work and found time in his busy schedule to write numerous letters to me and thus to show a fatherly interest in my work.

Father he is! Not only is he my abbot general, but I have the joy of being affiliated, as oblate and *familiaris*, with the Cistercian community of Hauterive in Switzerland, the community he brought into being and fathered as its first superior. It is my sincere hope that through this translation, many more readers will come to appreciate, as I have, the fatherly wisdom of the man I am proud to own as my spiritual father and *abba*.

J.G.S.

6 August 1984
Feast of the Transfiguration of Our Lord

# FOREWORD

SERVE GOD FIRST: there is here a norm, a measure, a hierarchy of values. It appears to be beyond question, yet it is not easy. We hear about the human crisis nowadays. A crisis is a reversal of values and criteria. Man has always had the tendency to want to be served first, but the formulation of a theory, a doctrine of self-service, has been reserved to our own day. An immense process of secularization is under way when God, having become an embarassment to man, is sent away to heaven's furthest corner, when indeed, he be not proclaimed dead. The world turns in upon itself and cuts itself off from God. In the past, secondary causes have sometimes been ignored; today the Primary Cause no longer counts. For many, religion has become a holiday ornament or a last resort against tragedy. Nothing remains of it in daily life, clinically purified as it is of the slightest practical faith. Man looks after himself, and religion becomes folklore or a refuge for those in trouble.

Now, religion is specifically the service of God. Serve God? Love God, yes; but serve? The word makes us uneasy. Yet we accept service to our brothers. Brotherhood is the religion of our times. 'Everything for man' is a slogan which pleases businessmen. Yet God, amazingly, has willed to adapt himself to that solidarity limited to man. In his Son, he became our brother. He came not to be served, but to serve. Having entered on an equal footing into human psychology, he made himself the servant of our salvation, our wellbeing.

He did all this, however, not to put man in God's place, but to introduce God among men, and to make us understand that we cannot establish durable fraternal relationships among ourselves without a Father who makes us brothers, who puts these relationships in order and gives us the Spirit of brotherhood: his Spirit. This Father is the God of justice, of love, of peace. It is through him that we are brothers.

3

To serve man well, then, we must know how to serve God. Where God is served first, man is served well. In reality, there is nothing more demanding, more absorbing, often more difficult than to serve man as he is. To be able to serve takes a good dose of self-forgetfulness. Jesus Christ teaches us this by making himself the servant of our well-being; in serving us, he did not turn his gaze away from his Father, because in giving himself to us, he served, obeyed, and loved his Father. Serving his brothers was for him the same as serving his Father. Besides, if man were to be served first, a thousand unanswered questions would immediately arise: who ought to be the first served? How and by whom ought man to be served in the first place? Ought the weak to serve the strong? Ought the strong to serve the weak? We are familiar with these questions.

To serve God first is to assure that man will truly be served, not according to beautiful theories which suppose him to be naturally good, or which impose a so-called universal brotherhood among the privileged while sacrificing others, but according to the divine plan whereby God is the Father of all without discrimination.

This is precisely the image which the Rule of St Benedict suggests. It is a rule of service to God and to one's brothers. From morning until evening, the monk is in service. On entering the monastic life, he learns to recognize 'the duties of his service' (RB 49:5). This is first of all the *Opus Dei* (RB 16:2, 50:4), but also the full ascetical and community life of the monk (RB 49, 71, 72). At the 'school of the Lord's service' (Prol. 45), the monk learns that all the services he renders to his brother end in God, and that the Lord is always therefore served first.

Vigorously trained by the Rule to seek God in everything he does (RB 58:37), to have God always present (RB 7, 14, 23), to realize that he is continuously seen and observed by God (RB 4:49, 7:13), to think of him and to love him above all things (4:1), the monk lets himself be carried along the way on which he has set out by the Rule he observes, and so does not turn away from his orientation toward God, who becomes more and more the center of his thoughts.

Is this a diversion of human energies toward a God who has no need of the poor services man may render him, while our neighbor remains in trouble? This objection is justified by certain disorders. Some people accumulate riches very negligibly ordained to the glory of God, while at the same time the poor lack basic necessities. The true service of God, far from neglecting man, sees God in one's neighbor and serves God in him. It would be an illusion to want to go to God without passing through creatures. Christ will not receive us if we have not seen him in the hungry, the thirsty, the pilgrim, the poor, the sick, and the prisoner (cf. Mt 25:35ff.). St Benedict has given his Rule a strong Christocentric bent. The monk sees Christ in the abbot (RB 2:2, 63:13), and receives Christ in the guest (53:7), the poor, and the pilgrim (53:15); he serves Christ in the sick (36:1). He who serves his brother serves Christ, God. For the person who believes, there is no problem of precedence in this service. To serve God first means that if he does not serve his brother humbly and sincerely, God is not being served. On the other hand, he will not believe that he can create an excuse from serving God by serving men, especially when he chooses by his own whim those whom he claims to help.

The Rule of St Benedict is imbued with an extraordinary force for normalizing the relations between God and man, and between man and his fellow. It has a rare wholesomeness and capacity for giving man an equilibrium both psychic and physical by re-establishing in him right concepts and by ordering an hierarchy of value in him. There is in it no neurotic affirmation of the rights of man. Where God occuplies his true place, everything sorts itself out in the best way for man. The rights of man are assured where the rights of God are respected.

More than ever, people today live in insecurity. The sources of their ideas are troubled. An anguish without outlet seizes them. Strong personalities make fun of this anxiety; others battle against confusion, even against despair. The remedy is simple; for many it seems too simple: we must order our values. Moral and intellectual health are restored only by re-establishing the normal order of things. The first commandment for man is not to have false gods, to give God his place. By that very fact,  man finds his own place, and the rest follows. The Rule of St Benedict possesses this charism of setting a man forcefully and smoothly upon the right track, of assigning him his special place. In this way it renders him happy, balanced, healthy. The logic of the Rule begins with God, and anyone who seeks God will seek man as well.

This is the orientation of Jesus' life. All of his thoughts, his work, his aspirations were directed to the Father. 'I go to the Father' (Jn 14:12, 28). This is the direction of his life. Everything he did he did to orientate his disciples toward the Father and to give life to the world by rendering to God what is God's. Therein lies the entire theme of the Rule: 'That in all things God may be glorified' (RB 57:9).

# THE CULT

# OF THE RULE

Some people use the expression the 'cult' of the Rule—what does it mean? First of all, that we have for our Rule, for that little book crowned with such honor, all the respect due it. Many illustrious men knew it intimately. Is the Rule not one of the most celebrated documents of human thought for the person who seeks God? A rule for a holy and christian life for the Church? Finally, a creative force of true culture for Western society? The expression 'cult' of the Rule expresses first of all a veneration for its teaching, its orders and directives, and the fidelity of the disciple toward the basic Rule (RB 3:7). Does it not teach the monk a simple and sure route to God?

In view of the extraordinary moral authority of the Rule, it is necessary to define its limits exactly and measure its meaning. Let us admit at the outset that the cult of the Rule could lead us to attribute to it a role which it does not fit, for example, to esteem the letter at the expense of the spirit, or to give a disproportionate importance to details.

First of all, we cannot isolate the Rule, putting it, without realizing it, on the same level as the Gospel. The Rule has no value except in relation to the Word of God. It leads us to the Gospel (Prol. 21); it is an exposition of its message, a manual, a practical résumé, designed for the use of simple men wanting to be monks. It is, through its institutions, a permanent reference to the Gospel and to its summons to the Lord, which it translates into sound practices, wholly bathed in the humble search for God.

If the Rule is a law (RB 58:10), it is one only in order to turn the Gospel to profit (cf. Mt 5:17ff.). For 'the object of the law is Christ' (Rm 10:4). The law of the Gospel binds us to Christ: chains us to make us prisoners of Jesus Christ (cf. Eph 3:1). The yoke of the Rule (RB 58:16) has no other function than to submit us to the sweet yoke of Christ (cf. Mt 11:30). It is our Rule, the norm of our life. The mentality of St Benedict makes him express himself in the same way when he speaks to us of God's service, of the school to which he sends us for our apprenticeship in that service (cf. Prol. 45) through the imitation of Christ (cf. Prol. 50; 7:34).

The role of the Rule as a guide to lead us to the Gospel and to Christ is thus summarily characterized. The Rule is a norm which refers us, in accordance with what is said in the decree *Perfectae Caritatis* (cf. no. 2 a), to the supreme norm of all religious life: the imitation of Christ.

In this matter, St Benedict, following his predecessors, set himself a task both delicate and difficult: to gather the marrow of the Gospel and extract from it a concrete way of life for his monks. It was necessary not only that he not betray the Gospel in any way by commentaries which might filter out the divine Word, but he had also to transmit all its fullness, all its depth, so that the teaching of the Gospel 'might be spread like the leaven of divine justice in the hearts of his disciples' (cf. RB 2:5).

The high esteem which the Church has given the Rule by

irrefutable signs through the centuries testifies to the success of St Benedict. If, along with paternal gentleness, he shows himself very strict in his insistence on the observance of the Rule (cf. RB 3:7, 64:20), this apparent severity, far from obscuring the Gospel's primacy of charity, is but a very realistic manifestation of a love which knows how to support human weakness.

In this way, we avoid another possible danger in the 'cult of the Rule', that of giving an exaggerated importance to small details. The careful reader of the Rule draws from his meditations, the distinct impressions of a perfect and harmonious balance. Each detail remains in its proper place and never in the spotlight. The spirit, with its energetic and clear principles so predominates that no amount of insistence, however strong on particular points, changes St Benedict's intention as to the pastoral aim of the Rule: to lead the monk to Christ. The Rule fades away as soon as the end is obtained, as John the Baptist made way for Jesus. The ladder of humility is an example of this. The day when the monk, having climbed to the top, arrives at perfect charity, all that had to do with fear, that is to say, with the effort of climbing, will have had its day and can disappear. One can see there the provisional nature of everything that is only a means.

The Rule itself therefore has only a relative value. Yet all of its prescriptions do not have the same importance. The novice who still lacks perspective can in his first fervor attach too much importance to rules at the expense of the Rule, and may have trouble establishing a hierarchic order in its prescriptions. One day he will understand that certain superior rules take precedence over secondary ones, and he will also understand that it is through fidelity to the Rule that a certain number of its prescriptions have fallen into disuse and that, paradoxically, it is the Rule itself which has caused the suppression of certain minor usages it mentions. For it is thanks to the discretion, pastoral prudence, a certain pluralism, and above all, the principle according to which means ought to be directed toward the end which individuals, concretely placed in a determined context of time, place, and circumstances, propose to attain, that the Rule of St Benedict adapts itself to very different situations. In this it proves itself to be a masterpiece compiled by one of the most remarkable spirits of all humanity, assisted by Divine Wisdom.

In the course of these conferences there will be no dearth of occasions to go back over the values of the Rule briefly mentioned here by way of introduction.

# THE RULE TODAY

Is the Rule still timely? Can St Benedict, the patriarch of Western monks, the fifteenth centenary of whose birth we will soon [1980] be celebrating, still be listened to and understood by people who spontaneously believe that they surpass everything the preceding centuries were able to discover? This author of a famous Rule whose style, diction, syntax, and setting take us back to the sixth century, the very thought of which often reflects situations of another age, how can he pretend to be able to tell us anything? Could not men of our own times transmit the message to us far better? Why spend time with this document from another era, whose language is, at least at first glance, difficult for modern man to understand?

This book sets out to give good reasons for attaching ourselves to St Benedict. The Rule has no need of being reformed or reshaped to be up-to-date; quite simply, we must know how to read it, as an ancient book ought to be read in our day. Holy Scripture is not outdated simply because it is dressed in well-worn garments.

Some may object that the Rule is not an historical or didactic book like the Bible, but a law written in a concrete sociological context which no longer exists in our age of technology and urbanization where education is wide-spread and where secularism and existentialism are rife. Who can deny that the human situation in time and space, in relationships to the world and to fellowman and even, phenomenologically speaking, to God, have changed profoundly in fifteen hundred years? The one thing that has not changed essentially is the human person. He remains what he has always been, having come from the hands of his Maker and been deformed by sin. Methods of education may have changed, but the fundamental laws of man's education remain the same. The image of man seen by St Benedict corresponds to the reality of man as truly today as it did in the sixth century. We need only to separate this image from the context of an age now past for it to maintain its vital worth.

This book seeks to show, without apologetics or polemics, the present value of the Rule of St Benedict and why it is still up to date. We should remember that the Church to this day places this Rule among the books richest in salutary effects, recognizing also that for thousands of monks and nuns and for thousands of the faithful of benedictine spiritual orientation, it ponders the practical and concrete norm of the christian life. Might we not add to these the religious who, more recently, and under different forms have drawn and continue to draw from the pure fountain of the Rule? This fact alone proves that the great Legislator is still up to date, as he was during the grand flowering of Christianity and indeed during the ages when the monks, far from the world's hubbub and notice, prepared the coming of better days.

In this precise sense St Benedict is for us, as it were, a contemporary. Under his guidance the person of today, often profoundly uprooted and neurotic, can find healing. Fundamentally, St Benedict does nothing but lead us to the living waters of the Word of God by means of a wise pedagogy embracing, without constraint, the entire course of our life.

# THE CHARACTER OF THESE TALKS ON THE RULE

This way of looking at the Rule, and through it at the personality of St Benedict, determines the end, the style, and the character of these conferences. The Rule is a source of life for the monk and the nun today just as yesterday. It has not lost its relevance and can by itself alone direct their spirituality. This is what the author wants to show. Hence the pastoral style of this book, taken from conferences [informal talks] given for the most part to Cistercian nuns at the monastery of Sainte Marie de Boulaur dans le Gers, who helped prepare them for publication. One must not expect to find here a systematic, much less an historico-scientific, commentary on the Rule, although care for an authentic interpretation is at the base of the author's effort to bring out the thought of St Benedict and to encourage fidelity to the Rule. Thus citations from other commentators will not be found here, although the conferences which follow are in a general way indebted to all those who have applied themselves to the Rule, and have made use of all their knowledge, their insights, and their study. The question of the dependence of the Rule upon the *Regula Magistri*, which seems evident, is not dealt with except at certain places where the difference of the Rule's thought and its greater maturity shed a particularly strong light on the meaning of the text, or make it stand out more clearly. The style of these conferences causes some repetitions and digressions; it also means that some subjects mentioned in the Rule are omitted. The references are borrowed from the division of Hanslik, introduced after the style of Lentini, which has been adopted in recent editions of the Rule.

These conferences on the Rule then have an entirely practical aim, while remaining as faithful as possible to the thought of the Legislator. In accordance with his farsightedness and good sense, we must not take as eternal what is only contingent, but must try to draw from the contingent the intentions which transcend the time and place wherein they lie hidden. In this way we will not fall into the error of attributing absolute value to what is only relative, nor of dismissing whole chapters as medieval simply because the orders found there cannot be carried out to the letter today. Even if Jesus did tell his disciples to go and evangelize people without taking shoes along (Mt 10:10; Lk 10:4), it is obvious that this order ought not to be followed in every climate. A certain amount of relativity is inherent in every text, and it is the task of good hermeneutics to extricate the permanent meaning without change or mutilation.

May these conferences help to turn to profit the treasures of human and religious wisdom contained in the Rule: a little masterpiece ranked high among the most precious books of human literature. And may these pages, full of balm and life, guide those who, stimulated by a longing for eternal things, strive with all their hearts toward the heights of knowledge and virtue (RB 73:9).

# The Meaning of the Monastic Vocation

# THE MONASTIC VOCATION IN RELATION TO THE WORLD

The mysteries of the Ascension and of the descent of the Holy Spirit are intimately linked one to another. At his last meeting with his beloved disciples Jesus said to them: 'It is good for you that I go away; for if I do not go, the Paraclete will not come to you. But if I go, I will send him to you' (Jn 16:7). In other words: In order for you to be able to receive the Holy Spirit, I have to leave.

Let us put ourselves in the apostles' place. They were dedicated men, faithful to their Master, even fervent. But they were also fearful, timid men, perplexed by the task the Lord was preparing to confide to them: 'Go, preach, convert'. It was just when they had most need of him that the Lord said to them: 'I am going to the Father' (Jn 14:12). What a paradox, just at the moment when they would have liked to cry to him: 'Lord, don't leave us! Why do you abandon us? Why are you sending us into the world now? You know us well enough. You see we are incapable of doing anything worthwhile, and you go away?' If we meditate on the Saviour's words at the Last Supper, we are immediately struck by the objections of the disciples which appear at almost every phrase: 'Why are you leaving us?' And the answer which comes as an explanation is like a defense plea: 'I will not leave you orphans' (Jn 14:18). 'Let not your hearts be troubled' (Jn 14:1). How clearly we can imagine the disciples' arguments; 'Now you are leaving us orphans, you are leaving us to our own shortcomings, our poverty,'

15

and many other words of the same sort.

'If you loved me, you would rejoice that I am going to the Father' (Jn 14:18). Now you are in sorrow; you do not yet truly love me, otherwise you would rejoice with me over this return to my Father. And, to convince them completely, the added affirmation: 'I will send you the Holy Spirit. Wait in peace, in joy, with patience. Wait at Jerusalem until I send you the Holy Spirit.'

This attitude of the Saviour poses the same problem for us as well. Why is he going to the Father? Why doesn't the Lord, now that he has in his hands the magnificent argument of his resurrection, manifest himself to the world? He withdraws. He hides himself. He leaves. We would like to say to him: 'But Lord, You came to preach the Kingdom of God, to save men, to convert the world. Now that you have everything in your hands, now that all the doors are open to you, why are you leaving?' His very simple answer leaves in us in our perplexity: 'If you loved me, you would understand and you would rejoice that I go to the Father'.

In these words all the depth of the mystery comes to light. It is much better for you, for me, for the world, that I go to the Father, 'for the Father is greater than I' (Jn 14:28), the Father is greater than all the rest. The whole mystery lies there. To be near the Father, at the right hand of the Father —that is what the Son prefers to everything and what he judged better and more useful for us, for his work among us, the redemption of the world.

Shall it be the same for us? Shall we prefer being with the Father to remaining in the world? To stand before the Father, is this not how we define the monastic vocation? Our Lord has not left us in order to let the world take care of itself while he is near the Father. He has entered into the eternal tabernacle: He, the High Priest, to complete His sacrifice 'ever living to offer intercession on behalf' of those who are redeemed (Heb 7:25). He is always there before the Father, interceding for us, showing him the wounds of his passion, offering him his death, speaking as our ambassador. The Lord prefers that attitude, that position, to any other. So it is with our monastic vocation. People say to us too: 'Why do you withdraw from the world? Why do you hide yourself in a monastery, sheltered from difficulties? Behind those walls, you abandon the world to itself. Let poor humanity do as it will; you are at the right hand of the Father, *ad dexteram Patris.*'

These are the objections we hear.

All right! Let us answer first of all that this life is not comfortable. It is not easy to live at the right hand of the Father, and it is not necessary that it be so. Let us understand this. Our Lord left all the work of converting the world, of preaching the Kingdom of God, to his apostles; then he withdrew. Our own task, then, cannot be to live quietly, to seek calm and peace in the ordinary sense of these words. We do not enter the monastery in order to find an easy life, good companions always ready to wait on us, pleasant, and considerate on every occasion. We ought not to imagine that we have entered an earthly paradise nevermore to meet the troubles of the world. We ought not to believe that to live in community means to live always at peace and charity with everyone. It is necessary to stand in spirit at the right hand of the Father, that is to say, to pray without ceasing as Christ himself continues to plead for his brothers. We must show the Father the wounds on the body of His Son; to them our own wounds should be joined, the wounds of our passion. We must understand that we are here, not to be sheltered from suffering, but, on the contrary, to live the redemptive passion with Jesus so that the Father may see in us the victim of sacrifice offered for the peace of the world, for its conversion, for the salvation of souls.

Consequently, we should not imagine that everything should always go well in a monastery, that we have a right to outstanding superiors who have all of the qualities which agree with us in such a way that we feel at home, surrounded by our father and our mother, with brothers and sisters who are sincere and open, kind and obliging, overflowing with charity toward us. The Lord will not always permit us to find such conditions in the monastery. Must we then declare that we have entered a bad community? This may, as a matter of fact, be the case, but is not the important thing. I ought to believe that my vocation is precisely in the process of fulfilment in that community, that I am able to do my duty there, that I carry out my promise of profession there by accepting the conditions where I live, because that life will be my passion so united to the Passion and death of Our Lord, that I may be at the right hand of the Father, letting him see the force of my faith and of my charity for humankind, for my brothers, and especially for himself.

These are some of the characteristics of the monastic vocation. How could anyone say to us after this that we refuse to serve our brethren, that we are fleeing from the world, that we are hiding ourselves, that we are afraid of not being able to resist the world's seductions, that we are timid, lazy, and all the other arguments you are familiar with. No, it is not for this that we live in a monastery. At the beginning of our vocation, our reasons for entering the monastery were not very clear yet or mature, perhaps, and God called us through more or less natural motives. You see young people coming who are attracted by the liturgy, by the countryside around the monastery, by the atmosphere of the place. They are attracted by the friendliness of the brothers or sisters, and the idea of sharing their life comes to them; they enter, and once there, the period of probation begins. Then they begin to realize that the demands of the monastic life go far beyond what they had imagined. Then comes the moment for them to enter fully into the Lord's intentions and into his passion.

In no case is our monastic life an evasion, a flight from the world (*fuga mundi* in the bad sense of the word). It is a flight from the world in the sense of Our Lord's Ascension: 'I am going to the Father'. This is how we accept it, and we follow the Lord, in his footsteps, when we agree to follow him wherever he goes. In this way we are justified before the world, before ourselves, before the Father, and before the Lord. One day we may perhaps be tempted to ask ourselves: 'What am I doing here? I am wasting my time while my brothers in the world suffer and perhaps cry out for my presence as the apostles did for their Master: "You leave and abandon the world to its misery!" ' If we have received the vocation of 'going to the Father' by the secluded life which is the monastic life, it would be giving in to temptation if we allowed ourselves to be carried away by the idea that we have to help our brothers out there in the world. For us it would be a real evasion, the evasion of our specific vocation. It would not be apostolic zeal tormenting us, but the mistake of thinking that the Father wanted us someplace other than where He had called us. It might even include the subtle temptation of avoiding the sacrifices imposed by the monastic life.

Once we have made profession, we should map out our life according to the theological fact it represents; we should admit that the Lord has led us here, and that we are obliged to continue, looking neither right nor left, nor especially back, but going straight to him; and to go straight means always to go in the direction of our profession, of the promise we made. Neither should we be struck with the fear of having taken the wrong road by entering monastic life. Let us realize that our imagination never lacks the ability of furnishing us with arguments against what may at certain moments appear too difficult to us.

Yet one final word: the Holy Spirit will not be absent from our monastic passion. He will be its great fruit. Why? Because we call him down upon the world, and because the monk who prays without ceasing calls the Holy Spirit down upon suffering humanity that he might fill all the earth, every soul, and every heart. That is our great and magnificent mission.

# THE DIVINE CALL: THE MONK'S RESPONSE

The Lord wants to begin a conversation with us, says St Benedict, and he expects us to respond by our works to his holy lessons (Prol. 35). He invites us to 'Listen, my child'. *Obsculta, o fili* (Prol. 1). We hear that call throughout the whole prologue. The Lord is speaking; we ought then to listen. *Obsculta:* that word, so thought-provoking, placed at the beginning of the Rule, sets the tone. 'Listen, my child'. There the conversation begins. To help us understand, St Benedict insists that the Lord is at the door and comes to seek his worker. 'Today if you hear his voice . . . come, my children, listen to me' (1:10, 12). And next the parable of the vineyard: 'The Lord seeking his worker' (1:14), and then at last, this invitation: 'What could be sweeter to us than the voice of the Lord who invites us?' (1:19). 'He has invited us into his kingdom' (1:21).

Then the Lord waits for our reply. He waits patiently (Prol. 36).

It is interesting that St Benedict, like a good Roman, began his Rule with an *oratio*, an allocution constructed according to the rules of discourse. The Romans were great orators and classic latin literature has preserved for us some very beautiful examples of their eloquence. St Benedict imitates them, and his whole introductory discourse is constructed on the theme of God's invitation. God calls us, and as a result, we should and shall respond.

Now let us look at some phrases in the Prologue and note the steps in the dialogue which has begun. First of all, we are invited to take up arms; then we need to get up, to run: *exurgamus ergo* (Prol. 8). 'Run while you have the light of life' (Prol. 1.13). By these imperatives St Benedict pushes us energetically onwards. The Lord arrives at the marketplace to hire workers for his vineyard; he seeks, he inquires on the right and on the left. And if it is you who hear his request, if that call attracts you, you answer the invitation with 'I come' (1.16). See how alive and animated the picture is. The consequences of the agreement are immediate: 'Let us, therefore, gird our loins with faith and the performance of good works' in order to undertake our journey (1.21). For only by running by good works can we attain our goal (1.21). To this new and pressing invitation, the invited responds by a question: Lord, who should dwell in your house? And the Lord answers: He who agrees to satisfy the demands of the master of the house. What then are the conditions for entry? 'He who walks without blemish and does justice, he who speaks the truth in the depth of his heart, he who has not used his tongue for deceit, who has not done evil of his neighbor, nor listened to slander against him (25-27), someone, moreover, who knows how to defend himself against the temptations of the devil (28). Finally, it is those who are not puffed up by pride because of their careful observance, but who realize that the good that is in them comes from the Lord (29ff.). And the conversation continues. Knowing what we must do, we respond: *Correndum et agendum est*, it is necessary to run and to act (44). We accept the invitation.

At the end of the prologue, St Benedict explains to us, the workers set out on their journey. They enter the school of the Lord's service (45). And little by little, in proportion to their progress in faith, in works, in the religious life, their heart enlarges and they run in the ways of God's commandments with an unspeakable sweetness of love (49).

Notice what the prologue is: a call, a response, an agreement, a conversation. The whole Rule is based on this conversation, and so we can say that our entire life is this conversation. It does not end at the moment we set out to follow the Lord once he has called. No, the Lord says 'listen' to us all our lives. He enters into this dialogue each day. Beginning in the morning we hear him. 'If today you hear his voice, harden not your hearts' (20). We must answer to the grace of that call. Then, during the course of the day, the conversation continues. Our Lord is always there to call us, to help us, to invite us to see the beauty of our life's pathway. He is there to fill us with his joy and his grace, and to bless us in every way. Yes, he is continually entering into conversation with us. That 'Listen, my child', continues throughout our whole life. What should we do but listen? We have to learn to recognize the sweet voice of the Lord, to dispose ourselves to receive it, to accept it; and then, we must answer him in our own way. Today, because of fatigue, the answer may be a little weary; tomorrow it will be braver. But never let us give way to the temptation to remain silent; let us always answer him, bravely and thankfully each time he invites us. The voice of the Lord is sweet and insistent. He loves us.

Yes, God loves us. This is why St Benedict presents him in this dialogue with the monks as his children. From the beginning we are his children, called to hold that place. And so he says immediately: if you wish to hold the place of sons, in order to be sons of the Father, respond like a son, lest someday the Father get angry with an attitude which is not filial and treat us like a *servus nequissimus*, a very bad servant (7).

It is interesting to see how St Benedict, from the very beginning of the Rule, contrasts the son and the servant. It is a way of showing clearly that he does not want to present us as serfs. Does he not speak of the *servitium divinum*, of our divine service, of the *dominici schola servitii*, the school of the Lord's service (45)? In expressing himself this way, St Benedict does not want to hand us over to a new servitude, or inspire us with its spirit (cf. 7, 8:15). We are and are called sons. As a result, the dialogue that takes place is a dialogue between father and son. 'Listen, my child, and willingly receive the admonition of a loving Father (Prol. 1). We are also soldiers, laborers, disciples. Obedience makes us take up arms for Christ our King (3); we are laborers, who work in his vineyard (14), and finally, disciples in the school of the Lord's service (45). The Lord meets us in different ways so that we may answer him in the monastic life in the way that best corresponds to our personal character. The call of the Father to his son may be for us the determining form of our fidelity, or perhaps, we may love to fight as soldiers under the standard of the Rule. Or finally, perhaps our desire to labor in the vineyard of the Lord will shine out with all the tools that St Benedict puts at our disposal. The person who wishes to be a disciple will also feel at ease with the Rule. Each one sets to work according to his particular personality, and his response is in harmony with his personal aspirations.

May the Lord's invitation to 'Listen, my child,' always resound in our ears. May we learn to listen, and may this openness to God become an habitual attitude of our hearts.

# "LISTEN, MY CHILD"

'Listen, my child'. This command not only begins the Rule, but is its program. St Benedict borrowed his Prologue almost entirely from the *Regula Magistri*, but with this difference: he knows how to strike his disciple by means of a turn of phrase which is unique to him: *Obsculta, o fili*, 'listen, my child'. In this way, he underlines its existential importance.

This command is addressed to a son—notice that St Benedict uses the word son only two times, and then in citing Holy Scripture (RB 2:3, 29); otherwise he speaks to his 'brothers'—for to listen with that naive freedom of a childlike spirit, without thinking of oneself, is unique to a son; to listen to one another among brothers on an equal footing is a procedure which naturally implies a personal, responsible judgment on the acceptability of what is said. This attitude is typical of St Benedict. Whereas the Master demanded to be heard by his disciple without questioning, St Benedict is more subtle, and he leaves to the Lord his role of 'only Master' (Mt 23:8). The abbot, in the image of Christ, who is the first-born among his brothers (Rm 8:29), is rather his monks' elder brother. But, for all that, the *obsculta* does not lose its force. 'To listen' is the attitude of man before God. The monk especially ought to repeat: 'Speak, Lord, for your servant is listening (1 Sam 3:9ff.). The entire Rule is there to educate the monk to that attitude of listener, attentive to God, to make him understand what a privilege it is to be called to hear the voice of the Lord seeking his worker, and to answer him: 'Here I am' (Prol. 14-16). And in fact, from the Prologue on, St Benedict eloquently makes us understand that above all we must listen: 'Let us listen with attentive ears (Prol. 9) to the divine voice: 'Let him who has ears to hear, listen' (Prol. 11).

God speaks to us in different ways. He speaks to us through nature, through creation. The Divine Office can join together the triumphant chants of creation celebrating the glory of the Creator, and nature itself serves him with a powerful voice. He speaks to us through history, through the events and circumstances of our life. He speaks to us through our brothers, through our community; finally, he speaks to us in a very special way through his Church, and through the Holy Scriptures.

In the daily schedule, according to the season, St Benedict sets aside four hours or more for *lectio divina*, so that the monk may always have time to listen to the Lord. He recommends that he 'willingly lend an ear to holy readings' (4:55), and he even draws up a list of the most important books: in addition to the Holy Scriptures, which have 'divine authority', there are the books of the holy fathers of the catholic faith, the *Institutes* and *Conferences* of Cassian, the *Lives of the Fathers*, that is to say, the biographies of ancient monks known at his time, and finally, the *Rule of St Basil*. The *Regula Magistri* is never mentioned. These books can serve, if they are well heard and followed, as sure guides to the heights of perfection (73:2-6, cf. 42:3). If 'faith is born of preaching' (Rm 10:17), the impulse toward perfection ought also to come from the teaching of our holy masters.

Without any doubt, if St Benedict were writing his Rule today, he would enlarge this list to include other authors, perhaps, for example, St Teresa of Avila, St John of the Cross, St Francis de Sales, Dom Marmion and others. Here we can ask ourselves, people of the twentieth century, agitated and short of time, if we do not lack that capacity for long, peaceful reading; if so, the method for nourishing us spiritually ought to be made up of shorter and more frequent reading. *Obsculta*, listen. This is much more indispensable for us whom waves and invading images assail without respite and leave no leisure to perceive the sweet voice of the Truth; yet we must force ourselves to listen, to lend the ear of our hearts (Prol. 1).

*Obsculta:* listen! It is first of all an invitation to hear 'the precepts of the Master and the instructions of a father who is full of tenderness' (Prol. 1). The Rule itself is the principal object of that *Obsculta.* It is not an inspired work, but it is like a compendium of all the monastic doctrine up to that time, a synthesis of the wisdom of the ancients. It deserves the full respectful and obedient attention of those who attend his school. It is the mistress: the mistress who should be followed in all things (3:7). For, 'as the role of the master is to speak and to instruct, that of the disciple is to be silent and to listen' (6:6). St Benedict presents himself here as master and father, and in his person introduces the abbot whose duty it is to teach by word and example, so that his doctrine may penetrate 'the souls of his disciples like the leaven of divine justice' (2:5).

The monks should listen to the abbot's teaching them. Herein lies a problem. On the one hand there is the written Rule, a book; on the other hand, there is the abbot, the representative of the Rule, a living person toward which one has sympathies or antipathies, a relationship of understanding or contention, a guileless openness or prejudices. Here the *obsculta* makes its whole force and weight felt. If the monk is not able to listen with a religious respect, as a disciple, he builds a wall of misunderstandings, of quarrels, and of destructive criticism between himself and his abbot, making it impossible for him to speak in Christ's name and discouraging him, paralyzing the relationship. The monk is not obliged to listen to the words of his abbot without examination—our intellect is endowed with the power of discernment—yet he ought to reserve for them the reception due God's word. St Benedict does not hesitate to apply to the abbot the word of Christ spoken to the messengers of the Good News: 'He who hears you, hears me (RB 5:15). The monk should receive his abbot's teaching with a sincere, frank, and open receptiveness that will create between them a trusting and productive atmosphere, bringing about salvation.

We realize that listening is not a passive, indifferent, sceptical, or bored attitude. We have to act. The command 'listen' precedes another: 'Accomplish efficaciously' (Prol. 1). The monk does not enter a school of philosophers where each preserves his own freedom of action; he enters a school of divine service where obedience is the order of the day, for there one obeys God. Consequently there can be no hesitation there (5:13) once an order has been received—that order awaited with great attentiveness—thus 'the sound of the command is followed by such a prompt reply that . . . there is no interval between the order of the superior and the action of the disciple' (5:8ff.). This is why the ideas of 'listening' and 'obeying' seem sometimes to overlay the entire Rule (5:5; 43:1).

St Benedict wants us in learning to listen, to learn to discern the voice of God. Yes, we want to hear the Lord speak to us through the Holy Books, the teaching of the Fathers and doctors of the Church, through the wisdom of the ancients, and through the Rule. Doubtless we will have to apply the rules of hermeneutics to distinguish the voice of the Lord from what may be purely human and mutable. For it is Him whom we want to obey; we know that 'the obedience rendered to superiors refers to God' (5:15).

And, as a matter of fact, our deepest duty is to perceive the voice of God. Jesus promised to show Himself to the person who loves him (Jn 14:21). We have complete confidence in his promise, and that science which, going beyond its limits, wants to cut us off from all transcendence and denies what it cannot reach by its own means we find deceptive. The human soul feels within itself a deep and secret correspondence with the voice of God, Creator and Father, and God Himself has seen fit to confirm our hope by his Word; we have great need of receiving God's message, we who have no certainty of ourselves. Our intellect is made for thinking, for knowing, for discovering, for finding, but it needs the voice of God if it is not to stray from its proper destiny. God has endowed it with a supernatural sense to perceive truths which are beyond it.

The danger which lurks for a man is that he may limit himself to the realm of the senses. This danger is all the more serious today when the mind is assailed by an overwhelming amount of information, impressions, and images; they monopolize our attention and bar the way of any transcendence.

Do we, in view of this mounting tide of impressions—from the monk cannot entirely free himself—possess the necessary discipline of discernment which enables us to hold on to the useful and to leave aside the frivolous and the evil? Does not a dangerous curiosity too often become our criterion for acceptance?—or indeed, do we allow ourselves to make a hasty and superficial judgment on the suitableness of some study of knowledge? We listen, yes, but too often to what flatters nature, our egoistical, vain, and sensual tendencies. And so we stop up the interior ear, the ear of the heart (Prol. 1) and render it incapable of perceiving the words of the Lord. Or indeed we hear ourselves, we close ourselves in upon our own views and personal judgments and no longer pay attention to others. How many dialogues are in reality monologues, because by letting another speak without really following him, we develop within ourselves the course of our own thought? How can we be open to God when we are closed in on ourselves this way?

To know how to listen is then an art, it is the very beginning of the spiritual art. It is knowing how to discern, among all of the words that strike the ear of our heart, the Word of God, the Truth which makes us free and is our true happiness.

The importance of the rule of silence (42:9) becomes clear in this light. By not speaking, the monk learns little by little to silence the discordant voices of his senses, and so he better perceives the divine Word. According to the measure of his recollection, he discerns the voice of the One who lives in him and is introduced into the secret of God three and one, where the Father shows him his Son, the splendor of his majesty, and baptizes us in his Spirit. 'Is there anything sweeter for us, dear brothers, than this voice of the Lord which invites us?' cries St Benedict (Prol. 19).

Our spiritual life has need of the milk of reading; it will always have need of it. But, according to the masters of the spiritual life, there may come a moment when our reading and our meditation will hinder rather than help us, when every discursive thought will turn us away from what is most important, that is to say, from catching the voice of the Lord, or at least from giving him free rein in our hearts. That happy moment may arrive once the soul is already detached from the desires of this world, free of its own self and its own desires, once it begins to take pleasure in the things of God. The Lord then becomes active in the soul. This state of passivity is not idleness, but the beginning of contemplation. If from time to time the Lord wants to give the soul the grace of simple regard, perhaps only for brief moments, the soul keeps itself entirely at his disposal, fully obedient. Then she is able to grasp all of the depth of the Rule's invitation: *Obsculta, o fili!*

When St Benedict speaks of prayer made 'with fervor of heart' (52:4), does he not mean precisely that interior, silent prayer, which manifests itself through tears and fervor of spirit? We may suppose that St Benedict wanted, without speaking of his own 'mystical experiences', gently to lead his monks toward the attitude of perfect openness to the sanctifying will of the Lord. To lend the ear of the heart to the Lord is to offer it to him, to offer him our selves. If, having heard his call, we show ourselves generous (Prol. 16), he will not let himself be outdone in generosity and will answer: 'When you act like this, my eyes shall be upon you, my ears will hear your prayers, and even before you call upon Me, I will say: "Here I am"!' (Prol. 18).

# CHOOSING

St Ignatius, a former soldier, devised in his *Spiritual Exercises* a famous meditation on two standards. After mature deliberation, the Christian chooses the standard of Christ. The idea of enlisting in Christ's army is already found clearly outlined in the Rule (cf. Prol. 3, RB 2:20, 61:10) and it is drawn from Scripture.

Now, to enlist in an army supposes a decision, an option, a choice. In the context of the mercenary troops of former times and of the non-obligatory service of arms, the necessity of making a decision before enlisting appears clear. Enlisting in the army of those who fight the good fight (1 Tm 1:18) supposes, therefore, a choice, a decision. The responsibility for making a good choice, moreover has been inherent in human life since the days of Paradise. Adam found himself seduced by the serpent. Man's lot is to be engaged in the dialectic of alternatives. These are often indifferent. But every life has its crossroads at which one chooses orientations of great importance. Every life has choices of great importance on the moral, religious, and material planes which involve the persons's eternal future.

The goal proposed is what determines our life; it should be proportionate to our strength and our means. Pursued with courage and perseverance, it gives our character firmness, and our life enthusiasm; and if it is to find in its realization a fullness worthy of our best aspirations, we must make a good initial choice, with prudence, generosity, and a full consciousness of its implications. Our happiness depends on it, and happiness is found only in its accomplishments and its success. Our perseverance and the firmness of our action depends on this choice; for where it is poorly made, there is hesitation (27:3) and doubt; man is like a reed shaken by the wind (Lk 7:24). On it depends even our faith in the eternal values which we bear; for a bad choice centers our energies on objects unworthy of our vocation and we risk losing sight of the eternal values.

The Rule of St Benedict proposes a choice to us. It is a question of life or of death. Seeking in the crowd the person willing to enlist, the Lord offers him nothing less than life (Prol. 14ff.). Is it a small thing to receive a promise of life? 'And if you answer, "Here I am" (cf. Prol. 16), "give me Your life." He offers you nothing less than "true and eternal life" ' (Prol. 17). Is the opposite of life not death?

St Benedict sets before us a fundamental dilemma. The choice is inevitable; how could we not prefer life? But to choose life, he makes us understand, is to choose the means, to prefer the path of life (cf. Prol. 20) to the paths of death (7:21).

We admit that the means to attain eternal life proposed by St Benedict are not the only possible ones, but those who adopt them do so moved by the ardor of arriving there by the narrow way (5:10ff.). They choose the path of monastic life, of obedience, of renunciation, of chastity for the kingdom of heaven. Here is where we see the admirable psychology of St Benedict at work, a psychology dictated by faith which enables him to lead a person seeking the absolute yet exposed to a thousand dangers, to a conscious, joyous, firm, and a definitive choice.

He invites him first of all to listen, really to open the ear of his heart (Prol. 1). He knew full well how difficult it is to be heard by a person withdrawn into himself, always tempted to seek answers within himself and going around in circles. To encourage us to go out of ourselves, St Benedict tells us that the voice of the Lord, the voice which invites and calls us, is sweet and pleasant (Prol. 19), but at the same time ever more urgent. We hear him throughout the Prologue using the entire compass of persuasion to make us understand the necessity of decision, the apparent paradox of a God both loving and at the same time demanding, and finally the absolute primacy of the service of the Lord made possible by his grace.

The person who seeks life becomes a disciple by beginning to listen. He decides to enter the school of the Lord's service (Prol. 45). He makes this choice with trembling, afraid he may fail (Prol. 48), yet certain of divine help (Prol. 18, 41);

girded with the faith and firmly resolved to practice the Lord's commandments (Prol. 21), he sets out on the path marked by the Rule. This first choice is often groping, hesitant. The person is looking. In his eyes one reads uncertainty, mixed with an authentic desire to pledge himself to the Lord's service.

He comes then to knock at the door of the school of life, the monastery. But, a strange thing happens to this ardent and enthusiastic young man: St Benedict does not answer right away (58:1). He does this not to drive the seeker away, but rather to strengthen his resolution. Knowing by experience that the novelty of a thing or the fervor fed by the unknown in the monastic life (1:3) may attract young men, he does not want to deceive them. The beauty of the liturgy, the need for guidance, the search for warm and brotherly friendship, the attraction of a dynamic abbot, may indeed create an illusion for them. There are even sometimes at the bottom of their hearts, selfish motives, such as the desire to be shielded from difficulties, or the temptation to flee commitments, or life's struggle, or responsibilities; it is easy to give in to laziness, considering the monastic life as an oasis of comfortable peace without risks. In spite of these too natural tendencies, St Benedict knows also that there may be in the person a real thirst for God. It is necessary to help him purify and free himself from these tendencies. On the other hand, some candidates for religious life are psychologically poorly balanced. Their nature obscurely seeks a counterbalance for their mania or their imbalances. Certainly, they are not capable of bearing the burden of the Rule, and if they were to be admitted, they would cause others to bear the burden of their eccentricities. St Benedict therefore wants the newcomer, whether layman or priest, to be tested (60:1) in order to lead him to make a choice which is fully lucid and completely responsible. At the same time, it can be seen whether the postulant is guided by human reasons or sent by God (58:2).

Methods of probation vary according to the circumstances. The important thing is to make him reflect carefully, to analyze his desire for monastic life. Later on, he will run less

danger of losing a good for which he had to fight. His decision
ought to be free of every sort of carelessness or childishness.
If the community leads a postulant to think that they expect
a great deal of him and are counting on him, this reception
will not help him be patient or humble, but may cause him
to become demanding. It will not help him really to appreciate the divine gift of his vocation, but will lead him to
believe that he is giving the community an important gift by
joining it. Acting this way dangerously mislays the emphasis
at the very beginning. Small wonder if later on, a vocation
chosen under such conditions fails to arrive at the firmness
of a humble gift of self to God. If it be necessary to make
the young man see the great value of the gift of his person, it
is also necessary to make him understand that the ability to
consent to this gift is fundamentally a grace from the Lord
and that he comes to the monastery in order to be helped in
the development of the grace he has received. Let him therefore be aware that in giving himself to the Lord and to his
brothers, he is himself the first beneficiary.

Once he has surmounted the difficulties of entry, the
newcomer is conducted to the guest house (58:4) where he
begins a new step in the testing process, one destined to cause
his decision to mature. Spiritually speaking, the person of
today may come from a great distance, and the baggage of his
religious knowledge and conviction is often meager. Nevertheless, a mysterious call led him to the monastery. Must he be
refused simply because his background is not perfect? Test
him, says St Benedict, to learn if his desire is inspired by
God (58:2). But it is not advisable to put him immediately in
constant contact with the community. He would find there a
way of life too different from his lifestyle, and this might dis-
concert him, discourage him, and in the end cause him to
leave. Such departures are great disillusionments for communities. The young man ought, then, to live at the guest
house, or in a similar place at the edge of the community;
there he will familiarize himself little by little with the
routine and its meaning. At the same time, this provides an
occasion for getting to know him better (61:5) and if he
seems capable of submitting to the final test, he may then

enter the novitiate (58:5). According to the text of the Rule, notice, the newcomer continues to live separated from the rest of the community for spiritual formation, for meals, and for sleeping (*ibid.*). That is important, for, as we said earlier, experience shows that young people in the midst of maturing suffer incurable spiritual wounds when they are involved too soon in community life. The time of the novitiate is very specifically set aside for probation. Everything there is orientated toward a final, perfectly conscious and slowly ripened choice. The novice learns to seek God (58:7), that is to say, to be faithful in his efforts better to know God and his love for us. He is introduced to prayer, to obedience, to humility, to all the virtues necessary to the common life. Nothing is hidden from him; on the contrary, he discovers the hard and difficult things which lead to God (58:8) or, in other words, deciphers the language of the cross, folly for those who are lost, but the power of God for those who are saved (1 Cor 1:18). The quality of the novice's decision depends on his good formation in the novitiate.

This year is entirely consecrated to probation. Yet, in the arrangement made by St Benedict, we see special times where the Rule is presented to the novice as his law of life. He is able to reflect for two months, then again, for six months. He is invited to be aware of the final decision. He is still free. If he feels he has the strength to observe this rule of the Lord's service, let him enter; if not, let him leave in complete freedom. The important thing is that he prepares himself well to make a free and responsible decision when the time comes (58:9-12).

The decisive moment comes four months later. It is the end of the probation. The novice knows the rule. Now he is fully aware of what he is pledging himself to. With mature judgment, he takes his decision before the assembly of his brothers; it is definitive and irrevocable (58:17ff.). Under present ecclesiastical legislation, that year of probation ought to be followed by an undetermined period of up to nine years before the final engagement. After such long reflection, there is no longer any excuse for throwing off the yoke of the Rule (58:16).

By this energetic attitude, St Benedict reveals his concern for complete honesty before God, before the postulant, before the community of brothers. It would, in fact, be to affront God and to deceive the community as well as the young brother if a candidate whose intellectual, spiritual, and emotional maturity was not genuine were admitted to solemn profession. How could that be called a free choice, involving one's entire life?

By what signs can maturity be recognized? St Benedict tells us: If he shows himself generous in the divine service, full of charity and devotion in obedience, and if in trials (58:7) he gives proof of having sufficiently overcome the self-centeredness of adolescence. Anyone who is withdrawn into himself is not capable of disinterested love; on the other hand, the generous young man opens his heart to objective values, to the rights of those around him, to the needs of others. He is capable of renunciation and sacrifice, not in the enthusiastic manner of the neophyte, but in a steady and virile way. He is capable of making vows and of depriving himself by them, for the love of God and of his brothers, of legitimate goods which people hold in high esteem.

The maturity of young people can also be recognized by their ability to order their judgments. Someone who frequently runs into difficulties with community life and with differences in character during the time of probation, like the Pharisees, sees the straw in the eye of others and makes his vocation depend on the perfection or imperfection of his companions. St Benedict, it is interesting to note, asks the novice only if he believes that he is able to assume the obligation of the Rule. He doesn't ask him if the site of the monastery, the community, or the abbot please him. Indeed, it would not be proper to subordinate the grace of a vocation to secondary contingencies. The call of God ought to be received in its purity, and followed simply because it is God who calls. The response made in this way will be much freer and surer.

Before concluding, let us pause a moment to understand

the thought of St Benedict. In bringing about a fully deliberate decision in the heart of the novice he shows a deep respect for human dignity and liberty. Throughout the entire psychological process which he employs to awaken a full awareness, he shows us that he fully measures the transcendant value of his act and intends to make the young man attain the highest summits.

And indeed it is a matter of an irreversible commitment when the candidate to the monastic life takes his destiny firmly in his hands. Is it presumption or folly to wish thus to arrange in advance his own future? Let us notice that often the simple choice of a job, an undertaking, a life's partner, is just as irreversible as is monastic profession. Besides, are we not counting on the all-powerful help of divine grace (Prol. 41)?

On the other hand, our life receives from this bold act of sovereign freedom a stimulus, an enthusiasm, and a richness which has no comparison with an untamed liberty which is always searching, where the present denies the past, and where the hypothetical future already throws the uncertain present into question. In teaching us freedom of choice, St Benedict, therefore, renders an immense service not only to monks by forming their personality, but to human society which draws from it a witness of courage and hope necessary for the construction of the city of God.

# BEING A DISCIPLE

This expression characterizes the relationship of a person to a master and is well known to us through the books of the New Testament. It corresponds to a deep need of man, conscious of his limitations, to entrust himself to the direction of another, to seek his advice, to familiarize himself with his teaching, and to follow him. The Jews have their rabbis, the Indians have their gurus, the Russians their startzi.

To get a concrete idea of what a disciple is, let us read

the moving story of St John as he recounts his own experience. There we see young, ardent men, enthusiastic, moved by the devouring desire to find the Prophet, perhaps the Messiah, to be able to follow a saint, a leader who gives security, light, peace, who has the wherewithal to satisfy a heart hungering for truth and unadulterated happiness, and then find John the Baptist. Humble and self effacing, he directs them to Jesus. John then recounts for us the great adventure of his life: Andrew and John, disciples of John the Baptist, at seeing Jesus, encouraged by their master, 'follow Jesus. Jesus turns around and sees that they are following Him. He says to them: "What do you want?" They answer him, "Rabbi . . . where do you live?" "Come and see", he says to them. So they went . . . and they stayed with him that day' (Jn 1:37ff.). John remembered even the hour of that memorable meeting. Later, Jesus called them: 'Follow me and I will make you fishers of men' (Mt 4:19). And from then on, 'They followed him', (Mt 4:22) everywhere, in everything, even to death. They became his apostles, the witnesses of his life, his teaching, his resurrection. That is what it means to be a disciple.

They remained Jesus' disciples, they did not found a new doctrine, a new school. Jesus said to them: 'For your part, do not be called rabbi, for you have only one Master and you are all brothers' (Mt 23:8); 'Neither let yourselves be called teachers, for you have only one Teacher, the Christ' (*ibid.* 10). The christian tradition has given these words their exact meaning while taking into account Our Lord's other words when he sent the apostles to teach the gospel to the nations (Mt 28:19), constituting them the teachers, while at the same time preserving their quality as disciples. They ought not, according to the manner of the 'Doctors of the Law' have the pretence of believing themselves judges of doctrine. They ought not either, after the example of the rabbis, to despise the ordinary people, 'this rabble which knows not the Law, these accursed' (Jn 7:49), or to believe themselves the sole masters of the gospel which, by the grace of faith, is deposited into the hearts of the baptized as a treasure to be discovered. They ought all to consider themselves disciples of the Lord, brothers with all of those who, thanks to them, were able to become acquainted with the gospel and the kingdom of God. The apostles were sent as the Father had sent his Son (Jn 20:21). Anyone who hears them hears the Lord (Lk 10:16). We know that the disciple is not above his Master (Mt 10:24)—like him they will be persecuted (Jn 15:20)—but those who have kept his word will also keep their word (*ibid.*). The disciple is one with the Master and shares his lot, just as he proclaims his word. The apostles, disciples of Jesus, are then, in our phrase, authentic teachers, but this is because they are disciples of the only true Teacher, who has come from the Father and who alone is able to attest to what he has seen in the Father's presence (Jn 3:11).

The apostles established successors to whom they entrusted the 'deposit' (1 Tm 6:20) of the faith. The Pope, as Peter's successor, exercises the 'ordinary *magisterium*'; he is therefore the supreme teacher of the faith, the vicar of the one Master. The bishops united with the pope exercise the 'extra-ordinary *magisterium*'; they also are teacher-disciples of Christ. In the same restricted sense there are many other masters. The title 'Master' is conferred with the right to teach. The Dominican Order was founded to 'transmit to others the fruit of one's contemplation' and their Superior is called 'Master General'.

As a result, those who listen and learn are disciples. Does this relationship of master and disciple exist in monastic life?

In the beginning of monasticism, anyone who wanted to become a monk could choose a master. This way of doing things could, however, lead to individualism. St Benedict, in writing his Rule for cenobites, wanted the master to be established juridically, so that one might not abandon him arbitrarily under the pretext, for example, of an order too difficult to execute or not to one's liking. To act this way would be to put oneself as master over against one's chosen master.

We have a master, then. This idea is deeply rooted in the Holy Rule. It is true that the relationship of master and disciple appears in the texts of the Rule, especially in the first chapters, under the influence of the *Regula Magistri.* But it is also true that St Benedict retained these texts in his own Rule. Might it be that he wanted to make the abbot and his brothers understand that, in matters of doctrine especially, the abbot and his monks find themselves in that relationship, whereas in matters simply of community life, the abbot ought to regard his monks as brothers? At any rate, the attitude of the disciple is strongly, and no doubt intentionally, marked from the very beginning of the Rule, which begins with the word: 'listen'. This is the essential attitude of the disciple, someone who listens. We are disciples for our entire lifetime, because to listen, to be a disciple, is, so to speak, a part of our state in life, of our profession. By our vocation we are disciples.

In order to remain always in this spirit, we must have the attitude of a disciple as we see it in the third degree of humility. Obedience is nothing other than listening. In German, the word for 'obedience' comes from the same root as that for 'listen'. He who obeys, listens: *Horchen, Gehorsam.* That is to say, to obey is essentially to listen, and it supposes that one listens, and listens not only with the ear but with the heart. One listens while acquiescing. For St Benedict does not fail to add immediately: *et efficaciter comple* (Prol. 1). It is a matter not only of accepting the teaching, but of effectively carrying it out. 'It befits the disciple to be silent and to listen', he teaches (6:6), and also 'to obey' (3:6), and, going still farther, to perform this obedience 'with a willing heart' (5:16ff.).

The disciple is by definition, therefore, one who listens and obeys. We know that the monk has the vital and inalienable human right humbly to express his point of view when there are serious reasons for doing so, leaving the final decision to the superior, for certain commands may be beyond his strength.

Who is the monk's master? From everything we have said it is clear that the Master is Christ. From him the monk expects the 'words of eternal life' (Jn 6:68). He knows that the fountain of living waters is the Lord. There he can draw, certain that these waters will spring up in eternal life. Is his whole desire not to seek (58:7) and to find God? He can discern, by the Lord's grace, the voice of the Shepherd from the voice of strangers (Jn 10:4ff.). The monk ought never to depart (Prol. 50) from the teaching of Christ, his Master.

But he also knows that the Lord has arranged his Kingdom in such a way that we have to help one another to walk on the right path; that there are guides set up by him and that we ought to have recourse to them with confidence so they may transmit to us and explain the words of life. The monk wishes to fortify himself against the treachery of his own self-will, and he withdraws to a monastery 'in order to live according to the will and good pleasure of another' (5:12).

Someone who wishes to become a disciple, therefore, will seek among his brothers for an 'elder' (5:4, 5:15, 7:34), a disciple 'greater' than himself. That is, a 'senior' (4:20, 46:5, 58:6), a person experienced in the ways of the Lord. For he seeks a 'master' (Prol. 1, 3:6, 6:6) capable of teaching him, forming him, and guiding him. He wants to find this master among his brothers, a man who has had to learn as he has, to fight as he has, and therefore someone able to help him more by his actions (2:1) and his example (7:55) than by his words.

More than a senior or a master, he will look among his brothers for someone who can be a real father to him. We are all, in the first place, disciples of our father, and the father is the natural master of his son. Instinctively, we connect the idea of our search for a master with the idea of fatherhood. St Benedict is particularly temperate when he touches on the fatherhood of the abbot. His thought leaves no room for ambiguity, however, for he adopts the name *Abbas* for the person placed at the head of the community, citing St Paul (Rm 8:15): 'You have received the spirit of adoption which makes us cry out: Abba! Father!' (RB 2:3). The notion of father, connected with the experience we have had in normal family life, brings to our minds pleasant memories and quite naturally, having become adults and seeking a master of the spiritual life, the ideal of fatherhood imposes itself on our minds.

Someone who wishes to become a disciple recognizes in the spiritual personality of the abbot as St Benedict paints it the master whom he seeks, and joins himself to those who 'desire nothing more than to place themselves under the leadership of an abbot' (5:12). He becomes a disciple for the love of God (7:34), recognizing the abbot as master in the place of Christ (2:2).

Like master, like disciple. The disciple will not be above his master. The disciple may surpass his master in virtue or knowledge, but he will remain deeply marked by his master. Holy masters have often had holy disciples. And here we penetrate the psychology of the disciple who wants to commit himself to a master, in the hope of advancing along the paths of wisdom by means of the wisdom of his chosen master.

The responsibility of the master, of the abbot, towards the disciple is therefore immense. This is why the abbot, once installed, must continually ponder the heavy burden which he has assumed (64:7). St Benedict draws up a whole list of duties, a sort of mirror to make the abbot understand the delicate mission he is charged with for his disciple's good. To go into details here would overstep the limits of this conference.

Let us instead pose one final question: In order to be a good disciple, need one possess certain natural dispositions? No doubt, a certain natural receptivity cannot help but facilitate the generous initiative of the disciple who is just beginning. But let it not be passivity! Of course, the heart of the disciple must open and be malleable to the teaching proposed to him. He must let himself be impregnated and impressed by everything good he sees. But there is here no question of indoctrination, of brain-washing, or of a kind of hypnosis or, worse yet, a return to a state of childishness. On the contrary, to be a disciple demands an attentive collaboration and sets into motion all of the faculties of sound criticism and discernment. Just as medicines applied to the body to speed up the cure ought to be assimilated, so also the disciple ought in a fully conscious and responsible way to integrate the things he learns which are conducive to his full development. The master will help him in this effort by the great respect he shows for his personality. Before all else, he will endeavor to supply him with sound principles and the intellectual tools needed for forming judgments. Thus instructed, the disciple will become capable of being a master in his turn, skilled especially in the art of following perfectly the great Master, Christ.

# THE SCHOOL OF
# THE LORD'S SERVICE

In hearing the words, 'We are going to establish a school where the service of the Lord is taught' (Prol. 45), we understand that our father St Benedict, after having delivered his discourse of the Prologue, wishes to draw from it the logical conclusion. It would be interesting to show how this program of a school of the service of the Lord flows from it, but let us try instead to study in depth this key idea of a school of the Lord's service.

At the entrance of the Generalate of the Order of Citeaux in Rome, the visitor's eye is caught by a large inscription upon the cornice of the pediment near the door of the chapel: *Dominici schola servitii* (School of the Lord's service). Could there be a better motto for a benedictine monastery?

The word *schola* strikes us first of all. We are at school—that is the literal translation of the word *schola.* For the ancients, the word designated a place, a site; later its meaning became more precise, and was limited to the ideas of 'discipline' and 'instruction'. As a matter of fact, the two senses become merged: to learn a discipline, to learn everything in general. It is obvious that St Benedict intends the word *schola* in both senses. We enter into a whole: into a discipline of life, for, the Prologue tells us, having abandoned discipline by disobedience, it is necessary for us to find it again through obedience. This is the first aspect.

Let us go on to the second: the school. All of our lives we are at school. Actually, we don't go to school all of our lives, but only until a certain age, so we think that once out of school, we pass as masters. That is not St Benedict's idea. On the contrary, he tells us very simply, without a long discourse, that we remain at school all of our lives. This is the tacit correction of a wrong idea which we might someday get: that to enter the monastery means to join an elite group. In the monastery, great center of the christian life, live the masters of the spiritual life. By entering, one in a short time becomes in his turn a master. No, St Benedict tells us we stay in school.

What is the goal of this school? The question comes immediately to our lips. St Benedict answers us: *Schola servitii.* He might have said for example: 'You are entering a school of meditation, of contemplation, of mystical life' or something like that. The Rule breathes not a word on all that. But really, are we not entering a school of prayer, contemplation, christian doctrine when we enter the monastery? We find all these there, but St Benedict avoids expressions which might mislead. In his day—still the first centuries of Christianity—Platonism exercised a powerful attraction on the spirit of certain christian philosophers. *Gnosis* held that through knowledge, science, doctrine, one might penetrate to God, that union with him was an intellectual affair. St Benedict wants to cut short these lucubrations and does not share this way of thinking. It is interesting to notice that he speaks very little of personal prayer and meditation —and he is reproached for it, I believe wrongly. He does not give any method for it. Our cistercian *Rituals* written at the time when ignation spirituality was at its height, and and when methods of meditation held an important place, says in the chapter on meditation: '*Optima methodus meditandi, nullam habere methodum*'—(the best method of meditation is not to have a method). St Benedict seems to have been of this opinion. It is true that in analyzing the chapters on the chapel (RB 52) and on the manner of singing the psalms (RB 19), as well as the chapter on reverence in prayer (20), we can find some ideas on the manner of praying, although our desire to possess an exhaustive treatment on the subject is not satisfied.

St Benedict does not speak, then, of a school of meditation. He could just as well have called his school a 'school of humility' (and with good reason, since the seventh chapter is clearly the center of the Rule from the spiritual point of view) or even a 'school of charity' (since charity is the end of all of the monk's efforts—7:67). But no, he says 'school of service'. Not everyone is satisfied with this. Yet today, in our post-conciliar times when people insist on ministry and service, the word *servitium* has regained a little of its prestige. The word today does not sound so bad. Far from recalling a state of slavery or the serfs of ancient times, it makes us think of Jesus who wanted to be the servant of our salvation. It would be artificial to believe that St Benedict, having with him perhaps some descendants of slaves, would have wanted to help them make the connection between a servile life and the idea of the Lord's service. The explanation is simpler. The word 'service' and what it stands for flow quite simply from what the Prologue proposes: the monk enlists in the service of Christ the King (Prol. 3). It is evidently not really a military service, but it is nevertheless a real service: the Lord's service.

This idea of the Lord's service is in conformity with the thought of Sacred Scripture. We repeat so often in the Psalms: Serve the Lord with joy (Ps 99:2), with fear (Ps 2:11), or similar words. In the New Testament, the idea of *diakonia*, ministry, service, is found everywhere. It would be easy to cite numerous texts on it.

But why service? Because to serve makes us go out of ourselves, it turns us from the egoistic self and opens us to a relationship with another. This is also why St Benedict does not speak of a school of prayer or humility or charity: all these would center us upon ourselves; we would be tempted to spend our time studying ourselves, to reflect too much on our own problems. For St Benedict, life is much simpler, more humane, more natural, and more balanced. He attempts, by freeing us from every exaggerated preoccupation

with ourselves, to fix our attention on what is outside ourselves. This psychologically sound idea gives our life an un-
selfish orientation and guards us from the danger which
threatens every spiritual life, especially the life of an
ascetic: to be busy with oneself, to think about oneself, to
meditate on oneself.

We are, then, in service. But in the service of whom, of
what? 'In the school of the Lord's service'. Our school
teaches us to serve the Lord. There also, we do not enter into
the service of an idea or a project. Nor do we enter into
the service of persons as such. The monastic life causes us to
enter into the service of the Lord. The Lord is the center of
our life; everything converges toward him. He is our
sovereign good, the goal of our life. It is to him that we
belong, he who condescended to receive us into his service.
St Benedict teaches us forgetfulness of self in the chapter on
humility. This abnegation takes us to the Lord, and it is not
negative. At the sight of a great good, one forgets the lesser.
That is what happens to us when we are in the Lord's
presence; our whole life tends toward him.

To serve the Lord; not to rejoice in him? St Benedict does
not put forward the idea of union with the Lord, and for
psychological reasons. It is evident that he wants to make us
arrive at that union, but he recommends to us the simplest
the most natural, the most sensible way to get there.

Serve the Lord. Who is this Lord? 'The Lord, he is God';
that is clear. By reading the Prologue we know from the first
sentence that the Lord is Christ: 'to fight under the true
King, Christ the Lord' (Prol. 3). People speak, rightly,
of the Rule and its program as Christocentric. All of our life
is centered on Christ. We could develop this idea, but let us
instead ask ourselves: Who is Christ? The 'whole Christ'—
St Augustine spoke of this—is not only God made man, the
Jesus of the Gospel; the whole Christ is the entire Church
gathered together in him, taken up into him through the
incarnation, the redemption, and the resurrection. All Christians, all the people of God: this is Christ.

We understand therefore that in entering the monastery we
enter a school to learn the service of the whole Christ, that is

to say, of Christ and of our brothers and sisters. To convince ourselves of this, let us recall how often St Benedict identifies our brothers with Christ: the abbot (2:2, 63:13), the sick (36:1ff.), guests (53:1,7,14), the poor (53:15), pilgrims (*ibid.*). 'All of us are one in Christ' (2:20). St Benedict is conspicuous in not missing a chance to insist upon this point. For him, the Church, the brothers, are Christ.

St Benedict's program is perfectly clear, then. His monastery is the place where one serves the brothers, but not in their purely human entity. They are served because of their relationship to Christ. What a beautiful arrangement! Our monastic life has as its guiding principle the service of Christ, not only the historic Christ who dwells at the right hand of the Father in heaven, but Christ in our brothers. It is through this service that we make our monastic life real. It is by means of this service that we come to the Lord.

Far from St Benedict is the idea that we are individuals who come together in order to organize an external institution which will help each of us in his personal journey toward the Lord, without having, after all, any more profound relationship among themselves. On the contrary, we form in Christ a community whose members unite to make Christ present through the exercise of mutual charity. We would be greatly mistaken were we to withdraw ourselves from our brothers, even finding them perhaps annoying, leaving them aside in order to live in our own corner, before the tabernacle, for example, with some idea that by doing so we will better encounter the Lord. This would be an illusion. We journey toward the Lord with the help of our brothers and through serving our brothers.

# SOLDIERS OF CHRIST

'In order to fight under the true King, Christ the Lord', the monk takes up 'the powerful and glorious arms of obedience' (Prol. 3). From the very first sentence, the monastic life is presented as military service under the standard of the great King. Far be from us, then, every illusion about a peaceful life in the shelter of the monastery walls after a flight from the world which we cannot resist, into a community of brothers who love us and are eager to help us develop our individuality by fulfilling all our wishes. St Benedict does not allow us to dream. This means going to war. The monk enlists in an army, a small one, surely, but a determined one.

This presentation of the monastic life cannot surprise anyone familiar with the language of Scripture. From it he has learned bluntly that 'man's life on earth is a time of military service' (Job 7:1); to refuse to fight is to waste one's life. All passivity, all false pacificism in the matter leads to defeat. In ì the language of the ancient monks, allusions to military life are frequent. Do we today, like this language, these comparisons with military service? Jesus speaks of the violent who take the kingdom of heaven by force (Mt 11:12) but he does not use the image of a fight for life. This image is not, however, foreign to the thought of St Paul, who is conscious of having fought the good fight (2 Tm 4:7) when he recommends that his disciple be a 'brave soldier of Christ Jesus' (2:3). But although Jesus does not speak of combat, he does not fail, far from it, to present life to us as a struggle which can go as far as martyrdom.

Without a doubt, there is a certain movement afoot to suppress the incentive of combat and mortification from monastic life. Some people would like to see it flow along peacefully in the sunshine of divine grace, in charity, with everyone haloed in serenity. The allegory of combat makes us think of wars, the fear of getting hurt makes us draw back, we are afraid of overreaching ourselves and of making efforts of the will which, after having been maintained for a time, will end up abandoned. Modern man thinks he no longer has in his physiological makeup the robust natural strength the Rule takes for granted. To wish to fight as it recommends would be, for him, to invite nervous depression. But let us not deceive ourselves: to give too much importance to this way of seeing things will lead us to becoming comfortably settled. Yet which of us doubts the need to struggle to gain a place in the sun, keep a place in society, or quite simply, maintain our human dignity? Is a struggle not even more necessary when the values in question surpass everything wonderful we can imagine? Yes, we have to struggle. We are soldiers, or, in St Paul's words, athletes running in a stadium in order to win a prize (1 Cor 9:24), an idea we also meet in the Prologue of the Rule (Prol. 13, 22, 44, 49).

With St Benedict, the idea of combat returns frequently. The type of life led by cenobites is characterized by the fact that they 'fight' under a rule and an abbot (1:2, cf. 58:10). The entire monastic life is 'a military service' (2:20), under the same Lord (*ibid;* 61:10). The idea which the expressions 'school' (Prol. 45) and 'service' (*ibid.*) cover is probably the same: at this school the monk learns how to serve the King who enlists him under his standard. The enemy of the King, and himself is 'the evil spirit' (Prol. 28) whom he engages in combat, supported by his brothers (1:45).

When St Benedict speaks of the 'stronger kind of monks, the cenobites,' (1:13) and of the 'mighty arms of obedience' (Prol. 3), he is probably aiming at the sarabaites who stay 'soft like lead' (1:6) and the gyrovagues, 'slaves of their own passions' (1:11), who want neither to fight nor to serve; but it is better to be silent than to speak of their miserable condition (*ibid.* 12). The monks' race is a brave, dynamic, energetic race. The combative spirit of the ancient monks of the desert and the anchorites 'hardened to single-handed combat' (1:5), vibrates throughout these lines of the Rule. It was a manly race which counted a little too much upon its own strength—Pelagianism is a heresy which grew out of the monastic milieu and mentality—a race which wanted to equal the martyrs in courage. St Benedict clearly rejects pelagian pride, but while keeping his distance from that error, he did risk falling into the semi-Pelagianism anathematized by the Council of Orange in 529 (the year of the foundation of the monastery of Monte Cassino). This doctrine which spread mainly in Gaul among such monks as Cassian, Vincent of Lérins, and others, is known chiefly through the difficulties they encountered with the doctrine of St Augustine. Later on, his explanation of the role of grace strengthening the free will prevailed.

Whereas the monk Pelagius had attributed the work of justification to the human will, semi-Pelagian doctrine assigned only its beginning to man's own effort, and credited grace with carrying it out. St Benedict, like any practical man caring first for the spiritual advancement of his monks and obviously wanting to avoid theological subtleties and not interested in the semi-Pelagian controversy, deliberately does not get into the question. So there is in the Rule no expression which is frankly semi-Pelagian, nor anti-semi-Pelagian for that matter, unless one interprets the maxim of chapter 4:42f. in the latter sense. If it is true that a semi-Pelagian meaning may be given to certain phrases, it remains no less true that these same phrases can be understood in a perfectly orthodox sense, because St Benedict never expressly reserves the beginning of a good work to free will. It is easy to understand why someone in a monastic setting might want to give an important role to free will: a practical concern with encouraging the monks to work, to observances, and to the struggle explains this insistence. Have they not been called to 'struggle with their arms and hands against the vices of the flesh and evil thoughts' (1:5)?

We will not digress here on the respective roles of grace and free will in the accomplishment of a good work. We know that an act which can please the Father requires the sanctifying mark of the Son Who is the universal Mediator between us and the Father. This is why the Son has declared to us: 'I am the vine, you are the branches . . . without me, you can do nothing' (Jn 15:5). We are happy to remain in him, and to bear fruit in him (*ibid.*) who works in both to will and to do (Phil 2:13). We realize no less that we have to 'work', to accomplish our salvation (Phil 2:12) and, to do this, struggle without reprieve. We speak, for example, of the 'militants' in Catholic Action. The monk is a militant in the 'Catholic Passion'. He needs no less courage and christian fortitude to endure this battle. Christ is the Leader, and the army of all the militants follow him and fight in his name. He carries the standard of the cross before us and proclaims that if we do not take up our cross every day, we are not worthy of him (Lk 9:23, Mt 10:38); this ought to make us tremble.

This cross is both a standard and a weapon at the same time. What does this mean concretely for the monk? The Rule tells us not to seek for it afar, not to seek for it in your own ideas and wishes; it is obedience which will show it to you hour by hour, day after day. In obedience you will meet the cross, one which does not deceive; by it you will be sure that you are in the army of Christ.

The monk's entire combat is given to concrete form by obedience; this is the gist of the Rule. What has been spoiled by 'the sloth of disobedience' has to be restored 'by the labor of obedience' (Prol. 2). This labor is our cross. Now because it is by the cross that we become worthy of the Lord (Mt 10: 38), it is through our cross as monks, that is to say, through the labor of obedience, that we are united to Christ our leader. St Benedict could summarize this logic in one forceful phrase: 'This obedience without delay is the distinctive mark of those who hold nothing dearer to them than Christ' (5:1f.).

Have we this love in us? Have we fully realized the central position of obedience in our life of combat in Jesus' steps? Let us not be surprised if the scandal of the cross (Gal 5:11), which therefore becomes for us the scandal of obedience, remains in our life like a sign of contradiction against which our nature revolts. And let us not be surprised that arguments against the scandal of obedience are presently rife. The enemy of Christ uses all his power to do away with the cross and blot out obedience. As a good strategist, he seeks to destroy the weapons of his adversary, 'the mighty arms of obedience' (Prol. 3). They are all the more powerful since Christ, we know, overcame the devil through his obedience unto death, even death on the cross. The struggle which his disciple wages is therefore obedience even unto death.

# MONASTIC PROFESSION AS THE GIFT OF SELF

The craft we exercise gives a certain orientation to our life, especially when it polarizes our interests and our energies. Certain professions require that a man consecrate to them a real dedication of his intelligence, the qualities of his heart, his physical powers, without however absorbing him entirely; he may still occupy himself with a family or a pasttime.

The monastic profession is a craft which polarizes all of our powers, because in adopting it, we renounce all the rest on principle. Everything outside of it is subordinated to it and ought to be abandoned to the extent that it is a hindrance or becomes foreign to it. Because it is the total gift of ourselves to the Lord, the monastic profession consecrates to him all our powers, all our physical and psychic assets, and even all the material goods at our disposal; and since the Lord identifies himself with his Body the Church and with his brothers, the elect, this gift of ourselves is likewise offered to the Church, to our brothers.

Let us remark in passing that in speaking of monastic profession we mean not only the solemn act of taking vows, but profession as it is lived each day, each hour of one's entire life *usque ad mortem*, even unto death. Monastic profession is the total gift of ourselves to the Lord. To give oneself: this is the definition of charity. Our Lord has told us: There is no greater love than to give one's life for one's friends (Jn 15:13). He could just as well have said there is no more beautiful quality, no greater perfection than to give oneself entirely: what could be more generous? This is the sacrifice of the martyr, but it is also the continual gift of self during the course of one's life, the sacrifice of the best of our life.

Generous charity is without doubt the noblest quality of the heart. The soul is precious to the extent that it possesses charity, or still better, to the extent that it is possessed by it. Monastic profession, the giving of oneself without reserve, perfects us from the supernatural as well as from the human point-of-view. Even in the natural order, the greatest human perfection is love: to love sincerely and without reserve.

Here we must ask a question: where does the power come from that lets a person give himself totally? Does an act of such scope, such range, such dedication not exceed his powers? And looking further, where does he get the charity, the capacity for giving self?

'God is love' (1 Jn 4:16). That is as much as to say that God is the gift of self. The Father gives himself entirely to the Son. This total gift of the Father is his divinity. The divinity as the gift and the breath of love of the Father is the Holy Spirit. By this 'gift of the most High' every total gift is inspired. 'Every perfect gift comes from on high and descends from the Father of lights' (Js 1:17). And again: 'the love of God has been poured into our hearts by the Holy Spirit Who has been given to us' (Rm 5:5).

Monastic profession, the total gift of ourselves, is, we might say, charity in action, and therefore a gift of the Holy Spirit. We participate then in that perfect gift of the Father to the Son and of the Son to the Father. It is therefore a sacred act, coming from God and directing itself to him. It addresses itself also to our brothers whom we receive from his hand, through this gift which we give him of ourselves.

The oblation of monastic profession is the perfect gift of self. We are invited to imitate God and to give ourselves to him and to the world. We respond to that gift of God to the world by making the same gesture—and it is the greatest act we could do. God is the good which gives self; He is the gift and pours himself into the universe. We imitate him according to our means; this is the apostolic aspect of religious profession.

We ought to be able to say that having loved our brothers so much, we have gone so far as to give ourselves entirely.

The oblation made to God is nothing else, and we are all linked together in this personal step, for the oblation ought always to be considered under two aspects: the one who gives, and the one to whom is given. Our oblation is offered to God and to the world, and therefore to our brothers as well, and to imitate the great love of the Lord, we are invited to give our will truly every day and every hour.

All this leads us to the question: 'What does the gift of monastic profession formally consist of for St Benedict?' According to the Rule, the total gift is made through obedience. In promising it and in living it monks renounce 'living according to their own wishes and desires, but rather walk according to the judgment and command of another' (5:12, cf. 58:15), in order to give themselves entirely to God who has called them to himself. Along with the document of their profession, they place their own wills on the altar (58:20). And therefore, this gift is united to that total gift of Christ offered at the Holy Sacrifice of the Mass.

St Benedict tells us in Chapter 62 that if a priest absolutely will not obey or submit himself to the rule, he should be expelled. Lack of obedience, therefore, is enough for expulsion from the monastery. St Benedict has the same attitude in regard to the deans (21:5) and the prior (65:21). Why? Because obedience is of the essense of our life. Faults against chastity, for example, do not require the expulsion of a religious, but serious and repeated and incorrigible faults demand it when they touch what is essential to our monastic life: that is to say, when they touch obedience. It is not a matter of wanting to expel a monk at any cost, but rather of making us understand that in our life obedience is essential. In chapter 71 (2) we read: 'Knowing that it is through this path of obedience that they go to God'. St Benedict, note, does not here mention the other vows, but speaks only of obedience.

*Obsculta, o fili*—listen. To listen is already to obey, because one submits himself by listening. It is necessary to listen. As disobedience separated Adam from God, so through obedience we unite ourselves to God. This obedience is simple, without restriction, without pretence, without distortion, without undue agitation. It is a frank obedience. We do not force our heart in an artificial manner, but with the help of God's grace, we obey those who hold the place of the Lord in order to know through them what he wants of us in any circumstance. This is the real oblation of the will. Indeed, if we speak of oblation, it means the gift of our will. To signify the offering of the whole person in paganism, he was burned. We place our will on the altar. We place our document of profession there and we mean in this way to symbolize the gift of our will made solemnly to the Lord.

To obey is to give oneself and to love. The secret of joyous obedience (5:16) is to be found in this love which moves us to obey. Obedience is the most formal act of profession, the one which embraces everything in it; it is the total gift of self, the gift of love. The monk who lives out his profession through the generous offering of his will will not be disappointed of his hope (58:21). He will receive the hundredfold, the love without reserve of him to whom he is given: 'He who loves me will be loved by my Father, and I will love him' (Jn 14:21).

# TOWARD
# THE NEW MAN

'If we wish, my brothers, to attain to the summit of perfect humility' (7:5), we must ascend by our works. The Lord invites us to settle down in his tabernacle, upon his holy mountain (cf. Prol. 25).

This morning, therefore, I propose an excursion. It is never very easy to make an effort, perhaps still harder to make a spiritual than a physical effort. This is a tension which touches the very root of our being. This, to give it away immediately, will be, the excursion to the mountain that Jesus made with his disciples. The three who followed him had to expend a great effort in order to climb with him.

The transfiguration! Man has always had this desire to go beyond himself. It is a desire inscribed in the very depths of our being, perhaps because our father Adam fell into sin, and because a nostalgia for another realization of our life still remains, or because, in spite of our limitations, we retain a fundamental need to approach God, to arrive at the stature to which Scripture alludes: 'You shall be like gods' (Gn 3:5). This is why the Transfiguration is a profoundly human theme. The person who does not know God, who does not deal with him, nevertheless dreams of a kind of transfiguration, especially the person of today. He dreams of a man conditioned, prepared, fashioned according to his desires, starting with the foetus, which would be perfect, always more perfect, thanks to technology, biochemistry, and all the scientific means at his disposal. In the depth of his heart lies the image he has built up of this superman.

But this human transfiguration does not satisfy us. With it, we would remain still very far from the limits to which we can reach out and desire. We aspire to another transfiguration which goes far beyond the dreams of science, one which would truly go beyond our being, beyond all we are. It is in this hope that we have become monks: 'to climb by the very ascent of our actions the ladder' of humility (7:6), by ridding ourselves little by little of the old man and, in time, arriving at the summit 'of divine charity' (7:67). Let us therefore ascend the holy mountain where Our Lord is transfigured before the eyes of Peter, James, and John. He had worked many miracles and preached beautiful sermons. But really, all that was in the order of nature, so to speak, in the order of human attainment; it appealed to their dreams and ideas. The day of the transfiguration, the Lord did something altogether extraordinary, something the disciples did not imagine or expect. St Peter tells us they were overwhelmed and beside themselves (2 P 1:16ff.).

It is clear that Our Lord was transfigured, not just to show us his true nature, but to invite us to penetrate a little further in our understanding of the kingdom of God. In the transfiguration, this call goes out to all of us: 'Follow me'. This invitation is an intention to make an excursion to the mountain. Our Lord invites us: 'Jesus took with him Peter, James, and John' (Mt 17:1). He is the one who has taken the initiative. We know that it is always God who begins the dialogue, God who calls us, who invites us to follow him. For us, that is a great assurance and a great consolation. We cannot follow him, it must be said, even on an excursion to the mountain if he does not first say to us: 'Follow me' (Mt 9:9), if he does not take us with him.

God calls us from the beginning of the world. The monks of Mount Athos call the wooden clapper which wakens them for the midnight office 'Adam'. Why? Because God's call began in paradise: 'Where are you?' (Gen 3:9) God asked Adam. Immediately after the fall, without wasting a minute, God invited man, 'Come to me. Where are you?' The Lord calls us. He calls each of us by our own name. It is easy to substitute our own name for the names of Peter, James, or John.

He invites us to climb this mountain. To climb a mountain—you know this by experience—takes some effort at first. Later, when you are on a high mountain, at the summit, you are completely changed. You left below and abandoned everything that weighed you down, everything that was superfluous. You left his burden down in the valley, shook off its dust, and made of the climb a liberation, a blossoming forth. This is why the Lord first of all requires an effort from us. But the effort, once again, is made through Our Lord's grace. He who takes us with *him* (Mt 17:1)—and also, let us add immediately, with our brothers. Peter, James, and John made this ascent in the Lord's company, encouraged by him and his grace, but also in their brothers' company. These three who had comprehended, understood, and loved each other so well, were moved in the very midst of their discussions by a force of brotherly understanding which helped and supported them when the moment came to make this effort of ascent.

And besides, it is always pleasant to take an excursion into the mountains in the company of good friends! And we are on that upward trail. The presence of our brothers, and our sisters helps us, encourages us, stimulates us. Little by little, we ascend, we are liberated; the air changes, the world becomes larger, almost limitless. Let us recall the day of the temptation, when Jesus saw the whole world at his feet. The intimate human desire has always been this great temptation to have everything in our hands, to be above everything, above ourself, above our weaknesses, above our limitations. We want to live beyond what we are, liberated, in full bloom. We still have within us the nostalgia of the new creature, which is the primitive creature, the true man. This nostalgia stays in us, and when we make the effort to ascend Mount Tabor, we feel the man in us change little by little. A transformation takes place within us. We sense ourselves growing in the Lord; gradually, a greater resemblance grows within us, a truer, more ancient resemblance to our guide on the mountain, to Jesus. That is transfiguration.

This transfiguration, let us repeat, is brought about first of all through the Lord's grace. We cannot do it alone. We can only follow Him, and in order to follow Him, He has to draw us, tug us, call us continually. He even wakes us up: 'Where are you? Are you sleeping?' He has to shake us all the time. But little by little a change does take place. Besides the initial grace of the Lord, there is the grace which pushes us, pulls us, and encourages us in various ways. We have heard the word coming out of the cloud: This is my well-beloved Son. Listen to him! (Mt 17:5) and follow him! We must listen to the Lord. For us this word is already a great means of change.

This word which is given to us, which we hear and follow continually in our monastic life, all day long, is a great means of transfiguration. It is not only a word coming to our ears; it is the divine word. It enters into our hearts, it changes us, and brings this transfiguration about. It is the divine word we chant at the Divine Office. It is comforting to follow the thought it expresses, really to listen to it. We cannot follow Jesus if we do not understand what he says, if the word is beyond us or passes through us without having sown the divine seed it brought us.

Our senses also lead us to this transfiguration, but it is our interior senses, those which see the Lord, and draw ever nearer to him, and touch him more and more, and see him transfigured, in his true being and which consequently make us approach him inwardly. They help us to change, to become a new man according to the stature of Christ (Eph 4:15). In a word, we become adults in him. We cannot be children and climb this mountain. We leave childish things below. God, through his word and sacraments, offers to help us make the climb. His word sharpens our supernatural forces, the spiritual energies of our will.

The word of God which we pronounce continually, which we sing joyfully in praising the Lord, ought to be our continual nourishment. And if St Benedict, our father, took the trouble to prepare this nourishment for us according to the traditions of the Church and in a practical way so we might be nourished and helped effectively, then we ought to accept it, assimilate it, be penetrated by it. Any one who makes an excursion into the mountains doesn't risk going unless he is well nourished. To go on an empty stomach would weaken us quickly and we would be condemned to being stuck in the middle of our journey unable to arrive at the summit of transfiguration. If we have entered the monastery, we did so to be transfigured little by little. This is the reason we wear clothes which are different from other people's, a white habit symbolizing in some way our vocation to transfiguration, a habit which invites us there always, all the time, so that the interior man may grow strong within us (Eph 3:16).

Let us therefore allow ourselves to be invited by Our Lord, let us allow ourselves to be called, and let us follow him on the path of our liberation and our union with him. It will be a liberation on the human level, on the level of our nature, a liberation from the burdens that crush us. It will be so above all through redemptive grace. Through everyday experience we know that this liberation is necessary, and we aspire to 'the glory that is to be revealed in us' (Rm 8:18).

Let us climb that mountain with joy then. St Benedict sustains our courage. From the heights of Monte Cassino he must have thought of the height already attained and of the pinnacles remaining to be scaled (73:9). Through the words of the Rule and the narratives of St Gregory the Great (Dialogue 50.2) we glimpse, as a light to guide our steps his human and mystical experience.

# FOR THE LOVE
# OF CHRIST

Our good actions are often in fact dictated by imperfect motives and even, from time to time, by devious reasons. We may do something objectively good through ambition, to show off, or to put on airs, or through a spirit of contradiction or even out of convenience. To analyze the motives for our actions, good, bad, or indifferent, to control our actions, to make a sincere descent into the depths of our conscience, is often a useful, even though disagreeable and difficult, thing to do, for we are often the victims of our imaginations, which tend to embellish matters. People have a certain repugnance to looking themselves in the face, and we prefer our fancied to our real appearance. We let ourselves be enticed by the mirage of angels which we are not, and we think we are prompted to act through charity, *caritas*, when what prompts us is really concupiscence, *carnalitas* (cf. *Imitation of Christ* 1.15.2).

St Benedict, as we know, is not gentle with those who make the satisfaction of their desires their law (1:8), who hold as holy whatever they think or prefer, and who regard as unlawful whatever displeases them (1:9). Nor is he with those whose judgment is perverted by the desires of the flesh, the eyes, or pride (cf. 1 Jn 2:16); these are 'men of corrupted understanding' (2 Tim 3:8). Among them, do we not witness that reversal of concepts by which obedience becomes an evasion by the weak, humility a lack of personality, and chastity a perversion of nature?

We are not safe from these subtle falsifications; nature is there to suggest them to us. Self-will, selfishness with all its tentacles, stimulates the imagination which then invents a whole series of justifications to cover our evil instincts with angel wings. In this way, we can be deceived by our apparently good intentions; as it says: 'There are ways that seem right to men, but which end in the depths of hell' (7:21). The danger of fooling ourselves about the purity of our intentions, and even of committing acts which are morally evil is a trap lying in wait for us. The monk by his vocation must tend toward purity of heart, which is above all purity, a holy simplicity of intention. Yet, even among good motives there is a ladder of perfection. The motives beginners have in the way of purification yield little by little to others which are higher and purer. St Benedict warns us of them.

The fear of hell (4:45, 5:3, 7:11, Prol. 42) can effectively turn a man from sin whose wages is death (Rm 6:23), especially the second death (Rev 20:6, 14, 21:8), that is, hell. Is it appropriate in a rule written for monks to speak of this fear of the Last Judgment (RB 4:44, 7:64)? The Gospels speak of it. Is it advisable today to pass over in silence this revealed truth? When the faith of christian people was simpler and hardier, the thought of the reality of hell doubtless exercised a salutary pressure. If Our Lord were to speak to the crowds today, would he speak no more of eternal fire, of the eternal torments awaiting the damned who refuse to perform acts of charity to their neighbor (Mt 25:41, 46, 45)? Should the truths of the faith be adapted to human psychology, or should human psychology be formed so that man can learn to adapt himself to the truths of faith? St Benedict supposes quite simply that his monks are not afraid of having a fear of hell because they believe at the same time in the mercy of God. And since the Lord excites the fear of hell in the souls of those who believe in him, St Benedict, as a faithful servant of his Master, does not hesitate to use the same language.

Although St Benedict speaks about the fear of hell, he knows other, more perfect motives for doing good, but he also knows that neither psychology nor theology obliges a man to use them all, beginning with the least noble and ending with the holiest. Each soul has its own history. The choices and motives which determine his actions and reactions will depend on his natural development and the influence of grace in his life. Perhaps the fear of hell will not make a great impression on some people, especially if the experience of sin has scarcely marked them.

Again, is it appropriate in this context to speak of the 'fear of God'? We must not confuse this with the fear of the eternal Judge. In the motivation of a monk's actions, the fear of God plays a decisive role. It provides a background (7:10). This fear of God, according to Holy Scripture—the source on which St Benedict draws—extends from fear to love (72:9) and develops, so to speak, with a man's spiritual maturity. It goes practically hand in hand with faith in a God existing and present (7:13), and it underlies all motivation of a supernatural character.

The Rule speaks of the motives behind our actions in analyzing those for obedience without delay. There it mentions the promise of 'sacred service' (5:3). Once made, the promise to persevere until death in the monastic life obliges the monk to persevere by fidelity in the state he has chosen (Prol. 50, 58:17). There we are touching upon a whole series of motives which guide many of our actions. Education, ordinary or religious, creates in our soul a certain number of principles, axioms, ways of acting, and habits which in concrete life act like dikes to channel our acts. Fidelity to responsibilities once accepted is one of them. It would be disloyal and shameful to fail in them. Our dignity as members of a society of honorable persons would be tarnished. We have received a mission, a task; we ought to be faithful to our duty. The community is counting on us, on the stability and firmness of our behaviour and this obliges us to remain in the path where our social background, traditions, unforeseen circumstances, and above all, our personal decisions have placed us. The promise made solemnly before God and our brothers to live as monks and to live as good monks, and the will to remain true to ourselves in following this way until death, may for many of us be a motive of very great moral force.

Fidelity to the Lord's grace and gratitude for the merciful

call he addressed to us can also exercise a good influence on our life. The Prologue of the Rule eloquently calls to mind the Lord's invitation and urges us to respond promptly and perseveringly (Prol. 35).

The hope of obtaining eternal reward is another motive for the monk's action (5:3, 7:11), a motive not only valid, but definitely desirable (4:46), since the possession of eternal life goes together with the love of God, the goal toward which all human life moves (5:10). Concerning this motive, it is fitting to repeat our remark about its value and its nobility being in proportion to the spiritual maturity of each person, for the love of God, just as love of glory or happiness, can be quite possessive and self-centered, or it can be centered on God, and worthy of a love of self-offering. And so we have arrived at the most perfect motive: the love of God himself, or more concretely, the love of Christ, since God has chosen to approach us by making himself thus more lovable.

St Benedict describes for us the painful ascent of the monk through the degrees of humility toward the heights of holy love where there is no longer fear, or menace of hell, or pain, and where he observes, 'as it were naturally and through a habit acquired of blessed practice and the very attraction of virtue, through the love of Christ, all that he formerly observed with a feeling of fear' (7:67-69).

*Amore Christi*, for the love of Christ. This is the wonderful motive toward which the Holy Rule leads us prudently, gradually, without wanting us to skip stages when the state of our soul may require we wait. There is no more attractive, persuasive, or vigorous motive than love. Love is inherent in our nature and it ravishes us. Why stop on the way then? Why not go directly to the love of Christ? Yes, we should run toward that love. St Benedict helps us understand why someone does not generally arrive there until he has gone through the degrees of humility. He needs to be purified of his vices and his sins (7:70) in order to arrive at that blessed state where the love of Christ possesses him completely. Impurity is an obstacle for us; it does not always come from serious sin, but from evil inclinations, selfishness, self-seeking, our self-will, in short, from a nature corrupted by original sin.

The monastic life with its fidelity to the practices of its observance, deepened by an ever more living faith (Prol. 49), offers the monk the means of acquiring purity and liberty of heart, and thus prepares him for the love of Christ, the gift of the Holy Spirit (7:50). Oh, how enviable that happiness is! To be able to act in all things through the love of Our Lord, to fix our gaze on Christ who himself always acted according to the will of his Father because he was entirely possessed by the love of that Father (Jn 14:31, 17:4). How ideal it would be always to be led by the love of Christ (2 Cor 5:14), carried along by the holy habit of scrutinizing and following in all things his holy will, just as he told us: 'If anyone loves me, he keeps my word (Jn 14:23), to know in exchange his love 'who loved me and gave himself for me' (Gal 2:20), and to be known by him who from his cross forever extends his arms to us to reveal the secrets of his love. May all the activities of our daily life, the acts commanded by obedience, by the horarium, by duty, originate in a response to the love of Christ who draws us irresistibly, if we truly pay attention.

Through contact with the most loving Christ, our Father St Benedict clearly experienced that expansion of the heart which makes one run in the commandments of God (Prol. 49) and fills one with the ineffable sweetness of love. His words allow us to catch a glimpse of his happiness, the happiness of someone who, holding nothing dearer than Christ (5:2), walks in love (Eph 5:2) while sharing the sorrow and the joy of his Lord's world.

Let us leave it at that, for here instruction ends and experience begins. St Benedict himself is content to show us the way to the tabernacle (Prol. 24) to which the Lord invites us by his strong sweet voice (*ibid.* 19). It is grace's privilege to guide us into that tabernacle, but the 'mother of fair love', Mary ever-Virgin, leads us there.

# The Supreme Rule:
# The Gospel

# ALONG
# THE GOSPEL PATH

St Benedict encourages the monk to walk in the path of the Gospel (Prol. 21). That is the principal norm of the monastic life as the decree *Perfectae Caritatis* (2) of Vatican II reminds us. The abbot ought not to teach anything outside the law of the Lord (2:4) and he ought to be well versed in the Word of God so that he can draw from it teachings new and old (67:9), and sayings as remedies to heal wounded and troubled souls (28:3). The Holy Scriptures form the warp of the Rule; the New Testament is cited there more than 130 times, the Old Testament more than 110 times—without counting the frequent allusions it contains. The marrow of its teaching is the Gospel. The Rule leads us to the word of the Lord; it is a summary of his teaching for those wanting to follow him by the path of the monastic life. This is why the monk proposes for himself nothing more than the integral development of the evangelical life, the divine life he received at baptism.

Is the lay Christian not also a full-time Christian? Does the monastic life add to the christian life some perfection to which the ordinary Christian cannot aspire? Let us be on guard against such thoughts, even though they no longer find much of a hearing. There was a time when marriage was often considered a second-class way for Christians and when perfection and sanctity were considered the reserve of certain modes of life. The Second Vatican Council has vigorously retained for all Christians the vocation to holiness. We are all called to seek God—let us recall the condition the Rule requires of the novice: 'If he truly seeks God (58:7)— we are all called to find him, to contemplate him, to be united to him. Through baptism, we all receive the Holy Spirit through whom we are made sons of God and have right of entry to the heart of God.

Monks are not therefore privileged by their particular form of life, as if they had received a coupon for getting graces refused to ordinary people. They have to deserve those graces like anyone else. All Christians are called to pass through the same pascal mystery of Christ, to live their joys and their sorrows, their success and their solitude, their combats and their death with Christ Jesus who, although he was God, emptied himself even unto death (Phil 2:6ff.), so that they may arrive with him at resurrection and eternal life.

In all of this, nothing sets the monk off from other Christians. He cannot pretend to have the halo of a man of God by the simple fact of his profession; he is not thereby more qualified than others to speak of the Lord's way, or to consider himself an expert in ways of prayer. And if by his mode of life, he attracts the admiration of humble Christians, let him repeat loudly that his only claim to distinction is authentic virtue.

The Gospel is the guide of every Christian, and St Benedict himself lets us understand that the Rule is subordinate to it in arriving at the summit of perfection, that is to say, at the charity which Holy Scripture in every word teaches is the most exacting norm of human life (73:3). Outside the religious life, the way to holiness is wide open; for everyone the entrance is narrow (cf. Mt 7:14; Prol. 48), but it leads to glory.

Yes, monks, like everyone else, are simple Christians. The Good News is their law, their hope, their lot, and their salvation. Their commitment to the Gospel is re-inforced by a supplementary promise. But do we not find among them some who are very observant and insist on certain rules, but who at the same time lack in understanding, discretion, and charity toward their brethren; lacking, therefore, in a fundamental law of the Gospel? Does it not happen to us sometimes in our monasteries that we think too much of efficiency, success, money, production, and not enough about the works of mercy and of justice the Gospel demands of each and every person according to his state in life? Life in spiritual high places is not exempt from deviation; history bears witness to this. A spiritual orientation inadequately balanced by humble fidelity to the Gospel can cause one to forget fundamental duties. This is why St Benedict does not hesitate to list in his catalogue of virtues (RB 4) precepts which may seem superfluous for monks (4:3f.), or useless (4:15, 17). By this he makes us understand that it would be vain or pharisaical to want to build an authentic spiritual life in any way other than upon the solid rock of an integral christian life. Mere good appearances can no more resist the winds of doubtful doctrine than those of temptation.

Can the failure of certain monastic lives not be explained by a lack of balance where a monk, exchanging the essential, that is, life according to the Gospel, for accidental forms or superstructures of the spiritual life, finds himself confronting emptiness on the day those forms are called into question? How important it is during the probation period carefully to establish the monastic life on the practice of the christian life, especially upon the concrete exercise of charity! The monastic state is also threatened by the danger of a sort of rectitude which, clinging to venerable but outdated usages, charges relaxation and ruin at every little necessary change.

Others, misled by such things, find a contrast between the Gospel and the Rule, as if the Rule had become for the monk a rival or a substitute for the Scripture. But the Rule serves the Gospel, that is clear! The aim of the Rule goes beyond that of the Gospel, because it is written for monks alone, but it remains in full conformity with the spirit and even with the letter of Holy Scripture. It is not, therefore, a sort of prolongation of the Gospel, a Gospel for the use of monks, although it is in fact a summary of the Gospel, a complete and succinct synthesis of its doctrine, but not a substitute for it.

But what is the real aim of the Rule in the christian life, then? Does it want to create a christian elite, a race of super-christians? No, the Rule has no such ambitions. It simply presents to the Christian specific means drawn from the Gospel for living his christian life and for assuring the use of these means within an appropriate structure and organization. But, let us add at once, even these specific means, these counsels, as the Gospel calls them, counsels of chastity, poverty, and obedience, are offered to all Christians and by their fundamental demands require of all the very substance of the Gospel. All Christians ought to obey the will of God, all ought to live chastely according to their state in life, all ought to be poor in spirit, for the rich enter the Kingdom with difficulty.

The monk endeavors, therefore, to follow the Gospel faithfully. In penetrating this Good News, he discovers there the lovable person of Jesus who attracts him. He listens to his words and meditates on his life. He begins to love him and to hold nothing dearer than him (5:2). He wants to imitate him as much as possible. He discovers that Jesus lived obedience, chastity, and poverty more strictly than he imposed them on most of his disciples when he preached *metanoia* (conversion) and the Kingdom to them. Struck by the example of his life, he wants to follow him.

St Benedict really seems to have had in mind this *conversio*, this conversion, this passage from the simple christian life to the decision to follow Christ in his special way of life. Disobedient to God all have sinned. All, without exception, ought to turn back through obedience (Prol. 2). But among those willing to make the effort of obedience, some choose special means; they want to go all the way in obedience: these are the monks, St Benedict goes on therefore: 'It is now to you that I address my words, now I am to a monk: to you who wish to renounce your self-will and to take up the mighty arms of obedience' (Prol. 3), that is to say, a special obedience: monastic obedience. He will explain this later on in the Rule. But we find here again that the intentions and the hopes of monastic life are in line with and in the spirit of the Gospel, and that, in living out his vocation, the monk remains, therefore, at the heart of the Gospel. In this sense, he is simply a Christian, and he lives his life *per ducatum Evangelii*, led by the Gospel, but he follows Christ *pressius*, more closely (Decree *Perfectae Caritatis* 1), by choosing the way of life that Jesus and his holy Mother chose (*ibid.* 25).

We must not therefore put monks into a special category

of people wanting to do more than what the Gospel teaches. On the contrary, they want to live it fully by accepting certain counsels which it proposes, and which everyone is free to embrace or ignore. They want to follow the paths of the Gospel very closely, and St Benedict leads them in a very realistic fashion. He sees and shows them the goal: the perfection of charity. But as a good psychologist and educator, he prefers to insist on the means. We go to God through love, and obedience is an expression of charity (5:2, 7:34, 68:5, 71:4); he stresses this less than the practical side of obedience: *mandata*, the commandments. In a rule written for monks, we might think it would be enough to emphasize the motive of love. St Benedict chose to have his monks advance *per ducatum Evangelii*, on the paths of the Gospel, on the road divinely marked out by him who is the way to the Father, the road he himself took, who loved the Father (Jn 14:31). But Jesus tells us again and again that he comes above all to obey his Father and do his will—to love the Father is to obey his commandments: 'I do as the Father has commanded me' (*ibid.*). Therefore, St Benedict insists, as did his forerunners, on obedience and the 'observance of the Rule and leads to perfection (73:8, 9).

The monks' road to salvation, is, then, every Christian's road. If the monastic observance demands of them things the simple Christian is not obliged to do, 'let them not be puffed up by their own good works' (Prol. 29). The goodness of the Father asks it of them personally for the good of their own souls and for the benefit of the communion of the elect. Let them glorify God who works in them (Prol. 30). The Lord is showing them a great mercy by calling them to the monastic life framed about by a community of brothers in order to make the work of their salvation easier.

The temptation to believe oneself better than others can be experienced by people who have followed the path of the Lord all their lives. The monk must not let himself drift into this spirit of pride. This is why St Benedict insists that man is fallen and disobedient, a sinner, someone who has gone astray and needs to be converted. By becoming a monk, that man is transformed and embraces obedience. Thus, St Benedict took it upon himself to empty vanity out of our heart. In becoming monks, we do nothing extraordinary, we are not the better part of Christianity, a chosen race. If the monk has often been considered a penitent, one need look for the reason not simply to a history of famous and striking conversions, but rather to the root, the Rule itself; it follows closely the Good News and calls us to *metanoia*, to conversion: the Kingdom of God is promised to us on that condition.

The Rule has no other goal, therefore, than to introduce us to the spirit of the Gospel. It is likewise remarkable to notice the degree to which the divine Word, the *lectio divina*, organizes the monastic day of which it occupies a large part. The Rule is not a screen between us and the Gospel except for someone who does not know how to penetrate it but stops at minor details. For that matter, Holy Scripture itself can act as a screen between God and the reader if he does not read it in faith, just as the figure of Christ scandalized many of his contemporaries. The monk who is faithful to the Rule learns the road of the Gospel, and under its guidance meets the Lord.

# DOES THE RULE SHACKLE THE DYNAMISM OF THE GOSPEL?

Nowadays we are afraid of anything which remotely resembles 'institutionalism'. In order not to extinguish the Spirit and his urgent, unexpected inspiration (cf. 1 Th 5:19), it is said that we must leave the way clear for inspiration and spontaneity. We will not take time here to discuss the problem of knowing whether the Spirit needs human spontaneity to inspire. He lives in our hearts; our attitude toward divine activity ought therefore to be one of complete availability. But how can we know if the Spirit is speaking to us at any given moment? How can we discern his voice among so many others? We have to undertake this work of discernment, sustained by grace. It is as necessary and difficult as the spirit of human reason, often influenced by the flesh, is boisterous and noisy. The Holy Spirit loves to speak in silence. To hear the Spirit of God, we do not need to have freedom of action or to be free of structures and rules; we must have true liberty of heart, that is to say, a discipline of heart, a purity of heart. The All-Pure reveals himself only to pure hearts.

Now, we have just learned to consider the monastic life, and, more specifically, the benedictine life, as a means of accomplishing this purification little by little, of clearing out the obstacles in us to the actions of the Holy Spirit. Does life structured according to the Rule, therefore, give a more flexible spontaneity and openness to hearing the voice of the Spirit?

Let us take a look at what this institutionalization is all about. By this word is meant the tendency of man to establish himself within a social organization, to immobilize himself in laws and customs which have had their day; in brief, to take the institution as an end in itself. Without doubt, some usages, and some institutions and sacrosanct customs weigh heavily upon the liberty of the children of God. Here and there we find communities with long pious common prayers added to the *pensum servitutis nostrae*, to the measure of our service (49:50), and maintained faithfully for generations. Some works of supererogation wear us out more than they raise us up to God. The exercise of authority sometimes involves irritating customs which make it hard to form one in obedience. In some of our religious families, we must admit, the accent placed upon secondary practices can obscure the view of the gospel essential. Routine is another little-esteemed by-product of the institution. A false conception of fidelity toward some holy person or some such outdated regulation piously preserved, sometimes reeks more of sclerosis than of watchful fidelity to the voice of the Spouse of our souls.

Now, undoubtedly, a rule or a constitution, can become an obstacle between a community and the renewal that must be made, between abandoning oppressive customs and rediscovering of the word of God.

Here we may ask ourselves: Can the Rule of St Benedict in some cases hinder the development of the true gospel life? Can it act as a screen to the Gospel, or indeed, does it weigh down our steps by holding us to a certain mediocrity or self-sufficiency? For those who are attached to it, is there a danger of sclerosis, a threat coming not from a false attitude on our part toward the Rule, but from the Rule itself, from its character, from its spirit?

This questions deserves an answer. The short-sightedness of man, let us immediately make clear, can transform even the Gospel into a stumbling-block on the path to God. The disciples of the Rule are not safe from such a paradox; the worshippers of the letter, forgetting its spirit, can easily be among them. But let us leave this problem aside in order to come back to our question: does the Rule bear within itself a tendency to misunderstanding; does it lead to the error of limiting itself solely to a good external observance, and thus of going to sleep spiritually by replacing the dynamic of the gospel with second-hand regulations?

To answer this question we should consider two things:
—The Rule is not an obstacle to going beyond oneself.
—The Rule provides an enthusiasm, a stimulus, to overcoming one's own limitations.

St Benedict, in the famous epilogue of his Rule, shows us that it is a starting point, a beginning of monastic life (73:1). To advance in the ways of holiness we must draw on Holy Scripture, and on the books and biographies of the Fathers (73:2ff.), and finally, having fulfilled the observance with the help of Christ, we arrive at the sublime heights of doctrine and virtue which he lets us glimpse (73:8f.). The Rule is not, therefore, an end; it is a beginning, an open door to spiritual heights and, as the title of this chapter indicates, it does not contain all the norms of perfection.

St Benedict's remarkable modesty characterizes the whole Rule. It is only a school (Prol. 45). Someone who has followed its teaching well may leave the school to go into the desert to single-handed combat (1:5). He will have no further need of the institution.

The Rule's whole texture shows the great liberty of spirit with which St Benedict regarded prescriptions. He is, on the one hand, very strict on those points which make up part of the indispensable inventory of the spiritual workshop of asceticism—and this apparent rigidity could cause someone to overrate their importance in different circumstances; on the other hand, he recommends discretion, that mother of virtue, to the abbot (64:19), and a holy moderation (41:5, 64:19, 64:17). The abbot is to keep the Rule and see that it is kept (3:11, 64:20), but the fundamental goal of the Rule, the salvation of souls (41:5, 2:33-38) comes before its ordinances. The institution is there to serve souls and not the other way round.

This fact does not, however, give the abbot or a community a free hand to change the Rule as they please. St Benedict has a very acute sense of discernment between what is necessary for the maintenance of good community and individual discipline, and what ought to be left to the initiative of each person. In other words, he recognizes both the danger of exaggerated institutionalism and the danger of a disorder provoked by the relaxation of important rules. One cannot with impunity renounce the prescriptions imposed by pastoral prudence and discretion without losing sight of the meaning of monastic life and thus endangering souls.

St Benedict, therefore, leaves great initiative to the individual in the midst of community life and its demands (7:55). By not giving a method for prayer, he allows the monk to find his own way (RB 19 & 20). This spirituality, based on the Divine Office and *lectio divina*, on humility, obedience, silence, and especially on charity, is very simple and evangelical. Its recommendations on personal asceticism are extremely restrained (RB 4), so as to leave a very large margin for one's own initiative (49:6) while still prudently guarding against possible excess by means of the abbot's intervention (49:8).

This hypothesis of institutionalization by the Rule must, moreover, undergo still closer scrutiny. By faithfully following a rule, does the religious risk being weighed down by useless baggage on his journey toward perfection? And for us children of St Benedict, is brotherly love really hindered by the Rule? It is true that the vow of stability does not allow us to preach the Gospel to the peoples of Australia or Oceania, but have we not by our profession freely agreed to maintain a certain order in our exercise of charity, an order which does not prevent it from being unlimited in its object, but which, by directing its activities, necessarily limits them? Does the Rule hinder our gift to God in the service of our neighbor? Actually, it helps us instead to give our full measure.

Pressing further, we come to obedience, which above all else is called into question in this regard. According to certain people, it places the monk in a state of inferiority, it changes him into a child and imprisons him in a state of passive inaction. It is the great culprit, it clips the wings of charity, bridles initiative, accustoms the monk to crossing his arms in a kind of inertia. Is this what obedience really is? Is it not instead the conformity of our will with that of Jesus, who by the obedience of love has saved the world? Is it not that awesome power (Prol. 3) which can let us conquer self and advance the reign of God in souls? This obedience will send us, perhaps, to labor at an apostolic work, to fight for justice and peace, to preach the faith. Perhaps it will keep us in the cloister to pray and serve our brothers in religion. The effect will be the same. A St Thérèse of the Infant Jesus works as hard for the advancement of the kingdom of God as a great missionary. The institution did not hinder her from it, but regulated, deepened, even multiplied her efforts. She would probably not have become the saint that she is without the great difficulties that she had to face in the common life. At any rate, the rule of Carmel did not hold her back on the heroic path of the full blossoming forth of her love. The Rule of St Benedict has formed throngs of saints. Did they become holy in spite of the Rule? Who would dare claim such a thing?

We have just seen that the Rule does not impede our journey toward perfect charity (7:67). It remains to be seen whether it helps us, encourages us, and carries us toward that perfection. By entrusting ourselves to it, are we guided toward Christ, toward God? Is the Rule a good teacher of the Gospel, does it know how to introduce us into its dynamism, or does it leave us to ourselves to find our own way in? Some constitutions may err in their juridical coldness; some declarations may suffer from a lack of evangelical enthusiasm and end by exhausting us by concentrating their spiritual forces on the incidentals, the means, or the forms. Can the Rule of St Benedict be reproached for this?

In answering this question we do not want to get involved here in a long discussion. To know the Rule is to recognize the ardent accents so akin to the language of Holy Scripture. St Benedict strives to bring us continually back to the teaching of the Gospel. This is why nothing alien strikes the person who opens the Rule after having had the Scripture in hand. St Benedict masticates, so to speak, the marrow of the

Gospel teaching in order to put it within reach of his monks and to insert his monastic teaching into it. In other words, the institutions of the Rule never prevent one from seeing clearly the unconditional radicality of the Gospel and the absolute of divine love. There is no equivocating about the absolute nature of profession (58:15f.); the poverty is likewise radical (33:3), the obedience must be *usque ad mortem* (17:34) and prompt (5:7ff.), the heroic obedience of the Sermon on the Mount (7:35ff.). We must love Christ with a total love (72:11) and tend toward a faultless fraternal charity (72). St Benedict thus proposes to us (5:11) the narrow way (Mt 7:14) in a total fidelity to the teaching and example of Christ.

How could the Rule cast a shadow on the Gospel, then? How could it, by its institutions, turn us aside from the fullness of Christ's teaching? It is, on the contrary, a limpid mirror and guides us with assurance to grasp its most authentic meaning. If, therefore, it is of no use to us, this is because we do not know how to use it.

Let us add three more remarks to these considerations. Without any doubt, in the Rule we find prescriptions which, while they retain their deeper meaning, can no longer be observed to the letter. Most of the time these are customs which have lost their meaning or frame of reference in the different conditions in which modern man lives. Other usages, however, retain all of their reason for being in contemplative communities or those little engaged in exterior works, but they cannot be maintained where the needs of ministry or the apostolate affect the horarium and the course of daily life. It is, however, well to be on guard against considering obsolete everything which gives a first impression of being outdated, because many of these usages retain their spiritual meaning and efficacy. Such purism would impoverish rather than purify.

Modern man has an obsession for simplicity and authenticity, and can easily be tempted to sacrifice forms, structures, and symbols which he has not taken the time to assimilate. At a time when disputation is sky-rocketing, he may risk throwing out real values without proposing anything to replace them.

St Benedict shows himself an advocate, not of immobility, we realize, but of stability and tranquillity of order. He does not like the restless (2:8-25) and he wants conversations with the abbot to be conducted with dignity (3:9, 68:2f.), and he especially wants the abbot not to have a turbulent or restless disposition (64:16). Along the same line, St Benedict puts us on guard against singularity: the orderliness of the community depends on this (7:55). For him, institutions which are well-tried, reasonable, firm, yet generous, retain their full effectiveness in guaranteeing that atmosphere of peace, serene security and brotherhood to the man whose gaze is turned away from the love of the present and fixed on the God of love.

It is impossible, and this is our conclusion, to live without structures, without a pre-established order, without institutions. Nor is it possible to do away with the danger of people attaching themselves to the institution, becoming entrenched in it, and even finding in the ritual performance of their duties a justification for infidelities in the essentials of their lives. The risk of Pharisaeism, given man's weakness, is inherent in every type of exterior religious activity or form. But one avoids it not by exchanging one formula for another, but by fighting tirelessly for sincerity in his religious practices, sustained by the effort of referring everything to God, the only pole of reference for our actions.

So then, neither the institution nor, in some situations, the absence of institutions shall separate us from the love of Christ. On the contrary, for the person who lives the spirit of the Rule deeply and lives out its inward meaning, the usages and the institutions will become integrated in his whole life. He will love his Rule without a spirit of contradiction, and will find in it a spiritual guide capable of opening to him the path to the heart of God.

# MONASTIC
# SPIRITUALITY

Monastic spirituality is a vast theme which cannot be treated in a day. And yet I would like to throw out some thoughts for your meditation.

Benedictine spirituality is based on the attitude described in the Holy Rule. Monks are Christians, Christians who do not abandon the ordinary ways of Christian life, but who want to go to the Lord with greater security, greater facility, and also greater speed. For this reason, they adopt helpful means which are not necessarily those of all Christians: the evangelical counsels and the monastic Rule. In his journey toward the Lord, the monk needs a guide; this is why he says: 'Your word is a lamp for my steps' (Ps 118: 105). The word and the example of Christ, are there to lead him, because the Father has sent his Son to be the way, the truth, and the life. The spirituality of the monk is therefore based on the divine word, on Holy Scripture.

In accordance with the whole monastic tradition, St Benedict insists very much on *lectio divina*. There we find the book of the divine word: the *verbum Verbi*. This word is the nourishment which sustains our life, our heart, and leads us to the heart of God. Holy Scripture marks out our day. We find it in the Office and again in the *lectio divina* which is, above all, reading these holy books. May our thoughts be concentrated on this divine word! Every day we have it before our eyes, and we can easily let ourselves be impregnated by a text, by a few words, both at the Office and during our reading. We are nourished by it, and we feel its energy and vigor in our heart. We have no need to seek our nourishment in books written by men. Some of these are excellent, to the extent that they resemble Holy Scripture. But all the same, these books remain men's words.

We are nourished above all by the very word of God, then.

In this context, what is the place and function of the Rule which we profess?

For our life, the Holy Rule is a practical interpretation of Holy Scripture, or rather, the concrete application of its teaching to the monastic life. It is impregnated by God, and for us it translates into concrete reality, what is presented to us as divine wisdom in the Holy Scriptures. It is a rule of life: *Regula Monachorum, Regula Monasteriorum.* This is why the Rule is the second book which can nourish us and can truly guide us. It is a practical book, filled with the Holy Spirit.

To continue, we nourish ourselves, then, in a very simple way on Holy Scripture. It is the divine Word. To find God, we need not seek first to be a master of some method of meditation. You know very well that it is far from my mind to deprecate methods of meditation. They are means, aids. It is surely necessary for us to know how to ruminate on the words of God. But too easily—that's the way we are—we become attached to the method, and we imagine that if we do not succeed with that method, if we do not become master of it, if we do not proceed by means of it, we will never succeed in meditating; and we get discouraged. Now, this preoccupation, this obsession with wanting to succeed according to some method of meditation, and the fear of not succeeding, already betrays a false attitude.

We ought to be extremely simple on our journey toward God, or, if you prefer, in our method of meditation. Let us make a comparison: when Our Lord wanted to have a heart to heart talk with his apostles, he sat down at table; he celebrated the eucharistic supper with them, and on that occasion he spoke to them in a very simple way, heart to heart, telling them the deepest things that we could hope to know or hear. Now, by this we learn that our way of assimilating the divine word ought to be related to that Supper. We sat down at table with Our Lord, and Our Lord entrusts himself to us. This also means that we ought to assimilate the divine word as we do nourishment, and to receive nourishment for the soul as we receive nourishment for the body. When you sit down at table to eat, you have no method; you do not say: 'How ought I to eat this? How is all this to be digested and assimilated?' We do not make a problem out of it; it takes care of itself. This is the secret: it takes care of itself. The divine word is not made to be re-prepared, wrapped up, ground up, under some pretext that we can then better chew it, swallow it, or digest it. No. The divine word goes into our hearts directly. God speaks to us.

And why does he speak to us? Because he loves us. We have heard him tell us with great animation, 'The Father loves you, because you love me and because you believe that I came from God' (Jn 16:27). Therefore, because the Father loves us, he speaks to us. Now when a lover speaks to the person he loves, he doesn't ask that there be methods and manners of understanding; he quite simply speaks his mind, and does it in such a way that he will be understood. He uses words that will be understood.

Bear in mind that monastic spirituality does not look with disdain upon those other spiritualities which do construct methods. Basically, its manner of action is also a method, but it is simple. We want to go with simplicity, directly, to the word of the Lord. Now, in saying this, we understand perfectly that before all else we must have simplicity. Because we lack this we seek methods and ways to arrive at understanding. Look at the apostles around the eucharistic table. Jesus spoke to them, and they heard and understood immediately. They did not understand entirely and in depth. The Lord had to repeat his words often to let them enter into their hearts. But in their effort to understand, they were simple; they did not have pretensions of possessing or developing a method to understand their Master.

Simplicity: where do we get it? We must draw it from the monastic spirituality, from the whole system of virtues—allow me to use the word 'system'—which the Holy Rule presents to us. The practice of obedience and of humility under its various forms makes us simple; it prepares more and more in us that simplicity of heart which permits us to understand Our Lord more directly. There is, if you will, a certain happy circular movement which we cannot escape. We must ever better understand and assimilate humility as the Rule presents it to us, the greatest monastic virtue, and we will better understand the Lord. And, if we understand the Lord better, our humility and simplicity will increase.

St Benedict has taught us what the divine word ought to mean to us and its applications in our life. Through the Holy Rule he helps us to understand the Lord better by means of a procedure that does not seem to be one. He teaches us to go more simply toward him. The Holy Scripture, if we read it with piety, with respect, with love, helps us greatly in a very simple way to enter into the mind of the Lord.

We must not think, however, that meditation on Scripture dispenses us from prayer. But this is the very way to be able to pray, to understand the Lord better. For praying is nothing but entering into contact with the Lord, listening to him, paying attention to him, and then talking to him if we have anything to say to him. Let us think again of that eucharistic supper. This is how he speaks to us. He wants to speak to us heart to heart. That is what it means to pray.

We prepare ourselves to enter into conversation with Our Lord by hearing his word. And then—in a more or less direct way, the conversation begins. Whether it continues half a minute, or ten minutes, is not important. Let us not be concerned about time. Obviously, it does take time, and we should organize our time for *lectio divina;* this is, in fact, very important. Let us remember that St Benedict gives specific times for it. How, after that, can we neglect this responsibility? But we must not be concerned about counting the minutes we spend in real conversation with the Lord. If, for example, we are distracted for nine minutes and have a really intimate conversation with him for one minute, let us thank Him for having given us the grace of that minute of real conversation.

To pray is to converse with the Lord. He sits down at table with us. And what will he tell us in that conversation? He will talk to us just as He did to his apostles. What will he say to us? He will tell us, for example, his thoughts concerning ourselves; he will talk to us about his concern for the souls of all those who have believed in him, about those who ought to believe in him, about people who do not belong to his fold, who are separated from him, about all those who are lost, in a word, about everything. He will speak to us especially about his Father to make us understand that the Father loves us (Jn 16:27). He will teach us: 'Ask, and you shall receive' (Jn 16:24). He will tell us all his thoughts, which we can easily find throughout the Holy Scriptures, especially in the Gospels. Finally, he will talk to us also about ourselves; his counsels and his urgent invitations will fill our hearts with sweet joy and holy strength.

During this meal, he will thus speak to us in a very simple way very beautiful words which will nourish our souls. As for us, we will listen to him with great attention and great respect, and we will feel our hearts enveloped by the fire of love, because no one can listen to him, as the two disciples of Emmaus said, without becoming enflamed with love. Exactly that is the final goal of all prayer, of all our monastic life, and all its spirituality.

# LECTIO DIVINA

St Benedict gives primary importance to spiritual reading, as the forty-eighth chapter of his Rule testifies. The translation 'spiritual reading' dulls a little the force of the Latin expression *lectio divina*. St Benedict conspicuously obliges his monks to it, something which, presupposed of them an education beyond the ordinary during an epoch when going to school was not common. Perhaps one should see in this requirement one of the reasons which led him to receive even children into the monastery. At that time, it was actually easier to assure a sufficient education by receiving young boys (63:19; cf. 2 Tim 3:15) than by accepting adults, who were often unlearned.

The monks' obligation of several hours of daily reading—how parsimoniously the time set aside for reading the divine word is measured in our days!—makes us realize the formative influence which St Benedict attributes to *lectio divina* within the monastic regime. Does he not go so far, if necessary, as to adopt means of constraint to assure it (48:17-21)? That is only a last resort, for he wants his monks really to love sacred reading (4:55). In short, St Benedict sees in *lectio divina* one of the principal occupations of the monk, inseparable from the monastic vocation.

Why this insistence? Why these minute arrangements of times and circumstances to guarantee the necessary time for frequent and attentive reading? Because, of course, it concerns leading the monk to listen to the word of God.

That word is a great mystery. The Father has pronounced it from all eternity; it is a unique word in which he expresses himself: his whole being, his whole will, his whole love. God speaks to us in many ways (cf. Heb 1:1). He speaks to us by the thousands upon thousands of voices of creation, for the universe and all its splendor were made by his word, and are in some way his word. In a more direct way, God sent his word to Adam, to the patriarchs, and to the prophets, and finally, his word has come to us in the person of Jesus Christ (cf. Heb 1:1ff.). How marvelous! God speaks to us through the voice of a man. The Word of God appeared in human form. 'Blessed are your eyes, for they see; blessed are your ears, for they hear,' the Word himself says (Mt 13:16). We are blessed; the Creator of heaven and earth, he who knows the most hidden secrets, speaks to us. All of the libraries on earth, all the learned men together cannot know what he knows who searches the heart (cf. Ps 7:10) as the number of the stars (cf. Ps 146:4) even to the depths of God (cf. 1 Cor 2:10).

He speaks to us. To be sure, he speaks to us in moderation, for we would not be able to bear everything (cf. Jn 16:12). But he has the words of eternal life (Jn 6:68). He speaks to us of the Father, of the Holy Spirit, of the mystery of his own person. Of what greater things could he speak to us? He speaks to us of everything that is salutary for us. He entrusts to us the word of his mystery hidden for all ages (Eph 3:5) to the extent that it is useful to us. He speaks to us of the truth, He speaks the truth to us (Jn 2:45). Now, to know the truth responds to a deep desire, and even to the fundamental structure, of man. The human intellect has truth as its proper object. Man therefore seeks the truth and is restless until he possesses it. Let us not speak of the disillusioned Pilates who, despairing of finding it, fall into intellectual disarray and cynicism. Man has need of truth in order to build his life; he needs to know how to distinguish between reality and appearances, between what is authentic and what is artificial, between what is contingent and what is eternal. He needs to know the meaning of his life, his destiny and the Master of that destiny. God wills that every man arrive at the knowledge the truth (1 Tim 2:4, Jn 8:32).

God has spoken to us. He has sent us his Son who revealed himself to be truth (Jn 14:6). He has sent us the Spirit of truth that he might lead us to the whole truth (Jn 16:13).

Since God speaks to us, should all of our powers not be straining to hear him? Terrible indeed is the judgment for those whose spirit is dulled, who have stopped up their ears and closed their eyes lest they see and hear (cf. Mt 13:15). St Benedict vigorously sets his monks to the task of listening and opening their hearts to the divine word. Does he not begin his Rule by crying out 'Listen, my son', thus giving the whole monastic life so fundamental an orientation of openness to the word of God and contemplation of it that the monk may be defined as a person who is attentive to God, a disciple of the divine word (cf. Jn 6:45). For it is proper for a disciple to be silent in order to listen (RB 6:6), and to be attentive. The purpose of his asceticism is to silence the annoying and troublesome voices in himself, so as to hang on the words of the Master as the good people of Jerusalem did (Lk 19:48) in order to hear Jesus speak (Jn 7:46).

Do we really listen to him? Do we apply ourselves seriously to the Scriptures in order to meet him? To appreciate man's position on this responsibility, let us recognize that he continually has a choice to make. Very dissimilar voices are always entreating him. The temptation is very strong to let oneself be distracted by the many human voices which are always more insistent, and no longer to hear the divine voice. The mobility and instability of the modern human temperament do not allow him the calm for prolonged reading or lengthy meditations, and making efforts in this direction would probably lead more to fatigue and distraction than to concentration. St Benedict circumvented this problem in prayer well, and this is why he wanted it, as a general rule, to be brief (20:4). Today it would be necessary to apply the same principle of reading the Bible, which should be more frequent because it must often be more brief. May it penetrate and be more fervent, a true intimate, existential contact with the mysterious Speaker.

To know how to read the Scriptures inspired by God (2 Tim 3:16) and to be capable of receiving the touch of the Spirit, one therefore needs a real asceticism of recollection, of silence, of interior calm, and of purity of intention. Above all, one needs a strong faith which can overcome the obstacles and give God what belongs to God. He makes man the confident of his thoughts; He lets him see into his heart. Let us grasp in depth everything that means for us. Has Jesus not said: 'I no longer call you servants, because the servant does not know what his master does; I call you friends, because everything which I have learned from My Father, I have made known to you' (Jn 15:15); and the Spirit of truth will say 'all which he will hear, and he will announce the things to come' (Jn 16:13)? The Father speaks to us as a father speaks to his sons, and Jesus treats us as real friends. What joy! Let us, therefore, allow ourselves to be penetrated by the light and the heat of the divine word. It teaches us how much we are loved. God seems to have no other preoccupation than to treat us as well-beloved children (cf. Jn 16:27, 1 Jn 3:1). The Holy Scriptures reveal this to us on every page. 'For all that was written in the past was written for our instruction, that the constancy and consolation which the Scriptures give may obtain confidence for us.'

The word of Scripture is translated into modern speech by many different voices, an echo of the divine voice. The *lectio divina* of the Rule includes every type of reading which faithfully interprets the word of God in developing it and commenting upon it. St Benedict cites the *Conferences*, the *Institutes*, and the *Lives of the Fathers* (42:3, 73:2, 5) as well as the writings of the Fathers of the Church (73:4). And one might add to it so many other books by authors both ancient and modern in which the *Logos* of Truth, the Word, manifests himself while adapting himself to today's reader.

In this reading of things divine, and especially Holy Scripture, we find all that our soul needs. For these are not words which are lost on the wind, but words of life. What God tells us enlightens our mind through clear and wholesome ideas. 'For the word of God is living and active, and more cutting than any two-edged sword; it penetrates even to the point of the division of soul and spirit . . . it is able to judge the feelings and thoughts of the heart' (Heb 4:12). The word of God does not allow obscurity and doubt to remain in the soul or ambiguities or loop-holes. It exerts on our attitude, on our thought-process, a purifying action of detoxication. It judges us and separates error from truth in us. Little by little it transforms our judgment and lets us perceive what is good and what pleases God, while keeping us from following the inclination of our nature, which likes to model its judgments on those of the masters of thought of the present world (cf. Rm 12:2). For the word of God is a consuming fire; it burns what is straw in us, while keeping and purifying what is gold. Indeed, how many of our personal and common problems are resolved through contact with Holy Scriptures!

Yes, the word of God is that fire brought to the earth by Jesus (Lk 12:49); it sets our hearts aflame (Lk 24:32), enlarges and expands it (Prol. 49). The frequent reading of the divine word familiarizes us with the thought of God and his great intentions, and makes us go beyond our petty horizons, our personal anxieties, and the narrowness of our spiritual poverty. It transports us to a higher plane, to the problems of mankind, seen through the eyes of Jesus, the true Saviour of the world. For he is the Word. In reading Holy Scripture, we read the Word who is in person himself the holy Book sent by the Father that we might open it, and even eat it (cf. Rev 10:9). He is the Truth (Jn 14:6). 'In him are found hidden all the treasures of wisdom and knowledge' (Col 2:3). Through prayerful and meditative contact with the written divine word, there is revealed to us the most lovable of men, our model, in whom is mysteriously incarnated the Wisdom of the Father of whom he is the mirror, although misunderstood and even ridiculed, but resplendent for those who have heard his call.

# *Purification*

# ASCETICISM

The Greek word *askesis* corresponds to the Latin *exercitium*, exercise. In the broad sense of the word, man ought to impose on himself a certain asceticism, that is to say, make certain efforts to maintain his physical equilibrium, and no less to cultivate his personality, his intellectual and moral formation, his outward behavior. A man cannot eat just anything any way he may like; he has to impose restrictions, limits, and rules upon himself. He cannot drink just as nature inclines him; he ought to impose upon himself an asceticism. We cannot sleep just any time and as long as we wish; instead, we ought to rise at a set hour. The schedule of our work ought to be respected. How demanding is the asceticism which we must impose on our tongue! Maintaining normal relations with our neighbor also imposes upon us an asceticism of vigilance, self-control, and discipline. The need to be sincere and honest demands continual vigilance, and a frequent examination of conscience.

This asceticism has as its object and its motive the natural well-being of man. It is indispensable for the person who has self-respect. Here we are going to envisage an asceticism with a religious, supernatural object, an asceticism which often coincides in its outward activities with rational asceticism, but is distinguished from it by its motivation. It envisages the supernatural well-being of man. If the ancient monks had the name and reputation of ascetics, it was on account of this type of asceticism. Indeed, one cannot separate monastic life from the idea of asceticism. The entire monastic life is an exercise consecrated to making the monk capable of receiving the touch of the Holy Spirit, to preparing him for meetings with the Lord, to putting him at the disposal of the divine will.

The word asceticism is not found in the Rule, but we are struck by the great number of synonyms we find there. At the very beginning of the Prologue (2), St Benedict already speaks of the labor of obedience. Labor indicates an effort

91

which must be made, an exercise. The image comes from
manual labor. The word discipline (7:9) expresses a similar
idea. To discipline oneself is the work of asceticism. We impose upon ourselves a discipline in our external behavior,
and even more an interior discipline.

Already in the first pages of the Rule, we find the word
*militare* (Prol. 3, 40; 1:2, 58:10, 61:10), *pugnare, pugna*
(1:4f.). The asceticism of the hermit is a single-minded
combat against the devil and vices (*ibid.*), whereas the
asceticism of the cenobite is a military service (2:20) in
Christ's army (Prol. 3). The words *opus, operari, operarius,*
also denote the effort expended by the monk in the work of
his sanctification. The Lord seeks his laborer in the marketplace (Prol. 14), a worker ready to put forth some labor,
some effort, that of asceticism, by wielding the 'instruments
of good works' (RB 4).

This leads us to the expression 'the observance of good
works' (Prol. 21) and to the words *observare, observatio,
observantia,* which are familiar to us because we are used to
designating the exercises of the monastic life by the collective word 'the observances'. We include under this word all
our typically monastic ways of doing things. They impose an
asceticism.

Next we meet such expressions as abstinence, fasting.
These words designate ascetical works in the sense of privations, restrictions imposed on the body (49:7). To abstain
from something, to impose a renunciation on oneself,
*abrenuntiare* (Prol. 3), signifies the acts of asceticism which
consist in cutting off things which are licit in themselves,
whereas the word *poenitentia* expresses rather the spirit and
the actions of repentance (Prol. 37; 25:3). On the other
hand, the Lord's invitation to renounce oneself (4:10) calls
for an asceticism.

Some expressions like *parcius, restrictius* (little, with
sobriety or moderation; with a bit of rigor) denote a rigor
imposed by the Rule, a limitation in the use of goods, or a
certain austerity (Prol. 47). 'Patience', as we find it in the
fourth degree of humility, expresses a high degree of
asceticism in imitation of the Passion of Christ (Prol. 50). The

word *conversatio,* the *conversatio monastica,* designates a specifically monastic way of living, a way of life which is not as that of people of the world. It is understood specifically as an ascetical way of life.

St Benedict speaks in the fourth chapter of the *ars spiritualis,* the spiritual art. Exactly what is this? An artist or an artisan has to impose on himself an asceticism of recollection, concentration, and withdrawal, in order to fix his work in his imagination. The creation of a work of art supposes a catharsis, a purification, an asceticism. The spiritual art includes rules, principles, and procedures which help the monk purify himself; it prepares for the Spirit a heart disposed to receive his imprint, the image of Christ. It is, therefore, a summary of monastic asceticism. The idea of the 'Rule' is the same: a collection of truths, of regulations, and of practices to direct the asceticism of the monk.

Having ascertained through the many expressions in the Rule that the monastic life is an asceticism with a supernatural goal, let us repeat that the field of action for asceticism is principally the natural man, and more exactly, the whole man, body and soul. Asceticism is applied to all the activities of the body which are subject to the will. Although the will cannot command the vegetative processes of the body in a direct way, it nevertheless exercises a strong indirect influence over them through disciplined eating, through a natural rhythm of movement and repose, of intellectual work and bodily exercise, through a regular life, sober and simple, avoiding agitation and unreasonable excitement and unmastered nervousness. It has been asked whether the life of monks is not a recipe for longevity. And as a matter of fact, St Benedict, in dealing with the monks' table, decided that two dishes are enough, along with bread and vegetables or fruits if there are any (39:1), and that it is absolutely necessary to avoid all manner of excess and indigestion (39:7). As for wine, he would have prefered to see the monks abstain from it (40:6), but given the customs of his time, he let them drink a certain amount, while exhorting them to do so with sobriety and even praise the Lord if there is none in the region where the monastery is located (40:8). If one adds to these rules the perpetual abstinence from the flesh of four-footed animals demanded by St Benedict, the entire regime gives us an impression of a table soberly but well served for the time; that is, of a reasonable and sane asceticism. All this is an application of the counsels given by St Benedict in the chapter on the instruments of good works: 'to chastise the body' (4:11); 'not to be a great eater' (4:36); 'not given to wine' (4:35). According to the Rule, the fast is, moreover, very prolonged and consists mainly in setting back the hour of meals and reducing them to only one (41:2, 6f.). In any event, St Benedict wants the monk to find in this regime a system of life which he is able to endure without complaint (40:9, 41:5) and even capable of making him love fasting (4:13).

Discipline regarding sleep is likewise dictated by natural reasons (8:1) which, it is true, cannot be applied to the letter in our days. But St Benedict does not demand anything too austere for monks of his time when he requires them to rise at the eighth hour of the night, that is to say, a little after midnight, so that digestion may be completed at the time of rising (8:1f.). There, too, we note, asceticism does not go contrary to nature, but adapts itself to its needs. The monk is thus formed in such a way as not to give himself to sleep (4:37, cf. 43:8, 22:8) but to hasten to Vigils, and thus to be spiritually awake (cf. Prol. 8).

St Benedict understood this restriction of food and sleep both as consistent with nature and as an ascetical exercise accessible to the common man. This is confirmed by his counsels regarding Lent. Since, according to him, the ordinary regime of life laid down by the Rule was less austere than that of monks ought ideally to be (49:1f.), he invites them to take advantage of the Lenten season 'by guarding their lives in all purity' (49:2), to avoid all negligence (49:4), to increase the accustomed burden of service by special prayers and by cutting back in food and drink (49:5), to limit the body in food, drink, sleep, conversations, and joking (49:7). Everyone, therefore, has his personal measure of asceticism to accomplish, set forth by the abbot (49:6). The monk proposes on his own initiative (49:6), but he does

no act of supererogatory asceticism without the consent and
blessing of the abbot (cf. ibid. 5, 8) and he awaits the Holy
Pasch with joy, the fruit of the Holy Spirit (cf. ibid. 6) and
'in the joy of spiritual longing' (49:7).

Let us note in passing that the monk will accomplish his
works of asceticism not only without complaining (5:14),
but with joy in his heart; for God loves a cheerful giver
(5:16). The monk who complains, even if only in his heart,
about the burden of his asceticism, will not derive any merit
from it (5:19).

Among the works of asceticism recommended for Lent, we
have seen that St Benedict mentions that disciplining of the
tongue, which is connected with corporal asceticism, since it
has to do with mastering an extremely agile member of the
body (cf. J 3:8). Nevertheless, the good and the evil which
it produces pertain to the spirit; 'life and death are in its
power' (Prov 18:21, RB 6:5). Asceticism of the tongue has
always been considered as an exercise proper to monks
(42:1). To place a guard on one's mouth (6:1) and to be able
to discipline one's speech requires a remarkable degree of
humility (7:56-60) and wisdom (7:61). The person who
controls his tongue is master of himself. The asceticism of
the tongue does not consist only in not speaking evil
(4:51, 39, 40), in not being loquacious and talkative (4:52,
53, 6:4; 7:57f.), but still more in abstaining even from
good and holy words (6:3) and in knowing how to measure
and weigh one's words (7:60f.) while still maintaining true
liberty of spirit and a natural spontaneity. The observance of
silence has, moreover, its special rules (42:1, 6; 25:2; 26:1;
38:5; 48: 5, 18, 21; 52:2; 53:23f.; 67:5f.), especially the
silence during the night (42:8ff.). Besides the control of the
tongue, although with much less insistence, the Rule also
calls for discipline of the eyes (7:63), of the ears (67:4f.), and
of the posture of the body (7:62-66).

All this helps us to see the extent to which the monk
ought to watch over his actions with an ever vigilant
asceticism: 'At all times to keep watch over the actions of
his life' (4:48).

So far, we have been seeing what concerns our bodies,

its members, and its organs as objects of our asceticism. *Askesis* in its classic sense refers to what has a corporal expression. But there is also an asceticism of the mind (Prol. 28; 1:5, 4:50, 7:12, 18, 44; 65:5), an asceticism of the will (Prol. 3; 4:60; 5:7; 7:12, 19, 21, 31), an asceticism of obedience (5), of humility (7), of patience (Prol. 50; 7:35, 38, 42; 72:5), of prayer (19), of stability and of perseverance (Prol. 50; 4:78; 58:9, 17), of poverty (33; 34; 54; 55), of chastity (4:64), of manual labor (48), of punctuality (22:6, 8; 43; 44; 47:1). One cannot live the monastic life without continual asceticism, just as every well-ordered life imposes self-discipline.

Before ending this conference, we need to answer a fundamental question: What is the object of monastic asceticism? The monk does not have only a purely natural object in mind, however noble that might be, as, for example, the development of the human personality; his asceticism is an effort directed toward the principal object of his life: seeking God through the imitation of Jesus Christ. The love of the Father is manifested in Jesus through the total orientation of his person to the Father. His virginity signifies an undivided love for the Father. His obedience is the most moving expression of his filial love in action. His poverty is the result of his complete liberty from all that the world can offer. The asceticism of the monk is the active expression of his nostalgia for the moral beauties of the person of Christ, perfect model of Father's love. In his meditations and his readings, the Lord has let him catch a glimpse of these marvels until, smitten by love and urged by grace, he sends all of his energies toward the height of holiness. Of course, he is conscious of his misery and realizes that he is burdened with faults, and he undertakes the work of purification; that is the immediate object of his asceticism (49:2). He will not, therefore, fall into the illusion of believing himself holy simply because of his efforts at asceticism (4:62). Neither will he let himself be tempted by pride; that would be the sign of ill-directed ascetic efforts (Prol. 29). But trusting in the help of the Lord who supports the humble efforts of those who seek him sincerely, he pursues his modest efforts in the hope of seeing increase in his heart, along with purity, 'that charity, thanks to which he will accomplish without pain, as it were naturally and through force of habit, all that which formerly he did not observe except with fright' (7:68). Thus he hopes to arrive at the power to act 'for the love of Christ', by means of a holy habit and of a sweet attraction to virtue (7:69). And his asceticism will pass by the Lord's grace, from a burdensome mortification to the joyous freedom of the risen Christ.

# DISCOURAGEMENT

When St Benedict, on the last page of his Rule, shows us our life as an *initium conversationis* (73:1), a beginning of monastic life, he is suggesting to us that we ought not give way to discouragement in the face of the very modest progress our efforts yield. Yes, discouragement may appear in the lives of those who have chosen the 'narrow way' (5:11), whose entrance is necessarily narrow and difficult (Prol. 48).

First of all, what exactly does discouragement consist of? More than simple fatigue, it is a real moral lassitude, a despondency sometimes leading to the abandonment of what has been undertaken because of lack of belief in its success. One neglects it, then one no longer cares, finally one puts forth no more effort. St Benedict knew this phenomenon and speaks of it more than once, as an attentive reading of the Rule shows us, even if he does not use a terminology which corresponds to our expression 'discouragement'. We have to be able to distinguish well between real discouragement and quibbling, complaining, or stubbornness which may cloak themselves with the more sympathetic mantle of weariness, overwork, despondency. To identify real discouragement, it is therefore necessary to study the phenomenon more closely.

Let us look at the causes of discouragement. The physical causes first. Physical dejection can have repercussions on the soul, which becomes dejected. We get sad, good for nothing;

we feel we are not wanted, or that we are not in the right place; our life seems to us to be a failure. St Benedict speaks several times of this phenomenon. We see him require that weak or delicate brothers, all those who possess small physical resources, have a work that will neither oppress nor dishearten them (48:24), lest they be tempted to run away.

The abbot ought, therefore, to be prudent, keeping in mind the discretion of holy Jacob who said: If I tire my flock too much, they will all die in one day (cf. RB 64:18). He ought therefore to be careful that everything is done in moderation because of the weak (48:9), for the neurotic and the weak can quickly become discouraged. The abbot ought to act with discernment and moderation in distributing work (64:17). An excess of fatigue would be the ruination of certain people; this is why we see St Benedict taking such care to teach the abbot not to neglect this factor and to give helpers—the word *solatium* is suggestive—to the weekly servants of the kitchen who are weak, so that they may discharge their duty without sadness (35:3), and not be discouraged. For St Benedict, that rule ought to be general, according to the means of each community and the situation of the place (35:4, 15:19f.). He should give helpers to the cellarer (31:17), the porter (66:5), and to those working with guests (53:18).

The Rule foresees, then, that there are more robust brothers and others less so, that certain employments demand greater effort, whereas there are, on the contrary, times that are more tranquil. But the abbot is responsible for the good organization, and he ought to make the burden supportable for everyone. He ought to know how to measure the energies of each, to listen to their wishes, make use of their natural dispositions and talents so as to avoid overwork and exhaustion which would put their very vocation in danger.

In addition to physical reasons for discouragement, there are causes of a psychological order. And often, the physical causes have repercussions on the soul and lead to dejection. For St Benedict, there are a number of categories of psychological causes. Already in the Prologue, he puts us on our guard against one of these causes when he advises his disciple: 'If there is [in the Rule] something a bit more rigorous . . . take care not to leave the way of salvation out of a sudden fear' (Prol. 47f.). The monk should not allow himself to be over-awed or frightened, or give into discouragement by running away. It is normal in the monastic life to be confronted now and then by painful situations; all human life has them.

St Benedict puts the monk on his guard, then, against the temptation to faint-heartedness (48:9). Let us realize that each one of us has his own temperament and his own strengths, and weaknesses, of character. Above all we must know how to put up with our own selves, and to arm ourselves against eventual attacks of despair. In the end, would it not be a lack of faith, that faint-heartedness against which Our Lord warned his disciples (Lk 12:28)? Discouragement sometimes leads to flight. St Benedict asks himself, therefore, whether someone who has left of his own accord and through his own fault should be received back again (29:1). Such a person was not able to resist temptation. Our Blessed Father recommends having mercy on him and letting him try again.

Discouragement arises also from faults and errors committed. In this case the abbot ought to act as a good shepherd and a real father. St Benedict shows how to treat a wavering brother (27:3), the brother who is hesitating between an honest repentance and a proud resistance. This is a form of discouragement; it prevents a return, an honorable apology, and an acknowledgement of one's faults. It is necessary to help this brother if he is not to be submerged in an excess of sadness (27:3). So the abbot will seek out consolers, *occultos consolatores* (*ibid.* 2) to encourage him and help him overcome this crisis. For the desolate monk, there is a real danger of sinking into total indifference and apathy. A brother can let himself become discouraged by small faults, close himself in, and let himself slide into a kind of mediocrity because he judges himself incapable of overcoming some particular fault. The surest medicine for overcoming this form of discouragement St Benedict recommends to us in the fifth degree of humility (7:44-48; Prol. 28).

Sometimes it is simply a change in the weather or, for the young who do not yet feel completely at home in the community, a feeling of emptiness, of being alone on a feast day, the absence of a helpful friend, a vague feeling of sadness or of dissatisfaction which puts one down in the dumps. In such cases, useful first aid might include a talk, listening to a place of music, some distraction, a walk. But to leave young people to themselves at times when their imagination refuses to react courageously would be pushing them, in their inexperience, to founder in an unwholesome melancholy perfect for confusing them.

Whatever the immediate cause of discouragement, the monk is not defenseless before this phenomenon so painful to the soul. Let us ask ourselves about the measures to be taken. First of all, it is for the abbot to keep his eyes open over the brothers. He must not be content to wait passively when he sees a brother sinking into this state, but he ought in his fatherly heart to find means inspired by wisdom and charity for struggling. When St Benedict puts into our hands the instruments of the spiritual art for consoling and helping the tempted and afflicted (4:18-19), it is evident that the abbot ought to be the first to use them in striving to find means capable of helping the brethren.

The afflicted brother, on his side, ought not to let himself slip into despair, which can manifest itself quite simply by the temptation to laxity. Let him go to his abbot or to a spiritual father (46:5) that is to say, a monk in whom he can confide. Let this monk, however, be aware of the great responsibility he is taking on. If he agrees with the opinion of the afflicted brother, he risks reinforcing his possible grievances and causing him to sink. The abbot himself ought, therefore, to take the initiative in comforting the tempted brother, prudently, and if necessary, secretly. The twenty-seventh chapter of the Rule indicates methods of fatherly help which can apply in any case.

Above all, each of us should take refuge, and comfort with God and the saints, his servants. Let us study the reactions of our heart to see where it applies itself to struggle in moments of discouragement, disappointment, weariness, or the *passio* we are undergoing. Is our first thought perhaps directed toward the heavenly Father who inspires us with complete confidence because he is a Father of goodness and mercy? Someone else may perhaps turn immediately and naturally to Jesus by thinking of the Lord's cross and Passion, of the man of sorrows. We are suffering. All right. Jesus has suffered before us. He has suffered loneliness, abandonment, disappointment, scorn. We can find strength and consolation in him; with him we can endure our *passio*. Yet another may find the Lord before the tabernacle in a very personal way, with all his understanding, his strength and his consoling word, the warmth of his love. There his affliction can change to true joy, there he can accept the weight of the cross, heavy at first, but in the end, light, because it is the sweet and lovable yoke of the Lord. The Virgin Mary is also the *consolatrix afflictorum;* she knows how to console because she is our mother. She is our Mother. A mother, like a father, knows the best ways of consoling a discouraged child.

If we find ourselves afflicted, then, instead of running away, let us run *forward;* instead of retreating, let us learn how to grow through that very existence. In that way, the discouragement or oppression overwhelming us will not fail to profit us. We will open our eyes toward God and understand even better that we have a Father in heaven. We will meet and join Jesus on his way, the way of the cross, and through the cross, the way of joy. Jesus will turn toward us if we are toiling upon his way, and his glance will be enough to encourage us. As for us, let us also learn to turn to him and call to him like the poor and needy in the Gospel. On this way we will journey side by side with the Virgin Mary, our refuge, our hope, our life. Whoever calls to her for help without being answered? She will lead us to Jesus, and we will be strengthened, consoled. This consolation will be like a health-giving balm for our soul and will cure it. Thus we will emerge stronger than ever from this temptation and from this experience of discouragement.

# HOPE

Hope! The very word charms, awakens, heralds the future, victory, newness, happiness, a fullness which does not deceive, does not mislead, does not end. Hope is innate to man. It makes him begin again after a failure, to wait patiently to win his case, to take courage in disappointments. It is the powerful energy he needs to set himself to arduous tasks, to triumph in competition, to carry his projects through successfully, and to find the means for leading a life free of cares and labors.

But in itself hope is a blind force, an insatiable hunger to live, first of all an animal life (Mt 6:27), to satisfy the desires of eating, of drinking, of pleasure (Lk 12:19), to accumulate goods which assure a peaceful life (cf. Mt 6:19). This is a hope aimed at, and in fact, preoccupied with possessing the goods hoped for. This hope of a happy life can lead a man to follow false messiahs (cf. Mt 24:11, Rev 13:3), puppets, masters of an easy sensual life (cf. 2 Tim 4:3f.), those whose novel doctrines (1 Tim 6:20) please the imagination because they extol formulas as perfect as they are unrealistic (cf. 2 Tim 3:5).

What then is our hope, the hope of our calling (cf. Eph 4:4)?

Christian hope, like faith, is made up of two elements. The first is certitude, because it rests upon a trustworthy promise. St Paul teaches this with assurance: 'The crown of justice is prepared for me; the Lord, the just Judge, will give it to me' (2 Tim 4:8). This reward is promised not only to Paul, but to all those who love and await the coming of the Lord (*ibid.*). The second element is incertitude. Hope does not possess the object of its desires (Heb 11:1) and is able to conquer it, or to lose it. Anyone who hopes while waiting tries, not without fear, to pierce the veil of the future.

Theological hope, the hope founded on God, unlike the expectation of contingent goods, tends, therefore, toward a future good, but one firmly promised, where the effort to obtain it and the active awaiting for it will not be disappointed. It is not only a possible good to come, but solidly promised, to whose possession we are called and even urged. Acquiring it is within our calling. We ought to work toward making the uncertain certain: 'Apply yourselves to assuring your calling and your election by your good works' (cf. 2 P 1:10). The motive force of theological hope mobilizes our energies to win the game. Now, that force is not a gift of nature, but a virtue deposited in our soul with the grace of baptism. It is a gift of the Father who, through his Spirit, calls his children in the depths of their hearts by offering them, if they are faithful, the ultimate reward: the heritage promised to children, but refused to those who have behaved like wicked servants (cf. Prol. 5, 7).

What, then, is this good promised to the expectation of the baptized christian who is faithful to his baptismal promises? Jesus tells us: He who perseveres to the end will be saved (Mt 10:22), will have eternal life (Mt 19:29), will enter the kingdom of heaven (Mt 5:12), will share in the glory of the Father (Jn 14:2), in the life of the Most Blessed Trinity (Jn 14:23); his reward, in a word, will be God himself.

Will the monk receive an extra reward? In substance, the reward of all the elect will be the same. Here as elsewhere St Benedict avoids any kind of theological deduction or amplification, and speaks the simple language of Scripture; his reward will be that of every Christian. The monk commits himself to the difficult way of obedience for the glory of eternal life (RB 5:3), and after having put to good use, day and night, the instruments of good works and having rendered account of them as of talents well used, he will receive on the day of judgment the reward promised by the Lord to all those who have followed him: 'Eye has not seen, nor ear heard what God has prepared for those who love him' (1 Co 2:9, cf. RB 4:76f.). And, as a matter of fact, the monk's expectation in committing himself to the monastic life is ultimately to obtain life (Prol. 15, 17, 42; 4:46; 5:3, 10f; 7:11; 72:2, 12), to be saved (7:36; 25:4); to have part in the kingdom of God (Prol. 21f., 50), in his glory (Prol. 7; 5:3), and in the heavenly homeland (73:8).

Yet the monk enjoys a hope which those who travel to the heavenly life by other paths cannot share. In using the instruments of the monastic virtues which are the observances (cf. Prol. 21), he has a right to expect on the part of the Lord who supports the humble efforts of the soul, conscious of its weakness and assiduous in praying to him (Prol. 29ff., 41), a special and effective help (Prol. 31). For it is he who is waiting for us and arousing our expectations (Prol. 35). It is he who calls and draws us (Prol. 19, 21). He gives the desire for life and also the grace to win it. He invites us to the battle (Prol. 3) and also gives us the victory, or rather, lets us share in his victory (Jn 16:33). The monk, therefore, has reason never to despair of the divine mercy and goodness and grace (RB 4:74), and he can entrust himself to God without pointless fear (4:41).

The monk, unlike those who have no hope (1 Thess 4:13), those who have not received true charity to be saved (cf. 2 Thess 2:10), is the man of hope. His whole life is hope. While others are busy building cities, raising a family, building up humanity, the monk is helping to build the city of God; its foundations are on earth, but its blossoms surmount the eternal thresholds, forbidden to those whose ambitions are limited to this earth; for in heaven, no one will take wives or husbands (Mt 22:30; Mk 12:25; Lk 20:35), no one will buy or sell, no one will build, and there will be no more change.

The monk, to the extent that he can escape the contingent rules of this earth, should be a man of the other world. He should not be preoccupied with food or with clothing for the next day (Mt 6:25, 34; cf. RB 55:7), but he should expect the things he needs from this heavenly Father (Mt 6:32) and from the father of the monastery (RB 33:5). He will embrace patience instead of protesting against injustices (RB 7: 35). Unshakeable in the hope of divine retribution, he will find his own advantage in all annoyances (7:39), and he will accept the yoke of a superior with a good heart, according to the advice of the psalmist: 'You have placed men over our heads' (RB 7:41; Ps 65:12). Obedient to the Lord's precept, if struck on one cheek, he will turn the other; and to him who would take his tunic, he will give also his mantle;

conscripted for one mile, he will go two (RB 7:42). With the apostle Paul, he will put up with false brethren and will bless those who curse him (*ibid.* 43). He will not be inordinately attached to achieving any personal success, nor saddened at having missed an opportunity or at having lost a friend or a favor. He will abandon to the Lord even his spiritual progress. With humility, he will not lose heart at relapses, but he will rise again without losing a minute.

Hope makes the monk begin each day with new enthusiasm, with new love. Leaving the past behind, he turns bravely toward the next day and wishes to see it better than the day before. He will never be impatient with himself, nor with the brothers whom the Lord has given him, nor with circumstances; with good reason, he can always consider them providential. Nevertheless, while resigned into the hands of the Lord, he will also remain as far from harmful passivity as from morbid restlessness. His eyes fixed on Jesus, he will follow him with the desire 'to be clothed with the new man' (2 Cor 5:4).

Is this asking too much perfection of the monk? Is he not still a human person like anyone else? The words of Jesus reported by the Gospel can be interpreted as metaphors or literally. We may think that Jesus, by using the oriental way of speaking, purposely wished to express himself in a way which would permit some to take his counsels in a metaphorical or symbolic sense, while yet inspiring uncompromising individuality and men on fire for the absolute to take them literally. Have we not seen some saints crossing whole countries barefoot in order to be faithful to the word of the Lord (Lk 10:4), and others at the same time taking a broader interpretation? It really seems that St Benedict, in the fourth degree of humility, recalls certain evangelical counsels of high perfection in order to propose they be executed literally. These counsels, at any rate, usually envisage isolated acts and not heroic attitudes of long duration. It is hardly realistic, St Benedict well knows, to demand of the ordinary run of monks exploits of constant virtue, because, he says, those who possess such great virtue are few (48:2). The monk, it remains no less true, ought to be

committed to the narrow way (cf. Prol. 48) and not to let
himself be disheartened by the height of the summits of
evangelical perfection. And why? Because he is more perfect
than other Christians? Not at all; but he trusts in the help of
the Lord. He is a person of great enterprise because he is a
person of great hope. Trusting in the help of the Lord (Prol.
41, 68:5) makes him climb to the summit of virtue (7:5,
73:9). Yes, by putting hope into the monk's heart, God
makes him generous and courageous in the humble effort
toward charity (RB 7), patient (Rom 8:25, 1 Tim 1:3) in his
effort to overcome, with the hope of attaining tomorrow
what he cannot accomplish today. Hope gives him great
security in seeking the Absolute (RB 7:39), and spreads calm
through his whole being and peace in his heart.

The whole Rule is full of this dynamism of hope. From the
beginning to the end it knows how to inspire the monk with
a calm, strong, and lasting hope if he will let himself be
carried by its spirituality and breathe its atmosphere. It makes
him overcome the temptations to run away (cf. Prol. 48) or
settle himself into a state mediocrity (48:23). It makes
him hasten (cf. Prol. 44) along the pathway of salvation and find the Lord there.

Thus the hope of a successful monastic life is mingled with
the hope of the final reward, as the entire Rule bears witness.
The last chapter again proves this by joining the effort toward
the summits of doctrine and virtue (73:9) with the haste with
which a monk should hurry toward the heavenly fatherland
(*ibid.* 8). The eschatological sense of the christian life, and of
monastic life in particular, is very clearly expressed. The
monk does not set his hope on riches or success, realizing
their insecurity, but in the living God (cf. 1 Tim 6:17); he
possesses a sense of the other world and attaches himself to
all the values which permit a man to attain his eternal goal.
By voluntarily detaching himself from the use of certain
goods, licit but unnecessary, the monk is a prophetic sign of
future goods which are indispensable to the happiness of each
and every person. A person can live without private property,
without raising a family, without the right of self-determination; a man can live a life without fanfare in silence and a

humble retreat, a life without external apostolic activity and entirely devoted to prayer, but he cannot live eternally without God. The monk, through his renunciation of certain values, gives striking proof of future happiness to those who want to understand, a happiness which is the lot of those who attach themselves to the promises of God. The mist of human imperfections enshrouds the works of man and obscures the light of even the holiest institutions. The monastery becomes, indeed, a lighthouse (Phil 2:15) of eternal life for all souls of good will who seek the true light.

Hope, like faith, is never seen (Rom 8:24) and is denied someone who depends only on accessible reasoning or visible evidence. Positivism contents itself with truths drawn from its observations and does not hope for anything beyond its grasp; materialism does not turn itself toward the realm of the spirit. The monastic ideal is altogether different. The monk belongs to the race of those who seek God, and he hurries past the things which are useless in that search. He is a sign, if he wishes to be and if he conforms to his ideal, but a sign of contradiction, for he signifies realities rejected by some. His way of life is often slandered; popular memory retains the history of debauched or unfaithful monks. Some people misread his meaning, and see in him no more than a witness of history and tradition, a learned man devoted to study, or a specialist in liturgy or prayer. All that is true, but accidental. His true signification is one of hope, of a man of God. He is, therefore, whether he likes it or not, out of the ordinary, set up like a celebrity. Let him always remember that. He ought to be fervent when others are not; he ought to be unyielding where others may compromise. He is on God's side even when everyone else takes the part of man. He will be an embarassment, and people will want to get rid of him. What is worse, people will try to turn him aside to other tasks than his own in order to bring him down to the level of the world. All this because he is an embarassing sign, a sign of contradiction, a silent preacher of the world to come. But where the monastic salt becomes insipid (cf. Mt 5:13) it becomes like the dung of the world, ordinary rubbish (cf. 1 Cor 4:13). Yet, even there he remains a sign of hope, a fallen sign.

But God is faithful. His fidelity motivates our hope. He has called us and we have followed his voice. He has made us the friends of his heart. We gain the victory through him Who has loved us (Rm 8:37; RB 7:4th degree).

# OUR SISTER DEATH

I have heard it said that the soul of a people, as ancient as it is venerable, is naturally turned toward the thought, subconcious no doubt, of the last things. For the person who, because of his religious convictions, is used to considering supernatural truths with the eyes of faith, death spontaneously integrates itself into his religious view of life. But the awareness and the anticipation provision of this reality vary greatly from one individual to another. The thought of death is more or less intense according to our personal encounter with such events as the death of our parents and friends, and the psychological reactions they cause, as well as our own experience of sickness or old age.

And then, life with all the energy which it gives us, robust health, a feeling of well-being, a productive activity, success, the consciousness of our own worth, the impression of being irreplaceable—life, then, and its manifestations remove from us the sharpness of a sensitivity which would make us feel the closeness of death.

As an instrument of good works to help us deepen our life of faith, as a source of virtue, St Benedict proposes to us the daily thought of death, or more exactly, the idea that death could strike us this very day: *Mortem cotidie ante oculos suspectam habere* (4:47): to have daily before one's eyes the death which lies in wait for us. First of all, this thought corresponds to the facts. We do not know the hour of our death. We know that it can present itself unexpectedly at our door. We know enough cases where a sudden death, a stroke, an accident, have broken off a life in full bloom. A violent illness of short duration can wrest us from this world. Let us think of some relative, friend, confrère, or schoolmate who, although our own age, was taken early by death. In a religious family, in a community, we often have the sad experience of death's visit: the separation, the solemn funeral rites, the prolonged prayers for the dead; enough about *memento mori*.

So then, life and death coexist in us. There is always something disappearing in us—cells, tissues. There is always a struggle in our body between the forces of life and the powers of corruption. Death dwells in us. It is the companion of our life. *Sorella morte* St Francis said; our sister death. If we stop to think, we will recognize it in many little things which occur in us and are familiar to us. The smallest physical pain is a presage of death. All the deficiencies of the intelligence, the will, the memory, our senses are its precursors. If we did not wish to see it, we would have to close our eyes. But too easily, this habit we have of living on the surface of things, of fiercely clutching at all the signs of life, even where signs of death are more numerous and more pressing, prevents us from looking it in the face.

Now, clearly we ought to love natural life. It is the most marvelous, the most extraordinary and the most precious of the gifts of the Creator. He has given us a love of life and an instinctive, even primitive, will to defend it against every threat. This vitality is effected, is renewed, continuously. Life is a spark of the godhead itself, the noblest participation in what God is: Being. He it is who possesses it in its fullness, Who is the absolute Master and Author of it. We do not have the right to dispose of it according to our own whims. We have the duty of preserving it, nourishing it, maintaining it, developing it, turning it to profit as the greatest of talents, and saving it if it is threatened. But how can we reconcile serenity in the face of death with this love of life? How can we become familiar with death almost as with a friend, a 'sister'?

First of all, realism teaches us not to deceive ourselves, not to hide the truth but to envisage with courage and dignity the short duration of our life, the erosion of our forces, and the irreversible approach of our end. Now these are the human

considerations in the face of a phenomenon inexorably
unrolling upon the course of our existence. But is that all?
This purely natural attitude arises from prudence, courage,
and strength. It is the foundation of every further consideration, but it alone could not be enough for us. Since Christ has
undergone death, it is no longer the fatal event, destroyer of
life; it is the gate, the pledge of eternal life.

But are we not going beyond the thought of St Benedict?
He was not thinking here of the whole theology of death
which Christ has destroyed by his own death—*mortem
nostram moriendo destruxit*—but warning us quite simply of
its coming in order to stimulate our spiritual life.

May the example of Jesus help us to acquire this serene
vision of death. He was a man like us, except for sin. He had
to undergo death. He knew its glorious outcome: the resurrection. He instructed his disciples by saying to them: 'The
Son of Man shall be delivered into the hands of men, and
they will kill him, and when he has been put to death, in three
days he shall rise' (Mk 9:31). This certain knowledge, this
tranquil and serene acceptance throws a marvelous light upon
his life. There is in his thought not a shadow of false illusion,
of deceptive hope. Nor of the fatalism of a revolutionary
who accepts his lot with a fierce fanaticism and a mis-
guided idealism. He faced his death because it was the will of
his Father, and because the Father so loved the world that he
gave his own Son as a ransom for sin (cf. Jn 3:16f.); his
redemptive death is the crown of his mission, of the work
which he was to accomplish (cf. Jn 17:4).

Here too Jesus has become our example: in having always
before our eyes the death which lies in wait for us. As with
him, this certainty of death will give to our soul a great
tranquillity, in spite of our uncertainty of the time and
ignorance of the circumstances. Accepting it in advance,
however it comes, as a manifestation of the Father's will for
us, will give it the sacred character of a gift of God. We will
understand that death, just as life, is a sign of the Father's
love. This thought will certainly not take from it the cruel
sword of separation and sadness, but it will give this sadness a
foretaste of blessedness and our whole life a special

enthusiasm for having done well the mission which God has chosen to entrust to us.

Thus we will recognize not only its meaning in our life and its apostolic bearing, but we will better understand our part in the work of the redemption of the world and what we ought to accomplish in our own flesh of the passion of Christ (cf. Col 1:24). We can attain, at least at moments of intense prayer and profound conformity with the will of the Father, not only the point of awaiting this death, but even of greeting it as a messenger of the Father, as it were, the gateway to him, as a ransom for ourselves and for our brothers according to the desire with which he inspires us. And we will think of the word of Jesus: 'I must receive a baptism, and how anxious I am for it to be accomplished!' (Lk 12:50).

According to the teaching of Vatican II (*Lumen Gentium* 44; cf. *Gaudium et Spes* 38), monastic life has a wholly eschatological sense, because it is a sort of prefiguration of eternal values. Because it modestly anticipates the life beyond death, it introduces us by that very fact to a greater familiarity with it. If the hope of the good things to come is alive and active in us, death cannot logically have that hateful face which it presents to those who have no hope (1 Thess 4:12). And because, according to St Benedict, the monk not only walks, but hastens, toward the heavenly homeland (73:8), how could he neglect to think of death every day? Since he in some way anticipates the experience of the good things that are to come, he begins that anticipation with the thought of death, according to the teaching of the catechism on the Last Things.

How does he go about this? His acts perhaps dispose him to it even more than an explicit thought. Twice St Benedict uses the formula *usque ad mortem:* at the end of the Prologue and in the third degree of humility, there in speaking of Jesus, the model of the monk. What is the full meaning of this formula? Is it a question of persevering in the monastery and in obedience until the hour of death, until one's last breath? Or should we not rather find in it that total perseverance, that full obedience which is a death of renunciation and not a physical death, the death not of the will but of self-will? Jesus was obedient by renouncing from the beginning the right to orientate his life according to his own personal views. He accepted the imprint of the Father's will upon his life, even in the smallest details, fulfilling the Father's plans in complete liberty, with joy and love, in complete abandonment and in total conformity of his will with that of his Father. Is this not a continual death of self-will? *Non mea voluntas* (Lk 22:42)—an obedience of his will even unto death?

The monk undertakes 'for the love of God' to follow Jesus on that road by submitting himself 'in all obedience' (RB 7:34) to those who have the duty of leading him in his everyday life. It is in this way that he imitates the Lord, obeying even to the point of putting his self-will to death.

This death through obedience introduces the monk to the frequent thought of physical death. To dispose his soul to obedience is to detach it from its useless desires and its inclinations contrary to the will of the Father, to make it free, pure. For nothing better prepares a man for death than poverty. Without baggage weighing him down, death seems to him to be less violent and less cruel than it is to the person who is used to doing as he pleases. Dead to many things already in his life, he is less frightened by the thought of death; he thinks of it with that liberty which is the lot of the man who possesses himself by possessing nothing.

He does not desire death's approach, and he does not sigh after it. Apart from certain special cases, it is not natural to desire death. St Benedict puts the nuances in their right places: although the monk ought to make provision for death, he will put his energies into desiring eternal life. St Benedict, in chapter four, precedes the thought of death, with that other counsel: 'To desire eternal life with all the ardor of one's soul' (7:46). The monk's thought does not, therefore, stop at the death which lies in wait for us; it goes beyond death. It passes from the fear of judgment day (4:44) and from the fear of hell (4:45), to avid desire of life in God which will know no more tears nor death, and will be eternal (4:46). He knows that if his death is like Christ's, his resurrection will also be (Rom 6:5); that having shared in the passion of Christ by his prolonged patience, he will also share in the glory of his kingdom (Prol. 50).

# THE FEAR OF GOD

## THE PLACE OF THE FEAR OF GOD

The main objection which is made about the anthropology of the Rule is the attitude of reverential fear which it seems to want to implant in the monk as if he were not yet an adult in full possession of his freedom. If his objection were justified, it could destroy the confidence we place in the Rule.

First of all a distinction is needed: Is this a matter of the fear of man or of the fear of God? According to the Rule's teachings is fear of the superior considered an element of education? Or is it simply a system of education? Quite obviously, St Benedict thought the abbot ought to be a father imitating the Good Shepherd in his love for the stray sheep (27:8f.), he ought to show himself a physician to the end (28), to make himself loved rather than feared (64:15) and always to let mercy prevail over justice (64:10). St Benedict wanted the abbot to be loving, gentle, and indulgent, while still being just, prudent, and energetic. There is no need to insist on this. As for the prior and the deans, the Rule does not demand that they show themselves severe. Why is it, therefore, that St Benedict has so often been represented holding a rod in his hand? The artists who painted him like this with a finger on his lips, have probably not understood his spiritual mien and have disfigured it. But, they do testify in their own way to the impression which a superficial reading of the Rule can leave on the reader. Although the abbot of the Rule does not inspire any particualr fear, St Benedict still wanted him to be feared— *studeat . . . timeri* (64:15)—and respected (63:13). In the Rule he has at his disposal a formidable penal code. The chapters dealing with faults, types of excommunication, penances, discipline including whippings, and even with expulsion, and all the threats relating to them, are as numerous as the chapters reserved to the regulation of the Divine Office. It would be difficult to deny it: the penal code of the Rule can frighten those who do not have a clear conscience.

However, and it is interesting to notice this, if the measure of the penance to be inflicted is left to the judgment of the abbot, the Rule does not present him as an executioner; instead the penances are set down and in some way attributed to the Rule itself (think of the fairly frequent expressions such as: discipline of the Rule, or correction of the Rule). Without doubt, the abbot is responsible for their application, and without him the prescriptions of the Rule would remain a dead letter. He judges, but he judges according to a penitential code independent of himself. The intention of St Benedict seems to have been not to define the abbot as a 'severe master' (2:24), which he ought to be only as a last resort, but much more as a 'tender father' (2:24) wielding with indulgence a penal code established independent of himself.

St Benedict may have been depicted with a rod in comparison with other legislators of the monastic life before him: he elaborated a more detailed penitential code, but a code all of whose elements he found among his predecessors, including corporal punishment, excommunication, and expulsion.

In the face of this system of disciplinary practices, a question arises: What were St Benedict's motives in showing himself so severe? Did he believe it necessary to treat men of his time harshly and with a certain psychological constraint in order to lead them to God? Did he consider them rude, primitive or infantile, unlikely to let themselves be convinced by persuasive methods? Or indeed did he, by the rigor of the Rule, want to counterbalance the possible weaknesses of an abbot too prone to be a 'tender father'? To answer this question, we must first clear up another question: In giving primary importance to the fear of God, was St Benedict acting in function of the moral structure of his contemporaries, or are his reasons as valid today as they were then? Does his teaching on the fear of God address itself to simple people? To all, even to those who are free of their passions and have arrived at full control of themselves?

In order to give an adequate answer, we must understand the religious climate in which the ancient monks lived. For them the essential thing was asceticism; not a stoic but a Christian and eschatological asceticism. In this perspective, life was a continual struggle, a sort of martyrdom; the rigor of the first monks was often extreme, and purity of heart was their great ideal. An extreme seriousness overshadowed their lives. Although these giants of the desert, experienced *Parrhesia*, mystical friendship with God, they remained penetrated by a profound fear of God.

We find that same religious climate in the Rule of St Benedict. His teaching on the fear of God is not a reflection on the quality of the men of those days, but a profoundly theological attitude toward a value which transcends time. That St Benedict insists upon the fear of God as the beginning of wisdom is easily explained by the fact that he is addressing himself to beginners, whom we must not confuse with primitives. Does the confusion of many a spiritual life not come precisely from the fact that one has failed, in the fear of God, to dig the foundations of humility before building the edifice of charity? Poorly built, it crumbles into superficiality.

This fear of God, as also the whole spirituality of St Benedict, it is said, is too impregnated with the spirit of servitude coming from the Old Testament: too narrow an observance of the commandments, a heavy spirit of reward for merits and punishments for little misdeeds, fear of hell, in short, a psychology of fear. This objection clearly exaggerates one side of the very complete spirituality of St Benedict at the expense of the other. Jesus did not come to abolish the Old Testament, but to 'christianize' it. And we need only examine the citations of the Holy Scripture in the Rule to have an eloquent indication of the spirit of St Benedict. The New Testament is cited more often than the Old, and these latter are mostly texts from the Psalms, which quite naturally present themselves to the memory of a monk who is used to reciting them in prayer. The fear of God and hell are not subjects typically belonging to the Old Testament. Hell frightens those who believe in it. But to live in the fear of God befits the person who does not want to fall into the error of the worldly who have no place in their daily life for God. The saints insist on this fear; it is one of the gifts of the Holy Spirit.

The system of reparation in the Rule finds a partial explanation in this context. The monastic life is essentially a seeking for God and ought, in its very structure, to teach the monk the attitude that he must have toward him—that is, fear. Since it is a community life, this happens through measures of a public nature, including coercive measures. In other words, it is through the rigor of its demands and sanctions that the Rule teaches a real acceptance of the rights of God most holy.

The fear of hell recommended by St Benedict—*gehennam expavescere* (4:45; see also Prologue 7 & 42, 5:3, 7:69, 72:1) comes down to the fear of God, the inexorable Judge into whose hands it is terrifying to fall. Today, the motive of a servile fear of hell is not much to our tastes. It is, however, a motive from the Gospel. Our loving Lord spoke of it often. So let us not be surprised: the spirituality of St Benedict is based on a complete theology. He does not want us to go astray with a false optimism which would hide from us the terrible reality of Satan and hell under the pretext that a monk does not need these 'crude' ignoble motives. On the other hand, we see him make a great use of other motives for virtue—of hope in the grace and mercy of God, of eternal life, of divine love and its delights.

Is the fear of God still suited to the mentality of modern man? That is the question. Well! Yes, in the sense we are going to explain. Today, even more than formerly, we need to learn the fear of God. To fail to recognize it is to permit a relaxation of morals which will stop not even at the gates of monasteries. Then too, the Rule is written so that each person individually might find what he needs there. All of us, to some degree, go spiritually by our own pathway through the journey which all of humanity has travelled through the ages, from the time of infancy into adulthood. Let us, men and women of our age, take great care not to fall again through pharisaical pride into the spiritual conditions of a stage we should have passed long ago.

May God grant us the grace, through the exercises of humility proposed by the Rule to purify our soul, to arrive quickly 'at the summit of divine charity where fear is banished' so that all that we 'were not able to do in the beginning without the support of that fear' we may 'observe, no longer through the fear of hell, but for the love of Christ' (7:68f.).

## THE MEANING OF THE FEAR OF GOD

St Benedict in his Rule undertakes to teach us the fear of God: *Timorem Domini docebo vos* (Prol. 12). These words are taken from Psalm 33 [34:11 Hebr], therefore from the Old Testament, where the fear of God was of the very essence of religion: the attitude of man before God.

In fact, man knows he is a sinner deserving chastisement. The thrice-holy God Who cannot allow sin to exist in his sight, inspires him with fear and terror. Even the just man who experiences and sings the divine mercies trembles at the thought of his sinful condition. This fear of God, as it is described in Holy Scripture, goes from the fear of chastisement to the fear of losing the grace of God, of offending him, and showing oneself unworthy of his goodness.

St Benedict penetrated with the spirit of Holy Scripture and the spirituality of the psalms, teaches and transmits to us that fear. Let us admit that modern spiritual literature hardly ever deals with fear; we find ourselves a bit out of our element when we encounter the Rule's insistence on it. Better to understand the thought and the language of St Benedict we should first of all remember that in the sixth century Christians probably still had a more vivid sense of the grace of election than we do. They were close to the age that believed that certain mortal sins, such as apostasy, could only be forgiven once. Baptism renders one innocent, but one must not lose that innocence. By St Benedict's time, it is true, that age had passed, but people retained a living remembrance of it. Against this background, we can understand the tone of the Prologue, which insists so much that the monk not show himself unworthy of his election nor of his calling, and that he not jeopardize the grace of the Lord. Then, too, the time of St Benedict was also relatively close to the period when the Church was the Church of martyrs, of the elect and predestined, of the *diaspora*, when Christians were dispersed in a pagan milieu, exposed to misunderstanding. In this context, we can understand that the attitude of Christians might have been determined more than it is today by the idea of the grace of election, of choice, of predestination. Then one felt in a keen way that to be a Christian, chosen, was an invaluable gift from God. How many today are Christians, by inheritance, so to speak, and tradition. Do they understand that their Christian life is a gift from God before being a gift to God? At any rate, the attitude of Christians at the time of St Benedict incited them to look toward the Lord, Giver of the grace, with some fear deep in their heart, of losing that grace.

The language of the Rule feels the effects of these historical conditions, and today we are aware of this. In its own way, however, it expresses a teaching which is also ours.

Thus any attempt to find the Rule lacking in the spirit of the Gospel would be doomed to end in failure. His language cannot be attributed to a predominantly Old Testament mentality. While it is true that Jesus infrequently called the fear of God explicitly by this name, he never failed to inculcate it (cf. Mt 10:28) and frequently to call to mind the judgment to come and the existence of hell. We must be watchful and keep ourselves ready for the day of the Lord. The Christians of the first centuries, and the monks in particular, took very seriously the categorical demands of Jesus; that is, someone who does not fulfill the conditions he laid down cannot be his disciple or worthy of him (cf. Mt 10:24, Lk 14:26, Mk 10:38). Jesus has his own personal way of teaching us a salutary fear.

A monastic rule, conceived for following the Lord, cannot teach in any other vein. It ought to inspire in the monks a sense of the absolute demands and indefeasible rights of God. It will exercise, therefore, if one may say so, a salutary pressure on souls by underscoring the fear theme. It will speak not only of *pater*, but also of 'an angry father' *iratus pater* (Prol. 6) and of an 'angry master' (Prol. 7).

We could trace this severity of concept, this seriousness which St Benedict gives the monastic life throughout its chapters. The first degree of humility, for example, prepares us to consider God always present, seeing our actions, as a father, but also as a judge. According to the words of Scripture, he watches us, follows us attentively, and listens to his angels informing him of our thoughts and actions. We must therefore be on guard and live decently in order to avoid punishment and bring favorable judgment on us. St Benedict often advises the abbot to consider the judgment (2:6, 34, 37; 3:11; 55:22; 63:3; 64:7; 65:22). The Rule depicts for us the man coming to the monastery as a sinner wanting to correct himself, desiring to combat his thoughts, his evil tendencies, his temptations. This is an eminently christian doctrine, strongly accentuated by the Rule.

The penal code is written from this same perspective and contains penitential regulations concerning a number of misdeeds. Although as a whole it makes us see St Benedict as a good and prudent father, much less severe than other monastic legislators, we are still struck by the very existence of a penal code. To understand St Benedict's thought, however, we need to define precisely the nature of that fear of God which the Rule teaches. Above all, we have to guard ourselves against falling into the equivocation which often threatens treatments of this question. In saying 'fear' people think of what is called servile fear, which is more the fear of punishment than the fear of God. Now the fear of God, already in the Old Testament, is far from being merely a fear of judgment or punishment. The just man of the Old Testament fears God the Creator, his Judge, because he is completely penetrated with his adorable grandeur, his unequalled holiness, his incomparable majesty, his inscrutable judgments. In this fear, there is an underlying reverence, a gratitude and respect on the part of the creature who is as nothing before the Creator.

St Benedict teaches us the characteristics of this fear in a little meaning-packed expression in chapter 72: 'Let them fear God with love' (72:9). Fear ought to be inspired by love. Let it therefore be the fear of sons. We understand, of course, that the fear of God has different degrees; the soul has to make a long journey, whose stages vary according to different spiritual itineraries. In any event, in the Rule the monk never finds himself only before an angry master who stands ready to punish him and who is incapable of love. There God is severe, but loving. In speaking of the fear of God. St Benedict speaks more as a psychologist than as a theologian who is forced to make distinctions. His idea of fear is simply that of Holy Scripture and includes the whole range of motives by which man may be animated before his Lord.

The seventh chapter furnishes us with proof. The ascent to perfection through the twelve degrees of humility (7:67) begins with the fear of God, which is its first rung. Already from the very beginning it contains all the motives: the fear of hell (7:11), the hope of eternal reward, the desire to please the Lord who is good and awaits our conversion (7:30). But, the servile element of that fear will give way to charity to the extent that one progresses until it disappears completely (cf. 1 Jn 4:18) when charity arrives at its fullness, excluding every sin, and therefore every reason for fearing judgment. This way of conceiving the spiritual growth of the monk shows us clearly that according to St Benedict, the fear of God is accomplished from the beginning by filial love, even if it is only a stammering love. To the extent that the ascent costs our nature something, that it requires work of it (7:68), the support of fear provides a useful motive. Conversely, on the day when the monk 'without labor, as though naturally and by habit' (ibid.) observes the precepts of the Lord, then love alone will be in command (7:69), and on that day, he will be perfected in love (cf. 1 Jn 4:18).

The beginning of the fifth chapter of the Rule look very similar. The motive of obedience is first of all the love of Christ (5:2), the second is fidelity to one's commitment, the third is the fear of hell, the fourth the hope of eternal reward (3). The act of obedience is prompt, accomplished under the impulse of the fear of God and of an eagerness (*amor*) to climb the heights of eternal life (9f.). According to personal dispositions then the motive goes from the fear of hell to love, without letting one totally exclude the other, except at the end of one's spiritual growth.

Does the Rule look at man's deficiencies too much? No. St Benedict wanted to avoid an angelism which would have discouraged a good number of his sons or set them on an unreal track; the Rule was written for 'imperfect souls' (27:6, cf. 73:7), even while it was drawing throughout its chapters a portrait of the perfect monk to encourage the strong (64:19) to attain the summit of the virtues (73:9). To neglect the motive of fear would be to try to build the spiritual edifice without a solid foundation. Does the mediocrity of so many spiritual lives not come often from this lack of the fear of God from the beginning, and from a lack of the spirit of penance? To claim that St Benedict instills guilt complexes or the fear of committing a fault is quite simply to misunderstand the teaching of the Gospel, which in a remarkable way sensitizes man to sin in order to bring him to purity of heart.

Does St Benedict keep us in an unhealthy frame of mind? Must we be seeing faults everywhere where there are none? Does he traumatize us by interdicts where there are only harmless failings? He is very moderate, let us notice, in regulating the details of the common life, and he leaves a great latitude to the abbot's direction. Even when he goes into detail, we do not have the impression that he is petty or that he limits too much the breathing space of individual liberty by creating taboos. The many threats of regular punishment seemed necessary to him to maintain peace and order in the community. Today, they do not affect men of good will and are not resented.

To sum up: the fear of God, humility, and obedience are strongly accentuated in the Rule, but they are not ends in themselves: they are meant to lead to charity. The Rule according to St Bernard is not only a school of humility, but by humility it is a school of charity. The balance between fear and charity derives from the teaching of St Benedict, and his insistence on the fear of God has no other purpose than to lead his disicple to the perfection of charity along the surest and most solid ways. In the final analysis, the preponderance of the fear or the love of God will always depend on the disciple and on the structure or the progress of his spiritual life.

If St Thérèse of the Child Jesus felt less need of fear, this was her special gift and that of souls of her calibre. St Benedict marks out for us an altogether ordinary way; if we follow it faithfully, it will lead us to the sole fear of loving the infinitely lovable Saviour too little.

# THE HARD THINGS WHICH LEAD TO GOD

For St Benedict the ladder to heaven is humility. We go from the bottom rung to the top by practising it (cf. Mt 20:16); this is why we are not surprised to see monks go from a cherished, but theoretic, virtue to the rude asceticism of deeds—to the hard things that lead to God—to *opprobria* (58:7).

But here too, St Benedict excels in his discretion. Nowhere in the Rule does he encourage us to follow the example of the Fathers of the Desert, whose imaginations were fertile in inventing vexing mortifications to strengthen their disciples' virtue. We do not find along the entire length of the ladder any such artificial trials, and the fourth degree is there to prove to us that all of the trials of which the Rule speaks come through fortuitous occasions and circumstances, or from the lack of human appreciation.

What does St Benedict mean to say, then, when he demands that the novice master carefully watch his disciple's attitude when faced with trials and to see if he is generous

(58:7)? St Benedict, we should notice right away, in no way demands the novice's master put his disciple to the test. Of course, he was not received into the monastery with open arms (58:3), but once admitted, he is sized up by his reaction to the work which the monastic day imposes, by his attitude toward the orders and commands he is given, sometimes going against his natural preferences or habits. He will very simply be shown the *dura et aspera*, the hard and difficult things which he will find on the road leading to God (58:8), in other words, he will be warned about all those things that may be contrary to the inclinations of nature in the practices of the monastic life. But even here, let us remember: St Benedict hopes not to establish anything too rigorous or too burdensome (Prol. 46). And if he does warn his postulant, he does it to keep him from letting himself be overcome by fear at the sight of the Rule's demands (Prol. 47f.), and rashly abandoning the way of salvation.

All this explains the sense of the word *opprobria* (58:7); it does not, therefore, include anything artificial and, as a matter of fact, people today will not tolerate being put to the test in arbitrary or unreasonable ways. Artificial humiliations would be, in their eyes, a reason for contempt for others and for themselves. That is not his object.

It is true that an humiliation ought always to retain its medicinal character, and be administered without producing a trauma. It has to be received and accepted reasonably. The superior, on his side, has the duty of preparing the monk to receive it in the right spirit, taking account of the principle of the Rule: Let the abbot act with prudence, lest being too zealous in removing the rust, he break the vessel (64:12).

The Rule addresses itself to people of all times, and not to those of a particular age, living in a certain context. By attaching itself to the things that are constant in man's nature the Rule tries to form him, without pausing at passing circumstances. Thus its anthropology retains all its value, for it has in view man tainted with original sin. We must not let ourselves be too impressed by certain fashionable ideas, but rather, study and apply to today's way of thinking, which has things to recommend it, the eternal principles of the

Gospel and the Rule.

The effect of a real trial ought to be to permit a man to discover himself as he really is, assessing himself at his true value, without either demeaning himself or overestimating himself. Serving the personality does not consist in serving human pride by giving a person so much liberty that his sense of independence no longer will admit any authority. To act like this would distort his education and would produce a result contrary to a true formation of personality. To try to diminish a person's just esteem for himself would be imprudently to unwind the spring of his energy and courage, so necessary for maintaining his human dignity.

The trials envisaged by St Benedict under the expression *opprobria* are, therefore, quite simply the obstacles which go contrary to our natural inclinations, that is to say, mortifications imposed by the monastic observance and a community life with all its demands. This latter especially can easily bring us sad surprises. Our feelings can be hurt at a change of office and obedience if we have the impression that other brothers are being preferred to us. We can suffer from a real or supposed misunderstanding on the part of our superiors, from a lack of delicacy in certain people, from exaggerated demands, from antipathies or perhaps even from mistreatment by some brother. The monastic life, we realize soon enough, makes us resemble Christ humiliated, despised, mistreated, scourged, crucified. So, instead of protesting, we apply ourselves to embracing the cross and bearing everything without slackening or retreating, conforming ourselves to the teaching of Scripture (Ps 26:14): 'He who perseveres to the end shall be saved' (7:35f.). The awareness of approaching Christ through suffering infuses the soul with happiness and the monk experiences this.

# HUMILITY

It is not easy to speak of the degrees of humility in just a few words. But it is a very important theme. I will try to give you at least some thoughts, which are manifestly not a complete presentation of this seventh chapter of the Holy Rule, but which may help you in making a synthesis of it.

What strikes us first of all is that St Benedict presents all of his asceticism under the aspect of humility. As a matter of fact, there is no teaching on it apart from what is set forth in this seventh chapter, along with the same ideas which refer to it, throughout the Rule. This chapter is a program of the monastic life, the kernel of the Holy Rule. What then are its key ideas?

Basing himself upon Our Lord's words: 'Everyone who exalts himself shall be humbled, and everyone one humbles himself shall be exalted' (Lk 14:11), as well as these: 'The last shall be first and the first shall be last' (Mt 20:16). St Benedict shows us that humility exalts and pride abases. He observes two contrary movements on Jacob's ladder on which the angels ascend and descend. When we ascend, we ascend through humility; that is to say, we ascend by descending, and we descend by ascending. By this fundamental movement which leads us to the Lord and to eternal life we ought therefore to descend. I need not explain all the theology about this movement which begins with Adam and the first sin, and even with the first sin of the angel who wanted to ascend by ascending.

The first degree of humility is respect for God, the fear of the Lord. In the Prologue St Benedict promises to teach it to us: 'I will teach you the fear of the Lord' (Prol. 12). What is the fear of the Lord? It is nothing but respect for God, faith in him, in his awesome and blessed presence. To respect someone means to think highly of him, to recognize his personal value, to appreciate him in all his greatness. Now we ought to have this attitude toward the Lord from the very beginning. We firmly believe that he is—consequently that he is here—and therefore we ought to try to be conscious of his presence, to respect him, because at the same time we believe he is here, we know that he is the tremendous divine Majesty. We make this point and reflect on ourselves in this first degree; we recognize our lowliness, our faults, our fundamental malice, which comes from original sin, and consequently we adopt an attitude in which we can be in his presence. This is why St Benedict sets forth in this first degree the things we must do to purify ourselves, to put our lives in order. This is the fear of the Lord.

In the second degree of humility, we come to detachment. The first two degrees of humility apply to all Christians. One cannot be a Christian without having the fear of God, faith in him, and the will to observe his precepts. But why speak of detachment in the second degree? Not to love one's self-will is to detach oneself from it insofar as it is inclined by nature to sin, and so at the same time to accept all that the Lord commands of us. It is, therefore, this general obedience which is indispensable if we want to approach the Lord. To respect him means to respect his precepts, to respect his word, to cling to all that he is by essence, to all that flows from his nature. This is to do his will. This is the second degree of humility.

The third degree of humility brings us into the religious and monastic life. There we find obedience to a superior who now holds the place of the Lord. In this way, we enter into an immediate concretization of our life. In the first degree, the Lord is the invisible divine Majesty in whom we believe, whom we accept. In the second degree, it becomes evident that we must follow what he tells us and accept what he commands of us. The third degree makes us find a practical means of putting this faith in the Lord into practice. We know that the Lord himself came to earth to show us how we can practise obedience, respect, and veneration in his place. He came to teach us by always doing the will of his Father, by obeying in everything, obeying even to death, and inviting us to do the same by submitting ourselves to a superior accessible to us, visible and palpable.

St Benedict tells us that we must obey 'for the love of

Christ'. This is the third degree of humility. As Christ was obedient to his Father, his Superior, we likewise seek someone to take the Lord's place and we submit ourselves to our superior with the same attitude we want to have toward the Lord, realizing, however, that this is a matter of substitution and our obedience ought to end in God.

The fourth degree of humility introduces us to patience. If obedience to the Lord and to his representative sometimes becomes difficult, patience goes into action. Most of the time, it is easy enough to obey because superiors generally impose on us only what is consistent with our vocation, our duty, our work. On our side, we understand the needs, the demands of daily life and community life, the tasks that have to be done. And supported by a spirit of solidarity, we set ourselves to the task. There are however, difficult moments when patience comes into play. We accept, indeed, what appears to us a tribulation 'knowing that tribulation produces endurance, and endurance produces character, and character produces hope', as St Paul says (Rom 5:3f.).

The fourth degree then, is patience. St Benedict knows that there are situations which sometimes make monastic life difficult. He repeats these beautiful words to us: 'You have placed men over our heads' (Ps 65:12). Those are perhaps the most important words in the fourth degree. In the third degree we have declared that we wish to obey that superior whom we accepted at the time of our profession. We did that with a certain ease, out of generosity, even with a certain naïveté. Later on, we find out that it is not always so simply and so easy, because this superior is a man; he cannot climb out of his skin. Sometimes he is hard to put up with, therefore. It must even be said that all by himself, he tests our patience much more than all our confrères. This is in the nature of things, because he is the one who commands us, who tells us what we have to do, how we are to walk and act, when we have to get up in the morning and go to bed at night, he gives us what we have to eat, he assigns us our duties, our work, he exorts us and corrects us. So, in time, his ways of doing things can annoy us. The time comes when we begin to analyze the superior, to judge him. This is when we need patience, but a supernatural patience, which comes up to the very object we proposed to ourselves at the time of our profession. With a good heart, with a sensible heart, with a strong will, and for always—*usque ad mortem*—we agreed to obey a superior. We made the first step in obedience with a certain naïveté, but not without thorough reflection. Later on, we do not want to go back on what we promised at our profession; but we have to carry it out in another way, on another basis, on a higher level, in a more supernatural way: this is patience.

You remember that our father St Benedict speaks of patience several times and at very important moments; for example, in concluding the Prologue, he tells us that 'through our patience we share in the sufferings of Christ' (Prol. 50). We see here the meaning of patience: it is the whole Passion of Christ in which we share. For Jesus came to accept this passion that we might be able to enter into it ourselves, to be purified and sanctified in this way, and to be presented with him on the day of God's judgment. It is therefore through patience that we share in Our Lord's passion. We accept it, understanding at the same time that the principal means of doing this is obedience, and that obedience is therefore the means of introducing us into the passion of Jesus. This is the fourth degree of humility.

The fifth degree of humility is openness of soul, sincerity, sincerity without a veil. When we find a community with this sincerity as a dominant characteristic, it is extremely attractive, and this should be maintained at all costs. Our nature is always inclined to falsehood; it readily searches for ways which will permit it to be simple and sincere while still keeping certain secrets well hidden, certain things it doesn't want to speak about, certain parts of the soul carefully locked. The unfortunate thing is that we easily get the idea that we are very simple and very sincere, very open. Since St Benedict speaks of this openness in the fifth degree of humility, this means that this practice already requires a good dose of humility. To open our soul to the superior demands of us this real humility. I will not go into the question here of its internal or external arena, confession, nor into questions of monastic formation and spiritual direction.

Let us remember here that we must distinguish within ourselves between the actual sins which we may commit and of which we render account in confession, and our temperament, our character which does not necessarily express itself in sin, but in our general attitude, which we should not keep secret, either from our superior or indeed from the community. Simplicity, which is so acclaimed nowadays, demands that we not appear different from what we really are. Within ourselves we have qualities and faults which are part of our personalities. We have some bad one, so why hide them? Others notice them easily enough! But if, by ourselves, we open our heart very simply, then we are practising the fifth degree of humility. If not, we are taking the chance of falling into hypocrisy.

I would define the sixth degree of humility as serenity, or jubilation of soul: being content with everything. It is possible to arrive at this state of habitual contentment. We are told that SS Romuald, Bernard, and Ignatius always had a joyful face and that contact with them immediately put joy into the hearts of those around them. This is not a question only of external attitude; it comes from a very deep disposition of soul. Such a person keeps himself in great interior serenity by being disposed to accept joyfully everything that comes as a disposition of Divine Providence, of the Lord's will. And this acceptance is always made with great charity, by being at everyone's disposal. That is what it means to be always content with everything. And the joyful face expresses externally this interior state.

'God loves a cheerful giver' (2 Cor 9:7). St Benedict cites these words (5:16) in order to teach us that we should do everything with great serenity of heart. First of all comes obedience. If my superior tells me to do something, what good is it to look stubborn, to act sulky? Is that the sixth degree of humility? Yet, we often feel reactions like that. But when this happens to us, let us thrash out our fault and say: 'Great! Here I am again all wrought up on account of my character; here I am sulking again, or giving in to a bad mood. No quarter for me.' And the next time, we will react serenely, an *hilarem datorem*. Let us not forget that humor is a child of wisdom.

In conclusion, let us not lose patience, especially with ourselves. It is obvious that until the day we die, we will always be falling into the same faults: *usque ad mortem*. We have indeed promised to be obedient *usque ad mortem;* is this obedience and this exercise of the degrees of humility not necessary for us *usque ad mortem.* So let us not lose courage, and let us begin again in spite of our difficulties, thinking about this sixth degree which is also so delightful.

We find perfection, the fruit of holiness, in the seventh degree of humility; that deep conviction that we are the least of all men. In certain saints we see, and amire with an unequalled amazement, the deep conviction that they were great sinners, and even a curse to humanity. Yet they were real saints. We have to admit that the seventh degree is quite rare. But if we cannot wholly fulfil it, we can nevertheless arrive at such a sensitivity from time to time. If, for example, we have transgressed God's command in some way, we can certainly succeed in convincing ourselves that on this particular point, our brothers, our sisters, and maybe even many other people are much better than we are. This is not very difficult. If we think about it a little, we can admit, in spite of a solid optimism about ourselves, that in certain points we lag behind others or are inferior to them.

The eighth degree of humility—and I will end here—is conformity with our community. All the following degrees treat especially of our attitude and our external actions. Let us recall that chapter of the Holy Rule which treats of obedience to all. We must have this ease in obeying to get to the point of doing the good pleasure of others. And above all, we must have this conformity to the community as community. In it the Body of Christ is made present. Not to be singular in anything. If I know that the community is doing its spiritual reading now, I will not go do some work which should be done at another time. If I see that the community is processing to the chapter room, for example, I will go neither to the right nor to the left, but I will keep myself right in the line that it follows. If I notice that at table everyone conforms to certain images, I will not go and demonstrate that I am free by affirming my personality in some primitive manner by acting differently!

Those are some very little things which form us and allow us to arrive at this conformity. Certainly, this conformity ought not to be a constraint in the sense of a nervous tension which I impose upon myself; that could make me neurotic. But it ought to be the eighth degree of humility. My way of doing things ought to come from a deep interior attitude of humility: I do not want to appear singular, or to make myself stand out from the others. The Rule, the community, and even the smallest usages, I wish to adopt. I want to act like the others. But we must add: not through conformism. True conformity is not conformism, which is a kind of cowardice. There is nothing in it to resemble humility. It is simply the manifestation of a weakness of character, sometimes with such a fear of appearing ridiculous that we set ourselves acting like the superior and the others in order to avoid it. This is not a good attitude. Conformism leads to a distortion of the personality. But humility does not destroy it; on the contrary, it establishes it on a solid base. This is how we are to understand the eighth degree of humility.

# OBEDIENCE

## OBEDIENCE WITHOUT DELAY

An act of prompt obedience was what the ancients demanded of a monk when he had received a command, and St Benedict witnesses to the monastic tradition when he affirms in the very first sentence of chapter five that the first degree, the principal manifestation, of humility is obedience without delay. The monk, convinced of the importance of his sacred commitments, will not hesitate to follow the order he receives with an act, for he sees in it a command from the Lord (5:1-4). He lives in faith, the source of respect and fear of God; he lives also in the love of Christ for whom he has chosen the path of monastic life.

St Benedict insists in a very special way on a quick reaction from the monk when an order has been received, and he gives it a description of surprising vigor: the monks immediately leave what they have in their hands and, like a soldier ready for action, they go so quickly when an order is given that the two seem to coincide in the eagerness the fear of God inspires (5:7-9). This quickness is explained by the zeal with which the monk should be animated to march to eternal life (10). Moved by this eagerness, the monk chooses the narrow way (11), and so this obedience without delay is a hard thing.

In the sixty-eighth chapter, St Benedict seems to modify this way of thinking, putting some water into this fiery wine of holy promptness, for he permits a brother to explain to the superior the obstacles which he thinks hinder the execution of the order. Can these two different attitudes be reconciled, at least in practice? And how can the monk who sincerely wants to obey reconcile an eagerness without delay with the reflection necessary in some cases?

Let us refer to our absolute Model, Jesus Christ, exact imitation of whom never leads us into error. That His obedience to the Father was beyond all compromise, that his attitude toward obedience was like a need of his nature, that to him it was as necessary as food (cf. Jn 4:34) is all beyond doubt. Nevertheless, in the Garden of Olives Jesus gives us an example of an act of obedience as human as it is sublime: 'Father', he said, 'if you will, take this cup from me. Nevertheless, may not my will but yours be done' (Lk 22:42). Is this obedience without delay?

First let us distinguish between the fundamental attitude of obedience and the act of execution. That Jesus was obedient to his Father appears clearly from the very same words: 'If you will', he said, 'if it is possible'. Any spirit of contentiousness is far from Jesus. It is a humble request he makes, wholly immersed in this will to accomplish what the Father desires.

These words of Jesus allow us to analyze the process of

obedience. First of all, there is, the general will to obey an order. This preliminary will of the person who obeys ought to be unconditional in order to be sincere, which does not exclude the hope that the order might be withdrawn or modified. The 'obedience without delay' of the Rule refers first of all to this fundamental attitude in the monk who is resolved to take his promise of obedience seriously. On this level, therefore, obedience without delay excludes hesitation and indecision, the slowness of someone who is in no hurry, who sulks or wants to express his disagreement; it also excludes apathetic slackness, grumbling, or contentiousness (cf. 5:14). However, it leaves the door open to a humble and respectful request for an eventual reconsideration of the order (cf. 68:3).

At the beginning the master's order finds this psychological disposition which elicits an act on the part of the disciple. If it were necessary to take the words of the Rule literally when it refers to the order of the master and the deed done by the disciple as taking place at the same moment (5:9), it would leave no room for reflection or a request of the sort Jesus addressed to his Father. We must therefore either admit that St Benedict knowingly modified his point of view from chapter five, borrowed almost literally from the *Rule of the Master*, and added chapter sixty-eight which is unique to him, or else see in the teaching of chapter five a general exhortation to be applied to special cases according to circumstances. For there are many situations in which an order to be followed is already more or less known in advance and in which obedience without delay is wholly advisable.

Today we are tempted to class this obedience without delay with blind obedience or passive, infantile obedience, without reflection and therefore without personal commitment. This is not the meaning of chapter five. The motives listed by St Benedict at the beginning of the chapter protects this rule from these distortions. The perfection of the act resides in the basic attitude. We have seen that this is nothing but the union of love with the Father's will. The apostles who responded immediately to the Master's call cannot be accused of thoughtlessness. They followed him in full possession of their faculties of judgment and decision: 'At once, leaving their boat and their father, they followed him' (Mt 4:22). The monk, acting in faith, convinced that the obedience one renders to one's superiors refers to God (5:15), intends to act as the apostles acted. For God and the love of God he submits to the superior through an unreserved obedience in imitation of the Lord (7:34).

Everything depends, therefore, on the strength of our faith. To the extent that we, with the help of the Lord, succeed by a generous act of faith in making the connection between God and the superior who represents him and in seeing the order of the superior within the most loving will of divine Providence, the love of God will move us to accomplish what we are commanded with a joyful eagerness—without reserve, without second thoughts, without inhibitions. Then obedience without delay will not cause us any problems. With spontaneity and in the serene security which the consciousness of finding oneself in tune with the divine, sanctifying will gives, the monk speeds his steps in the way of God's commandments (Prol. 49), among which he will include the precepts of the Rule and the orders of his superiors.

## MONASTIC OBEDIENCE

Is obedience as St Benedict understands it (5:1) out of date, behind the times? According to some people, the Second Vatican Council has modified the traditional concept to which so many generations of monks have appealed. What exactly is this all about?

It cannot be said that there has been an essential change in the manner of obeying or in the manner of conceiving obedience, for Christ is the absolute model, and the Church has never taught another obedience than the one  lived by him. It may be said, on the other hand, that certain aspects of obedience which were less highly regarded before the Council were strongly underlined by it; more at any rate than they had been in the past. A strongly awakened personal commitment, a greater sense of responsibility have been more highly esteemed through a concern for effectiveness. But this is nothing really new: a commitment is a fully personal act, supposing, of course, that one clearly discerns the legitimacy and the moral value of what one is doing. By saying that one must deny himself in order to follow him (Lk 9:23), Jesus certainly demanded the total commitment of the human person. And the Rule, by insisting on the renunciation of self-will, expresses exactly the same thought while pushing it to its ultimate conclusion.

That demand is now seen in a new light when we insist especially on the connection between the act of obedience and the work to be accomplished. Formerly, one set the perfection of obedience more in its formal context, in its interior attitude, in the spontaneity and promptness of the act, and in the intensity of the commitment, whereas now one looks more at its fulfilment, in its relationship to the work commanded, in the quality of its execution. It is obvious that these two aspects, far from contradicting, complete each other. Instead of considering the act of obedience mainly in itself, one now adds to it the aspect of the work to be completed, which obviously demands the commitment of all the faculties and powers of man, all his talents and personal gifts.

Did St Benedict neglect this aspect, that is to say, the result of the act? Let us remember first of all that our sanctification itself is a work which requires all our efforts to be perfect. And our obedience, our promise of conversion, are employed. But whereas our acts of obedience constitute this work and coincide with it, it is not so with the results, which are set outside ourselves. Now it is here that this completely new aspect opens up, the one St Benedict did not treat, and for a reason.

Among religious congregations founded for a specific apostolic work, the obedience vowed for love of God and neighbor is centered upon the accomplishment, as perfectly as possible, of their particular work. For St Benedict, the external work to be accomplished has much less importance than obedience itself. The monk does not obey in order to produce; he obeys for the love of God, thus attending to the work of his sanctification. When it is a matter of completing an exterior work for the community, it goes without saying that this love demands that he bring to it his whole attention. But it is not the work that occupies the monk's attention; it is his action that he wishes to be perfect. Of course, there are only shades of difference here, a shift of emphasis, yet it calls for substantially different spiritualities.

Some have wanted to see in this concept of the monastic rule an incomplete, deficient theology. Instead, it is a fundamentally different concept of the religious life, far removed from the pragmaticism which is praiseworthy and necessary in groups of men, priests, and lay persons devoted to the apostolate. It jars the rationalistic spirit which men of all ages carry within themselves, especially those of a technological age of calculation and efficiency.

The substance of obedience is, however, the same for all those who consecrate their lives to Christ. Just as Jesus freed an humanity subject to sin by his obedience to death, so also the monk, like every religious, contributes to the work of redemption not so much in accomplishing beneficial works as by uniting his will as perfectly as possible to the divine will. There is, therefore, no question of deficiency, of a hole to be filled. The Rule is representative of all ancient asceticism in its concept. The obedience of the monk who acts through love of Christ and abides in him certainly bears the fruits of eternal life. Measured by the obedience of Christ, it is necessarily apostolic.

But the difference of concept remains. St Benedict felt no concern with productivity, either economic or even apostolic, although he was conscious that the brethren depended on one another for their salvation (cf. e.g. 27:4; 67:1-4) and that the cenobitic life is built entirely upon the truth of the communion of saints and the solidarity of the brethren in Christ Jesus. There is no hint in the Rule of the line of thought so strongly developed today concerning the apostolic committment of every baptized person incorporated into Christ and made corresponsible in his redemptive work. St Benedict, who abstains almost entirely from considerations of a theological character, could not, even had he wished, treat this question, because in the sixth century it had no place among the great theological themes.

A simple look at the Rule proves to us that St Benedict set little importance on economic productivity or cultural efficiency. The artisans of the monastery are exhorted to humility, not to production. Their job should even be taken away from them if they become proud and think they are benefitting the community. The products of monastic work are sold more cheaply than that of others (RB 57). The abbot is exhorted not to let himself be worried by excessive concern for material goods (2:23), and even if the basic assets of the monastery should be far too small, he ought to put his trust in Providence and not in the activities at which he busies himself in solving the preoccupations of his office as administrator (2:35f.). In the chapter on the cellarer, there is no consideration of economic utility. As for harvests, the monks help only if local circumstances or poverty oblige them (48:7) and not to make more profit. It is clear from all this that St Benedict did little to connect obedience with material success. The monastery is in no way a business; its object is the salvation of souls (2:33; cf. 41:5).

We arrive here at a consideration characteristic of the monastic life. It is a life not only without a lucrative object, but a life that has no goal other than seeking God (58:7) and his love (7:67). Nothing is to be preferred to the love of Christ (72:11). To imitate him is to assure our salvation (Prol. 50).

St Benedict does not exclude other activities from the monastic life, as the Rule itself and his life, written by St Gregory the Great, testify, so long as they can be integrated and adapted to its principal exercises. In any case, every consideration, whatever it may be, ought to yield to the salvation of souls.

All this shows us that obedience according to the spirit of the Rule is not directed toward a set activity and that no activity ought to trespass on it, as would be the case if, for example, competence were finally to be substituted for it. Never, therefore, should obedience be conceived or modified according to the demands of a work to be done but the work remains subordinate to the fundamental importance attributed to obedience in the work of salvation. This does not mean that the abbot should not employ the greatest circumspection in both cases. Often, as he ought to realize, obedience does not present itself in its pure state and he cannot expect an act of obedience 'without delay' until he has prepared for it by dialogue, consultation, reflection, and prayer. But this aspect goes beyond the subject of this conference.

Coming back to our subject, we notice that St Benedict never speaks of the monks' co-responsibility, of participation in the decisions to be made. The abbot ought to consult widely, listen, become informed. But since St Benedict is concerned above all to have his monks profit by obedience, the principal and eminently salutary virtue, under the responsibility of the abbot (2:6), and since he hardly looks at it under its utilitarian aspect, the idea of solidarity in a common work to be done or in the administration to be made does not even come up. It must be admitted that the more a community of monks develops into responsible groups who take the direction of the monastery in hand, the more the obedience according to the formula of the Rule and as we contemplate it in the divine model is diluted and blurred. On the other hand, co-responsibility in the horizontal sense is strongly accented in the Rule, both on the spiritual and on the material level. Solidarity in the arduous march toward our common end, the kingdom of God, is the object and the meaning of the common life per se. Mutual spiritual help, although St Benedict speaks little about it explicitly, is essential in the monastic community. Co-responsibility in the material order is at the root of the idea of mutual service for which the Rule gives some simple and enlightening principles in chapter thirty-five.

If St Benedict stimulates the spirit of responsibility on the level of consultation while reserving to the abbot the decisions to be made, this is consistent with his concern to assure obedience without delay. Some believe they see here an inadmissible restriction on the rights of the human personality, a way of reducing monks to the state of minors.

This would be greatly to misunderstand the very supernatural intentions of our Father St Benedict, based on the teaching not only of other monastic rules but of other great teachers and founders in the religious life. Because he is convinced of the value of obedience, and considers it the most precious and noble attitude of the monk, he wishes to transfer the right of decision to a higher level, where the monk once and for all and every time the occasion presents itself, has decided to renounce it (5:12) in order to obey.

Is this too much to ask of people today, of 'adults'? Do we not retain the natural right to express ourselves in questions touching the destiny of the community in which we are incorporated and which necessarily have repercussions in our personal fate? The monk retains that right in essence; but he also has the power to cede that right to someone else, which he does with full freedom when he votes to elect an abbot. For centuries, moreover, monks have had the right to participate in the administration of the goods of the monastery. And it does not seem contrary to the Rule to invite them to a decisive co-responsibility in other matters. In these cases, the abbot's task to foster a serene, free obedience without delay, becomes more delicate, and much more difficult, too, is the effort of the monk to arrive at a real and frank obedience which depends on the command of the superior and not on his own judgment. But these acts of obedience will be that much more meritorious.

The essence of obedience will always remain the total and unrestricted consecration of the will to the Lord as proof of love and unlimited confidence; it is thus that the monk will share in the great designs of the work of salvation.

### RESPONSIBLE OBEDIENCE

The objection most frequently brought against the formula of obedience without delay (5:1) is that it risks being no longer human. Man ought to concentrate the higher faculties of his intellect and of his will in order to act in as conscious and free a manner as possible. It is proper to underscore the fact that, in the last analysis, a man is always personally responsible for his acts and has the duty before taking an action, of making a judgment on it; just as in obeying, he ought to take account of the value of what he is doing. Man cannot act as a robot without abdicating his dignity.

There can be no question of his rendering a complete judgment; this is often impractical and even out of place; because, for the monk, to do an act of real obedience is to act with faith in God. That act thus shares in the obscurity of the act of faith and in its risk. It suffices, then, to ascertain that it is morally good. If his own opinion regarding the value of the work commanded were to be the condition on which the judgment of whether to perform the work depended, and if he desired to reserve this right to himself, he would no longer be obeying the superior, but he would be relying on his own judgment. In any case, there would no longer be obedience without delay.

Now, it is a fact that people today often lack the joyous assurance of faith, and this is why it is not easy for us to practise this virtue. Sceptical, we hesitate. Concerned to maintain our human dignity, we reflect. And supposing that St Benedict is being a bit rhetorical in this beautiful chapter five, we hide under a less strict and less demanding interpretation, while still maintaining in our heart, we suppose, a firm and detached will to obey perfectly. We love to find, in chapter sixty-eight, the paternal indulgence of St Benedict and his exhortations for a prompt, entire, and available ready obedience, once the dialogue with ourself or with the superior has ended.

The dialogue with ourself: in scholastic philosophy they would speak of this process of reasoning, which ends in the *judicium ultimum practicum*, the ultimate practical judgment, which decides about the act which we are going to take without delay.

Now, in this reasoning before the act of obedience there is perhaps in man today a desire for a deliberation more profound than what formerly took place. He sincerely wants to be a disciple of the Lord, but he takes more time to deliberate than did men of the past. I am not saying that he resists, no; he takes more time. Formerly, there was, perhaps, a greater disposition to obey without examination. Democracy has made man more conscious of his right of self-determination. He has become of age, according to the popular expression, and he takes more time to cross the line between the command and the act of the will which decides, 'I will obey'. There lies the difference between yesterday and today. Obedience in our day clearly costs young people more. The young person wants to know the reasons for the act he is ordered to do. He asks questions. He wants, and rightly so, to obey the command in an active and convinced manner, not merely passively. True obedience, of course, cannot be passive and never was. Moreover, St Benedict insists that it ought to be energetic and militant (5:4-10; Prol. 3). Formerly, perhaps, people asked fewer questions before carrying out the command they received. They accepted the order of the superior with more spontaneity and more simplicity. Sometimes maybe a little too much ease slipped in: 'Let's go, it has to be done, the superior demands it; don't ask too many questions!' There was a risk of being superficial and of taking obedience lightly.

Persons today, on the contrary, tend to examine everything, to test everything. This way of acting sometimes gives us the impression of an obedience less sincere than formerly, as if the monk preferred to follow his own judgment rather than that of the superior, obeying because he understands and sees the reason for an order, and therefore that it is acceptable and perhaps even desirable. It is possible that this obedience carried out with greater understanding may be also more authentic. But it is just as true that as formerly people were tempted to obey without stopping to think, today in obeying, they can be tempted to an act of self-will which makes them say: 'Yes, at last, in this particular case, the superior has judged well and is right.'

There are, then, two dangers to avoid. Obedience must not be purely passive: 'He told us to do it, so I'm doing it', without making of it an action which is fully embraced and belongs fully to me. This would be to put too little of ourself into the activity. On the other hand, my act of obedience must not be in the last analysis a manifestation of my self-will: I do what I am commanded because it pleases me, because I am convinced, because I accept it, but not because the superior has asked me. In that act, there is no longer a trace of obedience.

In this context, we must mention again the special case of officers or those in charge of things. Let us take the example of the deans in the Rule. St Benedict, broadminded and convinced of the necessity of a relative sharing of power according to what we call the principle of subsidiarity (on this point cf. 65:11: 'Let the abbot have the full administration of his monastery in his hands'), St Benedict wants the abbot to entrust 'part of his burden' (21:3) to officers called deans who will care for everything in their deaneries according to the commandments of God and the directives of their abbot (21:2). They receive from that very fact a mission which is certainly universal, 'to care for everything', a delegation *ad omnia*, with precise instructions from the abbot, a sort of *loi-cadre* framework. Each one is made responsible for his respective deanery. A comparison with the *Rule of the Master* (RM 11) shows how great a margin of responsibility St Benedict allows the deans. In the chapter of the prior, St Benedict comes back to this point, moreover, using a very clear expression: 'If possible, let all the business of the monastery be run by the deans according to the orders of the abbot' (65:12). They find themselves, therefore, invested with considerable authority in making their own decisions. The qualities demanded of the deans (21:1,4) confirms the importance of their authority. The office of prior (21:7; ch. 65) and cellarer (31:2f.) are considered by St Benedict in the same way. And, due allowance being made, the principle of a mission received and a certain autonomy must be applied to every monastic officer.

Back to the question of obedience; it is clear that these officers have received, along with the investiture of their office, the mission of making themselves truly capable of administering their office. Their competence and their practical experience will very often surpass that of the abbot. In enjoining a determined order upon them, therefore, the abbot should use all required prudence. And they, on their part, will know by the very fact of their nomination to an office that they have received a more general mandate, to which will be subordinated particular obedience in the same area. Obedience has its own special logic. This is what obliges the officer to reflect upon a new order and conceive a clear idea of its compatibility with the norms, the demands and the experiences of the task incumbent on him. It is therefore, in the name of obedience that he ought to reflect whether the order given by the superior is in accord with his duty. In that case, he ought to be ready to obey without delay. If he discovers obstacles which hinder the execution of the order, he ought humbly and frankly to inform his superior to whom it belongs to decide, according to the dispositions of chapter sixty-eight. Let us not forget that in a monastery, everyone has the right to remain entirely a monk, that obedience takes precedence over all considerations of natural utility, and that even the most down-to-earth things take on a religious meaning and receive their real value from it. If in our monasteries the justice of the Kingdom maintains its decisive place, material affairs will not in the end suffer great harm.

Obedience is, therefore, of prime importance in a community. This is what gives it its spiritual outlook, for it is the most concrete monastic form of exercising the theological virtues which demands of us a commitment whereby our whole person, our conviction, and our will manifest themselves. The most frank and most limpid obedience is, indeed, a magnificent witness of faith in the loving will of God.

# SIMPLICITY OF HEART

*In simplicitate cordis laetus obtuli universa*—in simplicity of heart I have gladly offered everything. The Church has borrowed these words of David (1 Chron 29:17) for the feast of the dedication of a Church, that liturgy which is especially ours because our vocation is to be an offering to the Lord,

144

a gift made joyously—*laetus*—an offering made in simplicity of heart. Our Lord has invited us: *Praebe, fili mi, cor tuum mihi.* We recognize this text of one of the responsories. 'My Son, give me your heart' (Prov 23:26). And to this request we have responded by the oblation of ourselves, an oblation to be lived in the rhythm of each minute of our existence.

What does it mean: 'I offer everything'? Everything means my entire self; it is my heart as the expression of myself. In the Litany of the Sacred Heart of Jesus, this word 'heart' expresses all that the Lord is: all his aspirations, all his inclinations, all his desires, all his affections, all that is most beautiful in his heart, all the spirit of the offering he made. In making monastic profession, we have imitated him, and offered him all that. We have not, indeed, made one portion which we have given and another portion which we have kept. We have not said to the Lord: I give you this, but let me have the rest. No, we wanted to give him everything. That was, and that still is our will. Is that will always present, real, and generous in our hearts? This is for us an examination of conscience to renew.

Let us, then, place ourselves before Our Lord's cross. He is hanging there. His arms extended not only toward his Father, but also toward us. He gives everything, opening not only his arms, but his heart, to the soldier's lance, keeping nothing for himself, giving all his divine and human love; this heart, he offers it to the Father. Before that cross, we feel inspired and urged in our turn to give everything. We need this call of Our Lord hanging on the cross in order to become capable of giving ourselves. *Obtuli universa.*

Before our crucified Lord who gives us his love we hear his call: 'My Son, give me your heart'. And we answer: 'Yes, *paratum cor meum, Deus, paratum cor meum*' (Ps 56:8). 'My heart is ready, God, My heart is ready.' I am ready, Lord, to give all, and I am ready to love you with my whole heart (Deut 6:5), that is to say, holding back nothing, keeping nothing for myself: *universa.* We understand the meaning of this gift forever and without exception.

That is what we want to express in saying that we make this gift *in simplicitate cordis*, in the simplicity of our heart.

What is simplicity? Let us distinguish first of all between simplicity of the intellect and simplicity of the heart. St Benedict speaks once in the Rule of the *simpliciores* (2:12), of the simple who do not have a well-developed or trained intellect and who have remained simple. This is not what is meant here. This concerns simplicity of heart. What is that? When we take the train, we go to the counter to buy a ticket; we are asked: *'Simple ou retour?'* (One-way or return). *In simplicitate cordis;* this expresses the one-way, without return. Simplicity of heart is precisely that. If we have too many returns to self, there is no longer simplicity. If, when we give something, we unconsciously ask: 'What am I going to get out of this? Do I like this? Does this correspond to my aspirations?', then we are making a return to self. It is no longer one-way, it is a return to self. There is a going and a returning, a duplicity which is nothing but thinking more of ourselves than of the Lord, of making ourselves the ultimate criterion of decision.

Yet we should not be surprised at this tendency in our heart, which in one way wants seriously and sincerely to give, but on the other hand, following the pull of nature, immediately returns to self. This tendency has been innate in us since the sin of Adam. In the earthly paradise, Adam had one sole aim: God, the sovereign Good. He make no mistake, because God really was everything for him. But sin destroyed this blessed state, causing Adam to want to be like God. Then he made a deplorable return to self: believing and desiring to be the one toward whom all things converge and on whom all are concentrated. From the moment Adam became orientated to self, complications and disorder took possession of his heart. He opened his eyes, recognized himself, and abandoned the simplicity of innocence. At that moment, duplicity entered the heart of all humanity; it became inherent in it. We are no longer able to uproot it from our hearts, where it remains till the last breath of our lives. But we ought to fight it and try to reduce it as much as possible. We can and we ought to struggle to implant within ourselves little by little a real simplicity. But to want to become simple at any cost and without discernment brings with it the danger of imprudent returns to self which, instead of giving the desired simplicity, take us a little further from it by making us more complicated.

Simplicity of heart is, therefore, a virtue whose acquisition demands continual effort. It is not a gift; it is not a grace which is given us once for all. Much less is it a quality of our nature, our temperament, or our character. It is true that some persons are simpler than others; perhaps the cause is to be found in the make-up of some minds or in education. But the difference is only in degree, and appearances often are misleading. In every human heart there is the tendency to duplicity.

And yet we would love to be completely simple. What must we do? We should put ourselves again at the foot of Our Lord's cross. There we look in only one direction; in Jesus there is no return to self. He is in perfect possession of himself. Everything in him is given to the Father: everything. It is a complete abandonment; it is the perfect *simplicitas cordis.* Now, if our soul wants to achieve that simplicity of heart in the offering it makes of itself, there is no better way than to remain at the foot of the cross, and there constantly to rediscover our own cross, under whatever form it presents itself. It is through the cross that Jesus has re-established the correct orientation of humanity, the orientation toward God, vertical. If we do not take this path, we remain stationary, and will never go out of ourselves. It is through the cross that we rejoin the sacrifice of Jesus who was able to say excellently: *Consummatum est* and *Laetus obtuli universa.*

*Laetus.* This gladness, this sincere and perfect joy, this true gladness of heart, is only possible in simplicity of heart. Joy has different levels, so to speak; it can be very superficial. We amuse ourselves with trifles, with pleasantries. St Benedict does not like that (6:8, 7:59). There are other levels, nearer the heart, where it becomes deeper, truer. It may not appear so, outwardly, but it becomes more and more 'cordial'. St Benedict speaks of it in connection with obedience: God loves a cheerful giver (5:16). This gladness, this jubilation of heart ought to become more and more ours. It is a fruit of simplicity. We will possess it the day we have learned to renounce ourselves, when we understand that we must stop these endless returns to self; they end up only in fixing our attention on ourselves and on our insignificant progress. One day we will succeed in freeing ourselves from the commercial spirit in our relations with the Lord—I give so that you will give—*do ut des*—and at the same time, we will arrive at happiness, at true gladness of heart. That will be the fruit of the Holy Spirit (Gal 5:22); it will no longer be the joy which is nature's fruit. This too is lawful and good, and our soul feels need of it, but it is different from the joy promised by the Lord (Jn 15:11) for which we long. This joy is intimately linked with simplicity of heart, that simplicity which makes us want to render to him the things that are his, that is to say, ourselves.

Is it not the Father who, with a simplicity wholly divine, gave his only Son so that every man who believes in him may not perish, but have eternal life (Jn 3:16). And has the Son himself not said: In the simplicity of my heart I have gladly given all. He invites us to follow Him, saying: Anyone who loses his life for my sake will find it (Mt 16:25). How beautiful is that perfect liberty of spirit which seeks only what is of God, which makes us capable of giving our life drop by drop for our brothers! That simplicity of heart, which is, however, fully conscious of the gravity of its acts and the consequences of its offering, is an incomparable gift from the Lord to those who truly love him and who, with a pure heart, choose him over and over again unceasingly. They walk with an enlarged heart (Prol. 49) in the steps of Jesus 'going about and doing good' (Acts 10:38); in joyful simplicity of heart, they present to the Lord the total offering of themselves.

# ABANDONMENT
# TO GOD'S PURPOSE

From all eternity, from before the creation of the world, God has for man a benevolent purpose, determining beforehand that we should be his adopted children through Jesus Christ, who should be our only head, so that we might be incorporated in him and possess in him the promise of redemption and eternal life. In Him we are 'marked with a seal through the Spirit of the promise which constitutes the pledge of our heritage'. In the first chapter of his letter to the Ephesians, St Paul works magnificently about the purpose of the divine love for us.

These are the Father's plans. What should be our attitude toward them? Could there be any question of our preparing another project opposed to the divine plan, a personal project—this one human—of liberation based on human self-sufficiency, now that we are ready and able to take our destiny into our own hands?

Does St Benedict have us enter this path of abandonment to the purposes of God in the history of the economy of salvation as the Father has conceived it from all eternity? Does he try to make us grasp these divine plans? Once again, St Benedict does not speak as a theologian; he does not give us meditations along that line, but actually makes us enter into theology. If we take the Rule and open it to the Prologue, what do we see immediately? His will that we enter into God's plans. 'Listen', he begins. This is a way of saying: See God's plan. And in what does that plan consist? God offers you eternal life (Prol. 17), he also offers you the means of getting there, of entering fully into his magnificent plan, which is all for our benefit, of attaining eternal life. This is why we have this long section of the Prologue where St Benedict develops for us the means to be employed for entering into the tabernacle of God (Prol. 22ff.), into eternal life, to receive the promise, to share the wonderful light, to make His project ours. He shows us the path of redemption. Once again, this is no theological treatise, but an admonition: we ought to enter into the work of salvation in the way that God has conceived it and follow Christ— *ut Christum sequamur* (4:10)—our head, in whom alone our salvation is assured and accomplished.

So then, this teaching is linked with that of the letter of the Ephesians, of the New Testament. Entering fully into the plan of God, we march toward life everlasting, which, as you know, is not only the life to come. Starting now, our life is eschatological; begun at baptism, it continues during our passage through this earth to blossom in heaven, without interruption, without a break. Death is only an adaptation to ultimate life. The simple christian life, lived in faith, hope, and charity, contains the promise of eternity. Now, St Benedict does nothing but offer us in the monastic life a faster and surer way of entering it, by following Christ with fervor, committing ourselves to following him poor, chaste, and obedient, finally, following him in his passion so as to deserve a place in his Kingdom (Prol. 50).

St Benedict, therefore, has us take this road by giving us a rule of life. To enter upon it is to make the salvific plans of God our own by committing ourselves to a sure and clearly-marked path. There are many formulas for following Christ; the benedictine life is one of them. To enter upon it means an abandonment to the merciful purposes of the Father for those whom he has called to monastic commit-ment, which is only a means of abandoning oneself into his hands.

St Benedict teaches us this by the whole spiritual attitude of the Rule. Without giving us special chapters on confidence in God or the abandonment of our cares and problems and even of the whole tissue of our lives into the Father's hands, the Rule leads us there quite simply by means of the force of its teaching. It teaches us so great a liberty, so firm a will to cling to the divine will, that we are not even tempted to think of anything else, if we really follow it. We do not find in it any suggestion, any insinuation, which would invite us to be concerned about anything. Little by little, we set ourselves to follow very simply the plan of Providence.

Is not monastic obedience an attitude of loving confidence in divine Providence? 'All things work together for good for those who love God' (Rom 8:28). Far from being passive, it manifests a great love of God, going sometimes even to heroism. God, indeed, deigns to work with the obedient for their good.

To renounce for the love of God every kind of ownership is also the gesture of someone who, full of confidence, throws himself into the arms of the heavenly Father, entrusting his entire life to him (cf. Ps 22:1), and expecting everything from the father of the monastery (RB 33:5). The monk, for example, is not preoccupied with what he is going to eat. St Benedict, in the Rule, shows no anxiety over guaranteeing a supply of vegetables, the necessary grain, bread for tomorrow. Likewise with drink. If we have wine, so much the better; if we do not, let us be content (40:8). No concern for clothing: take what there is (55:7). If there is less work, very well, let us accept it from God; if there is a lot of work, in the fields, for example, let us not be disturbed; in that case, we can be good, real monks (48:7f.). Neither is St Benedict concerned about the number of members in the community. He sets down no minimum number. Nowhere in the Rule does he imply minimum limits or foresee ideal conditions regarding material questions. In no way does he hint at the image of a better or more agreeable tomorrow. Let us, therefore, not have any worries like this. St Benedict does not even advise us not to worry. He simply has us enter into this attitude of being open, of letting ourselves be guided by Providence, of not worrying about tomorrow. Isn't this the spirit of the Gospel? The Rule has us enter, without second thoughts, into this real spirituality of a naïve acceptance of all that God disposes, all that we find. Look at the directives he gives concerning the monk coming from another monastery; if he quite simply accepts what he finds, he says, he may be admitted (61:2f.). Nor is the novice asked what he expects, what he desires, and what responds to the aspirations of today's youth. Certainly the superiors ought to be attentive to the signs of the times, but it would be an aberration to organize the monastery indiscriminately according to the demands of the young, and it would be doing them the greatest possible harm by letting them believe they have the right to impose their wills, their plans, and their projects instead of accepting the designs of God. St Benedict—this is significant—has the Rule presented three times to the novice as a law of life, so that he will know what he is obliging himself to (58:12). For him, there is only one alternative: 'If you can keep it, enter; if not, you are free to leave' (58:10). There is no third possibility open: 'If you desire certain modifications, say so'. He is required, therefore, to renounce his personal views and to abandon himself to the divine plan. In the attitude of perfect trust, the novice asks the Lord: 'Receive me, O Lord, according to your word and I shall live, and do not disappoint me in my hope' (58:21). In this way, the monk abandons himself to God from the beginning of his monastic life, by an act of supreme renunciation, ridding himself at the same time of any inquietude over his own destiny.

St Benedict wants to see this total confidence in God in everything. He does not want any restlessness in the monk's heart, for himself, or for the future of other people or for the community, or for anything at all. The abbot is not to let himself be burdened by the cares of administration, by questions of price, by the lack of resources of the monastery (2:35). God will provide. 'Your heavenly Father knows that you have need of all that' (Mt 6:32). The abbot ought not to be passive, of course, and the cellarer ought to administer well the temporal goods of the monastery, but everything should be done without disquiet (31:12). Confident in God whose house the monastery is (31:19; 53:22; 64:5) one is always hospitable; guests are received with open arms, the poor with generosity (31:9; 53:1, 15). The father of the monastery ought to be attentive to the needs of his brothers (31:16ff.; 33), and to watch out that no one is troubled or saddened in the house of God (31:19).

St Benedict wants to have us enter into an attitude of openness, of acceptance of the designs of Providence. From this point of view, our life is without problems. For this reason, it is sometimes said that the Rule gives the impression of not being dynamic enough. But this is precisely its greatness: it does not develop in us a dynamism of unwholesome restlessness. The only care it wants to see in us is the seeking of eternal life. For this we ought to run, do things, not slack off (Prol. 44), St Benedict tells us, but for the rest, remain calm. We ought to put all of our energies into climbing the ladder of humility; the very idea of climbing shows us the necessity of some effort in order to progress toward God. But that effort, that restlessness, should be reserved for gaining eternal life (4:46). The cares of this earthly life, insofar as they are superfluous, ought not to trouble us.

In his first epistle, St John speaks to us of the three concupiscences: they are rooted in the human, and we feel a need to bend to their inclinations, present since original sin. They are the concupiscence of the flesh, the concupiscence of the eyes, and pride in possessions (1 Jn 2:16). The root of our troubles lives there. Selfishness asserts itself in these passions. Pleasure, success, possession are the springs which keep the human will in motion. By his eschatological orientation, the monk is placed in a command tower from which fortified by these criteria, he can judge the real value of things. He cannot confuse the good with what is simply convenient, pleasant, or agreeable, even though sometimes the good may also be all that. He will not be depressed if in spite of his efforts, he is not successful. It would be a counter-witness in the eyes of the world if we were to seek temporal advantage, or strive to extend our possessions or the area of our influence or renown. Where would the holy indifference so dear to St Benedict be?

On the other hand, sarabaites and gyrovagues are opposed to this attitude. The satisfaction of their desires is their faith (1:8). The gyrovagues cannot remain in one place. Why? Because they are never satisfied with what they have; there is always something better elsewhere, farther on; never satisfied, never stable—this is their life-style (1; 10f.). 'Let not your heart be troubled' (Jn 14:1). An agitated heart, troubled by a thousand cares, bears a counter-witness in the eyes of the world. It is not great buildings, in good or bad condition, which gives scandal, but the quest after security; superfluous conveniences, power, and triumphalism can create bad public relations for a monastic community. The attitude of perfect poverty consists in surrendering ourselves to God, in not undertaking projects which exceed our real needs. To be poor according to the Gospel, it is not enough to be able to say: 'Today I have no bread'. The poverty we seek is above all an interior freedom from everything that enriches with a wealth that passes away. St Benedict, if we follow his lessons, frees us and introduces us with a great simplicity to the practice of the christian attitude which opens to us the designs of God everywhere and always.

# Observances

# THE INSTRUMENTS
# OF GOOD WORKS

The fourth chapter surprises us. St Benedict, following the Master, offers us a doctrine of asceticism condensed into seventy-three axioms of christian life, almost all of them taken from the Holy Scriptures—their number corresponds to the number of chapters in the Holy Rule—and he presents them to us as instruments of good works. He is a teacher and a master; he is therefore ingenious in creating striking, convincing ways of making the laws and mechanisms of monastic asceticism enter the minds of his disciples, his brothers.

Now St Benedict was aware that he was dealing with men with a rather simple education and mentality, men from the peasant class, workers, or craftsmen. His monks were neither theologians nor philosophers. So he omitted reflections of a theological nature which he found in the Master. On the other hand, he followed him in this adaptation of the *praxis*, asceticism, to the psychology of the manual laborer. He speaks to him of the instruments of good works, of the workshop in which he works (4:78), of the spiritual art (4:75) which is the task for which God, his Master, entrusts to him appropriate instruments for which he will have to account on the day of judgment (4:76). All this makes us think of chapter thirty-two of the Rule, where the abbot, through his officers, distributes the instruments of work, while keeping an inventory of them, and watches over their specific and intelligent use. There it is a matter of tools necessary for manual labor, for the material art.

The spiritual art cannot be carried out either, unless one knows how to use the proper means to succeed at the work of sanctification. Man needs tools to work in either area, therefore. He needs intermediaries between him and the work to be done. This is an image. The spiritual tools required by the

157

spiritual art are obviously not in the same category as material tools. However, it is true that fundamentally they are handled the same way. It is easy for us to imagine a craftsman in his workshop with all the tools necessary for his craft. He is able to use them or to lay them aside, to make use of them or to neglect them. If he does not take care of them and leaves them in their drawer, then he is a man who does not have enough intelligence or enough ambition, application, or interest to carry out serious work. He does not know how to make the tools efficacious if he does not use them or uses them badly. So then the beautiful workshop is useless, even if it is the last word in technology.

Today, specialized workers are in great demand, because specialized equipment is becoming once more complicated and more indispensable. And consequently, capable operators are needed to run it. Think of a computer: an intelligent and well-trained operator is needed to run it. We would probably be quite incapable of making use of this instrument as necessary as it is expensive.

Now, in the spiritual art, we find ourselves in something of the same situation: we have a magnificent inventory of instruments of good works drawn up by St Benedict. Do we always use them? Do we know all these tools, their use, their meaning, their importance? Do we handle them with care? Are we like specialized workers, that is to say, have we studied these tools and how to use them well before handling them? Do we find ourselves a little awkward in this workshop of the spiritual art simply because we do not know how to treat with care the things put at our disposal?

Let us continue our comparison: we know that in the practical field, human intelligence is going further and further in its inventions and discoveries. In the same way, the spiritual art has various tools at its disposal. Some of them are very fundamental; others are of less importance; still others are secondary. All these tools—and this is very interesting—are taken from Holy Scripture, with one exception, according to the commentaries. This list was not drawn up by St Benedict; it is older than the *Rule of the Master*. It is found in various forms in christian antiquity. Human wisdom, natural and supernatural, has found these instruments of the spiritual art in experience and in the Bible, that is to say, in sources both natural and supernatural. It has drawn up lists, catalogues. Some of them have a natural character, and therefore have the perfection of the natural man as their goal. They are part of christian humanism, and serve to make man work toward an ever greater perfection to ennoble himself in his nature. Others are taken from the Word of God, from Revelation. They are of the order of grace, offered and given by Christ to perfect man according to the image of God, following the model of Jesus. The application, the use of these tools of the supernatural order supposes man as he actually is. Grace supposes nature. A Christian cannot be formed unless a person is deeply involved in his natural being.

There is, therefore, an inexhaustible arsenal of instruments placed at our disposal for the work of our natural and supernatural perfection. But it is necessary to know how to use them, to take them in hand, in order to make them uniquely effective, and that is the whole spiritual art. In this also, there is only one teacher, Jesus. *Unus est magister vester* (Mt 23:80). But in his name and commissioned by him there are persons who teach us the spiritual art, giving us the tools and training us to use them. These are the abbot and the other spiritual fathers. These are the foremen in the workshop of the monastery. St Benedict himself invites us in an urgent way to enter and remain in his workshop, in his school of the spiritual art: 'Listen, my Son' (Prol. 1). 'Here are the instruments of the spiritual art' (4:75), he tells us, 'by which you are able to arrive at perfection, at holiness'.

We ought, therefore, to take them well in hand and work with them. Craftsmen, whether they are painters, carpenters, or cooks are always trying to do better in their craft. Have *we* made any progress in the use of these instruments? Which ones do we really use, or prefer to use? Which ones do we neglect? There lies a whole *examen* to be made, and a very necessary one. Have we drawn up an inventory of the instruments we like to use? Do we know them and all their

160

possibilities well; do we know how to handle them? Do we
have the courage to enumerate truthfully those we do not
use? Such an *examen* ought to make us see the way we
practise this art, which is uniquely *our* art. All the other arts
and handicrafts are of secondary importance, terrestrial,
dependent on this life; but the spiritual art transcends time
and has an eternal effect.

Let us, therefore, make our *examen* in the light of
St Benedict's inventory. The cloister of the monastery is
a workshop for us, as the Rule says (4:78). Let us meditate
on what we must do, and let us get to work, beginning again
without tiring. We have very suitable instruments at our
disposal, simple to use, and very effective, tools which the
Lord, and the human wisdom he created, have offered us.

# MONASTIC OBSERVANCES

You know the book *Legatus Divini Amoris (The Herald of
Divine Love)* by St Gertrude\*. We see there what a profound
influence the entire liturgy, the Divine Office, the Holy
Sacrifice of the Mass, and also the observances, exercised
over the soul of this saint.

If we study her life attentively, we are immediately struck
by the place the observances held in her spiritual development, something which is, moreover, true in a general way
for all the ancient monks. Does the man of our day with his
mathematical mind not lose some of the sense of symbolism,
and by pushing sobriety to the extreme, does he not cut
himself off from this attitude characteristic of the ancients?
They, in fact, had a great conviction of the usefulness of the
observances in the structure of the monastic life, especially
the cenobitic life. So we need not be surprised at the care
given by the most ancient tradition and books of usages in
describing bows, prostrations, and genuflections, whether

---

\*English translation forthcoming from Cistercian Publica-
tions, 1985-6.

for liturgical celebrations or for the refectory and the dormitory, not to mention the observances of silence, solitude, and a humble and secluded life.

Let us mention in passing that the forms of the observances can change and be effectively modified according to human sensibilities. They are subject to the great currents of fundamental ideas and the behavior of each society. Many of them are, in fact, exterior manifestations of interior attitudes, and share, therefore, in the nature of a sign which is understood only if the person to whom it is addressed perceives it and grasps its meaning.

Let us return then to the spiritual life. It has to be cultivated. The monastic life likewise. And if we wonder what means are put at our disposal for bringing about this cultivation, we meet, among other things, a whole complex of observances. They concern not only the liturgy, but all the acts of our daily life which form the basis for it, the visible and external structure: our manner of walking, of dressing, of speaking, of meeting and greeting each other. Even external mortifications form a part of the complex of observances.

Here we come to a question: the observances are attitudes which are corporal more than anything else; how can they play a role in the work of our sanctification? We know the answer very well. The monastic life is based on human realities of soul and body. It takes into account the manifestations and palitations of life. Thanks to it, the monk runs a smaller risk of falling into the error of an exaggerated spiritualism and an inordinate excitement, where the body would be despised and its contributions minimized. Actually, it is the instrument through which the soul expresses and manifests itself. In turn, the soul is affected by the deportment of the body. As a slovenly body betrays a careless soul, so also a disciplined body exercises a wholesome influence over the attitudes of the soul.

Herein lies the meaning of the observances to which we referred. They are little ways of keeping us in order, training us, helping us lead a more disciplined life. They hoe, prune, and cultivate us, and to the extent that our efforts are made with the intention of opening up a way for grace, they help us grow in supernatural perfection; the soul develops, thanks to the body. Is not harmony between the two one of the goals toward which a man strives in the sunshine of grace, in order to arrive at a peaceful balance?

Now, we must admit that it is not easy to maintain the right attitude in the matter of observances. A double danger lies in wait for the monk. When he, perhaps, sees certain exaggerations, the fear of falling into this irregularity makes him show a sort of non-conformity, a nonchalance, a sort of disdain for observances. He maintains only the routine. Our imagination shows us a world of observances all ready to drown us and occupy our interior life. We think of the temptation to stop at gestures and signs without wanting to go beyond them. We are afraid of being regimented and categorized, of losing our personality.

We have to admit that that danger exists; and without doubt, it happens that we hold ourselves, if I may say so, at the edge of certain observances and content ourselves with that. In choir, we sing, maybe with a good voice which we cultivate, but we do not make the effort to descend to the marrow of what we are singing. We celebrate solemn ceremonies: do we think enough about their meaning? Likewise, we bow down at the *Gloria Patri*. Has it become a mechanical gesture for us?

And there is the danger: we can arrive at a certain conformity, at a formalism which stops with externals, at a kind of ritualism. Ought we then to give up the observances in order to avoid this danger? That would be to lack moderation and even to commit a fatal error.

Let us grasp the nature of the observances better. We realize that they are means, therefore instruments. Now what craftsman could do a good job without his tools? St Benedict has therefore drawn up a whole list of 'instruments of the virtues' (RB 4) to which must be added all those he describes throughout the Rule. The observances belong to this list. When we have used them well, we will one day be able with great profit to give them back to the Creator, rendering him an account of the use we have made of them.

We ought to think highly of the observances. The non-conformity of which people speak so much nowadays has this good about it: it puts us on guard to use them in the best way as 'instruments of the virtues'. Non-conformism contains an element of childishness, a lack of human experience. The activity of the soul cannot be separated from that of the body.

And then, in a community where people intend to share the same roof and to pray together, and in an orderly way, certain rules of life have to be established. Life in community ought to be regulated by rules, united by observances, and structured to a rhythm.

# THE ART OF SILENCE

From the very Prologue of the Rule, we are invited to listen. 'Listen, my Son' (Prol. 1:1). At the beginning of human life, Adam first listened to the words of God. And, throughout history, we see persons hearing and perceiving the divine word which is revealed and manifested to them. Now, for that we have to be quiet. We find silence then, from the very beginning. We cannot hear or receive God if we do not work at silence. The more we ourselves speak, the more we think we know and take ourselves for masters, and the less we listen to what the Lord says to us.

The Lord himself knew how to be silent, but his silences were of various sorts. Let us think of his silence before Pilate; he contented himself with not answering. In the presence of the adulterous woman, he was again silent. It was his way of forcing the Pharisees and the scribes who had come to accuse her to reflect, to retreat, and to take stock of themselves. The Lord moved them to this by a brief admonition, 'Let him among you who is without sin cast the first stone' (Jn 8:7). The result was that one after the other they abandoned their accusation and withdrew.

When we examine the ways of Jesus in the Gospel, we realize that with him silence and speaking are inseparable. It is as if he wanted to listen to his Father in order to repeat what he learned of him. 'What the Father has taught me, I speak' (Jn 8:28). 'I have not spoken of myself; but the Father who has sent me has himself commanded what I ought to say' (Jn 12:49). He listened in silence and spoke afterwards. This is why his remarks are well weighed.

The words of the Lord, therefore, were submitted to a great discipline. Even in his conversations with his friends, the apostles, we find the discipline of silence and listening. *Disciplina silentii.* We learn a lesson there; it concerns us. It is not only a monastic virtue, but a christian attitude. The Christian listens. Faith comes from hearing: *Fides ex auditu* (Rm 10:17), St Paul tells us. It cannot grow in us if we do not hear. And we cannot hear if we do not know how to be truly silent.

Here we already see what sort of silence is meant; it is interior silence. It ought to be preceded by a great interior tranquillity and an attention directed toward what is being said to us, an openness to what is going to be revealed to us. We are not speaking here of a lazy silence, or of a quiet and empty solitude where we busy ourselves with trifles; these are void of meaning for eternity, as is the silence of a frivolous selfishness occupied only with self.

Silence is, therefore, an interior attitude of listening. 'My heart is ready, O my God' (Ps 107:1), my heart is ready to listen. Does St Benedict not show us that this is the fundamental attitude of the monk? At the very beginning of the Prologue, he gives us this admonition: 'Incline the ear of your heart' (Prol. 1). The ear of the heart is the interior disposition with which we ought to welcome the word of God. The whole structure of our life leads us to this. We live side by side, yet our whole way of life is laid out in such a way as to facilitate interior silence.

Exterior calm, the practice of silence, ought especially to lead us to interior silence. What does that mean? St Benedict banishes from the monastery forever 'coarse jests, idle words which serve only to provoke laughter' (6:8). But it is not enough to avoid such behavior and such words. Someone who does not possess the discipline of silence can be tempted to speak every time he meets a brother, to have something to say at every turn in the corridor, behind every door; he can chatter a lot in a few words and concern himself with endless trifles. This is why a monastery is constructed in a way to teach us the discipline of silence. A sacred silence broods over the vast rooms of the building and we ought not to disturb it. What does 'enclosure' (6:8) mean if not a closing off, the exclusion of everything noisy, of all useless chatter or simply worldly talk which would violate these places, which would create a dissonance and break the harmony?

In what, then, does this silence consist? Is it absolute speechlessness, the simple fact of not speaking? The wise man, it is said, can express himself in a few words (7:61). His word is at the same time silence. What he says comes from his heart and not merely from the tip of his tongue. His words spring from profound meditation. That is true silence. A false, constrained, formalistic silence can make a person neurotic. True silence relaxes and liberates, unites us with what is great, keeps us from pettiness, and raises us to transcendence, makes us grow in God.

A charitable word does not break silence, people often say. That is true, without any doubt, provided we really understand what charity is. We can often deceive ourselves in this matter. Charity is an appreciation of the greatness of others, a correct attitude concerning the growth of our brothers and our own growth. If we both speak and are silent in this way, then both our silence and our speech are charity.

Here again Our Lord's example is a measure and a norm. At his school we learn to be silent, to listen, and to speak. These three attitudes are correlative. Someone who speaks without wisdom does not know how to be silent, nor how to listen, and vice versa. The discipline of silence leads to the discipline of discourse, to the art of speaking. That is why we place a guard at our lips (6:1), to allow to escape only such words as are capable of existing in the presence of Wisdom.

In light of this, we understand better St Benedict's thought when he speaks of perfect silence excluding even good, holy, and edifying speech (6:1, 3), even more, he sees a danger of sin in the very abundance of words (6:4f.). This

166

is why permission to speak shall be given rarely to the disciple, even if he is perfect (4:3). We see better, by these words, the fundamental state of soul from which this silence proceeds. We do not see there any constraint directed to maintaining external silence always and everywhere. The good order of community life manifestly demands that we keep silence in the church, the refectory, the corridors, and the cells, in short, in the regular places. But external silence is only the beginning, the exterior condition for gradually becoming a master in the act of silence.

The monk, the disciple of St Benedict, tends to live a generous and devoted charity toward his brother, by applying himself to maintaining a wise reserve and speaking in few words. He ought to succeed at showing great love in his words and nevertheless remaining habitually silent and moderate. This art of a silence overflowing with charity will lead him to that silent God who nevertheless chooses to reveal himself to those who have learned to listen in loving silence (Jn 14:21).

# ENCLOSURE

The term 'enclosure' evokes in many, at first, a feeling of uneasiness, mistrust, constraint, frus..ation, in short, a whole series of restrictive impressions. Enclosure seems to set an obstacle to the freedom of meeting people and things as we please. It makes us think of a sort of discrimination against the 'people outside' whose frequent contact would be quite undesirable, even harmful. Our times favor dialogue, sharing, the spontaneity of interpersonal relationships. Is papal enclosure not opposed to this sort of openness? How can a monastic institution separate those whom charity ought to unite?

Hearing all these reasons we understand why the papal enclosure is among the institutions being called into question; by some, it is even being relegated, in the name of the Gospel, to the rank of usages unworthy of persons who have finally been liberated from taboos. There is, therefore, a subject for reflection. Does the monk need to be cloistered? Does enclosure have a functional relationship to monastic life?

In order better to understand the complexity of this question, let us first of all place it in its natural context. The word 'enclosure', does it pertain only to canon law? Does only the monk need enclosure? No. Every person, whoever he may be, also needs contact with his fellowmen as much as he does withdrawal, distance, solitude, in short, a place of his own, inaccessible to the public. The artist, the thinker, separate themselves from others in order to find them better. The creative pause, in order to be beneficial, requires a reserved space. As water accumulates behind a dam in order to become a moving force, so a man needs enclosure in order to gather his resources. If some family properties are surrounded with walls, it is in order to guarantee the occupants some intimacy, a zone of independence, where family life can develop in freedom, away from an annoying and harmful casualness of contact. A good education cannot be had without a more intense association with certain people and a kind of separation from others. However repellent the sign 'No admitance' may seem, it affirms a person's inalienable right to the protection of his own personality, the right to create an area where he is able to live in full freedom and be himself. If he feels himself threatened, he has the right—which is, of course relative, since it is subject to safeguarding the common good—to put up a sign of non-welcome for those who might destroy or disturb his peace.

In line with these considerations, we understand why the monk has a need to withdraw. In order to be himself, to become a man of God, to meet the Lord and to discover himself in him as in a perfectly clear mirror, in order to know and love man, his brother, he needs a retreat, an enclosure.

We will see, then, first of all, whether what we call enclosure in the physical sense, existed for St Benedict. This study will also show us its spiritual meaning as an attitude of soul in the monk. Next, we will examine the object of enclosure, what is excluded in its active and passive effect. In other words, we will see what the monk renounces, and what he does to set himself apart for the love of the Lord.

Let us listen to St Benedict. In this area, as in others, he follows his predecessors while adding certain nuances.

In the chapter on the gatekeeper (66) the Rule presents the monastery as a closed unit in the manner of the roman *curtis*. Only one gate is provided, it would seem (66:1f., 58: 3), watched by the gatekeeper (66:1f.) and his helper (*ibid.* 5). Within the precincts of the monastery, the brothers find everything necessary: water, a mill, a garden, workshops (*ibid.* 6); this is as good as saying: within the enclosure. St Benedict speaks elsewhere of the *claustra monasterii*, the monastic enclosure (4:78, 67:7), designating those precincts surrounded by buildings, walls, and fences. The guest house (53:21) and the noviciate building (58:5) are probably found within those precincts. The chapel (RB 52) is the center of the monastery because the community gathers there to pray; it is also there that the monk is solemnly incorporated into the community (58:17). This entire en-closed unit is the place where the monk lives, where he exercises the spiritual art (4:78), from which he does not depart without the abbot's permission (67:7) and accom-panied by the prayer of his brothers (67:1f.), to which he returns as soon as possible, even without having eaten out-side (51:1). Because, St Benedict says, it is not fitting for monks to run around outside (66:7).

St Benedict wanted to arrange for his monks a real separation from the world. This desire appears clearly in his manner of receiving guests. On the one hand, there is no hesitation in receiving them because it is Christ who is received in them. They are admitted into the precincts of the monastery. On the other hand, complete cohabitation does not seem desirable for the monks. The guests, therefore, use a separate house (53:21) and even a separate kitchen (*ibid.*:16); no one has the right to speak with them except those who are especially assigned to care for them (*ibid.*:23). Here we see an enclosure within the enclosure.

St Benedict wanted to create for his monks a reserved

place and a structure perfectly adapted to their type of life and their aspirations. There is no doubt that he envisaged a clearly defined enclosure, an enclosed precinct, a *hortus conclusus*, a garden enclosed where monastic virtue may blossom without being troubled (RB 4). Those who persevere there until death (58:15) will pass from that abode to the kingdom of heaven (Prol. 50).

While they advocate this physical enclosure, we strongly sense in these texts that St Benedict intended to underscore its moral and spiritual character. Enclosure has absolutely nothing in common with that of a prison. The monk ought not to feel himself locked up. He enters there freely and is also able to leave freely (RB 29). We are not, therefore, surprised to see St Benedict avoiding expressions which might wound our sensibilities as free men. As for him, there is no concern with confining the monks, no explicit prescription about barring the door every time someone goes in or out, as we do find in the Rule of the Master. Yet, as a well-advised legislator, St Benedict takes into account man's need to be supported by restrictive institutions in order to realize his desire to remain in a situation freely chosen.

Now, the monk is a man of one desire alone, of one only love (72:11)—we love to explain the word *monachus* in this way. He desires to be free of all tht can turn him away from his quest. He flees, not in order to retreat, but in order to run to God; he hides in him (Col 3:3); he makes himself Christ's prisoner (Eph 3:1). This captivity in Christ is wholly spiritual and voluntary. So too, physical enclosure is observed and loved as the means and the expression of personal enclosure, of an interior discipline. To follow the Lord is a unique and difficult adventure (4:10), to abide in him (Jn 1:38), to belong to him, body and soul; so too, the enclosure, freely chosen, is for the monk a constant call to renounce all that could turn him away from that love of preference vowed to Christ (4:21).

St Benedict offers his disciple this abode, a blessed oasis. He shows him the road to the tabernacle of God, where he is invited to enter and live (Prol. 22-24, 29). The novice hears it said: If you are able to observe the law of the Rule, *ingredere*, enter (58:10) into that tabernacle. This idea of tabernacle is ambivalent and signifies both the physical place and the spiritual abode of the soul.

Since enclosure is an institution with an entirely spiritual end, we should not be surprised to see the spirit of the enclosure extend even to the space inside the physical enclosure. Enclosure is attached to the person of the monk. Even in the midst of his brothers, he lives recollected (RB 7: the ninth to the twelfth degree of humility). The spirit of silence (RB 6, 7:56ff.), the guard that the monk sets about his lips (6:1)—is this not an enclosure which is imposed? In the monastery, no brother ought to be near another at forbidden hours (48:21). Likewise, if a monk meets a guest, he ought to excuse himself and say that he is not permitted to talk with him (53:24).

The great St Teresa mentions endless visits in the parlor where one spoke all day with one's friends from outside. A grill, an enclosure, under such conditions, no longer keeps its meaning of real separation. Enclosure, therefore, attaches itself to the person even more than to the place. It is an attitude of discipline helped and supported by the institution. But even more than the walls of the enclosure, the community of brothers forms a living enclosure in which the monk feels at home in a loving atmosphere which holds him, incorporates him, and offers him a structure for the development of his being and for his religious quest.

We have just seen, with the text in hand, St Benedict's opinion of enclosure in its physical reality as well as in its religious motivation. The monk, the nun, in their enthusiastic desire to seek the Lord (58:7) want to have removed from them everything that could hold them back on their journey. They have therefore chosen enclosure by a free choice and for the love of Christ and his kingdom. Its immediate effect is negative; it is a refusal, a non-welcome, but in view of obtaining an entirely positive result: by withdrawing oneself, to gain liberty.

From what do they especially want to be liberated in entering the enclosure? Or, in other words, who is affected by it?

A first response to that question has been given us by Jesus, putting us on guard against 'the world' taken in its Johannine sense (cf. Jn 14:30, 12:31, 1 Jn 2:15f.). Certainly, evil is in us and does not halt before the sacred doors. To avoid it entirely, we would have to leave the earth (cf. 1 Cor 5:10f.). But the enclosure forbids the entry of what conveys the spirit of the world. The monk does not want to be of this world (cf. Jn 17:14); he flees the world which is opposed to Christ (cf. Jn 15:18f.). He wants to be sheltered from its deceitful clamor and its misleading mirages. The enclosure offers him a restricted zone from which messengers of the world ought to be excluded. That is why canonical enclosure, in order not to be a mere formality, ought to be a 'no admitance' sign against everything contrary to the spirit of Christ.

To keep away from the world and all its pomp is the Christian's clear duty. At baptism has he not promised to renounce it? Would this be the only reason for enclosure? No. Monastic enclosure is more demanding. It not only excludes evil, but opposes all that might trouble the monk in his effort at purification and clinging to God alone. In this way, monastic enclosure bars the way to people, usages, ways of acting, books, in short to everything that does not correspond to his orientation, is ambivalent, or inappropriate to his purpose. St Benedict does not speak of this explicitly. But when he forbids monks coming back from a journey to tell the brothers what they have seen or heard outside, this is to protect them not only from evil, but from all that could stir their imaginations disadvantageously; that would be, he says, to destroy much good in them (67:5). Likewise, St Benedict is strict about the tone and the level of conversations. The only time he uses the word *Clausura*—this is worth noting—is in order to condemn crude jokes, idle words, and words good for nothing but provoking laughter; we condemn such things everywhere, he says, with a perpetual ban (6:8; cf. 4:51). Within the precincts of the monastery, there are to be no useless or harmful contacts, no frivolous and superficial relationships; St Benedict would have it so, not through distrust of his monks or of their possible immaturity, we repeat once more, but in order to help them become more and more strangers to the world by sparing them contact with it (4:20). Under this consideration the advisability of allowing the means of modern communication to enter the house of God should be judged. That which is of the spirit of the world and its perversion should not have the right of access.

The expression 'canonical enclosure' leads people to think that men may not, as a general rule, enter the precincts of an enclosure of nuns, and that women may not enter the enclosure of monks. St Benedict does not speak explicitly about this. Did he receive women at the guesthouse? If the lodging for the guests (53:21) actually was within the precincts of the monastery, receiving women there would have been so unthinkable for the ancient monks that there would have been no need to make a law about it. On this point, St Benedict was relying on those abbots who, following the example of St Pachomius, could provide a separate guest house for women. He himself received his sister Scholastica this way in a dependency of the monastery (cf. St Gregory the Great, *Dialogues*, 2.33).

Without any doubt, another reason for enclosure is to preserve chastity, one of the foundations of the monastic vocation. But to wish to explain enclosure too exclusively as a protection for chastity would lead one to believe that it loses its meaning where chastity is not in danger and where monks are able to follow their vocation without this sort of protection. Protection for chastity is only one aspect of a much vaster problem. As a matter of fact, the monk entering the monastery leaves behind him not only the world, as a symbol of evil, but for the sake of the kingdom he also abandons the world of his natural relations. In order to follow the call of Jesus, he leaves home, father, mother, brothers, sisters, wife, children, and property (cf Mt 19:29, Mk 10:29); the enclosure, a place of separation and renunciation, lets him cut or control the ties which can hardly help him in his efforts to take the better part.

The withdrawal imposed by enclosure helps the monk, therefore, to cut harmful ties, or to apply a new measure to useful ties, a measure of purified love, or even to re-evaluate his contacts, his attachments, his relationships in the light of the love of Jesus and the Gospel (cf. Mk 10:29). Certain friendships useful to his vocation ought, then, to be deepened; others, though licit in themselves, will be cut off, applying the principle of the Rule regarding silence (6:3) according to which it is necessary to be able to renounce a secondary good in order to obtain a greater good.

St Benedict refrains almost entirely from legislating about relationships with people from outside, and in particular with the parents of monks. The fact of accepting child oblates (RB 59) certainly did not make the task of the legislator any easier when sensibilities, affections and blood-ties retain all their rights. Nowhere is there mention of what we call the 'parlors'. Nor is there any allusion to possible visits to be received or paid. He is content to settle one point when his concern for total poverty appears: the monk does not have the right to receive letters or small gifts even from his parents without the abbot's permission (54:1, 3). However, his relations with his sister Scholastica were so delicately arranged that they give us some idea of his thoughts in this matter.

We are able to conclude that the enclosure is first of all a monastic observance ruled by its own laws. But the law of enclosure ought to be understood as a help and a constant invitation to conform our heart to it by a lucid and free renunciation of all that it does not admit; without this it would lose its meaning. This process of heartfelt adherence to an exterior observance will result in transforming the monk's very soul into a peaceful enclosure where he loves to withdraw in order to *habitare secum*, to dwell with himself, as St Gregory says of St Benedict. But if the presence of God does not occupy that retreat, it will not really be positive. It is in order to seek him (58:7) and to receive his visits that the monk, the nun, gives up other visits. They want to follow the invitation of Jesus: 'But you, when you want to pray, enter into your chamber, and having closed the door, pray to your Father' (Mt 6:6). The monk, the nun, withdraws into an enclosure in order to abide in Christ; he calls them there because he himself wants to be their enclosure and their abode (cf. Jn 15:4ff.).

# MONASTIC WORK

Two aspects must be distinguished in the matter of work: the question of principle on the one hand, and the necessities of life on the other.

The question of principle: It is evident that in conscience we ought to be employed in useful work. As soon as he left paradise, Adam received this law. The Vatican Council reminds us in *schema* 13 of the duty of work. The Lord himself declared that he worked because he saw his Father work: 'My Father is ever at work, and likewise I work' (Jn 5:17). St Paul declared with justifiable pride: 'You yourselves know that these hands of mine have provided for my own needs and those of my companions' (Acts 20:34). The life of Jesus is there to let us see how we ought to value work. Let us be careful not to say that Our Lord did not work because he prayed or because he went about the countryside preaching. He labored in his workshop for many years, and later he worked in a different way during the three years of his public ministry. We ought, therefore, not only to accept, but even to want our monastic life to be, a life of labor, in order to satisfy the rule laid down for humankind on its departure from paradise, and in order to make our contribution to the development of society. Work is therefore compulsory.

Rhythm and variety characterizes our life of work, and St Benedict considers all our occupations work: the *opus Dei*, the *opus manuum*, the *lectio divina;* this last is also considered a work because anyone who cannot apply himself to it is to be given some manual work (48:23ff.). In addition, it is interesting to note that St Benedict treats the matter of occupations simply under the title *De opera manuum*, manual labor. All this, therefore, has its place in the concept and in the totality of our work. It is important, then, to assure a certain balance among these different forms. Monastic observances must not weaken us to the point that we cannot be employed in real manual work during the hours laid down by the Rule. We ought to be able to produce profitable work, and not merely busy ourselves with trifles. If our activity is not such that we can live from it, then we are parasites. Although prayer, beyond any doubt, is an activity useful to humanity, it is not permissible for us to live on donations or public charity. That can no longer be conceived today when our society is becoming orientated toward an ever more highly developed socialism; people cannot pretend to be living for God if they do not earn their own daily bread. In the beginning of chapter forty-eight, St Benedict speaks of avoiding idleness, not to slight uniquely theological grounds, but because he is speaking to monks as a pastor of souls and wants to save them from the evils that idleness brings.

Let us look now at another aspect of the question: the necessities of life, the need of having an adequately paying work in order to be able to live. Here we must formulate the problem exactly, in order to solve it, not with the rationalistic mentality of a society without God, but as persons vowed by profession to his service, for the monk ought to be a man of God.

To consider the *Opus Dei* in any way other than as real work would be to adopt positivistic and Marxist views, for example. To justify our existence, therefore, we should not yield to the temptation to suppress the *Opus Dei* or to adapt it to the point that society can believe that we work as they do, putting in as many hours of paid manual work as workers in a factory or farmers in the fields, and that in this area we are not lagging behind them.

On the other hand, we no longer live in a christian world disposed to understand that the *Opus Dei*, the activity proper to the monk, has a value from which humanity benefits, and which is therefore worthy of being remunerated by it. Nevertheless, we ought to keep clear in our minds the fundamental principle that the monastic life is entirely consecrated to the Lord's work. Nor should we give ourselves up to the illusion of believing that through adaptations we will arrive at making ourselves fully accepted by a society with materialistic principles. It will never be able to see the *Opus Dei* except as a useless pasttime, or even as an irresponsible waste of energy.

In countries where freedom of speech is not a myth, on the one hand, there are many who are not impressed by the petty objections which some people make about our way of life; their liberalism prompts them to apply even to monasteries the principle of 'live and let live'. Moreover, the fact that the mechanization of work has left an increasing amount of leisure to man, so that the number of hours of work each week tends to diminish, all permits the conscience of our contemporaries to admit more easily the idea of the gratuitousness of an occupation. But, we do not expect that today's society will consider the *Opus Dei* a useful employment, and less still, that it would pay us for it. We can hope that the people who come to the monastery will appreciate the work done within its walls as useful for humanity. 'Nothing ought to be preferred to the Work of God' (43:3). In the meet celebration of worship achieved through careful preparation, there is a manifestation of real work which is still perceptible to many people.

Having said that, we must—in order to provide for the necessities of life—adopt a system which will safeguard our monastic vocation while furnishing us with the profitable employment we need. Here, surely, we have a thorny problem. It is not enough simply to find sources of revenue; they must at the same time, while not prejudicing the integrity of our monastic life, be accepted by our society, smitten as it is with authenticity and a social conscience, as a real work and an effective contribution to the material wellbeing of our brethren. Let us not expose ourselves to their judgment by being employed in an activity which would be valueless according to these two criteria.

The choice of employment posed the same problem to St Benedict. We have to work, but the work ought to fit into the monastic life and its ideal. In his day, when class distinction was very marked in that feudal type of society, to work for one's daily bread was the lot of serfs, whereas monks could occupy themselves in other employments: a trade, for example (RB 57). The allusions to instruments (RB 4), to the workshop (4:78) as a symbol of the spiritual art strengthen this idea. Although the products of the monastery could be sold (57:4), this work does not seem to have been considered the only means of support for the community. In the sixth century, the general economy was based on working the land. People lived off the land and by raising animals. Agricultural work was the form of manual labor for communities which found it necessary to provide for reaping or harvesting themselves. Was this was because of the remote location of the monastery or because of a poverty, which made hiring laborers difficult (48:7)? But the text cited gives us clearly to understand that this working on the land was a rather extraordinary occupation for monks. The argument which St Benedict uses to encourage those who through necessity have to devote themselves to field work is valid for all manual labor. He is a true monk, says the Rule, who lives by the work of his hands, as the ancient monks and the apostles did (48:8). Now, the apostles did not work the land, and the monks of Egypt earned their living by making mats and work of that nature.

Field work is not necessarily imposed upon monks. The choice of work, according to the spirit of the Rule, is left to circumstances, with this restriction, that for St Benedict and his monks, work is conceived of as manual labor. Let us recall here briefly that on this point there has been during the course of the centuries an evolution leaving an ever larger place for intellectual work. Without any doubt, St Benedict, in his discretion, would have accorded the monk of an intellectual bent, longer hours for his studies or research, because he had to have had in his monastery teachers for the children (63:19), while maintaining for all the general obligation of daily manual work, as the title of chapter forty-eight suggests.

In this regard, the Rule insists upon three fundamental principles: We must work; we must be able to live, if necessary, from the work of our hands; this work ought to be chosen and organized to fit into the monastic life.

Today therefore, we must be very prudent in choosing our work and in finding a deserving and serious way of earning our living which at the same time will be accepted bo society. Each community ought on its own to resolve its particular problem. It is evident that the composition of the community, the location of the monastery, the economic possibilities of the place, open very diverse perspectives. How can we require a community made up of a majority of old or sick religious to carry on a really remunerative employment? Some are still able to celebrate the *Opus Dei*, but nothing more; others, elderly, do not have professional competence. Let us admit that there are cases which seem to have no solution and which may call for extreme remedies.

Let us add that each person is personally concerned with the obligation to work. We cannot be a burden to the community under the pretext of contemplation, saying our private prayers during the work hours. Once again, the work forms a part of the contemplative life. We should not fall into the mistake of believing that there is the contemplative life on the one side and the work on the other. It forms an integral part of our monastic life. St Benedict has well divided the day into three parts: Divine Office, spiritual reading, manual labor; he has even determined the hours, so that no one may think that during manual labor someone may quite happily go to church or apply himself to spiritual reading. If St Benedict has drawn up a rather detailed schedule, this is not because he wants to impose it upon us to be observed to the letter. Our age and the climate in which we live require accommodations. It is rather a question of proportion. In winter there is more reading because there is less work in the fields. In summer it is the reverse. On the contrary, in a monastery which has a school, work during the winter is more absorbing than during the summer vacation. The superior, in agreement with the community, on the general guidelines, ought to balance these elements so that in today's society the monastic life can be lived just as validly as in St Benedict's day.

In conclusion, let us understand, that in the matter of work, the monastic life ought to be wholesome and sound. Prayer and contemplation must never be a pretext to escape work. On the other hand, the necessity of a remunerative employment ought never to smother the peace of the soul or disturb its tranquillity. These dispositions are indispensable in raising the spirit to God. Each individual will resolve his own personal problem with work by fully integrating himself into the community life which is divided into hours of prayer, hours of reading, and hours of remunerative work. Entering into community life without bargaining, and solidarity with the brethren, will not allow false problems concerning the work to arise.

As Jesus saw his Father work and as he worked in filial obedience, the fact of working in a spirit of loving submission to the divine will manifested through the Rule, the constitutions, and the assignment of his task by the abbot, will be an efficacious means for the monk of arriving at a more intimate union with the Father, as well as at a sane balance in the monastic life; *ora et labora* will support and complement one another. Thus the monk will realize a little better each day that through productive work he participates in the work of the Creator, and helps him embellish the earth and perfect it. Also, he will experience that being occupied in work develops the personality, arouses creativity, and advances knowledge.

By uniting himself through his work with the Creator, the monk enters into profound communication with the energies of the divine Love which is at the beginning of all things, and thus he learns that the true source of all productivity and the first motive of his activity ought to be love, if he wishes to accomplish durable and authentic work.

# USING THE TOOLS AND BELONGINGS OF THE MONASTERY

In the excavations made to discover traces of man on the earth, the principle is followed that where there are instruments and tools alongside bones, these are human; where there are none, it is supposed that they are apes or hominoids. As a matter of fact, man cannot be separated from tools. With his intelligence, he possesses the power of induction, deduction, and combination, which makes him capable of making instruments to carry out his plans, materialize his ideas, accomplish his work. In order to make himself master of the material he handles, he needs equipment set between his hands and the material. These tools can be extremely simple, as in the stone or bronze age, or they may be developed all the way to the kind we use now. Think of the hammer which man's intelligence develops even to splitting the atom, of the lever which ends up as a crane, of the wheel which we find perfected in the watch, of the steam engine, ancestor of the rocket. Man has always and continually known how to perfect his tools for work. So St Benedict, practical and concrete, knew that these tools are precious belongings for the monastery, especially if they are complicated and sophisticated. Typewriters, calculators, automobiles, tractors, these all represent a part of the community's wealth. As for St Benedict himself, he was concerned with the tools in use at his time, more primitive certainly than ours, although alongside the most ingeniously combined marvels of technology, we have kept such basic tools as the shovel, the hammer, and the wheel which always retain their same value in the eyes of the *homo faber*. It is about these that St Benedict legislated.

In the thirty-second chapter, he speaks to us first of all on how to handle them, that is, the care we should take of them, the inventory to be drawn up, the control to be exercised in the use and the effectiveness of these tools. He wants the abbot himself to have an inventory at his disposal. He cannot not take interest in things of such prime importance for daily life, things man needs for his work just as he needs bread to live. It is only fitting to care for them intelligently. Concerning the care that should be taken in using them, the preceding chapter on the cellarer gives us a hint: they must be treated like the sacred vessels of the altar (31:10); in them we must recognize that sacred character which is conferred by the fact of being used by the monks to help them in their life of service to God, and to sanctify it. St Benedict did not want to give them a dignity over and above their natural value, still less to attribute magic power to them. His intention was to give the whole life of the monk its true dimension, putting all that he lives and does in its true relationship with God. As the monks' work derives its meaning and its dignity from his wholly consecrated vocation to God, so his tools also have an end which raises them above their purely natural value, just as a chalice is consecrated by its anointing to the service of the altar. We are here at the heart of St Benedict's *Weltanschauung;* for him man's destiny turns toward God everything he uses along the way, and from this it receives a special dignity and splendor. Here we are as far from an undue sacralization of things and natural processes as we are from a tendency to desacralize everything. St Benedict, precisely because he was a realist, left each thing in its place with its natural value, without at the same time cutting them off from God the Creator. Quite the contrary. By leaving them in the place nature gave them, he knew that they serve him and praise him as a reflection of his infinite beauty, participating thus in the dynamic unfolding of life.

The thought of St Benedict does not differ here from the way of looking at things which has so profoundly marked the attitude of christian peoples, and in order to understand it, we must grasp the sense of that little phrase *ac si altaris vasa sacrata* (31:10), which we may translate as 'as if they were sacred vessels'. St Benedict in no way intended to put the shovel in the same rank with the chalice; instead, he is using a comparison to bring out the theological reality which the objects at the monks' service possess. We recall there what he says about an order given by the superior to an obedient monk, who accepts that order *ac si divinitus imperetur* (5:4), 'as if it came from God'. It is faith which makes the monk see everything in this light. He has entered into a life entirely given to God; everything that he meets or touches in that life will be connected to God, and that relationship will depend on his own faith. If he remains *homo animalis* he will see only the material side of everything, and will perhaps even boast of that secularistic spirit. But if he becomes *homo spiritualis*, everything will speak to him of God.

Now we understand in what sense St Benedict insists that the tools, the belongings, the furnishings of the monastery be treated with care, that they be kept perfectly clean and in good state of repair. In his day, almost all these things were common and for everyone's use, and control was that much more necessary. Anyone who broke or lost something had at once to accuse himself of his misdeed or his carelessness before the abbot and the community (46:3). All this, in our day, has lost neither its meaning nor its validity. Even more, since today many monks have their own rooms where less oversight is exercised, a personal discipline is much more important for each individual. Let us remember that good order in the room excludes the deterioration of objects as well as untidiness, dust, and other undesirable effects of disorder. Every day we should take the time to put everything in its place, and nothing will be lost or deteriorate. The spirit of faith will help us to make our cell a little sanctuary in which there is a place for the objects consecrated to the service of our God, praised in everything and forever!

# STABILITY

May the monk change monasteries? This question arises in reading the sixty-first chapter of the Rule. To change stability according to the present legislation, let us note first of all, we need the appropriate permissions; but that discipline did not exist at the time of St Benedict. In his Rule he takes into account the laws of his time, which permitted a monk to leave his monastery for good reason and to enter another. St Benedict asks himself, therefore, what attitude to take toward the monk who knocks at the door since, on the one hand, a certain stability was part of the monastic tradition, and on the other hand, a certain liberty for changing monasteries was recognized. It was therefore necessary to settle this problem.

In this first chapter of the Rule, St Benedict intends to define clearly the different kinds of monks and distinguishes, along with the hermits and the cenobites, the sarabaites and the gyrovagues. St Augustine speaks very severely of these latter. These so-called monks wandered around for their whole life. At the foundation of this movement of pilgrim monks, there was a profoundly religious intention, the idea of a complete detachment leading to leaving one's homeland like Abraham and being everywhere a stranger like Jesus. The idea is beautiful and legitimate, and people held these monks in great veneration. St Benedict Labre in the eighteenth century was on pilgrimage practically all his life. But by the time of St Benedict and St Augustine, the gyrovagues had degenerated, and St Benedict warns us against them (1:10f.). Outside the Catholic Church, we note, there have always been pilgrim monks.

At the beginning of monasticism, then, there was no question of stability in the sense of belonging definitively to one certain monastery. On the other hand, it was understood that once a monk, one remained a monk. The habit was received as a sign of the monastic life. The receiving of the habit therefore, was and remains the beginning of that life, although the time of the novitiate is still a time of probation. For St Benedict, to take the habit was to become a monk, and the monk must remain faithful.

The person of modern times is marked by a tendency to instability, by the fast pace of his age when everything related to 'installation', 'stability', 'institution', is treated as a hated idol. Existentialism, the philosophy of the restless, obliges man to a continual re-assessment of life; it makes him constantly alert to respond to the call of the present, and thus to create himself and to choose himself by his actions. In all sincerity and in conscience, he has an obligation to change his life, if at any certain moment he believes that he sees that it ought to take another direction.

This philosophy—which is true in part—does not, however, correspond to the reality of creation. We have to distinguish between the substance and the changing phenomenon for which the substance serves as base. In God, everything is unchangeable; we can 'evolve', it is true, but only while retaining the identity of our person. We are perfectable, and it is our dignity to be able to become, in this way, more like God each day. But we arrive at a certain moment in our existence at a state where no further change intervenes. We prepare ourselves for eternal life through the continuity of our effort and through fidelity to God and to ourselves. The monastic life, like every life, is a preparation for eternity. In becoming monks, we enter into a permanent state of life, not merely an occupation or a profession. As marriage establishes an indissoluble union, a permanent form of life, so also the monastic life, in principle, does not change. The solemn promise is its sign and entry way. We have to remain faithful. This way of looking at it is traditional. The novelty, in the time of St Benedict, came only with stability in the same *congregatio* (4:78, 58:23). The word 'community' corresponds to the expression *congregatio.* This promise of stability in one definite community has further reinforced the sense of stability proper to our state of life.

Some people think differently on this point, and hold that, through respect for the internal dynamics of life, one may be led to appear unfaithful exteriorly to one's word once given. For example, in order to remain honest with oneself, one could be unfaithful to the promise given on the day of profession. Would that infidelity be only apparent? No, because in wanting to remain faithful to oneself, a solemn promise made to God would be broken, and consequently, in breaking a line of conduct established after long reflection, one would be changing course on an essential point which involves every dimension of the personality, therefore, shattering one's identity and the cohesion of one's most personal acts. Clearly such ideas lead to the denial of every obligation to a commitment made.

But God is faithful. He is so by the help of his grace, in calling us, in receiving us, in urging us continually on. He is an absolutely faithful friend, and would we not want to be one to him? Would we believe that being unfaithful to a promise could be a true faithfulness to God? No. This is a lie; it upsets all just ideas, and leads in the last analysis to a lack of absolute values in all things, to an extreme evolutionism, to an insecurity and an instability justified by by a so-called philosophy of existentialism.

Stability, on the other hand, not only corresponds to christian philosophy, but is a necessity of our moral life. We are conscious, each one of us is aware, of being always our own self. This does not mean that we do not follow a development, a wholesome evolution, which ought to be a continual improvement and to respond to our ability to grow. But the identity of the person remains: it is I who grows, it is I who am perfectible; and this 'I' remains identical. This identity is one of the greatest gifts we have received: to remain ourselves while yet growing in wisdom and age.

By introducing greater stability into our life, St Benedict has assured a greater continuity to the development of our personality. To remain ourselves, to remain in our own line, to grow harmoniously, organically, normally, without a break, without division, is the ideal which corresponds to all the fundamental notions of our philosophy and our religion. It would no longer be possible to think of a permanent God if that God had not given his creation the power to grow, yes; but a growth of 'oneself'.

With the sixty-first chapter, then, St Benedict opens the door to the monks who come to the monastery first of all as guests. Faithful to his principle, he wants the monks, if they are commendable, to fix their stability (61:5, 8-11). If, on the other hand, they do not fit this criterion, if they are nothing but demanding gyrovagues, they are not to be received (61:6f.). In this chapter, then, St Benedict takes a stand, although with flexibility, for stability in the monastic life and in the community.

# THE MONASTIC HABIT

We need only introduce the theme of this conference to raise a great number of current questions. Only a few years ago, priests and religious wore a distinctive habit. Today we are witnessing an abandonment of the ecclesiastical or religious habit fostered by an increasing movement of secularization. It makes sense, then, to study this question in the light of the Rule and the monastic tradition.

The Second Vatican Council, let us remember first of all, emphasized that the religious habit is the visible sign of the consecrated life. It ought to be simple, modest, at once poor and becoming, adapted to the needs of health and the requirements of time and place and ministry (*Perfectae Caritatis*, 17).

What did St Benedict think on this subject? Do we find in the Rule the description of a monastic habit properly so called?

On the occasion of the promise made before the community, the newly professed is stripped of his belongings, *rebus propriis*, and is clothed *rebus monasterii* (58:26). The word *res* designates all kinds of things, including clothing (58:24, 32:4, 55:10, 59:3, 5). The examination of the texts shows us that in the ceremony of changing vestments, in the clothing ceremony, there is nothing, according to the Rule, but the abandonment by the newly professed of a vestment which is his own property, in favor of another belonging to the community. We do not find any allusions to an exchange of a secular clothing for a religious, monastic, or sacred habit. Nothing in the text of the Rule permits us to think of the symbolism attached to that rite: the stripping off of the old man and putting on of the new. The texts preceding the description of the clothing ceremony also suggest clearly an act of disappropriation on the part of the monk and renunciation of all that is his own, rather than a taking of the religious habit (58:24f.). In accepting the *res monasterii* the new monk acknowledges that he no longer has anything as his own, not even his body (25). He becomes, in a certain way, himself a *res monasterii*. The symbolism of this act of dispossession is therefore very real. In itself, it does not signify a moral change to be brought about in the monastic state, but a juridical and notarial act of the total renunciation of every kind of property. In other words, instead of making an explicit vow of poverty, the monk, according to the Rule, makes a solemn act of disappropriation, 'reserving nothing whatever for himself' (24). The offering of a child is made according to the same criteria (59:3ff.).

This way of regarding the monastic clothing rite, although ancient, is characteristic of St Benedict. His interest is not directed at the ceremonies, but at what they express. The ceremonies signify a profound reality. Now, the more adequate the sign is to the thing signified, the more effective and impressive the ceremony is. For St Benedict, the clothing is, above all, the tangible sign of a change of ownership. From now on, the monk is no longer the owner of his vestments, nor even of the body covered by the vestments (58:25); the right of ownership which he had over himself passes to the monastery.

By interpreting the clothing rite this way does St Benedict exclude other interpretations, notably that of moral and spiritual change, the *conversio morum* of the monk? He does not speak of it. But the spiritual interpretation of the rite traditional in the monastic order (even though St Benedict does not speak explicitly of it) imposes itself as the supreme consequence of his interpretation. For in the last analysis, how would it help a monk to be despoiled of everything, no longer to be his own master, if that would not help him be entirely God's, a man of God, a *novus homo?*

Likewise, although St Benedict does not speak explicitly of the monastic habit as a distinctive habit, his realistic and sober interpretation of the clothing rite not only does not prevent us from seeing in the *res monasterii* (58:26) a religious habit properly so called, but even moves us to think along that line.

We should not forget that St Benedict himself, if we are to believe the narrative of St Gregory the Great (*Dialogues*, 2.1), received from the hands of the monk Romanus the *habitum sanctus conversationis*, the religious habit, which made him a monk in everyone's eyes. And, to limit ourselves to two witnesses, let us remember that for the Master, the habit is that of the religious life: *sancti propositi habitus* (*Rule of the Master*, 90:82). If the monk leaves the monastic life, then he is publicly deprived of that habit: *exutis sanctis vestibus et habitu sacro* (90:85). The distinction between the monastic habit and secular clothing was therefore familiar to St Benedict.

Did our legislator follow that tradition in practice? It is not easy to answer this question if we limit ourselves strictly to the texts of the Rule.

The indulgent pluralism which St Benedict shows in the fifty-fifth chapter (1-4, 20f.) reveals at any rate that his intention was not to prescribe a uniform habit, although the different parts of that habit are more or less defined (55:4-6, 13,19). Their thickness (1f.), color, quality, and size (7-8) obeyed the laws of adaptation to the requirements of work, climate, and local customs. The vestments provided by the Rule were those in use among the people and were neither reserved for, nor the distinctive sign of, the monk. Worn habits were to be returned to the wardrobe, the Rule tells us, to be given to the poor (9); those of the monks therefore did not possess any special characteristics. At the time of St Benedict, the words 'cowl' and 'scapular' were not strictly monastic terms.

We have the impression, then, in reading the fifty-fifth

chapter, that St Benedict's concern was not with establishing a special form of religious habit, but rather with assuring the simplicity and poverty of the monk even in his clothing. It was to be the proper size for each person (8), clean (10, 13; cf. 32:1, 4) and suited to the requirements of health (55:10); he did not want it to be worn threadbare (9, 12) and wanted the brothers leaving the monastery to receive clothing more suitable for the journey (13) and of better quality (14). In clothing, the abbot was to take into account the needs of each person (3, 21). This chapter shows us that St Benedict's principal concern is to teach the brothers the meaning of poverty. It is characteristic to find there three times the word *sufficit*, it suffices (4, 10, 15). Whatever is over and above the clothing provided is to be considered superfluous and ought to be eliminated (11). This clothing ought to be reasonably priced and generally worn in the region where the monastery is located (7).

It is difficult, let us admit, to find in the Rule concrete indications concerning a distinctive and uniform habit for monks. And Benedict's remark about the sarabaites lying to God by their tonsure (1:7) seems to indicate that the distinctive sign of the monk, according to him, was not necessarily the habit, but the tonsure. On this precise point, we today find ourselves in a different situation. Let us not consider the monks whose external appearance does not differ in anything from that of seculars, but the others—they have abandoned the tonsure, but keep the religious habit. The nun, on the other hand, proclaims her belonging to God by following the tradition of consecrated virgins of the earliest times, through the tonsure covered by the veil.

So St Benedict, on the one hand, was certainly familiar with the religious and sacred habit, but on the other hand, he avoids talking about it expressly. We may wonder about the reason for this rather reserved attitude. Although he does not exclude the idea of the monastic habit as such—poverty itself could serve as the distinctive sign of the monk—he does seem not to attach any importance to it. Where there are beginnings of culture, St Benedict realized, man's tendency is to impose himself by the richness of his clothing, to set himself apart from the masses, and to form groups with others in which the vestment becomes uniform. In this way, the individual proclaims his membership in a state, an office, or a class.

Let us note that the more the habit tries to manifest something spiritual, the greater the danger is of a discord between the habit and the life it signifies. 'The habit does not make the monk' runs the adage. One can lie by the habit as one can lie by the tonsure. The tonsure in itself is a matter of hair, not of soul, but it qualifies the man who wears it sociologically by classing him in a fixed and venerable category, that of monks. It therefore confers a dignity on him; it distinguishes him and represents him; it makes him holy.

Now, St Benedict's concern—the impression imposes itself when we read the Rule—was with seeing the monk humble, simple, and poor. He ought therefore to distinguish himself by his virtue and not by exterior signs which are necessarily ambivalent: some 'lie to God by their tonsure' (RB 1). For St Benedict, the brothers, the guests, the poor, the sick, the abbot, are holy persons, for we must see Christ in them, because he has identified himself with us. But this aspect of the christian person is purely theological and does not lead to making the individual person sociologically sacred. How close St Benedict was to the feelings of people today! The monk ought to be holy interiorly; this is the concern of our legislator!

All these considerations help us better understand the position of St Benedict concerning the monastic habit. Did he positively wish to exclude it? Nothing permits us to affirm this. There is not so much as one remark in the Rule to let us suppose such an intention. In speaking of the sarabaites' tonsure, he does not reject it, but accepts it as a matter of fact. His monastic habit received in his youth as a sacred vestment, was certainly dear to him. For him it was the constant sign and reminder of the conversion of manners which must be brought about with the help of divine grace, or, to speak with the Council (see above), of his congregation. Indeed, the taking of the habit in itself changes nothing in us, and any kind of magic efficacy is far from christian thought.

Yet, 'the monastic habit not only expresses exteriorly what someone is, but also gives him the interior consciousness of what he ought to be' (Paul VI).

This moral aspect, this constant recall to a consciousness and to a nobility of sentiments, is profoundly christian. Common sense demands we see the priest in the exercise of his sacerdotal functions dressed in liturgical vestments, not only in order to underline his dignity and his participation in the mystery, but also in order to remind him of the need for holiness which flows from his consecratory action. The monk is a man consecrated by his vows. The analogy recommends that he be marked first of all interiorly, but also exteriorly in order to retain a lively consciousness of it.

The Rule, moreover, lends itself by its arrangements to a certain uniformity of dress. First of all, all the monks wear clothing given by the community; next, the prescriptions of chapter fifty-five, in spite of the place allowed for justifiable differences, determine each part of the monastic habit in its general form; finally, the concern with avoiding every kind of whimsical freedom necessarily leads to a certain uniformity, as also do the consciousness of fraternal solidarity and the need of manifesting membership in the same group. Similar occupations and the demands of poverty also lead to the establishment of one set form for common clothing. All that is very human. The religious goal of our life causes it to take on a religious finality, that is to say, a profession of conversion of manners which is at the same time a profession of faith in God.

These considerations allow us once more to recognize the personal trait St Benedict had of going straight to the essential while leaving possible developments of lesser importance to the side or open to question without closing the door. He shows in his teaching that same discreet attitude which the Council manifested: the monk's habit marks the simplicity and the religious poverty of his state. In their detail, the forms may vary, taking into account wholesome traditions (cf. *Perf. Carit.* 2), the solidarity of groups, the requirements of place, time, and popular customs.

Superiors must not forget that their negligence or an

attitude of licence in the matter of wearing the monastic habit, through the logic of human weakness, ends up in laxity in graver matters. Research in this delicate matter ought therefore to be made with great spiritual tact. The principle of this research should be that of St Benedict: the monk is recognized in his fundamental concern to be poor in imitation of Christ—poverty of which his habit is the sign.

# GOOD WORKS AND REWARD

One characteristic strikes us in reading the Holy Rule: the emphasis St Benedict places on good works and the eternal reward. The Protestants repudiate all bargaining with God and any lack of faith and confidence in the work of justification by Jesus Christ. Such a position also sounds wrong to our ears. We are saved by faith, it is true, but there is no faith without works. And it is by faith and works that we are able to share in the merits of Christ and by his grace merit the eternal reward.

The teaching of the Rule illustrates this evangelical and catholic position. Notice the texts: 'Our loins therefore being girded by faith and the practice of good works . . . let us walk in his paths, that we may merit to see in his kingdom him who has called us' (Prol. 21). Or, again in the Prologue, 'the Lord seeks his laborer in the multitude of his people', that is to say, a laborer capable of working, and he says to him: 'Who is the man who wants life and desires to see good days?' (Prol. 15). I am making an offer, says the Lord: life. If you do the works—that is to say, 'keep your tongue from falsehood; and your lips that they speak no lies; turn from evil and do good; seek peace, pursue it ardently' (Prol. 17)—then you will have both peace and life. 'When you have done that, my eyes will be upon you and my ears will be attentive to your prayers' (Prol. 18, Is 58:9).

193

The entire Prologue energetically encourages the monk to commit himself seriously to the practice of virtue: 'Run while you have the light of life' (*Ibid.* 13), because 'it is impossible to arrive at the tabernacle of that kingdom if one does not run by good works' (*ibid.* 22). *Currendum et agendum est*—what dynamic words, and how strongly centered on salutary action!—'we must run and act now in a way that will profit us for eternity' (Prol. 44). The fourth chapter of the Holy Rule, 'On the Instruments of Good Works', is entirely built upon this idea. If we accomplish a whole series of good works, we will receive the reward of eternal life. If we do not satisfy this condition, we will not enter into the joy of the Lord.

'Behold, these are the instruments of the spiritual craft; if we use them day and night without respite, we will return them on the day of judgment, and the Lord will give us the reward he has promised, which eye has not seen, nor ear heard, what God has prepared for those who love him' (4:76f., 1 Cor 2:9). We are invited to work so we may receive a reward afterwards.

Today, our ear is less used to hearing such language, and modern man is not greatly attracted to systems of retribution. He prefers to be approached through disinterested charity and wants to have the accent placed on the happiness of the christian life. As for the idea of recompense, he admits it, but without insisting on it. Modern books of spirituality dwell more on a charity bearing in itself its own reward; is it not only the key that opens the doors of happiness, of which it is the beginning already in this life and its fulfilment in the next? Let us not forget, however: charity does not exist without works, they find their recompense in it. Our Lord tells us: I have not come to judge but to save, to give my life; no one can come to the Father without passing through me. He tells us also of the goodness of the Father, of divine mercy, and of the dwellings he is going to prepare for us near him.

If the Lord teaches us that he is leaving us in order to prepare a place for us near the Father, this implies, and He says, that we must obey the commandments. 'He who hears my

commandments and keeps them, he it is that loves me'
(Jn 14:21). 'If you keep my commandments, you will dwell
in my love' (Jn 15:10). He even encourages us to let our
good works shine so that others may glorify the Father
(cf. Mt 5:16), and he forewarns us that on his return he will
repay each person according to his conduct (Mt 16:27).

St Benedict always follows the language of Scripture; this
is why he particularly puts forward the importance of
works—so there is nothing surprising here. The mistake
would be to interpret this attitude as the morality of mer-
cenaries, implying a spirit of vile bargaining.

Moreover, one of the passages of the Prologue cited
above, where we see the Lord seeking his laborer and offering him life in exchange for his work, is nothing but a cita-
tion, more or less free and amplified, of St Augustine in the
*Enarrationes in Psalmos*, so that there we enter into the
thought of a theologian, of the greatest of the Latin Fathers
of the Church—the accusation of interested morality does
not hold when it comes to the place of good works in the
economy of our salvation since it exalts the work of divine
grace in us. In following him, St Benedict behaves as a realist
toward his disciples. First of all, he speaks to beginners, and
he realizes that with them it is not good to insist too much
on charity before they have understood what this really is.
For we discover love step by step in the course of our lives,
and how to act in love. Certain privileged souls, it is true,
awaken very early to a tender love for Jesus or the Father.
But more generally, in order to understand charity, we have
to fulfil the commandments; this is a basic attitude. We
learn the love of God by obeying Him; we show our love for
him, and he responds to it. This love grows; then more and
more it governs our actions. What we did at first under constraint, afterwards, aided by a good habit and by the attraction of virtue, we do through love. This is the teaching of
chapter seven. Now, love bears within itself the promise of
eternity; it will never end; it will be consummated in the
union with God, in blessedness.

To accuse St Benedict of having an Old Testament attitude
or to think that he had not seen or understood the function

of charity in the christian life would be wholly to misunderstand the teaching of the Rule. St Benedict is a realist, however. He had before him men coming not only from every level of society, but from every spiritual background. Most of them were beginners and they had to be taken as they are. We if we look back, see clearly that this love with which our heart burns, has been learned through knowledge and practice while we have been traveling on the road of the commandments and good works: To be attentive to God and to his demands, we have grasped it little by little; this is love.

The emphases in this matter are simply placed differently. St Benedict urges us to good works, but these give birth to charity, or cannot be accomplished in the long run without charity, which awakens hope and the taste for union with God with the desire of eternal life as goal and reward. Certain passages of the Rule put us more face to face with the divine love calling upon our love—thus the piety of each has freedom of choice—this love urges us to do what pleases God and makes us hope to possess him at last as our eternal reward.

We find ourselves, therefore, with a consistent teaching. Without faith achieved by good works, it is impossible to please God. The teaching of our father St Benedict is found to be confirmed: it is through faith and the practice of good works that we arrive at our goal: love, that love of Christ to which he invites us so insistently to prefer nothing else (4:21, 5:2, 72:11). We witness to this love through a very close and warm imitation of Christ; it will merit our being associated with him in the glory of his kingdom (cf. Prol. 50).

Finally, we should not forget that the insistence placed upon the effort to do good works (Prol. 2) is proper to the monastic state; our first Fathers hoped in this way to become emulators of the martyrs. St Benedict himself clearly felt the weight of good works, of monastic asceticism, and of the rigor of the life. Thus detached from the world, that is to say, from earthly concupiscence, he became free for spiritual desires. Does he not, in reality, want his disciple to desire eternal life with all the ardor of a spiritual concupiscence?

(4:46) St Benedict refuses to call up the beauties of this final recompense, which he allows to be glimpsed, however, through the hope with which the Rule is filled.

# THE GOOD ZEAL
# WHICH LEADS
# TO GOD

This little chapter, written by St Benedict near the end of his life, is a synthesis of the Rule and expresses its marrow. It is his spiritual testament and a last admonition to his monks. Its structure reminds one of that of the seventh chapter, of Jacob's ladder. To the ladder of humility he adds that of charity, or rather of good zeal. As the first includes two groups of degrees—that of the virtues as such and that of the virtues applied—here too we find two groups—first that of the virtues referring to fraternal charity, then that which concerns the activity of our zeal toward God.

Just as in the chapter on humility we must not consider the different degrees as a series of acts to be done successively, in order to arrive at the goal, so also here, we must not force the comparison in this way. But there is a certain succession. First St Benedict considers our way of acting toward our brothers; then comes our conduct, our zeal, toward God. This order corresponds to the logic of the love expressed by St John: 'If we love one another, God abides in us and his love is perfect in us' (1 Jn 4:12). Our love for the Father is known by our love for the brethren. And as the ladder of humility can work in two directions, for we can descend by pride or ascend by humility (7:7), on this ladder of charity we can likewise ascend by the good zeal that leads to God (72:2), whereas an evil and bitter zeal leads to hell (72:1). By descending, the monk withdraws from God; by

ascending, he withdraws from vices and draws near to God
and to eternal life (72:1-2).

How can we define zeal? First of all, as we use it, the
word designates an attitude which is not very nice. In
French to have zeal toward one's neighbor is to be envious,
to be jealous of him. In English, it often means excessive,
dangerous enthusiasm. This is evil zeal. St Benedict uses the
expression in this sense when he cautions the abbot against
this vice (65:22, 64:16), and again when addressing the
brothers (4:66). But there is also the zeal for God's house of
which the Psalm speaks. The disciple remembered this when
they saw Jesus chasing the merchants from the temple
(Jn 2:17). It is the *zelus Dei*, the zeal for God to which
St Benedict invites the bishop, the abbots, the christians
neighboring the monastery when the election of an abbot,
badly done, has to be called into question (64:6). Used in
this sense, the word 'zeal' is a synonym for fervor, eagerness.
In modern language, when we set two people vying with one
another at the same task, we say, 'Ils travaillant à l'envie'
[literally: They work enviously]. On the other hand, if
someone works sluggishly, apathetically, or indolently, like
a hireling, we say he lacks zeal; he does his work, perhaps,
but he takes much too much time and exerts too little energy.
Of course, the quality of the work will be affected.

Zeal considered this way becomes then a way of acting, a
quality of action. St Benedict speaks to us in this sense of
good zeal as a quality in the exercise of brotherly charity. We
must not practise it thoughtlessly or unwillingly or even
without putting our hearts into it. We must be zealous in
love. For to love without enthusiasm raises doubts whether
one is acting with true charity. The lack of good zeal
can be an evil zeal. To return to our image of the ladder: if
in climbing it we look around on all sides, taking the rungs
one after the other with sighs, without enthusiasm, and taking a lot of time as if we were afraid of putting forth the
effort, then what remains of our zeal? Nothing at all! This
climbing may well become a descent. A climb poorly made
is no climb at all. An act of charity poorly done may be
worse than an omission.

The zeal of Jesus for his Father's honor and our salvation is such a great example! Are we not moved at seeing him constantly repeat that he loves His Father, that he wants to do the will of his beloved Father in all things, and that he seeks only to please him. What zeal of Son for Father; nothing stops him! With admirable courage he accomplishes the mission entrusted to him and drinks the chalice to the dregs. This is the consuming zeal whose program he traced as a child in the temple of Jerusalem and which made him reply to Mary and Joseph, 'Why did you seek me? Did you not know that I must be about my Father's business?' (Lk 2:49). There is singlemindedness! Concerned solely with serving his Father!

We could make the same observations in meditating on Jesus' zeal in bearing the message of eternal salvation to his people. The Jews did not want to understand. But he did not allow those whom his Father had given him to be snatched away, and offered his own life as a ransom for us. His zeal was not stopped by any obstacle; he multiplied his efforts and defied death.

Here, then, is the authentic image of zeal. If St Benedict abstains from developing the subject at length, it is because he remains faithful to his literary form, and leaves the task of doing it to us. His succinct image of good zeal is very rich in suggestion.

There are in this chapter, then, if you will, two groups of rungs. First the group which treats of brotherly charity. They will respectfully anticipate one another's needs: the first rung. They will very patiently bear with each other's infirmities, both those of the body and those of the spirit: the second rung. They will vie in paying obedience to one another: the third rung. 'To vie with'—this is what it means: to put zeal into one's obedience. The expression is suggestive. One hurries to serve his brother, lest he beat him to it. No one should seek what he considers useful for himself, but rather what is useful for others: the fourth rung. Let them practice brotherly charity with a pure love: the fifth rung.

The perfection of fraternal charity leads us to charity toward God. This is why we find here the three degrees: the first degree: they will have for God a fear inspired by love. We are creatures; we must, therefore, fear the Creator, but that fear should be inspired by love. St Benedict sums up here in a masterful fashion the whole teaching of the Rule on the fear of God. Let us not be mistaken about this fear. Yes, it is surely fear, but inspired by love. *Amore Deum timeant:* let them fear God in love. The genius of the Latin supplies this precise and magnificent formula which expresses an entire theology.

The second degree: they will have a humble and sincere love for their abbot. Would it be trying at all costs to make an alien idea fit into a given system if when we try to see in this love for the abbot a degree of the love of God? Elsewhere St Benedict explains to us why he is to be loved. We have, in effect, received the spirit of adoption as sons by which we attribute to the abbot, in faith, the name and the quality of Christ, the father of our salvation (2:3). Love of the abbot has, therefore, as its reason, object, and motive Christ in his representative (2:2). The fact that this second degree is immediately followed by the sentence: 'Let them prefer absolutely nothing to Christ who deigns to lead us all together to eternal life', underlines even more the deep relationship there is between the supreme love due to Christ and the love due to his representative, the abbot.

The third degree is the summit of the ladder and sums up everything that precedes it. The love of Christ is the sum of all perfection. Thus this sentence is the synthesis of the spiritual teaching of the Rule. To Christ belongs the first place. St Benedict expresses this truth in the form of, an option a choice to be made, and forces us to the demanding confrontation of the love of Christ with every other love which ought necessarily to be subordinated to his. It is impossible to have other gods or demi-gods besides him. Every kind of falsification which might try to put one's neighbor in the place of Christ is excluded ahead of time. St Benedict does not like ambiguities. We know about his insistence on making us see Christ in our brother, but without confusion; the love of preference goes straight to the person of Christ. It is on that one condition that love for our brother will be authentic, without respect of persons, without discrimination.

'To prefer nothing to the love of Christ'. Thus St Benedict makes us understand that love for our brother is legitimate along with love of Christ, but that in every practical decision, where the two loves do not follow the same end, where into love for our brother there slips some tendency towards variance with the love of Christ as a sovereign and privileged love, we always know how to choose Christ. By this everything in us converges toward one summit: Christ.

Let us, therefore, climb this ladder by which, through our love of our brother, we arrive at the love of God. This is our daily task. The ladder invites us to exert ourselves and makes us understand that we must climb. For that, we need zeal, enthusiasm. We do not arrive at the top by adopting an apathetic pace, without a firm and serious determination, by stopping all the time, by looking back. The fundamental idea of this chapter on good zeal is to make us understand that the monk cannot content himself with half-measures, with mediocrity. His whole life lacks direction if it lacks enthusiasm. Let us remember the grave words of the Prologue: If we want to dwell in the Lord's tabernacle, let us realize that we do not arrive there unless we run by good works (Prol. 22, 44, 49). To run requires effort, energy, enthusiasm, zeal.

Lord, you know my lack of zeal, you know my weakness. Send me the irresistible breath of your Spirit, that breath, that inspiration which may push me and carry me to the summit of the virtues (73:9), of love (7:67), and of eternal life (72:12), that breath which quickens and spreads in my heart an ardent love, the gift of your love.

# The Monk

# in Relationship to God

# GOD PRESENT

It has been reserved to our day and age to speak of the 'absence of God', and even to invent a theology of the death of God. Certainly, the truth of God's presence is a mystery, a paradox for anyone who tries to reconcile it with the crying reality of evil, misery, and the mire which threatens to submerge our world. How, then, is it possible to think of a God who creates and rules the world, of a loving Providence attentive to his creatures? God omnipresent—is this not a flagrant contradiction, even a blasphemy? To believe in a real God, is this not the hunger and desire of many people today, and are certain forms of atheism not proof of it, even though a contradictory one?

Monastic life, the christian life itself, would be folly, nonsense, if God did not exist, if he were not present. Why seek God if he is nowhere? To want to believe at all costs in the existence of God, is this such a beautiful and attractive illusion that it deserves seeing someone sacrifice his life for it? A look at the motives for our actions teaches us that man needs psychotechnical references; they give him basic orientation and determine his choices, whether this is for a series of acts or in a general way and over a long time. Usually unconscious or subconscious orientations are present whose influence is all the more powerful because we are not in control of it. Some honor or advantage will influence one person's decision; the prospect of pleasure or profit will be the determining factor for another. Selfish passions preside over the actions of the animal man. 'Do not allow yourself to be carried away by our lusts', St Benedict urges (7:25). And to these psychological references to corrupt man (22) he opposes a sublime reference which may appear at first glance too elevated and therefore ineffective, but it redounds to another passion: fear. God is present always and everywhere, God sees me (27). Little by little, this reference to God present ought to take the place of other worldly and evil references (22) or to direct them to him. Little by little this motivation frees itself from the predominating fear and becomes a happy consciousness of the divine presence of the sovereign Good.

St Benedict does not engage in theological speculation. His theology is simple. This is the faith and its content. God exists. He is too great for men to be able to dare to pretend to discover him to a degree greater than he has himself revealed, lest they try to analyze the notion of God and tell his history. For St Benedict, as for every Christian, God exists; it is a fact. God is that immense, eternal Being transcending every concept, to be grasped only through analogy: 'the Lord God of all things' (20:2). The whole Rule is imprinted with the majestic grandeur of God as with a basic reality which occupies his entire thought. In the Rule we should note those attributes of God which concern us directly: his omnipotence (28:5, Prol. 29ff.), his justice (3:11, 2:6, 9), his mercy (Prol. 20, 4:74, 7:46; 53:14), and especially his omnipresence.

Concerning this presence of God, St Benedict declares straight out: 'We believe that God is present everywhere, that in every place the eyes of the Lord observe the good and the bad (19:1). St Benedict insists on this truth with unusual energy. God is here, and he watches us everywhere. To place this truth beyond any doubt is one of the most fundamental instruments of the spiritual art (4:49) and this is why the ladder of humility rests entirely on this first degree (which Cassian, more logically, simply made the base, the support, of the ladder) the fear of God, or, expressing the thought of St Benedict just as well, faith in the presence of God, the just and eternal Judge. The first degree of humility is therefore to preserve always the fear of God and to flee all levity (7:10). 'A man ought to be persuaded that God watches him continually from heaven, that his actions are everywhere visible to the eye of the godhead, and are constantly being reported to God by angels. The prophet teaches us this when he represents God as always present to our thoughts, saying, "God searches the heart and the reins", and again, "The Lord knows the thoughts of men" . . . And elsewhere he says,

"You have understood my thoughts from afar", and again, "men's thought shall praise you" ' (13-17).

> As for the desires of the flesh, let us believe that God watches us without ceasing; for the prophet says to the Lord: 'All my desires are before You'. One must guard himself therefore from evil desires; for death is near the gates of delight. Thus the Scripture gives us this command: 'Follow not your lusts'. If, therefore, the eyes of the Lord consider the good and the bad, if from heaven the Lord constantly watches the sons of men to see if there is someone who has understanding and who seeks God, if, finally, the angels assigned to guard us report our works day and night to the Lord who creatèd us, we must, my brothers, watch constantly, lest as the prophet says in the psalm, God should surprise us at some moment when we have fallen into evil and become unprofitable, so that, if he spare us for the moment because He is good and awaits our amendment, he would have to say to us later: 'You did this and I was silent' (7:23-30).

Do these texts not give us the impression that God is present only in a passive way, so to speak, watching our progress as a simple spectator? St Benedict clearly insists upon this kind of attentive presence of the Lord, it is true, in order to strike the imagination of simple souls more forcibly and, doubtless, to stimulate his disciples' zeal, too. The ancient ascetics attached great value to the efficaciousness of their own efforts, their own exploits, and here St Benedict seems to be indebted to their way of thinking.

Nevertheless, it would be inaccurate to believe that St Benedict limits himself to this. At the base of this way of looking at things there is for him the idea of an alliance between the monk promising his fidelity before God (58:18, 7:38) and the ever faithful Lord, and the monks' efforts are supported by God's grace. The monk ought to be loyal; he has made a commitment, God has the right to expect that he will fulfil his promise, for He is loyal by nature and by covenant. So, when the disciples whom the Lord has invited have presented themselves to acquire 'life and see good days' (Prol. 15f.) and have applied themselves to the work of asceticism (17), he will answer them: 'When you have done these things, my eyes will be upon you and my ears attentive to your prayers, and even before you call on me, I will say, "Here I am". What could be sweeter to us, dear brothers, than this voice of the Lord who invites us? Behold, in his goodness, the Lord himself shows us the path of life' (Prol. 18-20). God is not, therefore, a passive spectator watching us run in the stadium from afar in order to distribute the prizes in the end, or to reject those who have run badly or who have abandoned the race and become useless (7:29). He is instead the Lord patient (Prol. 37) and good (38) who offers us his help, expecting to see us make good use of it (7:30). He is present to us, therefore, like the father of the Prodigal Son; he watches us from afar with his infinitely merciful gaze, ready to help us as soon as we begin to turn our back on evil (7:30). From him, model of all goodness, the abbot learns to be a tender father and a good shepherd (Prol. 1, 2:24, 27:8).

God is not only present in a general way; he is present to each thing, to each of us in particular. Inasmuch as we are creatures, we already live and move and have our being in Him (Acts 17:28). But we dwell in him and he in us in an infinitely more intimate way still, as the chosen of his love: 'Abide in me and I in you' (Jn 15:4). The Most Blessed Trinity establishes its dwelling in us: 'If anyone loves me . . . we will come to him and will make our abode with him' (Jn 14:23).

This blessed permanent presence, going beyond our expectations, causes us to bow deeply in honor of the Most Blessed Trinity at the 'Glory be to the Father and to the Son and to the Holy Spirit' (9:7), and makes of our monastic life a continual grateful *Jubilus*, especially in the liturgy where the presence of God manifests itself with a special fulness. St Benedict reminds us: 'Let us be even more persuaded that this is true [that God is everywhere present] when we assist at the Divine Office' (19:2). And so it matters little whether the Divine Office is celebrated in the chapel

(11:13, 24:4, 25:1, 43:8, 44:2, 6, 9; 45; 50:1; 52) or else-where (50), since God is everywhere present and hears us in every place.

For us the Divine Office is the period of audience with the divine Majesty. Now if we want to ask some favor of power-ful people in this world (20:1) or honor them, we comport ourselves in their presence with humility and reverence. At the canonical hours distributed throughout the day we are admitted to that audience, and even to dialogue. God is there. He is waiting for us; never miss your appointment. Are we also faithful to these meetings? He is on time. Are we also punctual? Do we hurry to be in his presence (22:6, 8, 43:1) or are we habitually late (43:4-12)? We ought to reflect on the duty of being present, not just any which way, half absent mentally, distracted, or sleepy, but fully, with our whole personality, as committed and alert persons. We ought to be present to God with our whole heart, our whole soul, with all our strength (4:1), to live in the presence of the God-head (19:6), to listen, to speak, to love, in full possession of ourselves. And this not only for God, but also for the brothers in whom God reveals himself and in whom Christ is present (2:2, 63:13, 36:1-4, 53:1,15). Obedience itself does not become reasonable and responsible unless it includes God present in the person of his representative.

Finally, we ought also to be present to ourselves, atten-tively gathering and controlling all our senses and powers, even of the body, as far as we are able, in order to be truly at the disposal of God and of others. We must be present before the Lord, present in the present time, in the circumstances of our life, with an ever renewed freshness and liveliness through which the ever youthful God constantly renews our youthfulness of spirit and keeps us from a premature and somnolent senility. We ought to be present with equal attention to things both old and new (64:9), without letting ourselves be carried away by the whirlwinds of fashion.

Realizing that we are constantly under the eyes of God gives us the right sense of proportion about ideas and things, persons and events, and it allows us, in all that presents itself as new and valid, to separate what is doubtful from what deserves our esteem; finally, it furnishes us with sure and sovereign criteria in the judgments which we are led to make about these things which demand our taking a stand. Gazing upon God furnishes us with a real 'tele-vision' of things, under the light of the 'signs of the times' (cf. Mt 16: 4) which are the signs of the will of the sovereign Governor of the world. Only in the intimate union with God present are we able to interpret the signs and the needs of the present time.

We cannot end this conference without saying a word about the God-Man present in the Eucharist: his sacramental, mysterious presence, visible through his sign, the bread and wine. St Benedict does not speak of it, not only because he does not touch on the truths of faith unless they have a necessary and immediate relationship with the practice of virtue and the monastic observances, but also because his theology of the divine presence allows him to follow an exclusively moral purpose: to make the monk conscious that God sees him everywhere. Now, the eucharistic presence is limited to a place. Moreover, we must note that the early Church did not especially dwell on this aspect of the mystery of the Eucharist so familiar to Christians of today. Even with St Bernard, Christological mystique was not centered on Christ sacramentally present. But God has willed to put himself within our reach, and Jesus present exercises a decisive attraction on us. The monk holds nothing dearer than Christ (5:2), discovers God by following Christ (4:10), leaves all in order to be with Jesus (cf. Mt 19:28f.), finds in the eucharistic Lord a master, a brother, and a friend. Close to him, he receives the good advice he needs, finds tranquillity, patience, and charity. With him he learns to integrate himself into his community, to be reunited with the brothers whose orientation and opinions differ from his. With him he learns to be present to himself, to love himself in the way Jesus loves him. Looking at Him he becomes aware that living truly in his presence in intimate union with him is one of the greatest values there is.

# PRAYER

What we call prayer is an absolutely extraordinary thing, for through prayer we contact God himself. He deigns to listen to us, to let us talk. God knows that most of the time man cannot maintain a lofty conversation with him, and along with a great deal of love, he is also capable of a great deal of stupidity, and often lacks respect for him. Yet, in spite of this, God allows us to speak to him! It is unheard of!

Jesus invites us urgently to: 'Ask and you shall receive' (Mt 7:7). More than once he returns to this theme, because he wants to help us. He is on the lookout for our needs to supply our deficiencies. He expects us to count on him, to need Him.

Our vocation is a vocation of prayer. We want to know then how we ought to pray. This problem interests every person whose heart is turned toward God (cf. Ps 84:9), all those who feel above them a benevolent Power, a God of goodness who wants to dialogue with man. Christians and non-Christians, all believers, feel the need of knowing how to pray. The problem of prayer is a human problem. The apostles expressed this need in a moving way when they asked Jesus, 'Lord, teach us to pray' (Lk 11:1) and Jesus gave them a confident and vigorous formula for a prayer of unornamented simplicity.

In speaking of prayer, St Benedict remembers this sober and substantial style. His method of prayer, the *disciplina orandi*, remains in the gospel tradition. He does not explain the *Pater Noster*, as the 'Master' does, but tries to let us enter its spirit by speaking to us about what seems to him necessary without further development. What does he teach us? Aside from the chapters regulating the arrangements made for the Divine Office, St Benedict has left three chapters on his thoughts on the manner of praying: On the Manner of Singing the Psalms (RB 19), Of Reverence in Prayer (20), Of the Oratory of the Monastery (52). We should not seek there for a definition of prayer. He doesn't give one. Yet it is easy to formulate one from it. Not to misrepresent his thought, let us take as our theme for this little discussion, the title of chapter 20: *De reverentia orationis:* Of Reverence in Prayer. Prayer is a reverent act toward God, the Lord of the universe (20,2). Man, aware of his condition before God and in relation to him, raises his soul toward him—there we have arrived at the classical definition of prayer, the one the catechism taught us. The man who prays opens his heart and his whole being to God.

Here we ask St Benedict: What should we do truly to pray well? His answer is simple: the quality of our prayer depends on our disposition. And if we insist: But what are these dispositions? he replies: the reverence to be observed in prayer (RB 20, title).

St Benedict seldom speaks to us of the physical dispositions and postures to adopt for prayer, although our body, associated with the life of the soul, can intervene even in our spiritual efforts as either an obstacle or an instrument. Fatigue in its many forms may hinder us in our spiritual activity. Did not St Paul for this reason desire to be freed from his mortal body (Rom 7:24)? On the other hand, vigils, fasting, silence and solitude foster prayer. Exercises, such as yoga, can also dispose a person to a meditative attitude.

To pass different methods of meditation in review here is not our purpose; in any case, St Benedict does not propose any, unless it is *lectio divina* to dispose us to recollection and thus to prayer. Methods of prayer simply order and regulate the acts which prepare and sustain prayer. Some people imagine that by these 'methods' and a strict observance of the means they propose one arrives automatically at the goal. It goes without saying, it is perfectly obvious, that the acts suppose an attitude of soul, and only in function of this do the means animate us and attain their goal.

St Benedict, we should add, does not distinguish between vocal prayer and mental prayer, a distinction having little bearing on the point of view he takes. Indeed, he speaks of vocal prayer even outside the Divine Office (e.g. 49:5), not wishing anyone to raise his voice while praying (52:4). However, it matters little whether our prayer is purely mental or if it is vocal, as, for example, ejaculatory prayers. That a prayer be real, reverence is necessary. And St Benedict explains: 'If we wish to present a petition to men of high station, we do not presume to do so without humility and respect; how much more ought we to entreat the Lord God of all things with humility and pure devotion' (20:1f.). Without clearly recognizing our total dependence on God, Master of the universe, we cannot hope to be heard. As there is no adoration without this reverence and this fear toward our sovereign Lord (RB 19), so also there can be no real prayer, no hope of being heard, without this reverence.

Analyzing this attitude of reverence, we find that its foundation is faith (19:1). Without faith, there is no access or opening to God. How can we ask something from someone in whom we do not believe, or believe in very little? Faith opens our eyes simultaneously to the greatness of Almighty God and to the nothing which we are.

Humility is a child of faith and with simplicity it shows us our exact place in our relationship with God as well as the conduct which befits a creature before its Creator. *Humilitas* means to be of *humus.* Yes, we are of earth, and we are aware of it before him who is our Creator, Greatness itself, very Majesty. We prostrate ourselves to the earth before him. Reverence means humility. The Pharisee (Lk 18:11) knows nothing of reverence. Proud, he remains standing before God and boasts of his good works. Such an attitude closes heaven to him. It is not that God wants to humiliate us, to abase us; prayer is not an abdication of our human dignity. On the contrary, being able to talk to God is a recognition of that dignity, as likewise is receiving a response from him. But if a person presents himself before God as someone having a right, like a feudal lord, his prayer, far from being a prayer, becomes a demand. Even among equals such an attitude would be intolerable, and the comparison with which St Benedict introduces this twentieth chapter has lost nothing of its force since the disappearance of feudalism. To pray well, a person therefore needs to have a basic attitude of reverence which comes from faith, fear of God, confidence, and humility. Jesus himself in the days of his earthly life, was heard for his reverence (Heb 5:7) when he addressed his supplications to the Father.

To humility, St Benedict adds another expression: *puritatis devotione* (20:2): this is surely an amplification of what the word 'reverence' expresses. This formulation, dear to the Romans, is an example of the *genetivus substantivi pro adiectivo* (Hauslik) and is therefore equivalent to *cum pura devotione*, with a pure devotion. Translations do not agree on the formulation. The meaning seems to be clear enough. In order to be able to present ourselves before God, we ought to be sincerely devoted to the Lord in total submission. This expression, therefore, links up with what the word 'humility' expresses.

The *puritas cordis*, purity of heart (20:3) required next by St Benedict of those who pray represents the much desired goal of ancient monks and remains so always: purity of heart, of intention, liberty from passions, *apatheia*, peace of soul, perfect interior equilibrium, all these give a person the necessary detachment to entrust himself to the word of the Lord who promised that anyone who asks will be heard (Mt 7:7ff.) in abandoning himself to his divine will. Pure hearts are nearest to God's heart (cf. Mt 5:8). This is why they have no need to raise their voice when they pray (cf. RB 52:4) or to multiply words (20:3). Purity of heart is closely linked to humility and reverence because it detaches us from ourselves, keeps us from self-centeredness, and gives God the first place.

*Et compunctione lacrymarum*, with compunction of heart (20:3, cf. 52:4, 48:4). The history of monasticism furnishes us with several examples of great sinners who, once converted, became monks and penitents. These exceptions have had too much of the limelight. St Benedict exhorts us, it is true, to daily and persevering penitence (4:58, 7:64), but his words were not aimed at great sinners, nor were they intended to give us a guilt complex. Yet if we say we are without sin, we deceive ourselves and the truth is not in us (1 Jn 1:8). The attitude of the Pharisee boasting of his good works (Lk 18:11) is not befitting even the holiest monk (cf. 4:62). The words of St John cited above have a very special flavor, because usually the more a person is a sinner the less he sees his sins, and the holier he is, the more he believes himself to be a sinner. This explains the holy monks' insistence in recommending compunction of heart, tears, and the 'gift of tears'. How is it possible not to see ourselves as evil-doers, ungrateful and wicked servants in comparison to a Lord so rich in goodness as is the Lord our God? Once this is understood, the tears become liberating tears, easing the tension and the shriveling of the heart caused by our pride and our thoughtlessness. These tears, therefore, bring us close to the basic attitude of purity of heart. Yet tears are not the result only of compunction of heart. Gratitude, charity, the very joy of meeting the Lord can be accompanied and manifested by tears.

Someone who wants to pray ought also to love to withdraw into himself (cf. Mt 6:6). Intimate conversation with God the Father does not allow indiscretion. Remaining alone (RB 52:3) with God alone is a need, as is withdrawing apart (52:4). Respect in the presence of God, reverence, already requires separation from all that is profane or secular. Even in a monastery, a special place is needed for prayer, the chapel (RB 52), where nothing profane is admitted (52:1). Our cell is also a place reserved for us, not provided by the Rule. It can be a meeting place for trifles or a sanctuary for meeting with the Incomprehensible. Above all, we need spiritual space, a humble expectancy. Our heart ought to be stretched out toward God, welcoming; the arms of the soul open to him who does not refuse himself to anyone who loves him. This is the *intentio cordis* of St Benedict, the attention of the heart (52:4). It is in the spiritual space of prayer that contact is made between 'Thee and me', between God and man, dialogue with him. It is there that man, having become simple, arrives at the prayer of simplicity (20, 52). We keep ourselves withdrawn, but we do so in order to open ourselves delightfully to the God of delights, to him who pursues those who seek him with understanding and love (7:27).

There in a few words is what St Benedict tells us about prayer. It would therefore be vain for us to ask him for some sagely constructed techniques for arriving at prayer. If there is one technique to learn, it is based on a very simple, clear truth: As the body grows in a harmonious way, as one arm does not grow faster than the other, so the spiritual person grows in the same balanced and organic way. Growth in prayer depends on growth in faith, in reverence, in humility, in charity. The monk who has not yet learned reverence toward his abbot (6:7) and toward his brothers (cf. 72:4) cannot possess reverence, obedience and charity toward God—dispositions which are, however, indispensable for anyone desiring to pray successfully. The growth required for prayer is not only mental or physical exercise, or even concerned only with the will, therefore, but an asceticism of the entire person, especially in the exercise of the theological virtues of faith, hope, and charity.

To learn to pray, then, takes time. It takes that growth in faith which allows us access to prayer. Maybe we unconsciously believed that the moment the monastery door opened we would enter completely into an atmosphere of prayer and quickly become masters of prayer and of what we thought to be contemplation. Oh no! The monastery is specifically a school of prayer. We have to serve an apprenticeship of humility there, understand the naiveté of our expectations, and perhaps even their pride. It will not be until the moment we have arrived at ground zero of humility that we will begin to ascend seriously in prayer.

But we should not forget in all this that prayer, like virtue, besides our own efforts is a divine grace and that the Lord is the origin of our bursts of virtue and prayer (20:4) which, like the moments of exceptional spiritual lucidity, go beyond our ordinary spiritual age. God pushes us harder from time to time, and we can call this 'consolations' or 'inspirations'. The Lord leans down this way toward us so we will not become discouraged on the hard and narrow road which leads to him; but let us not be deceived: this consolation or inspiration is of short duration. It is not prayer itself and we must not confuse it iwth the art of prayer. And then, they are brief moments: a fleeting sense, a sudden light, a clear vision of certain things. In the background there may also be a favorable physical disposition. But let us especially see in this a special divine grace which touches us. We do not know, of course, why the Lord is knocking at our door. He only knocks by exception and does not keep us in a continual fervor; that is the angels' job. At any rate, prayer becomes easier at these privileged moments. But we should not become disappointed or discouraged, if, after this happy experience, we fall back into dryness and feel ourselves empty and abandoned. The saints experienced such states of soul acutely, sometimes for years. Let us realize, though, that the feeling is not the prayer and does not make the prayer. Nor is it an indication of prayer. St John of the Cross has shown the total independence of prayer from feelings. Let us not, therefore, believe that we have failed in our vocation to prayer even when the feeling of knowing that we are praying is refused to us for long periods. These are the trials of purification, necessary for attaining purity of heart, the indispensable condition of praying well. If, therefore, we sometimes feel this inspiration of divine grace, an interior joy, the pleasure of praying, let us rejoice, let us thank the Lord, but let us not think that tomorrow he ought to do it again.

Through all these considerations, we are able to understand that the prayer described by St Benedict in chapters twenty and fifty-two is, as a general rule, short (20:40). Now, therefore, can we reconcile this teaching with that of Scripture according to which we must pray without ceasing (Lk 18:1, 1 Thess 5:17), and with the example of the Lord passing the night in prayer (Lk 6:12)?

When St Benedict speaks of prayer of the heart (52:4), he envisages, following the teaching of his predecessors, a sort of prayer, of contemplation, a simple gaze, and not prayer in general. This mystical prayer is, according to the witness of those who have experienced it, of very short duration (cf. St Bernard, *On the Song of Songs*, Sermon 32. 2). But the rock bottom basis, the dispositions for this prayer, are permanent and identical for all the types of prayer. Without faith in the existence and presence of God (19:1), without reverence and humility, without purity of heart, our prayer remains that of children of the world who, being selfish, do not know how to integrate their requests into the plans of the Lord and his Providence.

These dispositions would not, therefore, be serious if they were only momentary, passing. The more enduring and truly ours they are, the more the spirit of prayer abides in us. We are not capable of maintaining prayer in our heart in the form of a continuous act, but by divine grace the spirit of prayer, the milieu generating prayer, its seed, remains in us. Thus our fundamental attitude becomes a prayerful attitude. The favorable and paternal answer of the Father of heaven is assured to this prayer and to this constant union with him.

This prayer is likewise a prayer of the heart. Even if we might be mentally absent, we remain united by the force of this basic attitude to the Lord. The desire of the hymn expresses this: *te cordis alta somnient*—may the depths of our heart dream of you, O Lord. For even during sleep, it still watches—'I sleep but my heart watches' (Cant 5:2). This prayer attracts the pleasure of the Father, because while our passions sleep, it cries out to him, disengaged from all selfishness. As sleep does not interrupt this prayer, neither does manual or intellectual work, however lowly or absorbing it may be.

But aren't there still our distractions, our fatigue, our harrassing worries, hurry, and noise? Do they not impede this direct commerce with God the Father, with Jesus our elder brother? And in our prayers, do we not stay so attached to the earth that in spite of all our confident will, we remain seduced by it in our requests to the Father?

The Lord God who created us and has seen us fall in Adam's fall knows what we are made of (Ps 102:14). And truly, we do not know how to pray as we ought (Rom 8:26). The day we understand our helplessness to pray well but know that Jesus has promised to send us his Spirit to be with us always (Jn 13:16), he who in person unites himself to our spirit in order to witness to us that we are children of God (Rom 8:16), on that day we will know how to pray, for the Spirit comes to the help of our weakness and intercedes for us with ineffable groanings (Rom 8:26). Our prayer will be the prayer of the Holy Spirit, charismatic prayer, if you wish. Yes, it has such a need of being inspired, elevated, inflamed by the Spirit of God. Left to himself, doesn't it remain bound by our horizons and our weakness, incapable of really attaining the immense divine Majesty, and of letting our soul really breathe? For this is a magnificent truth: we are not left to ourselves in prayer; the Spirit of light and love, the divine Breath, is with us. It is the ardor of the inspiration of divine grace of which St Benedict speaks (20:4). And it is reverence before this action of the Holy Spirit in the soul of each monk, action to which St Benedict does not wish to substitute himself but which he has to protect, which makes him create this holy place called the chapel (RB 52) from which every foreign object (52:1), every kind of noise (2,4), and obstacle (3,5) is to be removed. Exterior, and especially interior, silence is, as a matter of fact, a preliminary condition for being able to hear and receive the touch of the Spirit.

Can the *Opus Dei*, our official prayer which punctuates the rhythm of the monastic day, be a prayer of the heart? By being spread across time, it is another application of Jesus' counsel to pray without ceasing (Lk 18:1). For this, too, St Benedict requires faith in the divine presence (19:1f., 50:3), the fear of God (19:2), sincere commitment and serious attention (19:6f.). Why, then, did St Benedict think it necessary to admonish us to put our soul in harmony with our voice (19:7)? A similar admonition is not given us where he expresses his thoughts on private prayer. The reason is simple. Whereas private prayer generally responds to a personal need and to a particular ardor of grace and ought for that reason to remain intimately linked for the duration of that grace (20:4), the Divine Office occupies us at fixed times to which a subjective need for prayer does not necessarily correspond. The rhythm of the canonical hours is far from always corresponding with the rhythm of our personal religious sensibilities or with our attraction to prayer. Could we then withdraw from the duty of our service (50:4), from the Divine Office, on the pretext of remaining authentic?

As a matter of fact, although the music often carries us along, the multiplicity of texts to follow may tire us. Harassed by our work, or emotionally empty, we run the danger of responding badly to our duty. Yes, the celebration of the Divine Office costs effort. It can be drudgery. We should add that although the content of personal prayer naturally mobilizes, as it were, the powers of the person who prays, it is much more difficult for the monk to put himself into the rhythm of the official prayer of the Church, even if it is the prayer of Jesus himself. Its quality may suffer, too, from the official length of the monastic and ecclesial prayer, which supposes a much greater abnegation in the participant than private prayer. Any Christian may find the same difficulties at Sunday Mass.

Every prayer is a matter of contact with God, of raising the soul toward him; everywhere, the arrangements ought to be the same. For someone who prays in private, the texts of the Divine Office furnish a very rich selection of aspirations to animate his prayer, to discipline it, direct it, and preserve it from deviations. This is why the Rule supposes that private prayer is like an ardent prolongation of common prayer (52:2, 5). On its side, the *Opus Dei* is enriched by the contributions of personal prayer whose piety and fullness are easily transferred to the Divine Office.

In conclusion, it seems that prayer is one. The Divine Office ought to be truly a personal prayer, and private prayer will be much more authentic insofar as it withdraws itself from self-centeredness with the aid of scriptural texts. We reach our goal by closely uniting these two forms of prayer. In separating them, we necessarily sacrifice first of all the Divine Office, dashing through it for better or for worse; next, by impoverishing our private prayer, we cause it to pass from a prayer of simplicity to a prayer which runs the risk of being frustrated by human moods and caprices. But, let us admit, there is often prayer in suffering, and any kind of triumphalism rising from the bliss where some experience of a divine grace or even our natural moods, may put us, would be illusory in this case. God is so close, and at the same time so far from us!

Our fundamental prayer, therefore, will always be: Lord, teach me to pray. Direct my steps toward the paths which lead to your heart! Teach me total abandonment to your love! Remove from me what separates you and me, what hinders me from approaching you, O God of all goodness. You promised us that we would be answered if we asked anything of the Father in your name, in full union with his will. Father, have pity on my weakness, my slowness, my lack of fervor to seek you truly! Deign, however, to find at the bottom of my heart that ardent desire to be able to fix my eyes on yours. Father, be my father!

# CONTINUAL PRAYER

What is continual prayer? What is its relationship with the monastic life? Continual prayer is commended to us by Our Lord. It is not necessary to remind you of his teaching. 'We must pray always and never lose heart' (Lk 18:1). And what we call our contemplative life, does it not have continual prayer specifically as its substance and goal?

Now, if we talk here about continual prayer, the expression may frighten us. Immediately we make a comparison between the state in which we are and these words of Holy Scripture, 'Pray always and never lose heart', and we find we are far from it. Consequently, the thought comes immediately to our minds: have I wasted my life? We have not arrived at the state of perfection, but are *in statu perfectionis acquierendae*, that is to say, we are seeking it. We realize very well that our brethren in the world may be ahead of us. But, by the grace of the Lord, we have chosen the monastic state, and modestly, humbly, we strive to tend to perfection.

Let us, first of all, define continual prayer going back to the latin expressions; they will help us better to understand *Oratio*, prayer; *oratio, orare, os. Orare* is then in modern terms, to speak. The *oratio* lets us speak with the Lord, with God; we speak to the Lord with our mouth, *os;* that is vocal prayer. The expression still keeps its meaning when we come to prayer of the heart. Our heart speaks to the Lord who is invisible and to whom we cannot speak as we speak among ourselves, unless by the mouth of the heart.

If we speak about the heart and the language of the heart, we know immediately that this language is different from that of the mouth. The heart expresses itself in a much more universal way; it speaks by love. The action proper to the heart is love. Now there are two loves, we might say: the love of self and the love of God. You may be surprised that I do not speak about the love of neighbor; but let's be honest: the love of neighbor ends up being either the love of self or the love of God. That is to say, we love our neighbor through love of self or through love of God. This is why Our Lord tells us that the love of God and the love of neighbor are basically one and the same thing, since the motive of a generous love for my brother finds its source in my love of God my Father.

Now if the language of the heart is love, then the language, the *oratio*, the prayer addressed to the Lord, is love; and if there is continual prayer, it evidently does not mean continual vocal prayer. Nor is this a matter of a continual thought of the *mens humana*, of the human heart; we would not be capable of it. There is a language of the heart which is always possible and which can be continual because it is a manifestation of our love.

Here we must ask ourselves what prevents our love of God from being continual. It seems natural for our heart to turn itself by immanent necessity toward the sovereign Good, the object which alone is able to satisfy it. But that supposes that it can recognize and understand it as its supreme Good. What force holds our heart back then?

The love of self, in fact! If our power to love has self as its object, if, to use a phrase that we understand well, we are centered on self, then, in proportion to our self-centeredness, we are not turned toward the Lord. This love limits us and prevents our heart from rising toward him. By that very fact it is not possible for us to love him with all our soul, and prayer, the prayer of the heart, is no longer continual.

Consequently, we may say that, in this sense, continual prayer, is purity of heart (20:3). We should not love ourselves in an inordinate way. Let us pay attention, because love of self may also be a love ordered by the love of God. The opposite of an inordinate love of ourselves is purity of heart. Our heart is pure when its motives are truly purified in the crucible of God's love. So, in this sense, continual prayer is really purity of heart. If our heart is pure it is always reaching, always directed, orientated, toward the Lord. If our heart is completely pure, there is no longer anything in it to make it turn in upon itself, but everything in it reaches for the Lord.

Therefore, if our monastic life is to be truly contemplative, a continual prayer—it is basically the same thing to contemplate God, to reach out toward God, to love God; they are similar terms—our monastic life, then, is to be truly contemplative, to be a continual prayer, then it ought to be a life wholly turned toward the Lord, a life of love for him. Here we already understand that perfect contemplation, the vision of God, is not for this life.

Thus—and I limit myself to essentials—in this way we see that there are many degrees in this continual prayer, and that these degrees indicate the degree of our purity of heart. Our prayer will be continual in proportion as our heart is pure. All that is pure in our heart is of itself reaching out toward the Lord, because to reach out to him is by definition the opposite of self-centeredness, that is to say, the exaggerated and inordinate love of ourselves.

Therefore it is clear that there are numerous degrees in continual prayer and that there are also many forms by which it is realized. It can be found in any state of life, any situation, any vocation. A craftsman in his workshop can live in continual prayer while going about his work. The same is true of a cook in his kitchen. A priest at the altar or in the confessional, or at table eating, can be in a state of continual prayer, or not. A monk in his monastic life, with all its observances, all the usages the life implies, may have a pure heart or not. You see where the essential of our life is.

But a question immediately comes to the mind: why enter

the monastery when we can have this continual prayer, this contemplative life, anywhere? A text of the Council says that every person is called to the fullness of the christian life (L.G. 40), which is as much as saying that every Christian is obliged to tend to a life of continual prayer. In saying, 'we must pray without ceasing', the Lord was not speaking to a group of privileged individuals. He made no distinction of persons in calling to continual prayer. But then, why enter the monastery?

We know the answer: Around the essential of which we have just spoken, there are many means which can help us to continual prayer, as there are also obstacles which hinder us from arriving at it. We can single out very well what is capable of increasing our purity of heart, on the contrary, what is inappropriate or ineffective in increasing it and instead distracts us from the love of the Lord. Consequently, we will rightly choose a state of life where we find a whole battery of means, situations, and possibilities which help us grow in that love, while withdrawing from our heart all that might hinder it in the exercise of the love of God. But, once again, it is not the external situations which make us pure or impure. We can fall into great impurity of heart in a very holy place. The place does not make the saint, and the habit does not make the monk. This purity of heart depends on us and on our personal relationship with the Lord. Everything lies there. An aid is only an aid. We can profit by it, as we can also toy with it. The monastic life with its legislation is not necessarily an assurance against eternal death. And a person can be in a hell of sin while keeping his heart pure, if he refuses to let the environment in which he lives turn him away from seeking the Lord.

Yet, we are human beings, and because of this, we are necessarily subject to various influences coming from without. These influences can be good or evil. Now it is quite obvious that if we place ourselves in an environment of useful influences, our soul will profit from it, and this will increase the probability of an experience of divine love. Consequently, to choose the monastic life is a good thing. But, once again, what makes us holy is not the monastic life; it is divine love.

Monastic life includes many observances, and we may ask ourselves about the usefulness of these practices in helping us attain purity of heart. Silence, for example, separation from the world, poverty, or rather, the spirit of poverty, detachment from self-will, meditation of the Scriptures or other reading. It is clear that all this is extremely useful for increasing purity of heart in us. But the closer these means are to the heart, the more effective they are. For example, poverty and detachment from self-will are close to our heart since detachment from self-will is specifically opposed to self-love. And self-love is the opposite of divine love.

Silence is useful to us because it speaks to the Lord. The silence which surrounds me prevents opportunities for distraction, for going out of myself or being busy with everything except God. If silence is a result of self-centeredness—and often a solitary who observes silence can be tempted to turn in on himself—then the result obtained is the opposite of that intended, for silence is naturally contrary to distraction and a dissipated life. Well understood, it ought to help us acquire purity of heart. But it is a more remote means than is, for example, poverty. Poverty touches us more closely; it takes away from us the possession of many things whose enjoyment is a temptation to self-centeredness. All the conveniences, money and the ease of buying things as we please, all that does not help detach us from ourselves, whereas poverty is an effective help for us.

Are extremely absorbing occupations a hindrance to prayer? The basic answer to this question has already been given. No occupation is a hindrance in itself if it does not absorb our heart. But some of them which are not in themselves absorbing, take over our heart because we are attached to them.

Do we need to distinguish between monastic life nad contemplative life? Is there a difference? We embrace the monastic life in order to arrive at continual prayer which is nothing but contemplation. All monastic life is, therefore, contemplative life in this sense, ordered to continual prayer.

In closing, we may contemplate our Lord who has given

us an example of this continual prayer. When we read in the
Gospel his words which are truly divine, words of God, we
find that they are all related to his Father, either directly or
indirectly. He was always with his Father.

# PRAYER AS DIALOGUE

St Benedict presents prayer to us as an approach to God, an
attempt—both timid and at the same time audacious—to
suggest something to him (cf. 20:1), to present a humble request to him, or, speaking generally, to enter into conversation with the divine Majesty. Prayer, therefore, the Divine
Office which punctuates our monastic day, as well as
*lectio divina*, ought and wants to be our conversation with
the Lord. We knock at the heart of God, we speak to him, and
we love to receive his response. It is a dialogue we engage in.
Does God answer us? Does he remain silent?

We are very anxious to experience a union with the Lord
which permits us to converse with him, so to speak, face to
face. This is the great desire of our heart: to know the great
Unknown, to approach him whom the intimate voice of our
heart says is our God, our origin, and our end.

Thus presented, is the problem well stated? Is it really we
who knock at the door of heaven, at the heart of God? Is it
God who seems to remain silent? The Book of Genesis tells
us that God called Adam: Adam, where are you? (Gn 3:9).
That does not mean that God had never yet conversed with
Adam, but rather that up till then it had never been necessary to call him; he never had to look for Adam, hidden in
the woods of paradise. Every evening, Adam was in the
garden of delights and God conversed with him. This is an
image to show us that between God and Adam no obstacle
existed. After the fall, the situation changed. Adam hid
himself, and when God called him, he excused himself: 'I
heard your voice in paradise, but I was afraid because
I was naked, and I hid myself' (Gn 3:10). Adam
had a troubled conscience; he realized that he could

not meet God as he had in the past.

So Adam hid himself; it was not God who hid his face from Adam. That is why when we speak of God's revelation, we should remember that God has no need to unveil himself in order to be revealed, but it is man who covered his face with a veil. St Paul tells us, in speaking of the Israelites, that when Moses is read, a veil is drawn over their hearts (2 Cor 3:15).

God was no longer manifest to man because man hid himself; he did not dare lift his eyes to the Lord because he did not judge himself worthy to appear before him, to hear him, to receive his visit. This is the state which has perpetuated itself from generation to generation on this earth.

We have the impression now that God is silent, that he hides himself, more so since human conduct has become distrustful. After withdrawing into the forests of paradise, he lost his way. And when God called him, he no longer wanted to hear him. Withdrawing further and further from him, he got used to this withdrawal, this separation, and decided or believed that God no longer existed, did not reveal himself, was not there at all. Remember what Gagarin [the cosmonaut] is supposed to have said—he did not meet God in space.

Man has built his life without God, has organized his city and his future according to his own ideas and concepts that please him. Man dreams of being the master of the world, of creating man himself, no longer needing a creator. He dreams of a marvelous interhuman solidarity which would exclude any necessity of God, of Another who is not human or who dominates him. Look where Adam has come, Adam who hides himself and stops his ears in order no longer to see or hear the Lord.

Yet God speaks, and he begins the conversation. He wants to approach us. In the last analysis, it is not we who seek him, but rather God who seeks us. And as St Augustine says, we would seek him in vain if he did not seek us first. It is because we are sought that we seek; it is because God accosts us and speaks to us that we also dare to speak.

In poetry we often meet such exclamations as: 'God, where are you? I speak to you, and you do not answer me.

I am in solitude without you.' You remember the poetic exclamations of the man who arrived at the conviction that God exists, a God whom he wishes to approach and whom he commands to appear. What an aberration! He wants to speak to us; He accosts us first: Adam, where are you? (Gn 3:9). He speaks to us, but we are far away because we have hidden ourselves. For ages and ages humanity has drawn away from God.

God calls us, he loves us, but we live in dissipation. And if we make an effort to approach him, we find ourselves still inclined to dissipation; it is characteristic of our nature. We have to be continually reminded: Adam, where are you? We are lost in the distance, and we have a bad conscience. Very sincerely, we imagine we are making continual efforts. But a sly doubt opposes these efforts: Is it possible that God is speaking to us? Do we refuse to believe that he can be great enough, generous enough, full enough of love to speak to us?

And still he speaks to us, reveals himself to us, lifting the veil which covers our eyes and ears. He reveals himself to us continually through creation. We have only to open our eyes and we discover God at every step. The person who knows how to open himself and let himself be approached by the Lord hears him crying: Adam, open your eyes and see! Creation proves to him that God exists; He is revealed in his beauty, in his perfection, in his love, in his omnipotence, in his wisdom, and creation is his road toward us. Man meets God in nature and meets him in his brother. This is how he speaks to him, quite differently from the way people mutually responsible in malice and wickedness are used to speaking among themselves. The brother we meet is a revelation of God's love; through him we hear the voice of God.

We hide ourselves continually from the face of God, and we do not see him clearly revealing himself in the persons who surround us. Our eyes do not penetrate down to the mystery hidden in the depths of the being of our brother, the mystery of God reflected in him. But when we meet him through prayer we begin to glimpse through him the divine splendor which makes us discover all the marvels that God has willed to put in him. Then we understand that man is

God's most beautiful creature after the angels and that the face of God is truly revealed through the face of our brother. We understand why God has chosen man to enter into this creation, that He chose to become man to reveal himself personally. In becoming man, God did not have to span so very great a distance, for the splendor of his divine revelation already illumined the face of his creature.

And then, we meet God especially and above all in Christ who is the very Word of God. In him, God expresses and knows himself, and that knowledge, that Word, that exclamation, that Logos is very God. God appears in man, in Christ. This is the greatest of all revelations. Through him, the Lord God speaks to us; he comes to us and begins a continual dialogue with us. What remains to be done on our side except to open our eyes and our ears: see and hear, aided by the grace of God? He calls us, he knocks continually at the door of our heart: Behold I stand at the door and knock (Rev 3:20). We ought then to open ourselves to his word, that unique word which is always the same: I am God, I am he who is the fullness. If he invites us to come, it is because—we know in the bottom of our hearts—he is our blessedness, our happiness, our salvation.

An atheistic philosopher once uttered this beautiful phrase: 'May a hand be stretched out to me'. Man feels in himself the need of someone more powerful to be his complement, and even a fullness which will cause him to bloom until at last he becomes truly himself. God holds his arms out toward us. Did the Lord not promise the apostles that he would manifest himself, reveal himself and speak to anyone who loves him? (Jn 14:21). When we go to prayers, to the Divine Office, to *lectio divina*, to pray, we go to meet the Lord. He is always there, wherever we are, all day long. 'A man ought to be persuaded that God is watching him continually from heaven at all times' (RB 7:13). He has promised us at our entry into his holy tabernacle, the monastery: If you have done well, 'My eyes shall be upon you and my ears attentive to your prayers, and even before you call upon me, I will say: Here I am' (Prol. 18, Is 58:9).

Let us grasp well that God wants to talk to us continually.

Let us be ready to listen, and always in that readiness of heart which makes us accept his revelation and his word; may an eagerness to accept the manifestation of his love grow in us. *Manifestabo ei meipsum* (Jn 14:21). Our Lord has promised to show himself to us. May this be in our hearts as a continual invitation to him.

# THE PSALTER

St Benedict, in presenting the list of the instruments of good works to us, clearly wanted to leave to another chapter the question of the psalter, for this is an instrument which holds a very large place in our daily life. The Church, in fact, places in our hands this musical instrument, the Psalter, that we might use it continually and, by means of it arrive at orientating our thoughts and senses toward God. The psalter itself encourages us to take the psaltery to sing the glories of the Lord: *Laudate eum in psalterio et cithara* (Ps 150:3). St Benedict wants us to know the psalter perfectly and to master the art of using it with facility (RB 8, 3, 48:13). And he arranges in detail the way to use it, consecrating to this important question twelve chapters of his Rule and returning to it incidentally in the course of his teachings.

St Benedict does not hide from us the fact that the use of the psalter requires an effort; the name he chooses, *Opus Dei*, makes that understood, as does the idea of the Office as the 'duty of our service' (16:2). It is an honor for the monk to be able to intone or sing the psalms before the community. That honor falls, therefore, only to those who are able to fulfil this function to the edification of their brothers (47:3). It is therefore logical that those who have not mastered this art, or who make mistakes, should acknowledge it humbly and make satisfaction (45:1); they ought even to be submitted to serious correction if they further display their negligence by refusing to humble themselves for the faults they committed.

It is also logical that St Benedict does not permit the ex-communicated to intone the praise of the Lord before the community in their order (24:4, 44:6), nor those who by being late to the Office through their own fault show their lack of enthusiasm for the *Opus Dei* (43:4, 5, 10, 11). It is an honor to lead others in the common concert of psalmody, an honor which falls first of all to the seniors, then to the juniors, each according to the place which the call of God and the decision of the abbot have assigned him (63:1, 4).

But let us look more closely now at this instrument of psaltery which the Church entrusts to us. It is an instrument of quite extraordinary sonority and richness of expression, surpassing even the most celebrated organs in the world by the variety and depth of its accents. The strings are without number, and the nuances infinite. The warmth of its intonations is limitless. There are the high strings of adoration, gratitude, and delightful intimacy with the God of mercies and the Father of goodness, mellow strings of the warm conviction of confidence in the God of hosts, the God faithful to his covenant, and the bass string of unshakeable faith which provides counterpoint to all the melodies. There are the delicate strings of love, devotion, promptness, and that obedience which unites us to the divine will; there are those of generosity in sacrifice and of mystical union with God, who is the joy of our hearts and the happiness of our life. There are numerous strings which express the spirit of repentance, penance, and contrition; and then, ever repeated, that song of invincible hope which experiences the God of promises, of a future of light, of truth, of glory: I will stand, O my God, 'at your right, everlasting delights!' (Ps 15:11).

In another register, the strings of sadness and suffering, of anger against the enemies of God and his people are not lacking either. The greatness of God is sung there in all its manifestations, in his holiness, his justice, and his mercy. He is the God near at hand and the God of majesty. The Creator is adored there in the beauty of all that his hands have made, and he is sung of as the God of the covenant in the history of his chosen ones. Truly, this powerful instrument of the psalter has at its disposal an unequalled variety of expression. Someone who knows how to use it can bring out the entire range of feelings of which the human heart is capable.

Do not think the psalter is cut off from the daily realities of human and mortal life, that it is concerned only with God and that the person who plays this instrument is a disincarnate man, oblivious of this earth in his effort to look at God. It is true that the gaze of the artist who plucks this instrument will remain fixed on God, but it is a living person, in his real existence, in all his vitality and weakness, who is portrayed in the psalter. This is why we find there a multitude of practical sayings, of advice, of remarks which have an extremely life-like realism for people of all times who meet the most diverse situations, in weakness and efforts, failures and hopes.

To know how to play the psaltery is extremely important, and this short outline tries to show that. It is an art which we must try to acquire during the course of our whole monastic life, ceaselessly perfecting it. We must not stop trying; St Benedict teaches us this in chapter nineteen: On the Art of Psalmody.

The fundamental frame of mind requires for it is to keep alive in us a faith in the divine presence (19:2, 6). As David played the harp before Saul, our task is to pluck the strings of the psaltery under the eyes of the Lord. And since the angels stand before the face of the thrice holy God, we find ourselves continually exposed to the gaze of angels (5), masters in the art of making the most mysterious instruments resound before the divine majesty. The awareness of being before the throne of God will not only make us more easily avoid every kind of carelessness and distraction, but will permit us to make our instrument send out sounds and melodies of an ever more perfect quality and finesse, and with time and perseverance we will make it express the searching and delicate feelings to which our soul will then be able to attain. Let us not allow ourselves to be discouraged by fatigue or the inertia inherent in our nature, even if they too often get the upper hand in our humble efforts.

At any rate, it is only in this way that we can arrive little by little at harmonizing the strings of our heart with those of our instrument (19:7), until we blend more and more with it. Yes, that is what the aim of our efforts ought to be: that our heart sing quite naturally on the strings of the psaltery, that its accents become those of our heart, assimilated more and more even till unison is attained with it and with the sentiments it expresses.

Yes, may its feelings become those of our heart! Is it not the Holy Spirit who has inspired them? Is not He the principal cantor of the psalter; has he not made of it the instrument of his all-powerful love? Has he not fashioned the psalter essentially for him of whom he is the personal love, the Son of God become man? It is, in fact, from the lips of Christ that his bride, the Church, receives the chants of divine love which the psalms are, and in his person she repeats them untiringly. And all those who sing them in the name of the Church form with the angels (19:5f.) an immense choir and orchestra tuned to the sweet and solemn melodies and rhythms of the psalter.

The more the art of using the psaltery according to the wishes and intonations of the principal Artist becomes the art of our heart, the more the Holy Spirit will make that same heart an instrument of his love. It will no longer be the stammerings of our heart which praise infinite Wisdom and Beauty, but rather, in the most adequate manner worthy of the majesty of God, it will be the ineffable sighs of the Holy Spirit (cf. Rom 8:26) which will make its strings resound.

# IN THE SIGHT
# OF THE ANGELS

The Rule speaks to us of the holy angels. Are they, in the spirituality of St Benedict, an ornamentation of joy, a bit like the cherubim which make baroque art rejoice, flying about its altars? Without being theological, St Benedict again shows himself to be a good theologian by assigning to the angels the place in the monastic life of messengers of God, intermediaries between God and man, thus essentially ordered to announce to man the glory of God and the salvation he brings them.

The holy angels, then, are beings highly placed, near God, very powerful, of dazzling purity and truth. As such, they enter truly into our life, and having been sent for our salvation, they are our true friends. We should above all have precise ideas about them. Our early instruction and the pictures, which are well suited to capture the childish imagination, often hinder us later from penetrating more deeply and stop us from attaining a more mature concept of the nature and personality of angels, a concept which ought, however, to impress itself on the mind of the religious person.

St Benedict, recognizing the importance of the very active intervention of angels in our life, acts therefore according to the logic of his right and simple faith, and makes us see their activity while remaining strictly within the limits of orthodoxy. He reminds us first of all that God has entrusted us to the angels who care for us day and night (7:28). We rightly call them our guardian angels. This truth, so beautiful, harmonizes well with our monastic spirituality, wholly centered on the service of God. It is marvelous to realize that we are accompanied at every moment, day and night, by beings of such rank.

And what is their role, then? St Benedict limits himself to telling us twice (7:13 and 28) that the angels constantly report our actions to God. This brevity is typical of his style and leaves us hungering for more. The aim of these short sayings is not, at any rate, to give us details concerning their activity.

When he comes to the control the angels exercise, does St Benedict not use a childish expression, or one tainted with anthropomorphism? God, who is all-knowing, has no need of an information service to collect data which might tip the scales in one direction or the other at our final judgment (7:30). Besides, we should notice that St Benedict does attribute this control of our acts to God personally, who, according to the wise man (Prov 15:3) and the psalmist (Ps 13:2), looks down from heaven to see the good and the wicked and to observe if among the children of Adam there are any who who have understanding enough to seek him. If St Benedict mentions the action of the angels this way, it is because God specifically chooses to use his messengers, his nuncios, whom he does not need to complete his own information, but whom he has created as an integral part of his work (cf. *Summa Theol.* 1a, q. 50, a. 1), and to whom, in his Wisdom, he wills to leave the exercises of the function he has assigned to them.

In reflecting on the passages of the Rule where he refers to angels, we may get the impression that it attributes to them more a function of control in our lives than a function of help. Now if it is true that St Benedict's concept of the world is based upon a deep, serious awareness of the last ends of man, and that everything in the Rule is designed to imbue us with this, then we would misunderstand his thought by seeing there a sort of police system. No, the holy angels, according to him, are destined to help us, not as disinterested observers, but as warm friends who, while creatures like us, may appear to us to be closer to God and thus, in some way, to share our lot.

The most exact explanation of these words of St Benedict, moreover, is furnished for us by the expression of chapter nineteen: *In conspectu angelorum.* We are honored by the constant gaze of God and his angels. We live under their eyes. Our life, therefore, ought to be made worthy of that honor even in its smallest acts. Our life itself ought to be angelic, according to the formula of the ancient holy monks.

It is a fact. The monks' life is close to the angels', and this idea appears in the Rule especially when the monks' occupations are identical with those of the angels, as in the divine praise, where the same interests unite them in a similar action and where the angel, while an intermediary and a messenger, is in even greater solidarity with man. St Benedict recalls this fact in citing Psalm 137:1: 'I sing to you in the presence of the angels' (19:5). Seeing God face to face, the angels are in a perpetual state of adoration and celebrate without interruption the heavenly liturgy of which the Apocalypse gives us a faint idea. In this, therefore, they are not only our models, but the best authorized and most effective promoters of the eternal praise: our masters and our inspiration in our vocation as worshippers of the Father in spirit and in truth (cf. Jn 4:23f.). We perform the Divine Office in their sight. They are our teachers, and we are linked with them.

Once I saw a picture showing monks chanting the divine praises in their church. They were bowing deeply at the singing of the *Gloria Patri.* Above every stall was an angel, the guardian angel of each, his face turned toward heaven, glowing with the reflection of the divine glory. Is this not the expression of a reality and of our prayer linked with that of the angels; does it not make us sing with one voice: Holy, Holy, Holy? They are present when we celebrate the divine praises in common, something done, therefore, *in conspectu angelorum.*

This loving presence permits us to leave our place in choir empty for good reasons, that is to say, for tasks by which we acquire greater charity (RB 35) and to see our angel substitute for us there at the *laus divina.* Yet, by good logic, would it not be necessary to think as well that if we miss the Office for insufficient reason, our angel will not be found there?

It would be good, too, not to forget the action of the wicked angels, always prepared to gain ground on us. St Benedict warns us against the wiles of the devil (Prol. 28, 58:28, 1:4); he seems to want to make us understand that, without any doubt, our carelessnesses give him a chance to gain influence over us (54:4) inspiring us with wrong attitudes or reactions. Between God and us exists another world which, by the command or permission of divine Providence, exercises an important influence over us for good or for evil. St Benedict notes this and draws from it a practical lesson which he applies to our monastic life.

So let us entrust our affairs to the holy angels; the goodness of God has destined them to the service of our salvation. Our angel will be wise and prudent when our view is short and our understanding dim. He will be strong and energetic when fatigue and discouragement overtake us. He will not let us go astray if, strengthened by his fraternal help, we truly count on God. Let us not think, however, that our angel will be the solution to all our problems; we ought to face them with the powers placed at our disposal by our Creator and Redeemer. Yet the angels are our powerful and devoted friends, let us not forget it. We can count on them to help us succeed in the course of our eternal salvation, and especially to defend us against the attacks of evil spirits.

Thus St Benedict, in speaking to us of the angels, allows us to have a complete vision of the friendly forces with which the love of the Lord surrounds us. Without any doubt, devotion to the holy angels will be in certain cases a powerful cure against those psychic illnesses whose origin is a heart troubled by enemy forces interested in snatching peace and tranquillity from the soul.

Let us close, then, with the Compline collect: Visit, we beseech you, O Lord, this habitation, and drive from it all snares of the enemy; may your holy angels dwell in it that they may keep us in peace, and may your blessing be ever upon us. Amen.

# The Abbot
# and His Assistants

# THE ABBOT

At the beginning of chapter two, we are struck by the definition of the abbot: *Christi enim agere vices in monasterio creditur* (2:2). This is a very important declaration: The abbot holds the place of Christ in the monastery. We believe it. What does it mean? Should we simply admit that there is a superior to whom we bind ourselves by a sort of contract, as was done in the Middle Ages between the lord and his vassals when they needed someone to lead them in battle? Or do we, like the monks of the desert, expect to find in the abbot that spiritual father whom we freely choose and whom we can leave when we wish? Is belief (*creditur*) based on a personal conviction, on a subjective necessity, or rather on a supernatural faith rooted in an objective truth independent of us?

Without any doubt, it is this true faith which St Benedict means. As we believe that God is one, so we believe that the superior holds the place of Christ. On what foundation does this faith rest? Quite simply on the incarnation of Christ. The Son of God has come to us, sent by the Father, to bring us a message in his name. The Father has accredited his messenger by these words: 'This is My beloved Son in whom I am well pleased; listen to him' (Mt 17:5). The Son has delegated this mission to His apostles and their successors: 'He who hears you, hears me' (Lk 10:16). A very simple, suggestive, convincing, concrete formula.

The person whom the Son designates holds his place. You see, it is not a question of a fiction, 'as if' the superior held the place of Christ. It is upon a reality that my attitude and my obedience to the superior are based. I believe that he holds the place of Christ. Sometimes, unconsciously, in our way of thinking, this fiction may take shape: 'I follow my abbot *as if* he held the place of Christ.' But it is not a fiction. And although the road which goes from the abbot (very real in our eyes) to the place of Christ which he occupies may seem a bit long, it remains no less true, for we believe 'that in the monastery he holds the place of Christ'—it is a reality, a true belief, an authentic supernatural faith.

The abbot, although he holds the place of Christ, is not Christ. Why mention that? It seems obvious. And yet, this fact has importance in the act of obedience. It is not Christ who commands us, but we obey 'as if' Christ commanded us, according to the very suggestive formula of St Benedict: *ac si divinitus imperetur* (5:4), as if God himself had commanded it. Yet it is not a fiction, but a substitution. A comparison can help us understand this reality better: When a chief of state listens to the ambassador of another country, he knows that he is listening to the voice of another chief of state. A good ambassador does not follow his own politics, but faithfully executes the instructions which have been given to him. In this sense, the abbot ought to teach the doctrine of Christ faithfully. That is the job of his embassy.

So we grasp the meaning of this formula: *Christi enim agere vices in monasterio creditur.* The superior is not Christ; he takes his place. His teaching ought to be that of the Lord (2:4f.). If in his own life, he does not perhaps follow the teaching he gives, that teaching nevertheless, remains right in itself, and he always holds the place of Christ (4:61). I believe that with a supernatural faith; Christ has commanded it saying: 'He who hear you, hears me' (Lk 10:16; RB 5:6). Through the intermediary of the Church he has concretely delegated the abbot to take his place, and in the strength of that mission he may say with St Paul: 'We are ambassadors of Christ' (2 Cor 5:20). He has to transmit to his disciples the words of eternal life (Jn 6:68), that ferment of divine justice (2:5) which little by little changes our souls by nourishing them and filling them with its strength and its marrow.

It is true that it was to the apostles, to the Church that Jesus said: 'He who hears you hears me', and not to abbots. But the monastic tradition, especially the *Rule of the Master*, has applied these words to abbots, thus placing them, perhaps voluntarily, on the hierarchical plane; we will not get into this debated and debatable idea. It is enough to put ourselves on the level of the thought of St Benedict who, with the Master, and without being too concerned about the exegetical problem, applies these words to those who exercise over others a spiritual and moral, more than a dogmatic, *magisterium*. The Church at the time of St Benedict recognized in practice and without discussion the right of the pastors of monks, that is to say, abbots, to exercise such a *magisterium*.

But here a delicate question arises: Would the abbot truly hold the place of Christ if, God forbid, he were to teach a doctrine different from that of Christ? Without a doubt, he would have fallen down on that point of his mission—one does not hold the place of Christ with false teaching—but he would not fall from his office as Christ's representative because of an isolated error, especially if his general teaching remains modelled on the Lord's.

The practice of obedience poses practical problems for us. But what is important is meeting them with that deep and supernatural faith which lets us see in the abbot the delegate of Christ, his vicar, his ambassador. And this is why—let us add at once—if the superior shows us by his general conduct that he follows the law of Christ, he is not only an ambassador coldly executing what the chief of state instructs him to say, but he accomplishes Christ's work really and concretely. It is then that he truly holds the place of Christ, in trying to manifest him by his own life.

Now St Benedict specifies, in fact, that the abbot should declare the Gospel teaching, the Good News, in two ways: by his works even more than by his words (2:12). Mandated by the Church, his office is to teach in the name of Christ the word of the Lord. He is the representative of Christ in the institutional order. The abbot of today is recognized by the Church as the juridical, canonical, vicar of the Lord within his community. Even if his actions were not in conformity with his teaching, that teaching, if it is done according to the Gospel, remains the word of the Lord, and the disciples ought to obey, because in the institutional order, the abbot speaks in the name of the Lord. 'Obey the precepts of the abbot in all things, even if, God forbid, he himself does otherwise, remembering the words of the Lord: Do what they say, but take care not to do as they do' (4:61).

The monks' obedience does not, therefore, depend on the way the abbot acts, still less on what he imagines the abbot does. Such an obedience would be very fragile. As long as the abbot remains in line with the institutional order, that is, as long as he preaches the Gospel, the Rule, the constitutions, as long as the orders he gives are not contrary to principle, the monk ought to obey him as Christ himself. That is what the institutional order requires.

On the other hand, the moral order is more demanding. In this order, it is not enough for the person who speaks in the name of the Lord to be only the channel through which the word of life passes or a sort of mechanical apparatus transmitting what it has recorded. No, the abbot ought to preach the truth, give orders more by his example than by his word: *Factis amplius quam verbis* (2:12), and to make himself useful more by the example of his life than by his ability to command: *Prodesse magis quam praeesse*, let him try more to be of service than to be the master (64:8).

We understand here that for the ancient monks the question of the source of the abbot's authority was not a canonical problem. His authority was founded on the conformity of his life with the Gospel—*factis*—rather than on a mission to preach the word of life—*verbis*—without completely neglecting this juridical aspect of authority. The chapter on the election of the abbot attests to this.

We must not, therefore, confuse the moral order and the institutional order. Very often the criticisms that we may hear in community result from this. Because the abbot, according to the opinion of someone or other, does not act as he should, somebody considers himself dispensed from obeying. In reality, in seeing it this way, one is the victim of a great confusion. We ought always to obey the abbot. On the institutional level, when he speaks in the name of the Lord, there is no question, even if his personal way of life is not in harmony with what he commands in His name. On his side, however, the abbot ought to try in his life to imitate Christ whose place he holds. He is juridically his legate. But what abbot would not feel the need of showing himself to be a true disciple of Christ among his disciples, to be the first among equals in the imitation of Christ? It is then that he responds truly to his task, for he ought to make himself obeyed much less through precepts than in leading his monks by his example to a free, joyous, spontaneous, and responsible obedience. On the other hand, he will be judged if he has made himself culpable for his monks' lack of obedience (2:6).

The abbot should not, therefore, think that he bears the responsibility for the obedience of his monks only in the canonical sense. He has it even more in the moral sense, according to the teaching put forward by St Benedict in the second chapter. May he lead them to obedience, then, by the example of his life and the sobriety of his conduct.

# THE ABBOT'S DISCRETION

St Benedict advises the abbot in chapter sixty-four: *Non sit nimius* (64:16). The word is difficult to translate into modern languages. But its meaning is clear: Let him not overdo anything! In fact, the difference between the ideology of the *Rule of the Master* and certain concepts of the Rule of St Benedict is profound. It manifests itself especially in the person of the abbot and his task. The *Rule of the Master* presents the abbot as the omnipotent master, the *magister;* the monks are his disciples, his students, and in a certain sense, his children. The abbot has all the rights; if he commands he must quite simply be followed and obeyed. The monk listens to the abbot's teaching and submits to him. In the Rule of St Benedict, the abbot is a master also, the master of the spiritual life, master of the community, but above all he is father, pastor, even physician.

On the subject of the virtue of discretion required of the abbot by St Benedict (64:19) the profound difference between the two rules appears strongly. In chapter sixty-four, St Benedict gives us, as in a mirror, a portrait of the abbot, an image so human, lovable, and sympathetic that one remains fascinated by it. The abbot is indeed the keystone in the vault of the monastic community. By the virtue of discretion, he is obliged to consider above all else who he is and what he ought to obtain from the monks in order to work in all things for the benefit of souls (41:5) not one of which he is to lose (27:5). Is he not God's steward (64:7) responsible for the salvation of the souls of his sons (2:31, 33), to whom he ought above all strive to be useful (cf. 64:8)? If is *omni sagacitate et industria*, with all diligent know-how (27:5), with all prudence that he ought to try to save them all. So let him try to be more loved than feared (64:15), let his goodness prevail over too strict a justice (64:10). Let him be especially prudent in punishing (64:12-14).

This discretion is the cardinal virtue of prudence; by it, every act is performed in balance, in measure. This faculty of knowing how to distinguish and weigh with justice appears throughout the whole Rule. It permits the abbot, *miscens temporibus tempora* (2:24) because he knows how to evaluate the circumstances, to show sometimes the severity of a master and sometimes the gentleness of a father; he also knows how to treat each person according to his personal character (2:31). He knows how to use discretion in the arrangements to be made concerning daily life, caring for the needs of each person (RB 34), whether it concerns clothing (55:21), the measure of food (RB 39) or drink (RB 40). The principle of the Rule according to which the abbot 'should adapt and arrange all things in such a way that souls may be saved and that the brethren may do their work without just reason for complaint' (41:5) ought to be considered fundamental.

St Benedict's profoundly humane and balanced attitude has often given rise, and still gives rise, to broad interpretations of the Rule. We must not forget, however, that if St Benedict on the one hand 'hopes to establish nothing rigorous or painful' (Prol. 46), if he even sometimes allows a choice among several possible options (18:22), he still insists that the Rule be observed well (3:7), and in fact, most especially for the abbot, it is a strict obligation (64:20). For it would be easy, on the pretext of justifying some arbitrary change, to appeal to the Rule's spirit of discretion while tending against this very discretion by wanting to tip the scales too much in the direction of imprudent or uncalled for mitigations.

St Benedict's attitude of discretion appears particularly important and incisive when he faces the fundamental question of obedience. We read in chapter sixty-four: 'In his commands, the abbot should be far-sighted and circumspect; whether the work he enjoins concerns God or the things of this world, let him act discreetly and moderately, and let him recall the discretion of the holy patriarch Jacob, who said, If I tire my flocks by over-driving them, they will perish in one day' (64:17f.).

If we analyze the fifth chapter, 'On Obedience', borrowed by St Benedict almost entirely from the *Rule of the Master*, we see obedience presented as a virtue which allows no exceptions. One must obey, one must submit. Obedience is to be prompt, immediate, and the true disciple shows himself precisely through his obedience. It is a good and exact teaching, impressive in its logic, but lacking, perhaps, certain nuances. St Benedict, the aged abbot of Monte Cassino, realized this very well. For him, obedience is not only a theory, it is an act of a being of flesh and blood, of a real person. He knew that account must be taken of certain situations, and that a Rule lived by monks, to be complete, ought to speak of these. That was why he added to the *Rule of the Master* the words cited above, even adding the sixty-eighth chapter—let us admit that he wanted one who added them—'Concerning the Case Where a Brother is Commanded to do Something Impossible'. So it is a matter of a *casus*, a case of casuistry, if you wish, where St Benedict admits the possibility, the eventuality of the abbot imposing something impossible on a monk. We see in reading the Rule and in studying its sources that St Benedict was acquainted with the ancient monastic literature. He probably knew the Rule of St Pachomius and especially Cassian.

Now in the biography of St Pachomius, the first abbot and legislator of cenobites, we find a significant anecdote. St Pachomius, on arriving at one of his monasteries to make the visitation, heard it said that the children destined for the monastic life were using the moments when they were left without supervision, to climb a fig tree to eat the figs! Here indeed was an unforeseen situation! St Pachomius ordered the gardener, Brother Jonas, to apply the radical solution and cut down the fig tree. Brother Jonas was an excellent monk, and wanted to obey; he said to the abbot visitor: 'But, my Father, these fig trees give us a lot to eat, it would really be a shame to cut down this tree'. St Pachomius, like a true wise man, took the objection into account, did not maintain his order, and let the fig tree continue its existence.

There were in the desert spiritual masters who commanded their disciples to do impossible things, for example, to water a dry stick planted in the ground; this was to train them in obedience. History even recounts that once the fruits grown on one of these dry sticks, watered without respite and without discouragement by an obedient monk, were displayed in a public church.

St Benedict, therefore, adds this sixty-eighth chapter to his Rule to tell us how the abbot ought to act in this matter: 'If it happens that a brother is commanded to do something difficult or impossible, he should receive the command with all meekness and obedience. If however he thinks the weight of the burden altogether exceeds the measure of his strength, he should present to the superior the reasons for his inability'. St Benedict permits the monk who has been given a difficult assignment to explain himself, requiring at the same time that the abbot, for his part, lend an attentive ear. In place of a rigid commandment, we find a precept, firm, no doubt, but linked to the possibility of reconsideration if all else fails. The abbot ought, then, to join firmness to flexibility, authority to prudence, resoluteness to an open mind and dialogue. To lead souls to God is the principal goal of the monastic life; thus, discretion demands that this never be lost from sight in his commands. He ought to be neither inflexible nor easy-going, but a father who treats his monks as a father, with that love which can find the right balance. He ought to be disposed and open to dialogue when he deems it necessary. The abbot ought not to let himself be turned back from what he considers just and salutary by the trifles presented by some monk or by the community, and not let himself be drawn into endless and useless discussions. Let him not be worried (64:16) about risking his authority by listening quietly to the opinions of a monk, nor obstinate when real and sufficient proofs counsel him to withdraw a command. Prudence demands that he remain master of his judgment in the sense of what is better.

This spirit of discretion and prudence is characteristic of St Benedict. The monastic world was won little by little by this sane balance to his Rule, until it became the only monastic rule in force in the West. And if eventually a new formula of religious life is again born of it, it will probably not depart from the spirit of St Benedict on this point.

Does not the abbot imitate the absolute uprightness of the heavenly Father whose place he holds if he strives to learn the virtue of magnanimity? It will help him remain above the attachments and petty passions which risk falsifying his judgment and making him tip the scales until he has lost his balance and his *discretio*.

# THE ABBOT
# AND HIS OFFICERS

The exercise of the abbot's power and the latitude he gives the officers in their respective charges is a problem which sometimes troubles communities. The peace of the community depends largely on a good balance between these two factors.

On the one hand, the abbot, according to the Rule, is responsible from beginning to end for the good order of community life. He appoints deans who are subject to his instructions (21:2,3), the prior (65:15) who ought to undertake nothing against the will or the arrangements made by the abbot (65:16), and the cellarer who ought to do nothing without the abbot's consent (31:4). It is the abbot who must make decisions after having consulted the community (3:5). He is the father of souls, and his monks owe him a faithful obedience in their spiritual conduct; without his consent, they ought not to take the initiative in ascetical matters (49:10).

On the other hand, St Benedict's spirit of discretion and his utter sincerity do not allow us to think that he would install a prior—a bit reluctantly, true—deans, a cellarer, or other officers as simple titulars for imaginary duties they do not exercise. He desires that reality correspond to the title and that the officers use their abilities. In other words, St Benedict has observed and practised what is called the principle of subsidiarity, which recognizes a real competence and authority for all those who occupy a lower rank in the social hierarchy of the community as necessary for carrying out a task properly. It corresponds to the thought of St Benedict: everyone ought to be capable of using his initiative in the place he occupies.

Without a doubt, St Benedict did not want to have the sort of management from the abbot which regulates everything, meddles in everything, and treats the monks as if they were children. An abbot who would not leave a wholesome liberty to the initiative of each one, would be fostering a kind of childishness in his monastery. The Rule, on the contrary, leaves us with the impression that St Benedict wanted to foster the normal development of his monks' personality. We find this first of all in the area of general personal attitudes, whether it concerns freedom for prayer (52:4), initiative in work (57:1), or, more still, in the exercise of asceticism and the monastic virtues. Obedience should not suffocate liberty but steer our efforts toward what is better.

In what concerns the officers' freedom of action, let us take the example of the deans to whom St Benedict obviously allows broad possibilities for initiative. 'Let them exercise a universal supervision over their deaneries in conformity with the precepts of God and the orders of the abbot' (21:2); St Benedict says clearly that there is a sharing of jurisdiction and responsibility between the abbot and the dean (21:3).

Another case is that of the cellarer. The fact that he is considered a father of the whole community (31:2) is already significant. In attributing to him the same characteristic as the abbot, being a father to all, St Benedict shows without equivocation that the cellarer exercises a veritable paternal power, and that he is not only the abbot's shadow. He also gives him this charter of universal jurisdiction: 'Let him have care of all things' (31:3).

One may wonder at the reason that made St Benedict set down vigorous restrictions to the liberty of action he gives the prior, the cellarer, and the deans in such a way that they may not venture to act beyond the precepts of the abbot—e.g. RB 65:16: 'he should do nothing contrary to his will or regulations'.

Among the principles of social life which enter into play here, the most important for St Benedict is the one which maintains the unity guaranteed by obedience, and this, for the good of souls. It is more than obvious that an abbot who is too authoritarian contributes to the devaluation of the spirit of obedience, first among the officers who are tempted to independence, and next, among the monks in general until the virtue through which the monk approaches God crumbles gradually away (71:2). To act this way would be to undermine and cause the entire edifice of monastic life to crumble. The principle of subsidiarity comes second. The abbot is above all concerned with and responsible for the good of souls, for the success of the monastic life; safeguarding the liberty of his officers' action comes afterwards.

It remains no less true that St Benedict wants to allow his regents a real autonomy; probably this explains why he threatens them so sharply about insubordination. He hopes to gain their obedience by this and to safeguard their liberty within the given limits.

Fundamentally, this attitude arises from the double orientation of the principle of subsidiarity. As the superior allows his regents autonomy of action when they are able to act by themselves, so he retains the necessary control and the right to intervene in a case where intervention is necessary. St Benedict refrains from creating a theoretical disquisition on the subject. If he does not warn the abbot against the danger of authoritarianism, so also does he not mention the case of an officer who does not possess all the necessary capabilities for his office, but still remains a fairly good officer. To protect himself against the difficulties which circumstances may cause to arise, St Benedict quite simply appeals to obedience, that is to say, to the abbot's power of entrusting his officer with some jurisdiction while withholding another; the case of the cellarer is typical in this regard: 'Let him have charge of all that the abbot has entrusted to him; but let him not meddle in what he has forbidden to him' (31:15).

It can happen that there is no one in a community capable of assuming some duty. The abbot ought then to substitute himself to the extent necessary. By the same token that he is responsible for announcing the hour of common prayer (47:1), he is also responsible if the infirmarians fail in their duty (36:6,10), and he has to fill the gaps left by other officers. This is normal, since he is the father of the family. Now in a family, if a son fails in his responsibilities, or if he lacks the competence which is demanded of him for the execution of certain duties, the father has to fill the gap, judiciously, prudently, and charitably, according to need, so that all is done well. As a matter of fact, the abbot cannot excuse himself in any way and say: 'This is his business, if he does it wrong, it is his fault, it's none of my business!' He ought to realize that in the final analysis, he is responsible in the house of God because he is the administrator of both its spiritual and temporal aspects.

This fact should in no way remove the sense of responsibility of all those who are put in charge of an office. Each one ought to proceed with competence, but according to the abbot's instructions. Here again, let us notice St Benedict's prudence. It is easy to draw a theoretical portrait of this or that officer as St Benedict did of the cellarer. But a concrete man in real life perhaps only remotely approaches that picture. St Benedict knows that we must take the concrete situation into account. So the Rule leaves the abbot the right of distributing duties according to ability, for example, sharing responsibilities among the cellarer and the other officers. The cellarer, by the very fact of his nomination, does not enter into a series of rights and duties whose invariable list is already drawn up. On the contrary, the prudence of the abbot ought to give him all the necessary instructions: verbal instructions and even written ones. We see here once again with what prudence St Benedict defines the role of the abbot. No authoritarianism on his part. He is above all a father, not a lord with absolute power. If he had to see to everything, control everything, he would weigh heavy on his sons, his monks, and the atmosphere would become oppressive.

The abbot ought to be like a father with his children. How do things work in a family? Let us consider, for example, a man who has a big business and three sons; what does he do? Little by little he has his sons get into the running of the business. They know that someday they will succeed their father, and quite naturally, they become more and more interested. They remain sons and do not wish to supplant their father. But the father, because he is a father, rejoices in his sons' interest. He transfers responsibility to them gradually, to the extent that he sees that they can cope with it; he helps them enter into affairs, to understand them better, giving them every opportunity to study, expand, and modernize the business. He facilitates their opportunities for carrying on negotiations, because he is a father and he is interested that the negotiations fare well in his sons' hands.

That is an example. The abbot is very interested that his sons, the monks, work properly, that their personality develops, that it becomes an integrated personality, and to achieve this, he leads them to develop the sense of responsibility proper to an adult. Since the abbot ought to be a loving father, he is able to measure the abilities of each person. His charity stimulates the potentialities of all so that they truly work up to their abilities. In that way the monastic community is a real family. A deep understanding reigns there. Everyone feels appreciated by the father, even though he does not hesitate to point out mistakes committed along the way. It is far more an encouragement than a correction or a humiliation. In doing so, the abbot truly forms his community. He trains men, superiors, cellarers, abbots. He forms men of worth who will be capable, when the day comes when he disappears from the scene, of taking over the helm, or in any case, of having the necessary knowledge to take on some responsibility. Is this not the mark of a real leader, to find or to train men capable of facing the tasks which new times bring?

By way of conclusion, let us consider the father abbot surrounded by his officers. He appreciates them and allows them great freedom of action in the exercise of their activities. That very liberty makes them feel the importance of their duties and at the same time the obligation of competence always incumbent upon a leader.

Let the abbot not be jealous nor annoyed; let him not give the impression of being restricted in his power by that of his officers. He ought to think sometimes of the words of St John the Baptist: 'He must increase and I must decrease' (Jn 3:30). He will thus experience what every true father experiences in his life. If he forms good sons, it will come about that he retires little by little as old age approaches and his sons enter the business and have the necessary competence to run the house. The abbot can die in peace, or perhaps, when the time comes, retire from affairs if God, or Holy Church wills it, as she now asks us to retire.

On the other hand, the officers should know how to act as sons and as faithful collaborators with the abbot. They will not lose any of their initiative if they know how to exercise it in accord with him. If they know how to have confidence in him, the confidence will be mutual. And the house of God will be administered wisely by wise men (53:22).

# THE EXERCISE OF POWER AS SERVICE

Christ has given the ecclesiastical authority the extraordinary power of binding and loosing, of opening the gates of the kingdom of heaven and of barring the entrance. In conferring on Peter a power which set him over other men, he made him leader, master, pastor, and judge of his brothers and gave him the keys of the kingdom of heaven. The apostles also received the power of binding and loosing in which all who exercise jurisdiction in Holy Church since then share.

The abbot in his monastery holds the power of binding and loosing. At his installation, he receives the keys; these are not the keys of Peter, and one does not say to him the words of Christ: 'I will give you the keys of the kingdom of heaven'. These are, first of all, the keys of the monastery whose gates he can open or close; but they also represent indirectly that power of the keys of the kingdom of heaven. The abbot can receive someone into communion with the community and he can also excommunicate. He has the power of the keys in all the acts of the exercise of his jurisdiction.

Ecclesiastical superiors are brothers among brothers, but, since they possess a power, they are in some cases above other men. Equality, superiority: two poles, two situations which pose some problems nowadays. If the emphasis is placed on the notion of superiority, then people of today speak of the Constantinian Church and declare that it was not the Lord's intention to underline so heavily the pre-eminence of those who hold power. A cross, a ring, a miter, all distinctive signs of prelates, do they correspond to the Lord's idea in sending his apostles into the world to be ministers of salvation for their brothers? People today, however, admit that the Church is a hierarchical society built on the rock of Peter, the Peter who holds the keys, but they also like to underscore the Church is also a brotherly society: 'You are all brothers' (Mt 23:8).

As a matter of fact, the pope is our brother, the bishop is our brother, the abbot is our brother, but because superiors have jurisdiction in the Church they possess a real power ordained to the salvation of others. Through it, the whole person can be plunged into the grace of the Lord, to use an image borrowed from baptism.

More than once, Jesus let us know his thoughts on this subject: You know, he said, that the leaders of the nations command them as masters and that great men make them feel their power. It ought not to be so among you. On the contrary, he who wishes to be great among you will make himself your servant, and he who would be first among you will make himself your servant. So also the Son of Man did not come to be served but to serve and to give his life as a ransom for many (Mt 20:25ff.). Let there be no question of domination, but of brotherly service. Power is service. It is necessary to serve much more than to dominate (64:5).

Let us add that all of us share this condition in different degrees, for often we find a certain power given to us. The abbot or the prior do not hold the power of the monastery alone; every act of power is a service. Even the cook exercises a power over the brothers who work in the kitchen, and even over those he feeds—a power which can be formidable.

This requirement places the man who exercises power in a continual dialectic: to exercise power, to exercise it as a service. It is necessary to know how to serve, but to serve in such a way as not to betray the power which is given specifically to be useful. You see the extent of the problem and the weight of the spiritual responsibility. The exercise of power presents itself in our life, therefore, as a dilemma which must constantly be mastered; and it is to the extent that we are able to master it that we will show that we understand a little of what Our Lord, the servant of us all, wanted to teach us, and that we are walking in his footsteps.

Where is the profound solution to the problem of power and of service? We must seek it in a force which surpasses the two contraries, embraces them, and absorbs them in order to unite them. What is it? It is brotherly love which helps us unite these two poles. Through it, we intimately mix the powers of ruling and of being truly servants. By it that love, whose characteristic is to penetrate, will penetrate us in making us brothers. What is it to be brothers? To be brothers is precisely to love. The relationship of fraternity is a relationship of intimacy. And since Our Lord used the word brothers he wishes to express by it that the relationship among us ought to be the most intimate one there is.

Perhaps we have not learned well enough to be brothers, while perhaps learning a little too much how to exercise power. In spite of this, we know perfectly well that this power is a service. But this theoretical knowledge does not always lead us to actions which would truly make us servants.

Another thing which impedes the spiritual development of the superior is the fact of being father and brother at the same time: little children do not always understand sufficiently that those who serve them have the right and the duty to govern them, and, they have on their side the obligation of obeying them. This lack of maturity is found sometimes among monks in the form of a kind of anti-paternal complex. Such attitudes do not help the superior to harmonize in himself the exercise of power and service. The education of superior and inferiors—I hesitate to call them that—has to be done mutually. The abbot will find it harder to act as the servant of all if he is too often forced to use his authority. It is very clear that even in this case he is making himself useful, serving his brothers, but they will distinguish less easily in an act of force the act of service being performed.

It is also clear that monks ought to possess the good sense and the maturity necessary to appreciate the humble and fraternal services of the abbot when he corrects them, exhorts them, so that he is not forced to act more as the *dirus magister* than as the *pius pater* (2:24). In other words, the abbot's action ought always to be a service, but the form of that action, of that service, must be adapted to the circumstances and temperaments (2:31).

Moreover, the Rule very clearly teaches us the manner of interpreting the power of the abbatial office. In chapters two and sixty-four, he is presented to us not only as the man responsible for running the monastery but also for the progress of each soul. Everything is referred to him. He is the father present everywhere in the house, leading everything, at least indirectly through his officers. Expressions of this sort might lead us to believe that St Benedict bestows a sort of universal authoritarianism on the abbot. Not in the least. St Benedict gives the abbot such power that nothing ought to escape his attention; this is to guarantee beginners, which we are, and the weak, which we remain, the constant support of his solicitude. So the abbot is presented as the servant of salvation. In following such a master, the disciple in his turn learns to make himself a servant and to give himself utterly.

The abbot must have the gift of discernment in order to lead his monks and give to each according to his personal needs. He ought to lead souls to the Lord in the spirit of Christ, with a profound respect for the personality of each and for what grace is working in him. If he sees a monk truly blossoming in Christ, he ought to employ reserve and restraint with him, for God himself has taken the formation of this soul in hand, and he should go so far as to say to him: 'My dear son, you have arrived at a state where you no longer need me. Go into the desert.'

In other words, he ought to adapt himself to the state of each person. What efforts (28:4) he should make on behalf of those who have gone astray! He ought to show the greatest care, *curam maximam* (36:10) for the weak, giving to each temperament what suits it: coaxing one, reprimanding another, scolding yet another (2:31). He ought to adapt himself to the character and state of each, *multorum servire moribus.* This willingness to adjust to different states of soul is the authentic expression of the will to serve the community. It follows from all this that the exercise of authority is always a service, even if that authority presents itself under the form of a punishment, or excommunication, or, in an extreme case, expulsion, provided the superior has no other aim than the individual's good and the common good.

The abbot is therefore truly a servant in his monastery; all his power is a power of service; he cannot pride himself on a power of domination. His only pride is in being his brothers' servant. To the extent that he has entered into this spirit of service, he has entered into the spirit of his duty as abbot.

To be father among men means to be a brother, but with a father's affection. To unite these two poles is not easy, but it is nevertheless the task incumbent on the abbot. He is not placed above the others, but laden with a burden even heavier than that of others, since he is not only a brother among brothers, but must know how to be a father to them. God himself has created this problem of duality. They are all brothers, but among these brothers are fathers and others are sons. Yet Our Lord demands that they all be servants.

By our whole attitude we should manifest our understanding of this great apostolate which is given to the pope, the bishops, the abbot, all superiors, and all fathers. Let us truly have within us that respect due the father and the confidence of always finding in him a brother. In this way we help our abbot to be at once father and brother and the servant of our salvation.

# THE "SENIORES"

In studying the structure of the monastic community, we may be struck by the importance the Rule gives the *seniores.* In taking up this theme, we need a definition at the very outset. As a matter of fact, the word *senior* does not necessarily mean an old man, as the reader quickly discovers. On the other hand, chapter thirty-seven of the Rule deals with old monks, for whom, as for children, it demands a special regime, because of their physical weakness. As porter of the monastery, St Benedict seems also to call for a monk of mature years (66:1).

On the other hand, the word senior by itself expresses a relationship of age between two or more persons, one of whom is older than the other. It is not necessarily a matter of advanced age as is the case with rank, established according to the priority of entry into the community.

Before studying this notion of *senior* in the Rule more closely, let us take a look at the same notion in Holy Scripture. Already among the Israelites, as indeed among all peoples, an important role fell to the *seniores* in family, social, and religious life. In the early Church, the *seniores* appear beside the apostles as holding authority with them (Acts 15:6,22f.). The very name *presbyteri*, the Christians appointed to the churches of the cities (Tit 1:5) makes one think of persons who are preferably elderly. But Timothy's example shows that this seniority was to be taken on the moral level, in the sense of experience and wisdom.

We meet the same idea of *senior* among the first monks. In the primitive monastic life, in fact, the *seniores* were the masters of the spiritual life, witnesses to the monastic tradition and wisdom; they were able to give the *logia*, the savings, the good counsels, which their disciples were to follow. In this sense, abbot and senior were practically synonyms.

In St Benedict the expression *senior* takes on, first of all, a juridical meaning. Like a good Roman he wanted his community to be well structured. For him this structure is furnished by ranking the monks in order of seniority. The *senior* is someone who entered the monastery before the *junior.* Someone who has entered the monastery at the second hour of the day must know that he is 'junior' to someone who entered at the first hour, whatever his age or dignity (63:8). By this notion of time, the *senior* is, therefore, the person who is 'prior' (63:10,12,15; cf. 71:4,6,7). At first glance, it may seem to us that ranking brethren among themselves like this is based on chance: one entered an hour before the other. But, as the examples cited by St Benedict show Samuel admonishing the high priest Heli, and Daniel confounding the wicked judges of Susanna, St Benedict sees in the priority of entrance a priority of vocation and divine grace. It is, therefore, in some way God himself who has established the ranks by his grace. In some way, for with his good sense, St Benedict knew that in human acts, even if they are determined by grace, so many human elements enter in that no one can say with certainty that priority of entry is an effect of grace. For this reason, St Benedict allows the abbot to change the ranks when he thinks there is a just reason for doing so (63:1,4,7; 2:18f.).

There we have the structure of the monastic society,

established by order of entrance into the community. The rank of the brethren, now established in an objective and juridical way, is to have many consequences. First of all, there is the matter of precedence in community life and community functions. The senior precedes his junior at the kiss of peace, to communion, in intoning the Psalms, in his place in choir (63:4; 2:19; 60:4,70; 61:11). Priority of entry may enter in even in cases where the abbot judges it well to give a monk a rank higher than his own. Thus, a priest promoted above his rank ought to return to it in matters preliminary to an election or in deciding an important question (60:6f.).

Besides, the senior–junior relationship gives St Benedict a line of conduct to follow in applying the precept: 'Give one another precedence' (72:4, from Rom 12:10). The junior ought, therefore, to show concrete signs of his respect for the senior (63:10,12; 4:70); he rises when his senior passes in front of him, he offers him his seat and does not sit until invited by him (63:16); if he meets him, he greets him and asks his blessing (15). Even mutual obedience lends itself to the criterion of seniority, and thus the juniors owe an obedience full of charity and eagerness to their seniors (71:4). And if a junior sees that the senior is displeased with him, he ought to hurry to make satisfaction and so calm his spirit (71:7f.).

St Benedict, it is characteristic and very interesting to note, does not want to leave the exercise of obedience, mutual respect, and fraternal affection to chance or simply to the good will of the wise, but he organizes the use of these virtues to facilitate them and assure their practice. We today might be tempted to think that this system would take the spontaneity out of virtue. St Benedict, a better psychologist, was not of that opinion. Knowing man and his tendency to justify himself in his own eyes, to believe that he is right to refrain from taking the first step, to minimize his own faults, St Benedict knows that without established rules to help and encourage us in obedience and mutual charity, no one will budge. He does not, let us note, intend to correct faults on the basis of justice, in many cases impossible, but through humility. This is why he institutionalizes the procedure in obliging the junior to be the more humble, since he is the inferior. This makes the act of humility easier for him; the senior, given his rank, would find it more difficult. This way of organizing the exercise of virtue may seem simplistic to us, but as a matter of fact, it is full of human wisdom.

It is, moreover, the non-observance of these simple and wise rules that causes persistent and frequent misunderstandings, suspicions, antipathies, calumnies, and even hatred in communities shaken profoundly by 'unsettled accounts' that lead to mutual aversion, to divisions, and to departures which a well-ordered charity could and should have headed-off in time.

For St Benedict, we understand, the hierarchical order which he establishes in the community with his remarkable juridical sense is not simply a social organization necessary for maintaining peace and tranquillity, but above all, a system for aiding and even inspiring virtue. Rank in the community is a constant call to the exercise of humility and charity. The over-estimation made today of certain forms of charity, such as spontaneity, creativity, simplicity, at the expense of such other forms as renunciation of personal satisfaction and freedom, causes many no longer to understand the language of St Benedict. They sincerely and ingenuously believe that the average person today no longer needs the aids and stimuli offered by the Rule. Very learned psychological analyses confirm them in their opinion. Perennial human pride plumes itself today on an exaggerated optimism, to its own detriment.

Confronted with this highly hierarchical system of St Benedict, could someone ask whether the seniors did not find themselves in a privileged condition, poorly suited to ease the practice of virtue in them, and even capable of fostering in them a certain arrogance toward the juniors? St Benedict's own thought gives us the answer, provided it is well understood and applied by all. Let us not forget that for him there is not one group of seniors, enjoying the advantages of the system, and then a group of juniors forming an inferior class. According to the Rule, each of us is junior to someone or other, while being perhaps senior to certain other brothers. We are, therefore, senior and junior at the same time. This fact puts the monk constantly in a demanding situation among his brothers.

Especially should we not think that being senior to another brother dispenses us from being constantly alert to becoming worthy of his respect (63:10,12,15f.), to showing him the affection due him (63:10; cf. 4:71), to serving him as a model of virtue (7:55), a counsellor and a spiritual guide (4:50, 46:5), as a stimulus in fraternal correction (23:2). Yes, it is necessary to have the supernatural spirit awake to accept the tokens of obedience (71:4) and the junior's humility with modesty and discretion (71:8), and especially to practise the natural and supernatural esteem which he owes the person of the junior, his brother in Christ (63:12), that junior who may bear the word of God more, if it please Him, than all the seniors (3:3).

In short, being a senior indicates first of all a social rank. But to see nothing in it but that, or especially that, would be to remain in a narrow legalism, to be incapable of understanding the aim of the right which is precisely instruction in a moral attitude. To be socially 'senior' ought to lead to being senior in the intimacy of oneself and all one's person. In this way, we will merely be following the thought of St Benedict, for whom every structure is a means to perfection, charity, and holiness. This is why he energetically insists on teaching us not to see in physical age a right conferring superiority over others (63:5), for example, over the children (cf. 70:6). Even the dignity (63:8) of priesthood gives no title to believe oneself superior to others (60:5, 62:3), or to non-priests. To be a senior means to have to precede others by one's virtue, and especially by the virtue of humility, the mother of wisdom. Those who pretend to deserve their brethren's consideration by reason of their years of profession are far from the spirit of St Benedict, as are those who, for the same reason, make much of honorary titles! The Rule excludes false clericalism and all undue forms of discrimination. Only virtue counts (2:21). Yes, they are far from a real understanding of the Rule who think they can take all these wise prescriptions lightly.

We see, therefore, how the concept of 'senior', juridical at first, is connected with the moral signification of that notion. We have already met this signification in the Holy Scriptures.

So now we understand better who these seniors are of whom St Benedict speaks so often, and to whom he gives a lofty position in his monastic society. Certainly, they are not necessarily the eldest according to time of entry. In analyzing the content of the notion of *senior*, we find there, first, an element of experience, then wisdom born of experience, and finally, stable and solid virtue.

First, experience. We may suppose it among the seniors advanced in age, because life itself is the mistress of experience, that precious gift, if at least, it is lived with openness and intelligence. Experience gives us serenity, preserves us from judgments that are too quick and superficial. And since it is the fruit of reflection, it furnishes us with clearer notions of life in general, of the spiritual and monastic life in particular, and of the ways of the Lord. Here we see well that old age is not necessarily the same as the wisdom of old age, because not everyone knows equally well how to be disciples of life. The true senior, therefore, is a wise person, and the two notions of experience and human wisdom are blended. Wisdom supposes knowledge, but adds to it the reflection, sympathy, and prudence of the adult. Now, experience and wisdom, in order to grow, need a certain time, which enters in like a constitutive element of experience. It is, therefore, experience and human wisdom which characterize the senior, while the juniors, still at the beginning of their exploits, little by little acquire what will with time make them seniors.

This evolution costs an effort, the effort of persevering virtue. It is by climbing the ladder of humility that the spiritual beginner becomes, in greater or less time, a senior in virtue. A young person is easily led to overestimate himself and does not yet recognize sufficiently his own limitations. The senior, on the contrary, has had the, often painful, experience of his limitations, his virtues, his abilities, and his talents. By making this apprenticeship and having experience of himself, he has had the chance to become humble, and more moderate in his judgments on others, and more compassionate provided, however, that he knew how to profit from the means of virtue which life has offered him. This makes him a real *senior*.

Neither human knowledge nor training, unless it be that of the heart, necessarily enters into the notion of *senior*. Often a man who is simple but upright and wise, preserved from the deformities of poorly assimilated knowledge, keeps the eye of the intellect clearer and the heart purer for the truth. He may be a true *senior*.

St Benedict does not give a definition of the *senior*. But one is easily deduced from the Rule, as we have just done. A glance over the functions he gives to the senior confirms this interpretation. For these functions, of a moral character, specifically presuppose experience, wisdom, and virtue. The seniors ought to be, as it is said of the deans, 'brothers of good reputation and holy life' (21:1), capable of giving spiritual counsel if it is asked of them (46:5, 4:50). They also oversee good order, whether of the dormitory (22:3,7), or, in the absence of the abbot or the responsible superiors, of the refectory (56:2), or during hours of reading (48:17). They are not only given an office of supervision to forestall human weaknesses, but also to correct them. The superior is not necessarily called on to admonish and correct first, but, according to the Gospel (cf. Mt 18:15ff.), it is above all an obligation of charity for the monk to give his brother the gift of fraternal correction. When St Benedict lays this duty on the seniors (23:2), he stays entirely within his tendency prudently to institutionalize this service, for reasons we have seen above. The office of *sympectae* with its similar aim, is therefore entrusted to wise seniors (27:2). As the master of novices is chosen from among the seniors (58:6), so too are the deans and the prior taken from among them.

In a monastery, the function of the seniors appears, then, to be of a decisive importance for community life and the goal it pursues: holiness of life. Have we the impression

264

perhaps, in reading some author or other, of a monastic life
overly centered on the person of the abbot? We are not here
lessening his preponderant role, but underlining that he is
solidly supported and at the same time moderated by the
activities and functions of the seniors who, obviously in
accord with the abbot and in intimate union with him,
exercise a real and decisive authority. St Benedict speaks of
'orders' given by the seniors (23:1), he insists that obedience
be given to superiors (5:15, 7:34); that recognizes, therefore,
a right and an obligation they have of participating in the
salutary function of authority. It would not be exact to
speak of a collegial exercise of authority set in motion by
the abbot and the seniors whom he has chosen, but nevertheless, St Benedict probably had the intention of decentraliz-
ing the authority in order to give it greater credibility and
better to underscore its entirely spiritual and religious
character.

This same intention made St Benedict decide to prescribe
that the abbot take counsel with the seniors rather than call
the whole community together if the affairs to be dealt with
were not of the greatest importance (3:12). The decisions
made by the abbot, surrounded and supported by the seniors,
generally carry weight with the community.

What are we to think, after all this, of the widespread
custom within monasticism, of having a certain number
of religious elected by the community as members of
the council? St Benedict, you realize, says nothing about
this. Do we stay within this concept by substituting elected
counsellors for the seniors? If these counsellors correspond
to the criteria held by St Benedict in defining the seniors,
the spirit of the Rule is safeguarded, but on the express
condition, for those of the community allowed to express
their preferences by way of a vote, that they respect the very
supernatural criteria advanced by the Rule. Considered under
this aspect alone, the establishment of senior deans or
counsellors by vote could be approved. If, on the other
hand, too-natural criteria preside at the elections, then the
candidates could not be considered as seniors according to
the Rule, and the goal envisaged by St Benedict would not
be attained.

In ending this long conference on the seniors, we make one observation: often the young people of today dislike to hear of such matters. Many do not understand the seniors and are not understood by them. They claim to live in a different world. And this is sometimes true. But, then, these elders are not the 'seniors' of the Rule. Maybe they understood their own day, but not well enough to draw from it the positive and practical lessons necessary to new times. The young people, on their side, close themselves up in their own ideas, which are often incomplete and unrealistic; their views have not yet been purified by the baptism of fire of a sane and painful life. Both the young and the old ought to understand that there is no progress without tradition, nor true tradition which is not open to progress. As a family without children dies, so the life of a monastic community is assured by a mutual understanding and trust among age groups. The function of the seniors is to gain souls (58:6), to love the juniors (63:10), therefore, to open themselves to them, to know how to bring out the good and the true which is in their young ideas and desires. The young, for their part, ought to open themselves to the wisdom of living, the patrimony of the monastic community handed down by the seniors. St Benedict showed great respect for the *doctrina patrum*, the teaching of the Fathers (73:2,5), and their traditions (18:25, 48:8), upon which the whole Rule is based. A young man who does not succeed in understanding sincerely this obligation to respect the seniors (4:70), a respect including not only their person, but their teaching (23:1) and their examples (7:55), would be mistaken on an essential point of the ideology of the Rule and of the healthy functioning of the monastic community. He would have no place in the benedictine life. With time, he would constitute a contentious and disruptive element dangerous to peace. Similarly, the elderly who systematically shut themselves off from the spirit of openness, which is the fruit of a sincere love for the young (4:71), could be guilty of a great loss of vitality for their community.

If it is well followed, this simple formula of the Rule: 'Let the juniors respect the seniors, and let the seniors love the juniors' (63:10)—assures the balance and the dynamic peace of the community, and makes of the diversity of ages not a source of problems, but a force of spiritual and human wealth.

# SOME ADMONITIONS FOR A NOVICE GUARDIAN

Does the Rule of St Benedict, written in the sixth century, answer the real needs of modern youth, and can it be understood by them? Is it able to satisfy their rightful and wholesome aspirations?

We cannot solve this question with generalities. Before entering into the matter, let us remark that the question of the relevance of the Rule could have been posed by every generation since the time of St Benedict. The manifestations of the past run the risk of not being believed in because they are not up to date. Our fault, but it is the fault of people of all times, is that we do not penetrate enough into the meaning of the traditions, their substance, the reasons for their origin, because we do not know history well enough and we see too little how it concerns us. As a consequence, everything is perpetually new and unprecedented for us. Now, if we immerse ourselves in history, we find that, under different aspects, man has always been the same. Certainly, structures change, society evolves, but man is always man, with his faults and virtues, his abilities, desires, aspirations, inclinations, and tendencies. In the past he did not go to the moon, but he always hoped to go. The technical means he uses today, are the fruits of long research. Let us study our history, and we will find there the man of all times. Yet the human tendency is to call what it discovers 'new' and to consider the past outmoded.

Let us pose a question here: The experience of life, the basic usages, the norms recommended by the Rule, the human experiences on which they are based—can they say anything to the person of today? Can their language, their message, be grasped by the young people of our time? In order to examine the Rule in this light, let us take a concrete example whose interest is applicable to young people in an immediate way. It will provide its own answer.

In chapter 58, 'On the Manner of Receiving Brothers', St Benedict discusses the reception and training to be given a candidate to the monastic life. He responds there to the aspirations of the young man, consequently. He ought to be 'won', according to the expression used concerning the master of novices, who ought to be capable 'of winning souls' (58:6), of attracting them. He must know how to lead the young man to ask with St Paul: 'Lord, what would you have me to do?' (Acts 9:6). The Gospel itself ought to be preached in a way that really reveals it as good, as wonderful, news. He ought to act, St Benedict says, in such a way as to convince him and win him for Christ's army.

Today, as in the past, the task of the novice master, charged with 'winning souls' in order to enroll them in Christ's army by taking up the arms of obedience (cf. Prol. 3), remains the same. The question is instead whether the way the Rule envisages that task still corresponds to the aspirations and the needs of today's youth.

Let us admit at once that St Benedict does not give us a complete pedagogical doctrine, and we must not seek it in the Rule. Obviously, we have to complete it by our presentday knowledge. What interests us is knowing whether the pedagogical principles of today can be reconciled with St Benedict's teaching. Before answering, let us first look at the difficulties which young people today encounter, and the positions they take on certain basic problems of human contact. Next, we will take note of St Benedict's positions on the same problems.

In the first place, young people do not easily accept authority. Ready-made rules annoy them. Next, they accept only what they are convinced of. They dislike uniformity. Finally, stability poses serious problems for them. Let us take these points one by one.

The difficulty in accepting authority. It is a fact that the young person of today seeks a friend and not a master in his teacher. He does not like having an authority which imposes itself in compelling fashion. Such methods do not lead him to an interior conviction. Can St Benedict understand such a person? The candidate, obviously, ought to be led, in time, to accept authority; this is indispensable. Without it, the Church itself would crumble. We accept God's authority and also human authority rightly constituted in civil life. Without authority, life in society is no longer possible. In the religious life, the problem is the same. There is the hierarchical order to accept, a social order based on the idea of the mission received from God and transmitted by the Church.

How does St Benedict go about getting these ideas accepted? It is necessary, he says, to give the novice a 'senior' (58:6). What is a senior? A brother capable of 'winning souls'. St Benedict does not speak of a 'superior' who would assert himself; but, on the contrary, a man who knows how to win souls gradually. He is first presented to the novice as a friend, an older brother, able to help him penetrate into the Holy Rule (58:9,12,13). It is as a friend that this novice master little by little gives the young man the ideas that he ought to understand, to assimilate, and accept. This friend, this father, this older brother, ought to be concerned for his novice (58:7), follow and watch him in a friendly way, but with a great attention (58:6). The way in which he himself exercises his authority ought to introduce the novice to an understanding of true authority, at once firm, patient, brotherly, and one which, by the way it is exercised, indicates its source, God. The novice master is charged with showing the aspirant what the monastic life is. He will explain to him beforehand all the hard and difficult things by which we go to God (58:8). While doing this prudently, little by little, and as a brother, he will hide nothing from the young man. By nature, he is generally courageous and idealistic, and much more enthusiastic for what goes all the way than for half-measures. Thus obedience, the young man will learn, is the road which leads to God (71:2). Without authority and without the obedience which accepts and recognizes authority, the monastic life would only be a beautiful and deceptive illusion. To want to go to God as a free agent would be to end up in disaster.

A second difficulty to be overcome by young people today lies in having to accept a standard rule. Formerly, it is said, it was easier to accept and respect a rule which was presented as well-established and which had age-old experience in its favor. But, that way of thinking is less familiar to the psychology of today's young people. They understand the need for a rule, but one they have established themselves by their own observations they like to control the experiment and discuss it. It is quite obvious that we cannot place the Rule in question, since neither the young people nor even, often enough, the eldest monks have what it takes to undertake the job. To write a Rule takes a saint, not commissions and dialogues. Nevertheless, it is right to take this attitude of the young into account. Let us see if St Benedict allows us the possibility.

Obviously, haggling over the Rule is not permitted. Nevertheless, St Benedict gives us the commission of proceeding in such a way that souls may be won (58:6). From the time of his entry, then, we need to educate the young man little by little according to his own way of thinking and his capabilities. We need to show him the Rule, not as a sacred monument, but through dialogue, to let him seek and find a spiritual path which permits him to some of it. Then, once he has arrived at some knowledge and interior acceptance of the Rule, if we may hope he will persevere in his efforts (58:9), we need to say to him: 'You see now what the Rule is. You can take it or leave it. If you do not yet understand it very well, do not lose patience (10f.). Three times it is presented to him in this spirit. But it is not at all necessary to present the Rule to the novice as a sort of formal notice; we must give him time to reflect calmly in the patience of faith and hope. And it is only when he has a real grasp of it that the possibility of a choice is presented to him: 'If you are able to observe it, enter; if you cannot, leave in complete liberty' (10). He is entirely free in his choice. Let us notice the importance St Benedict gives to 'deliberation' (58:14,16): it ought to be long and well thought-out, to prepare for an act on the part of the novice which is definitive, firm, and stable.

Although a relaxed atmosphere is suitable for the novitiate, this does not mean that life there should be without a rule. The task is to find a method of making it understood and accepted. Let us not forget that the young man arriving at the door of the monastery, moved by the desire to meet the Lord, is generally very little prepared psychologically for monastic life, and because of this, a too abrupt introduction to all that this life implies may have the effect of a shcok on him. The novice master ought to suppose that God has sent him to the monastery, and that he himself has to answer for that vocation before Him Who is its Author. The Rule is there for the sake of souls, and not the souls for the Rule. Let him act, therefore, as a true father, and open its treasures with the keys of charity.

Let us pass on, now, to the third obstacle: to accept a rule before being convinced of its value. Everyone, of every age, sometimes finds himself confronted with this problem. But for the candidate to the monastic life, there is a solution. The novitiate is there precisely in order to give him the time to become convinced little by little. The community ought, therefore, to recognize the speical situation of those who come to it. It ought to take into account a tendency to non-conformity which the young man likes sometimes to display in order to express his liberty of spirit before allowing himself to be convinced of the legitimacy of some requirement. Is it not on account of this concern that St Benedict wanted a separation between the novitiate and the community? He did not use the word 'separation', but its reality considerably surpassed what we practise today. In the old cistercian monasteries, the novitiate was separate, in a house distinct from the rest of the monastery. The community life of the novices actually ought, in terms of the Rule, to be spent there. There was even a refectory and a dormitory there for them (58:5). The community, on their side, saw them at the Divine Office and thus shared in the task of the novice master by observing their behavior (7). Apart from this, they had to live separate from the community. This is still practised today in certain monasteries. Why is this arrangement in the Rule? Because the young man entering the monastery is not a little monk; he is a postulant or a novice. One must allow him, or to speak more exactly, one must close one's eyes to certain peculiarities of his behavior, to certain juvenile compulsions, to certain experiments he has to try on his own. A good community will not be disturbed in its stability, its convictions, or its peace by them. It should know how to give him time to adapt himself gradually. It should understand that it has to allow the young a certain margin for maturation, and that certain inopportune or premature contacts can have disastrous effects. With certain people, the process is slow, and this requires patience and charity. St Benedict does not demand perfection in virtue of the novice. As for us, we think, without reflecting, that he ought already to be virtuous and that if he is not a holy novice he will not be a good monk. A saying goes around in monasteries: 'A perfect novice will be a good monk. A mediocre novice will be a bad monk. A bad novice will not be a monk'. There is much truth in that. But are we not tempted too much to see perfection according to a pre-established concept to which a young man will succeed in conforming only with difficulty? Someone who enters, let us not forget, is not yet a religious, he is not yet a monk, and he still thinks of the monastic life in his own way. It is normal, in this situation, that he manifest his vitality and his juvenile enthusiasm in a way which is not always too monastic. But in his character, in his habitual attitude, in his way of acting, in his deep desire for God, and especially in his fervor, he shows that he is on the way to that life. So let us not in our demands make him attain an immediate perfection which we ourselves, if we were honest, did not attain in one leap.

Now, the fourth point. Young people today are easily contentious, in the sense that they want to be different from others. Uniformity weighs them down. The young man has his budding personality, and he wants it respected. Therefore he challenges standard moulds, does not like being put into a category, balks at forms and formulas which he cannot yet assimilate. It costs him not to be able to dress or to cut his hair as he pleases. He criticizes some outward attitudes which are called 'monastic' and vows in his heart not to submit to certain secondary customs which he believes outmoded.

On this point, it is interesting to know on what basis people nowadays discuss the suitability of the taking of the habit. The idea of leaving the novice in secular clothes seems to be gaining ground. They think they are recovering an idea of St Benedict who, as a matter of fact, does not speak of a vesture in the sense in which we understand it today. For him, the 'clothing' takes place at the time of profession (26). At that time the young man puts off his clothing and receives that of the monastery. What clothing is involved? In another chapter we have the list: a cowl, a tunic, a scapular. The novice, therefore, does not yet wear the cowl, or any religious vestment; he wears his own. Have we not distorted the tradition on this point? We have made the candidate, the postulant who knocks at the door of the monastery, a sort of monk. Going further still, the boys in the monastic grade school, dressed in habit, have been transformed into little monks and assimilated, in some way, to the child oblates of whom St Benedict speaks in chapter fifty-nine. This way of doing things was perhaps positive in a psychological sense, in past times, but is no longer suitable.

At any rate, the young man of today refuses what is artificial, or what does not correspond to reality. This attitude is excellent, and shows us that he possesses a sense of the authentic.

To be complete on this fourth point, we must speak of the difficulty produced by the apparent uniformity of the spiritual life. Perhaps there, too, we may still find a tendency to consider the spiritual life according to a fixed plan and want to apply it to the novice. That would be neither right nor fair. In the benedictine tradition, the teaching of St Benedict has long been interpreted as leaving place, at its root, for different spiritual ways. The spirituality of St Thérèse of the Child Jesus or that of St Teresa of Avila, for example, fit without difficulty into the spirit of the

Rule. Even the spirituality of St John of the Cross on many points only makes those of St Benedict more explicit. And obedience according to the Rule is no less absolute than that taught by St Ignatius. St Benedict, we may say, is far from wanting to make his sons march by rank in a rigid spiritual line. On the contrary, he allows them every possibility, for his plan is very simple: Divine Office, *lectio divina*, work, in humility and in obedience to the Rule, under an abbot.

We have just said that young people today have a sense of the authentic. They do not like false situations or seeing reality dressed in borrowed garments. They cannot stand to see the accidental and the superficial mask the essential, and instead they allow what is exterior to fall aside in order to remain faithful to the essential, so as to be honest all the way. It happens, however, that they go beyond the limits of what is reasonable and fall into the excess of iconoclasm. But let us not forget that behind such regrettable action may be a passion for the authentic. The spirit of the Rule is completely limpid and forms the monk to the truth. The Fathers of Cîteaux understood this, and this quest of the authentic led them, like so many other reformers, to return to the spirit of the Rule, to that natural and supernatural balance which is its hallmark and which corresponds to a deep human desire.

The last great difficulty encountered by the young man or the young woman embracing the monastic life is found in the obligation to stabilize oneself definitively in a fixed state of life. Perhaps the times in which we live, the wars, the migrations and uprootings, the upheavals which have followed upon each other for half a century have contributed toward making man an unstable being. However that may be, instability unsettles him to the very core of his being. A type of monk of whom St Benedict speaks in the first chapter is tending to re-appear in our days: the gyrovague. This is a formula which would please some people very much. Here and there we meet these characters who lack only a hobo's clothing to play their role fully. These are the 'pilgrims of the absolute'! Is there not, in the final analysis, in the present vogue for eremitism—however praiseworthy the life of an authentic hermit may be—an indication of unwholesome tendencies toward individualistic instability? Some people do not want community life, where they feel too cramped, too constrained, too crowded. It is clearly more pleasant to become an adventurer of the Lord, a man of endless quest who sees in success a hateful establishment! St Benedict did not share this opinion. His whole being was opposed to what is not regulated and well-ordered. The Rule teaches us stability to the point of making of it an essential element of the balanced life, an element so positive that it has left its mark on the whole Middle Ages, helping Europe greatly to structure itself. If St Benedict is the father of Europe, it is because of this sense of stability to whose implantation he contributed; it is more necessary than ever in the troubled times in which we live.

By what means can the young man who presents himself at the monastery be led little by little to understand the constructive value of stability? Young people, it is true, after a period of adventure often grasp quite quickly the need for order, for tradition, for the Rule, in order to free themselves from vagrancy of ideas and actions. It is then that they begin to discover the liberty of the children of God and the guarantee supplied by the benedictine life. During this period of transition, they should be shown the danger of a life where the immoderate use of liberty turns into spiritual debauchery, into a license which ends by destroying the constructive forces proper to youth. Dedicating oneself to following Christ, contact with the Gospel will teach them, is a one-way street which does not allow backward glances or everlasting hesitations.

To understand all this takes time. In practice today the novitiate is longer than it used to be. In addition, after this probation the Church allows a latitude of nine more years for reflection. Is this a condescension to modern instability? One must be careful, nonetheless, not to prolong this probation beyond measure. The young person ought really to settle down and not give himself up to endless experiments all his life. This is why St Benedict leads him gently but firmly to a conviction of the necessity of stability. With a strong, but entirely paternal, pedagogy, he makes him realize the seriousness of the promise he is going to make; it is a promise without return. He invites him insistently to reflect at length on the uncompromising character of the Lord's call and on the definitive character of his act (58:15f.); he could not do it without a very special grace from the Lord (58:21), without the help of the saints (18f.), and the prayers of his brothers (23).

In conclusion, let us note how our Father St Benedict has penetrated the ways of God's merciful patience. This patience calls us, waits for us, and, as a sort of reprieve, prolongs the days of our earthly life (Prol. 36). It is in this sense that our legislator, as someone who understands human nature well, demands that his novice master be able to discern spirits (58:2), not be discouraged by the actions, apparently ill-conformed to the rules, of some, perhaps turbulent, young man—turbulent but well suited to the monastic life—and lead him little by little, with firmness and gentleness, to seek God alone and to love Christ by submitting to himself to the life of monastic brotherhood.

# SPIRITUAL DIRECTION IN THE MONASTERY

The spiritual direction of souls, especially souls conse-crated to God, is an activity, an institution, extremely use-ful for the health of the interior life. In speaking on this theme, we touch on a delicate problem, in the area both of the individual spiritual life and of the common life. We take up this subject because, unfortunately, it is not always clearly understood, and requires some explanation. By 'spiri-tual direction' we mean the direction of the spirit, of the soul, or perhaps the direction of the soul in the Holy Spirit.

In a religious community, one must first distinguish between general spiritual direction and individual direction. The general spiritual direction is, in the first place, a doc-trinal direction of the community and of its members insofar as they are part of the community. According to the Rule, it is the abbot's duty to be the spiritual master, *magister;* and in the Rule no one else is given the title *magister* (cf. 3:6, 5:9, 6:6). It is interesting to notice that in chapter fifty-eight, St Benedict does not speak of a novice master, a *magister.* The senior assigned to the novices is not 'master' in the sense in which the word is applied to the abbot. Cer-tainly, the master of novices ought to teach, since without doubt, he also ought to show his students the hard and diffi-cult things on the road to God (58:8). But he is not a 'mas-ter' with his personal doctrine; he ought to teach in accord with the abbot. The prior and the seniors, according to the Rule, do not seem to have any doctrinal function; their duty —like the novice master's (58:6)—is to supervise their deanery or the community, to organize the life, to guide their brothers as good assistants according to the precepts of the abbot (21:2, 65:16).

The abbot is the 'master'; he ought to teach. But he like-wise has no personal doctrine, for his doctrine is not his but the Gospel's. The abbot ought to teach nothing, establish nothing, command nothing which might be contrary to the precepts of the Lord (2:4). The negative turn of this sentence shows St Benedict's insistence that the abbot's teaching depart in no point from the commandments of the Lord. He ought to be in perfect conformity with them. The abbot may not venture out into personal theories, into practices or peda-gogical systems which do not bear the seal of the Gospel. He is leading souls who belong to the Lord and who have the right to hear his word from their abbot's mouth. The general spiritual direction of the community, therefore, is the responsibility of the abbot.

Let us point out here that the abbot owes his monks a doctrine which is eminently practical and not theoretical and abstract. Already the meaning of the word 'master' implies the practical application of the doctrine. The 'severe master' (2:24) suggests a committed master who ought not only to teach, but also to make sure that the knowledge is applied, and in his manner of teaching to follow the advice of the apostle by refuting, rebuking, and exhorting (2:23 from 2 Tim 4:2).

Since the abbot is his community's instructor, its master of the arts of the soul, its pastor (2:7), it follows that the monastery has a unity of doctrine, orientation, and spiritual direction. From the unity of doctrine proceeds unity of spirit in a community and, in spite of a diversity of char-acters and even of opinions, charity and peace in mutual respect.

This general spiritual direction, along with prayer, medita-tion on the Gospel, spiritual conferences, and reading, is enough for a great number of monks and nuns who do not feel themselves inclined to seek individual spiritual direction. Others need it, at least at certain moments of their lives. So let us speak of individual spiritual direction, what we spe-cifically call spiritual direction.

First of all, who are the spiritual directors? A first distinction is necessary, that is, between the confessor and the spiritual director. The confessor, a priest, is not neces-sarily the spiritual director. He is not always called to that;

278

he is not even always capable of it. You remember the difficulties that St Teresa of Avila had with some of her confessors. The priest receives from Christ the power to forgive or to retain sins in His name. That is his power; it is sacramental. The confessor ought to help the penitent recognize his sins. On the other hand, spiritual direction is intended to help the person being directed to overcome his evil tendencies and to grow in virtue. Its aim is spiritual progress and it is not a sacramental operation. Although the sacrament of penance tends to the same end, its immediate final goal is the remission of sins. The confessional is not, therefore, necessarily the place for direction. Whereas the sacrament supposes a power, spiritual direction supposes instead a charism, the gift of wisdom, the knowledge of the ways of God and of the work of his grace, as well as a penetrating knowledge of the soul of the person being directed.

We must not, therefore, confuse confession with spiritual direction. St Benedict himself seems to make this distinction. Formerly, in the monastery, everyone had to go to the abbot for confession. And this obligation was so grave that a confession made to someone besides the abbot was not even valid. This discipline was mitigated later by allowing confessors who could give absolution, at least in certain cases. St Benedict, it seems, does not speak of the sacrament of penance, but of confession to be made either to the abbot or to the spiritual fathers, the seniors, in the case of secret sin (46:5). Does this mean confession alone or also spiritual direction? The spiritual father of whom St Benedict speaks, does not necessarily have to be a priest; he may be a lay monk, as the abbot himself in principle might have been in those days. The penitent, therefore, does not receive a sacramental absolution. The qualification given this spiritual father, 'Who knows how to heal his own wounds and those of others' (46:6) may be interpreted in the full context in the sense of spiritual direction distinct from confession.

Among the instruments of the spiritual art, there is one which runs in the same sense: 'To break evil thoughts against the rock which is Christ as soon as they come to mind and to reveal them to the spiritual father' (4:50-51). Dealing with thoughts which are not yet necessarily sins, the confession mentioned by the Rule is an ascetical confession, made in order to maintain perfect purity of heart and to escape the dangers which a false shame may cause a soul left to itself in its combat with the powers of darkness (cf. Eph 6:12, Prol. 28).

Let us hear what St Benedict says in the fifth degree of humility: 'The fifth degree of humility is to hide nothing from one's abbot concerning the evil thoughts which present themselves to the mind nor concerning faults committed in secret. The Scripture exhorts us to practise this humble confession' (7:44f.). It is to the abbot who holds the place of Christ that one humbly confesses his evil thoughts and even his sins. He is the first of those spiritual seniors who are supposed to know how to heal the wounds of the soul (46:5). He is, therefore, what we call the spiritual director. And he is in principle the spiritual director of all his sons. No monk, in fact, escapes the spiritual direction, even the individual direction, of the abbot. In view of his pastoral charge he is obliged to encourage, to exhort, to give counsel and directives. He is, above all, the father of the souls entrusted to him, and his first duty is to lead them in the paths of the Lord (2:31, 33f., 37). Was he not elected precisely by this criterion of being able to direct and govern souls (64:2)? Here we link up with what we have said on the subject of the abbot's general spiritual direction. No one in the monastery will challenge that right and that responsibility of spiritually directing his community and each member in particular, because the monks who compose it establish his position before God.

But is this what we today call spiritual direction? On the side of the person who feels the need to be directed, this means a trusting approach to a father in whom he hopes to find the ability and the willingness to help him. Here we find again the idea of the monks of the desert about their spiritual director, their *Abba*. And since the image of the abbot has changed a bit in the course of time, we understand that not everyone necessarily feels inclined to open his soul entirely to his abbot. Canon law, defending liberty of conscience, has gone one better in this matter.

If spiritual direction, then, were to imply the complete baring of conscience, we could not speak of an obligation on the monks' part to take the abbot as their exclusive spiritual director, although they would be perfectly free to open themselves entirely to their abbot and to trust his direction. In comparing the texts of St Benedict cited above (4:50, 46:5 on the one hand, and 7:44f. on the other), are we not permitted to think that St Benedict himself had on this point a more liberal idea than the *Rule of the Master*, according to which the abbot is in theory and in fact the only spiritual director of his monks?

But if the abbot is the director of each and every monk, and if they may nevertheless have a special director, how can they avoid differences, even disputes on the spiritual plane, disorders which are all the more serious because the welfare of souls is at stake? Here we are touching upon a very delicate point. It goes without saying that such troubles would be deplorable and very capable of disturbing souls and the peace of the community.

Did St Benedict not want to make it understood by his attitude, at first sight ambiguous, that the monk ought to enjoy the freedom of conscience which is necessary, and might address himself to other spiritual fathers than the abbot, but that, on the other hand, the abbot is the primary spiritual father of everyone? In fact, is the aim of this direction not to lead souls to Christ? Can anyone exercise this ministry in the monastery while by-passing the abbot, who holds the place of Christ (2:2), while neglecting his teaching, which is in conformity with the Gospel and for which he is the person ultimately responsible (2:4, 64:9)?

Certainly, the abbot will not prescribe methods of meditation, ways of purification, and so on. In other words, as long as the teaching of the other spiritual fathers is orthodox, the abbot will find fault with nothing. But spiritual direction touches the practical attitude of those being directed, the monastic virtues, and especially obedience to the Rule and the abbot, the integration of the person directed into the life of the community, the entire range of monastic discipline; what a deviation if the spiritual director, instead of encouraging his disciple, were to insist on his own opinion in the case of conflict with the superior! What a bane for souls if, too inclined to see some difference of opinion through his disciple's eyes, he were to defend him (RB 69) either openly or in the course of conferences with him. A pious conversation could degenerate into murmuring this way. When obedience, the basic virtue of the monk (71:2), is called into question, when its sincerity is impugned by arguments which may seem to be highly spiritual, the essential of the monastic life are affected. Does the angel of darkness transformed into an angel of light not often mislead the most innocent souls on exactly this point?

The gift of directing souls is a charism, a gift of the Holy Spirit. The abbot knows that he is not the only person in the community who possesses the Spirit. St Benedict speaks of the spiritual seniors (4:50, 46:5) who also possess the Spirit and he even foresees the case of a younger monk to whom the Spirit of God reveals what is better to do (3:3); he recommends that the abbot use *sympectae*, seniors entrusted with consoling the brother who is tempted to rebel or to challenge authority (27:2f.). But although there is a diversity of spiritual gifts, it is the same Spirit (cf. 1 Cor 12: 4 ff.). The Holy Spirit does not contradict himself. If the abbot holds the place of Christ, he is entitled to the assistance of the Spirit of Christ. From this fact, we must not draw just any conclusion, but without a doubt, counsels given outside of or contrary to obedience, contrary to the respect due the abbot and the praiseworthy customs maintained or established by legitimate authority, do not come from the Holy Spirit. Where He is, there is charity, harmony, peace, respect, obedience, and unity. Where there is division, evil spirits are at work.

No one is a spiritual director who does not possess the true Spirit; he is recognized by his fruits (cf. Gal 5:22f.). It remains nonetheless true that in the community there can be spiritual fathers besides the abbot capable of leading souls.

An abbess or a good nun, are they able to direct souls?

Although a woman does not have access to the sacrament of Holy Orders, she also possesses the Holy Spirit. Woman and man are equals through baptism (cf. Gal 3:28) and the same Spirit descends upon them (1 Cor 12:13). Without any doubt, therefore, a woman, like a man, may receive the gift of wisdom to give good advice and direct souls. The great examples of women in the Church filled with the Holy Spirit are too numerous to dispute this fact. Besides, has the Church not bestowed the title 'Doctor of the Church' on women?

The abbess holds the place of Christ in the monastery by the same right as the abbot. Just like him, she has received the pastoral charge at the time of her abbatial blessing. Jurisdiction or priesthood are not part of the question. Everything that is said about the abbot as the spiritual director of his community can be applied to the abbess. The restrictions that must be made in certain cases are due to a difference, not of position, but of training. But the abbess too ought to study the Sacred Scriptures, be educated, and know from which sources to draw (64:9). There can be nuns in a community capable of giving good and wise spiritual counsels. Care must be taken, however, that unity of spirit and community charity be safeguarded. Let no sister claim the right to direct others unless she is ordered or authorized by the legitimate authority.

Communities of nuns often have a regular superior (the 'father immediate' in the cistercian terminology), a chaplain capable of directing souls, or other spiritual counsellors. These ought, before all else, to direct them according to the spirit of the Rule, and according to the wholesome spiritual traditions of the community (7:55), encouraging them in obedience, and helping them resolve the conflicts which are never lacking, in a spirit careful to safeguard unity and charity. It is of the greatest importance that they know how to maintain souls in peace, in the joy of the vocation they have received, in the generosity to accept the adversities which mark the steps of the journey toward God for consecrated souls. The day when the spiritual counsellor begins to instill trouble or division into a soul by letting himself imprudently criticize authority, he does a destructive work and shakes the foundations of the monastic life by his personal views.

Because the common life plays a preponderant role in the monastic life, it is obvious that the multiplicity of directors of souls constitutes a danger. All too often we see division rearing itself between the nuns and the internal governance of the community, making itself more or less deeply felt. Nor is it advisable, at least not generally speaking, for the nuns to keep the spiritual director who led them to the monastery, unless he is the spiritual director or confessor of the community. This is very important in helping the novice become integrated as quickly as possible into the life of the community; a priest who does not know the community except in a general and theoretical way, even though his knowledge is very accurate, is not playing a proper role. The newcomer ought to entrust herself to the abbess in order to be truly introduced into the community. One must be a member of it in order to be able to love it not only truly, but also practically.

Let us add to all these considerations on the spiritual director, a word on what the direction requires of both parties in order to be effective.

St Benedict is quite sober about the role of the person directed. Yet that is natural, because it is for the spiritual director to teach him little by little to know himself. Such a goal cannot be attained without a sincere openness on the part of the person being directed, especially on the subject of concrete facts in his past. The biography is woven beginning with this knowledge. The person being directed will tell the director his thoughts, desires, inclinations, habits, temptations (4:50, 7:44, 46:5), his difficulties in his vocation, in prayer, in work, in the common life. But, it is altogether inadvisable to make him or let him talk endlessly, because the result can only be a centering on self, which may go far as an unhealthy pleasure in being occupied and seeing others occupied with his own person. It lies, therefore, especially in the insight and the experience of the director— see why the director is called and supposed to be a senior?—

to arrive gradually at an objective knowledge of his disciple. He should not allow himself to be stopped or turned aside by the person's secondary elements of character, but let him keep to discerning the essential in him in order to help him to hold onto it.

St Benedict gives the abbot the responsibility of leading the souls of his sons. Likewise, he traces out a concise and substantial program for the novice master: 'He will take care to assure that the novice truly seeks God, that he shows himself generous in the divine service, in obedience, in trials' (58:7). The pedagogical program of the spiritual director is the same; yet, he ought resolutely to avoid encroaching on the territory of the abbot or the novice master by wanting to substitute himself for them in the sight of the monk he is directing.

In conclusion, we must recognize that the task of a spiritual director who is neither the abbot nor the master of novices is difficult and delicate in a monastic community. So the monk has every advantage, if there are not special reasons for doing otherwise, in going to his abbot for his spiritual direction—this does not necessarily coincide with confession or presuppose it—he thus assures himself of a unity of orientation and protects himself against useless and harmful troubles which are almost inevitable with double spiritual direction. The nun will act, *mutatis mutandis*, in the same fashion to her advantage. This attitude takes for granted in the monk or the nun that trust which is an act of filial love, a gift which the son gives his father, the daughter her mother. It has a very solid foundation: the mission which the abbot and the abbess have received from the Church to *regere animas* (2:31), to direct the souls who have been entrusted to them.

# THE CELLARER

The chapter on the cellarer is one of the most beautiful in the Holy Rule. If we compare it with the chapter on the prior, we are a little astonished to see with what love St Benedict draws the portrait of the cellarer, whereas he seems to have little sympathy for the prior. The cellarer, then, ought to be a man who is judicious, sober, mature, charitable, humble, a true religious, in short, a father for the community. We get the impression that St Benedict would like to paint the image of a father again for us as he already did in the chapter on the abbot.

It is well understood that what is meant here is a father on the material plane, a father providing for the needs of daily life and not for the spiritual life. Nevertheless, the cellarer ought to be a spiritual man, because unless he is, he cannot look after the material affairs of a religious community. The cellarer, history often shows us, is tempted to become a businessman. Such an idea of this office simply does not enter into the views of St Benedict, as a study of the Rule shows, for the abbot himself ought to avoid this danger and discharge his duties in an evangelical spirit (2:33). So the cellarer ought to be a father and to have for the community and for each member of it, a truly paternal affection.

One phrase strikes us in this chapter, the more so as we find it in other forms in the Rule: the cellarer ought to do nothing without the abbot's order; he does what he is commanded (31:4f.). St Benedict is formal. Elsewhere we find: 'He will take care of all that the abbot entrusts to him; but let him not interfere with what is forbidden him (31:15). In reading these texts, we might get the impression at first glance that the cellarer is the executor of the abbot's orders. Is the abbot the sole instigator, the one who sets in motion all the action, all the movements of the life of the monastery, leaving to others only the charge of executing his orders? Such an attitude would be the case with the *Rule of the Master.* St Benedict does not share this point of view. We read, regarding the cellarer: 'Let him have charge of everything' (31:3). In fact, in this chapter we find three times the expression: *Curam gerat* or: *habeat sub cura sua* (31:3, 9,15). Read without prejudice, it leaves us with the impression of a cellarer truly responsible in all the material affairs and managing his office with initiative and great liberty of spirit.

Then why does St Benedict insist several times, 'Let him do nothing without the order of the abbot' (31:4)? It is not a case of the abbot giving orders to the cellarer everywhere and on all occasions, but simply of the cellarer acting in obedience to, and according to the orders of, the abbot. In a well-organized community, there cannot be two heads. It has often been discussed whether the administrator of the monastery ought to be the abbot or the cellarer. The abbot is the administrator of the monastery on the spiritual plane and likewise on the material plane; the Rule and monastic tradition clearly show this.

The cellarer is, therefore, the agent of the abbot, while still being in charge of the business of the community. He is a father of the community, established by the abbot for the good of each and every member. Not only ought he not to sadden the brethren (31:6), but he ought to be ready to give what he is reasonably asked for (7) if he has it; if he has nothing, let him at least give a kind word (13f.). The cellarer ought to be punctual and distribute the brothers' portions on time (16,18). He is a man who is always ready to give, a real father. Far from him be all proud conceit, all need to dominate. To make it plain to the brothers with a certain arrogance (*typho*) or by unnecessary delays (16) that they depend on him and his bounty would be to put their patience to the test unduly and to scandalize them (16,19). On the other hand, he ought not to be bothered at unreasonable hours (18).

The care which St Benedict takes in painting the figure of the cellarer, in this following the earlier tradition, shows his desire not to burden the abbot with the actual administration of the goods of the monastery. Thus the abbot remains faithful to the instructions he is given (2:33): not to allow himself to be tempted to neglect the good of souls under the pretext of being charged with the temporal administration.

# TEMPORAL ADMINISTRATION

The last part of the second chapter on the abbot introduces us to a problem discussed in every age: the construction of the earthly city and our share in the commitment to build it.

You know the type of spiritualism which would like to see the abbot and the monastic community disinterested in the realities of this earth in order to live only in God. In the desert, the abbot was simply the spiritual father. He had nothing to administer. The only goods of the desert were the good things to come.

Now, benedictine mentality is not like that. The head and the mind of St Benedict are turned toward heaven, but his feet are on the ground. He was, according to St Gregory's account, a mystic, but the Rule shows him to be eminently practical and realistic. The benedictine community is therefore built on a sound material foundation. It possesses fields (4:4, 48:7), a garden (66:6, 7:63), a mill (66:6); what is necessary for the subsistence of the monastery (2:35, 31:10, 12; 66:6), the house itself, the novitiate (58:5), the guesthouse (53:21), the furniture, tools, and clothing (31:10, 32, 55) of the community. This monastic community sells the products of its craftsmen (57:4ff.). The harvests of the fields and the garden (RB 40) were to be gathered in and their prudent consumption organized. All this demands wise administration, exercised by wise men (53:22). The abbot cannot fail to take an interest in these things and ought to attend to his administrative duties as well as to his spiritual and pastoral duties.

Obviously, there is within all the tension characteristic of human life, the whole problem of our nature composed of a body and a soul, therefore, the ambivalence of this problem. Men are not angels and cannot live without a minimum of material conditions, and a community is the more caught in the problem of its daily bread to the extent that it is more developed; the abbot, according to St Benedict, is the person ultimately responsible, so he cannot pretend to be exclusively occupied with souls. St Benedict, in admonishing the abbot not to be *too* occupied with transitory things, gives him to understand that these questions do concern him (2:33, 35f.), he is also the administrator of the goods of the community, and he ought no more to count simply on the benefactors than he ought to impose beggary on the brethren or require them to live in extreme poverty. His duty is wisely to administer the temporal goods of the monastery in order that they may live reasonably. St Benedict, genius of moderation and discretion, here expresses his whole balanced mastery of life.

The danger exists that the abbot may occupy himself too much with the temporal administration. The material, it cannot be denied, asserts itself more than the spiritual. The visible is closer to us and more urgent than the invisible. St Benedict was aware of this danger, and he multiplies his warnings to the abbot that he must care for souls. Let us look at these impressively insistent texts:

'Let the abbot take care above all not to neglect or to make little of the salvation of the souls entrusted to him' (2:33). 'Let him always remember that he has undertaken the government of souls' (2:34). 'Let him realize that it is souls whose government he has undertaken' (2:37). 'Let him know for certain that on the day of judgment he will have to render an account to the Lord for all these souls' (2:38). 'Living thus in continual fear of the examination which the Shepherd will make over the sheep which He has entrusted to him . . . ' (2:39). The abbot ought always to be careful not to lose souls for reasons that are material, especially for the sake of too much work (48:24f., 41:5, 64:17f.). All these texts by themselves speak a language loud and clear. 'The salvation of souls: this is the supreme law'. Let the abbot not be anxious (64:16) if the good of souls imposes on him decisions which, on the level of the general economy of the monastery, seem hardly justifiable.

You have noticed that St Benedict goes so far as to threaten the abbot with the judgment of God. He does not appeal to the visitor, nor to the Holy See; he threatens by Christ himself. The abbot will have to present his accounts and his balance sheet to the Eternal Judge. This judgment, it is true, is a final one, more or less distant, and one could refuse to think about it. But a good administration cannot be maintained without good accounts. The abbot, therefore, should keep his always ready. In dealing with souls, he cannot neglect them for a moment or act like the wicked servant in the Gospel (Mt 24:48). On the contrary, after having served his brothers well in both the temporal and the spiritual areas (64:21), he will hope that the Lord will establish him over all His goods (64:22, Mt 24:47).

One last question: What should be done if economic difficulties surpass the measure of endurance? We should not expect from St Benedict formulae or recipes which, as if by magic, could transform a precarious or dramatic situation. His final advice, even in these difficult-to-solve situations, sends us back to the Gospel. Let the abbot not panic; let him have no fears or worries which would make him lose the proper scale of values; it is written, and he should not forget it, 'Seek first the kingdom of God and his justice, and all the rest will be given you besides' (Mt 6:33) and again, 'Nothing is wanting to those who fear Him' (2:35f.). Let him remain confident! 'Nothing is wanting' (Ps 22:1). What beautiful words from the psalm! Yes, remain full of confidence. In the administration of a monastery, this is the basic principle of all our economic activities: to have a great trust in the fatherly care of God. For those who love him, he works together in all things for their good (Rom 8:28). Would this attitude be too simplistic? It goes without saying, that we ought to act according to the means at our disposal. Yet does the heavenly Father not feed the birds and clothe the flowers of the field? So, before all, we must trust and believe in him. Does he not care much more for us? On the other hand, neither ought we to fear the cross. It can present itself in the form of poverty, even penury. Moreover, economic difficulties often have the effect of uniting a community and of educating it in a spirit of trust in the Lord.

Above the entryway of one monastery, I once saw a swallows' nest built on the arm of a crucifix. Is this not a beautiful image of confidence? As that bird had entrusted its little family to the cross, so our own nest is also on the cross. This image lets us understand that everything in the course of our life will not run perfectly in economic matters. Cares will not be lacking, but neither will trust in the Lord. We ought to realize that our nest is placed on the cross and that, while sharing in the passion of Christ, we nest in that tabernacle which is the open side of the heart of Our Lord; yes, we dwell there. In this nest, we feel the love of the Father, his concern for us touching even the smallest questions in our daily life. How could the Father forget us in our daily cares? Not a sparrow falls to the ground without his knowing it (Mt 10:29)! Thus we are able to find an harmonious balance between our concern for earthly and passing things (2:33) and the demands of the kingdom of heaven, a problem which is of such concern to the abbot and his collaborators in temporal questions.

In the earthly paradise, a breach occurred between these two requirements of life. Now, we want to see restored, little by little, that harmony in us lost through sin. Love alone is able to give its true place to each of our needs. It alone is ultimately able to indicate the right measure that must be given to the body without harming the soul, and what must be given to the soul without neglecting the body.

# THE SENSE OF RESPONSIBILITY

'The abbot, once in office, ought to ponder constantly the burden which he has received' (64:7). St Benedict wants to impress on the newly elected abbot the sense of responsibility inherent in his office. He works hard, therefore, to depict the most important qualities that a superior ought to have. Thus the abbot accepts his responsibilities with a knowledge of the facts and commits himself with all his strength to the office which has been entrusted to him. His office is not a kind of sinecure for him while he makes others work. Quite the reverse; it is for him a real personal commitment.

This exhortation to the abbot is of interest to every monk. In fact, St Benedict insists throughout the entire Holy Rule on what we may call the spirit of responsibility. It has to do with the zeal with which each person fulfils his duty, the obedience which he receives; with the devotedness with which he must give himself to his task by giving of himself. This is the spirit of commitment. In fact, in the very first sentence of the Prologue we meet a word at which we must pause. After having invited us to listen—*obsculta, o fili* (Prol. 1)—St Benedict adds another little word which is no less important: *efficaciter comple* (*ibid.*)—put into practice the teaching received. Let us note that St Benedict does not only say *comple*, accomplish, but *efficaciter comple:* be effective in practising what you have learned. So we enter into a vocation which must be taken seriously. It is not just a matter of listening to interesting lessons, a doctrine of sublime life; we ought to be effective and put the lessons we learn into practice. Already in the sentence following this first exhortation, St Benedict speaks of *desidia* (Prol. 2) in order to contrast it with this spirit of spiritual effectiveness, a word he clearly underlines: the *desidia* of disobedience, the *desidia* of carelessness. Du Cange translates the word *desidia* with nonchalance, *paresse* (carelessness, laziness). This translation seems, in fact, to correspond rather well to the intention of contrasting the laziness of disobedience with the effort, the labor, of obedience. *Desidia* is, therefore, the tendency of our nature not to be attentive, not to commit ourselves, not to take things seriously, to drift, in a word, to let ourselves be pushed by circumstances or by those in office. Now St Benedict let us understand from the very beginning of the Rule that such an attitude is contrary to the very character of our life, because it is essentially a commitment in the ways of the Lord.

In looking through the Rule, we find other expressions which show the same insistence on the spirit of commitment. In the Prologue, St Benedict compares the monk to a laborer (Prol. 14). We might be tempted to imagine the contemplative monastic life as a life of spiritual quietude. One sort of quietude, an error condemned by the Church, waylays some monks. It is tempting to imagine a life quite shut in, peaceful, beyond the tides of the world, not in the sense of a fleeing from the world and making a serious contemplative commitment, but a life without clashes and without problems, as it is also without fervor.

St Benedict works hard to make us understand that we are laborers who ought to apply ourselves to our work. We ought to set to work *non trepide, non tarde, non tepide*— without hesitations, without delay, without carelessness (5:14). How should we obey? Have we obeyed well if we content ourselves with not disobeying? To obey, is it enough to do as little as possible, to act reluctantly, to do our duty slowly, without interest, like people who are in no hurry, doing their jobs after a fashion? In the end, it is not done well, but it is done.

St Benedict loves promptness and in another place in the Rule we read: 'Let them vie with each other to arrive first at the Divine Office' (22:6). One may object: 'We ought not to get out of bed too quickly, it is not good for our health, but peacefully, tranquilly, to arrive at the beginning of the Office, even at the last minute.' St Benedict is not of this opinion. Not only did he expect the good monk to hurry to get to the Divine Office, but he wanted him to be eager to be among the first there, competing in promptness with the others, without, however, losing his composure. He wanted to see the monks encourage each other (22:8), amiably and gently, to hurry. There is in this whole attitude recommended by St Benedict a holy dynamism worthy of him who said: *Currendum et agendum est* (Prol. 44)—we must run, we must act, we must prepare our body and soul for combat (*ibid.* 40), because the Lord is waiting for us (*ibid.* 35) and allows us time, as a respite (*ibid.* 36) for our conversion. The entire Prologue overflows with energy to awaken us from the torpor inherent in our nature (*ibid.* 2). The monk ought to seize his responsibilities.

St Benedict asks us, therefore, to commit ourselves actively. He asks it in a special way of the officers and, above all of the abbot, as we have already seen. He ought to accept his responsibilities. His task is not easy. He cannot take it lightly, and ought to be committed. The election is hardly over (64:1-6), where the abbot, before God to whom he will have to render an account and whose representative he is (64:7), sets himself to his task. The monks are not his (2, 7, 30, 34, 37-39; 64:21). What a responsibility! He is placed at the head of the community, that is to say, he marches before them, and this *factis amplius quam verbis* (2:12, 2:12f.) by giving an example, by his behavior and his actions much more than by his words. He ought to walk at the head of the flock, giving each and every one the chance to follow him.

It would be interesting, Rule in hand, to go deeper into the doctrine of St Benedict as he defines the abbot's attitude toward the responsibilities of his office—culpable brethren, for example (RB 27) or the sick. On the latter, St Benedict insistently reminds him of his responsibility lest they are neglected (36:10), repeating twice: *Curam maximam habeat abbas* (36:6, 10)—let him watch with great care that they be well served.

The cellarer and the novice master also receive a list of obligations. St Benedict teaches the first not to neglect anything (31:11). Let him take care of everything and everyone (31:3) and carry out the abbot's orders diligently (31:15). With what care ought he to treat the material possessions of the monastery (31:10)! That is a pressing appeal to commit oneself, no doubt about it. Likewise, St Benedict exhorts the novice master to apply himself to his duty. *Sollicitudo sit* (58:7), he tells him, let him bring all his zeal to discerning spirits to see if a novice truly seeks God, if he really has the qualities required for leading the monastic life; and he should do this *curiose*, says St Benedict (58:6), with very great attention. The servers in the refectory also ought to apply themselves to their duties. If they prove to be distracted, inattentive, and careless, everyone becomes annoyed; such disagreeable vexations disturb the good harmony of the arrangements made to assure the peace of the community. It is the same for the brothers who work in the kitchen. This is a demanding service, and it is really necessary to give it all one's attention. The brothers' meals ought to be served by the cook or the cellarer *sine typho et mora* (31:16). Bound to their task without resentment, they are to be punctual. Imagine the community's righteous displeasure if the cook's bad mood risked making the soup late!

Every officer of the community bears, without doubt, the spirit of responsibility. But for every cenobite, the structure of the community is basically essential to his effort for perfection and his will to commit himself flows from his very profession. Through it, he is incorporated into the concrete community with its joys and its pains, its prayer and its work, its interests and its responsibilities. The commitment of profession leads to unrestricted sharing with the brethren. By his profession, the monk, in accordance with the order of the community and the arrangements of the abbot, assumes responsibility for his brothers. He becomes co-responsible for their spiritual and physical well-being. He cannot sneak away when the burden weighs heavy, when the task is difficult, when his brothers annoy him. He has entered with his whole being and all his talents into a relationship of complementarity. From now on, he ought, if he is able, to give whatever is lacking to his brother, he ought to help plug the holes, fill the gaps, stop up the cracks. The rule of fraternal solidarity, which we Christians call charity, will henceforth condition all his actions. He will neither be a semi-hermit, nor a sort of pseudo-spiritual solitary taking refuge in the chapel in order to escape the burdens of the community: he is committed. The monk ought to realize that if he allows himself negligences or even simple forgetfulness in the place which he occupies in community life, his way of acting will affect and burden his brethren.

Is this way of looking at things too material? In the monastery, is one chained to his task like some factory assemblyline where the worker has just enough time to do the task assigned him? No. Monastic life requires the development of each person's personality; but the monk never putters around; he performs a work worthy of the name, and he gives himself to it without hesitation. He knows that if he fails in his part, the life of the community will be affected. This co-operation of the monk, we should add in passing, in fostering the common life and his interest in that life, always has as its goal the flowering of charity and the spiritual building-up of the kingdom in souls.

In the monastery, everything converges in the construction of the heavenly city, and it would be a mistake to judge the daily work imposed by human life as too commonplace to enter the scope of monastic existence. Quite the contrary, the least details of our material life, well regulated, make up an integral part of our day, and they likewise demand our commitment.

Let us, for example, consider the Divine Office. We ought to be present at it, do our best to fulfil our role as hebdomadary in our turn, edify the brothers by intoning the antiphons and the psalms (47:2f.). We have to make ourselves heard when we sing in choir (47:3) or in the refectory (38:12). We ought to try, then, to articulate well, to learn how to read in public. Those who are silent in choir, or do not sing out, or sing out too much, annoy others. A choir is more than a group of people. A choir is where each person tries to take part by singing out in the useful measure indicated by the one directing and training it. The liturgy will be more beautiful and harmonious when everyone's action is truly common, 'choral'.

There are many other ways of taking seriously one's role as a member of a social body. Another example: St Benedict insists that the tools of the monastery be treated with care. *Si quis sordide et negligenter res tractaverit* (32:4), if someone handles things with a lack of cleanliness and carelessly, if we misuse tools in the garden or the fields, if we are careless in doing the dishes, negligent with the linen, or the utensils, if we mistreat the choir, or the library, books, if we let dust accumulate in our area, we put the community out.

Our spirit of responsibility ought to be especially watchful if we are asked for special help in an emergency. Obviously, this task keeps us for the moment from doing our regular work, but are we able to leave it aside on the pretext of having to render a special service? If it were a matter simply of furnishing a certain number of hours of work, the workman could content himself with doing the unforeseen work in place of ordinary work on the excuse that he cannot do two things at once. For him, only the work responsibility enters into account, he is not concerned with the combination of interests at work, and sees no reason to stir himself to do both jobs as far as he can. The paid worker works above all for a salary, doing, if you like, his strict duty, but leaving the work unfinished if the bell for the end of work rings. For us monks, these added services are an occasion for showing our spirit of commitment and responsibility.

We may often be asked to help a confrère. But when that service is finished, we return to our regular work. St Benedict deals with this case in his chapter on the reception of guests (53:18) where the spirit of solidarity also shows itself. If, in order to finish a job, someone needs help, the brethren must not pass idly by like the priest and the Levite in the parable of the Good Samaritan. How often we find ourselves in situations like this! Have you noticed what happens when you poke a stick into an anthill? All the ants hurry to repair the damage. They have a terrific spirit of solidarity. Without thinking of their own business, they concentrate their efforts on the damage done to their home. That is a manifestation of community spirit which suits us very well. Does each one of us not have, in the bottom of his heart, that spirit of dedication? Yes, certainly, but with the grace of God that family spirit grows in us little by little; if not, how would we be able to say: *Abba, pater,* if we did not have this spirit of adoption (2:3), of incorporation into our monastic family? The father of the family, the brothers, ought to be able to approach us with confidence to ask our help without the risk of being refused (5:14), or getting a grouchy or even an aggressive answer. St Benedict took it much at heart to recommend to us this quickness to mutual service when he invited us to obey each other (RB 71).

The community spirit, therefore, calls for a willingness to commit oneself. The person who commits himself with the intention of serving his brothers, his community, gradually goes out of himself and out of the narrowness of his own interests. He frees himself gradually from the sad tendency to relate everything to himself, to reflect on his own pains and little inconveniences, to pause over those pettinesses of which human relations are never wholly free. This willingness to commit oneself is the daughter of generosity, of charity; it is nothing other than good zeal (RB 72). We see it open up into the joy of faithful obedience and help the monk to be at the disposition of the silent invitations of the Spirit.

# THE COMMUNITY'S PARTICIPATION IN GOVERNMENT

Any community needs regulations to guide it. It is necessary, in fact, to be able, in certain circumstances, to refer to decisions born of common agreement. Now, how does one make decisions in a religious community, and more precisely, in a community governed by the benedictine Rule? Today this question underlies many discussions and opinions. A democratic tendency urges us to favor majority rule as in civil and secular society. So the community draws up regulations for its assemblies, deliberates, establishes commissions, if needed, and finally, to finish it all, takes its decisions by majority rule. Does this really correspond to the character of the monastic community?

When we use here the word 'democracy', it must be understood in the sense of a true democracy. In our modern states, the people only influence the manner of government in a remote way. Our Rule, on the other hand, is profoundly democratic, as we will see. Nor do we use the word 'democracy' in the modern sense of universal suffrage, where all the decisions are taken by a majority of votes. Moreover, this is no criticism of that way of doing things. In modern society, it would be unthinkable to champion past systems, Greek or Roman, founded upon distinctions of class, society, training, or education, systems which were followed by Christianity. In recognizing the basic equality of all men, humanity has made a leap forward, and today, it matters little what the social milieu might be of the person who wants to attain a top position. Present society more and more levels the inequalities of birth which once existed, and class distinctions and educational differences disappear more and more. All of which does not say that there are not profound differences of ability from one man to the other.

But let us come back to the problems of the monastic community. Is it desirable that it take its decisions by majority vote? Let us ask Holy Scripture: it is our norm. We do not find any example to support this way of doing things. On the other hand, we find several cases where there is a consultation among the apostles. The meeting at Jerusalem is the most remarkable example of this. The apostles and the elders have a discussion, then come to an agreement after having heard St Peter and St James (Acts 15:22). There is no question of voting. When it was necessary to find a replacement for Judas, it was decided by lot (Acts 1:26) and not by majority. The apostles and the first Christians got together to pray that the Lord himself might decide (Acts 1:24f.).

In the Church, the use of the simple majority vote system entered relatively late and in a rather limited way. The Church is an hierarchical society, organized on the plan of a mission received from above. As Christ sent his apostles, so they in turn established bishops and presbyters. From the beginning, the decisions concerning the good of souls were made by the pastors. Certainly, they were in the habit of of meeting to discuss and decide major questions in a democratic system of government. In monastic history do we find examples of decisions taken by vote? According to the ancient rules, starting with those of St Pachomius and St Basil, many community assemblies and discussions existed, but without majority vote. On the other hand, consultations were in use from the beginning of monastic life. In our Rule, there is no trace of majority vote; that point is clear. What system does St Benedict use, then, for arriving at a decision? We will speak of this in a moment.

Very early, the election of the abbot was made by majority vote, but let us leave this aside for the moment.

Decisions of an economic nature ought to be taken by means of vote; this is the law of the Church. This was to combat the abuses which were rife in the days when abbots could dispose of the monastery fortune as they pleased.

They considered themselves, and were considered, lords of property. Often the patrimony was subject to mismanagement, but, having the power to act as they pleased, abbots were seen more than once to squander the goods they administered. That is why the laws of the Church imposed a limit on that administration by demanding the consent of the community for the validity of acts of financial and economic administration.

Should this way of doing things today be extended to all the decisions of disciplinary and administrative character, in general those which concern the life of the community? What should be our attitude? Should we adopt a more democratic way of doing things, in the sense in which modern democracy is understood? In other words, should the will of the community be made known by letting secret ballots bear the power of decision?

Before examining the system of government of the monastic society in the light of the Rule, let us note that we are dealing with a community of a religious nature, of an ecclesial character, and not with a civil society or community. The purpose of our community as such is the journey toward the Lord, toward eternal salvation. Our life is therefore organized according to an evangelical and ecclesial model. Although there is no reason why questions of an economic nature cannot be decided in the Church by a vote of those concerned, yet the direction of each soul to its eternal goal cannot be made except by pastors personally responsible for the souls to be directed. Now, even questions of a disciplinary nature usually, if not always, have repercussions on individuals, so that for monks, their enforcement depends on the discretion of a competent superior. Most often, the establishment of disciplinary norms in cases where there is a choice of morally possible options should in the last analysis, to be left to the person who has to enforce them. That is why the bishops in the Church make laws for their flock, of course, within the structure and limits established by the authority of the supreme pastor, of the councils, and, now of the episcopal conferences.

The monastic community is, in a restricted sense, a local

Church, for we find in it a number of the elements of a complete ecclesiastical society. For that reason, it is 'exempt'; in terms of canon law, the abbot is its 'ordinary', and the Church even accords him the external signs otherwise reserved to bishops. The ultimate purpose of such a community is to assure the salvation of the souls which make it up.

Let us now see how St Benedict intended to have the brothers participate in the government of the monastery. Let us open the Rule to the third chapter.

It is important, first of all, to notice that this government cannot freely dispose of everything that concerns the life of the community. There exists a fundamental law, a constitution which no one, not even the abbot, has the right to touch: 'All must follow the Rule as the universal norm from which no one should have the audacity to withdraw' (3:7). With that unique law laid down—for St Benedict it went without saying that the Gospel is the norm of norms (Prol. 21)— the legislator distinguished between the major affairs of the community (3:1) and the minor affairs (3:12). Let us notice that the abbot ought never to act without consulting the brethren, for besides major and minor affairs, no third category exists: 'Do nothing without consultation', he says to the abbot (3:13).

For every type of consultation, St Benedict establishes three precepts directed to the brothers:

—The first is fundamental: 'Let no one in the monastery follow the inclinations of his own will' (3:8). It would be difficult to find such a law in the constitutions of democratic republics; so let us take this precept into account in order to understand the basic differences between the model of government called democratic and that of St Benedict.

—A second precept further explains the first: 'Let the brethren give their opinions with all humility and submission, nor venture to defend their opinions obstinately' (3:4).

—Finally, the third: 'Let no one presume to contend insolently with his abbot, either in the monastery [according to some manuscripts] or outside the monastery' (3:9).

With these articles of the constitutive law of the Rule

stated, let us now look at the procedure for consultation.

When there are important matters to decide, the abbot will call together the whole community (3:1); for matters of lesser importance, he will take the counsel of the seniors (3:12). The entire community is, therefore, the consultative body for major affairs without exception, with the obvious exclusion of the novices and of those in temporary vows who, in a certain sense, are still in a state of probation and do not make up an integral part of the community. As for the seniors, St Benedict does not specify either who they are or whether they ought to be called together in common for consultation.

Let us note that in both cases, the abbot calls and consults. St Benedict does not make any provision, as is the custom in modern states, for a distinction between the person who presides over the legislative body and the person who holds the executive power. With good reason. If, in the monastery, a sort of moderator were to exist alongside the abbot, the abbot would very quickly no longer be the father of souls, and at the most a friend.

Now let us go back to our original question and look at the procedure provided by the Rule to work out valid decisions.

The abbot himself convokes the community (3:1) and then explains the matter at hand. It is he who proposes the agenda. St Benedict obviously does not want the brethren to be the first to introduce certain subjects on which the abbot intends to consult them at the proper time. Here again let us note a difference from the procedure of political legislative bodies. But if the abbot reserves to himself the presentation of the theme of the consultation, he need not necessarily explain the entire question himself. In certain cases, he will do well to present it as a problem to be solved, or as questions. He should especially avoid making it felt that he himself is inclined to one certain solution; that would take away much of the brothers' spontaneity of expressing themselves freely, and would deprive him of their honest and good advice. The abbot is obliged to do everything in his power to create a relaxed atmosphere capable of opening hearts and loosening tongues. There is nothing against the abbot having a question studied by a commission whose secretary would explain the results to the brothers in his name.

If consultation with the brothers is done in a peaceful and orderly fashion, according to the principles laid down by the Rule, it falls to the abbot to think it over (3:2) and to weigh the force of the different arguments, without losing sight of the moral authority of those who proposed them. Having thought it over, 'it will depend on the abbot to decide what seems best to him' (3:5). He will judge, therefore, what is objectively and without prejudice *utilius* (2), *salubrius* (5), most useful, most opportune, best.

Note that we are not concerned here with cases where, according to canon law and the constitutions, the abbot is obliged to obtain the consent of his community in order to act, as in admissions, certain acts of an economic nature and others. Nor can one introduce important changes into the constitutions without the consent of the community obtained by majority vote. It goes without saying, then, that canonical norms should be applied in the best possible way. But it would be a mistake, surely, to have recourse to a plebiscite every time an important question comes up. That would be going against the spirit of the Rule. Let us remember that even where the abbot needs the consent of the community, it is his business to propose a question to the brothers' deliberations or to abstain from doing so.

We should study here more closely the profound difference which exists between a benedictine monastic community and every other association. We will leave aside many considerations in order to limit ourselves in this regard to the examination of two revealing aspects offered by the Rule.

First of all, the important thing for St Benedict is to assure and by all means to facilitate a holy obedience, and to exclude all that could lead the monk to cultivate his self-will (3:8). Let us recall his teaching; it appears throughout the entire Rule (RB 5: 7, the four first degrees of humility.). Now, the power to manifest his opposition effectively by vote, and perhaps in this way to challenge the abbot, the superiors, and even, in some sense, the community, might give some monk a taste for affirming his point of view in a way that is contrary to the spirit of humility. St Benedict we notice, is far from treating his brothers like children. They ought, by freely and frankly giving their opinion to the abbot, to affirm their personality, while renouncing the desire to see their opinion triumph through discussion.

Another consideration, which we find implied throughout the Rule, leads St Benedict not to recommend the procedure of voting. In order to justify his regulation of calling to consultation not only the seniors, as one might think from other passages in the Rule, but all the members of the community, he declares: 'The Lord often reveals to someone younger what it is best to do' (3:3). The Lord is the Master of the community; he calls each one to that life, all are traveling toward him. All ought and want to do his will. When should we not then suppose that in important affairs, he himself should inspire, *revelat*, the best decision? To discern the voice of the Spirit, it is not appropriate to poll the community by means of a vote, for that might lead someone to suppose that the divine will reveals itself ultimately by that means, which St Benedict does not mean to suppose. The brother prior of Taizé said on this very point in one of his books that to vote with an absolute majority in order to know God's will would lead one to believe that the decisive vote came from God. It is the abbot who holds the place of Christ; by his office he is the one who ought best to know how to discern the voice of the Spirit of Christ. Let us notice, moreover, that St Benedict refrains from claiming that the abbot has received the Holy Spirit in deciding. No, his task is rather to listen, to discern the voice of the Spirit in the midst of human noise. Once the general consultation has been made, there is nothing against the abbot questioning other brothers whom he considers particularly gifted in knowing the ways of the Lord, before making his decision.

Here we find ourselves in the arena of faith. Is there not, at the bottom of certain tendencies toward 'democratization', a purely human and natural reaction which imagines that it will find the salvation of communities by secular procedures and which places the abbot, the brothers themselves, and the whole consultative procedure on so base a level as to deprive the communities of the lights coming from above?

But, someone may object, does one not risk on the other hand to falling into a base spiritualism, as if all decisions about the most material questions ought to fall from heaven? Ought we not, especially today in the age of specialization, to chose who will be consulted from among those who are competent in the field? Even in great enterprises the leader often does nothing but ratify the decisions prepared by his associates, and a prudent abbot (64:17), who ought to 'dispose of all things with foresight and equity' (3:6), will doubtless do as much. Yet the head of an enterprise does not submit a decision to be made to the majority vote of his engineers; likewise, it would be naïve to believe that a community of monks could show more competence in the affairs than an abbot surrounded by good associates. And if the head of some enterprise holds that position precisely in order to take the responsibility himself, for an even greater reason the abbot, established first and foremost to care for the souls of his brothers, cannot excuse himself from the affairs of the monastery by means of a secret and anonymous vote of the brothers, precisely because these souls have been entrusted to him.

Some people think that it is not possible to have a real participation and a real co-responsibility among the brothers if they cannot manifest their opinion by voting, and if they are only called on to give counsel. Surely, if, in the course of consultation, the climate is neither favorable nor attentive—if the propositions made by someone with little competence are laughed at or treated with derision, the brothers will hardly be moved to partake in a fruitful dialogue, and the number of the apathetic, the malcontent, and the grumblers will grow. But if the consultation is made seriously, every effort at finding a good solution will be concentrated on it, since it is there, basically, that the decision is prepared. Then, one will no longer see an attack on the personality of the brothers in the system of the Rule, which for good reasons leaves the decsion to the abbot.

And then, is it truly realistic to expect from just any

member of the community a competent opinion on any matter whatever? Let's be honest! Someone can explain a problem to us, do everything necessary to make us understand it, but this does not yet mean that we understand it well enough to be able to judge it in full knowledge of the case by a fully considered vote. There is nothing more depersonalizing than to have to vote for or against propositions whose full meaning we do not grasp! Of necessity, we begin to follow a party, we vote by groups, following too easily those who seem to be authorities.

In short, St Benedict follows a criterion which those who are above all preoccupied with defending what they believe to be the inalienable rights of the human person find hard to understand. For him, the abbot possesses all the elements which make him fit for the task of governing: a very broad possibility for consultation and information, the services of associates at his easy disposal; a natural desire to succeed as well as possible in the affairs for which he is responsible, help if he needs it in making a decision, a good knowledge of his brothers, and especially, his duty and his responsibility as the pastor of souls, which make him the most authorized and the most competent person when it comes to making a decision for their welfare.

St Benedict, we think, with his usual serenity and wisdom, takes in this question the position which is at once the most equitable, the most reasonable, and the most religious.

# The Community

# CHARITY CREATES
# THE COMMUNITY

The most Holy Trinity is the mystery of love. The Father speaks his Word, and sees himself in his Word, his Son. He loves him, and the Son loves the Father. And this mutual love is the Holy Spirit. This profound movement of the Father to the Son, of the Son to the Father, is a movement of love, the Spirit of God. God is love. St John tells us this (1 Jn 4:8). He is love because all that happens in him and all that comes from him is love.

St John ends with a very practical conclusion: 'Anyone who does not love has not known God, for God is love' (1 Jn 4:8). It is a simple and direct conclusion. Anyone who loves, loves because he knows God. If we have even a minimal experience of God through faith, we understand that God is charity, and that no one can entreat God or be convinced of his existence without imitating him. We cannot live without love. We know that God, who is love, spreads it abroad in our hearts through the Spirit which is given us. And we know that, having received this divine gift, we can communicate it to others.

If we realize that we do not live as solitaries, but in a society, we understand at the same time what constitutes the relationship to the other, what the constitutive element of society, called charity, is. There may be many kinds of human relationships, but there is only one which involves a person in his depths, in that which is most human in him; and that is love. An interhuman relationship involving man is necessarily dictated by charity if it is authentic and positive. Human society is, in fact, formed on the ideal of the divine society existing among the three Persons. That society is love, and between the Father and the Son, the Spirit—Love— is the link. From him the order and the grace to love our brothers comes to us, as does being one with them, as the

309

Father and the Son are One, and forming with them, one mutual 'society' in charity.

Among men there is a sort of peaceful co-existence called courtesy which covers a whole list of customs practised in order to permit us to live in good relationships with our neighbor, with expressions of politeness and deference. But this is not true charity. In order for it to become charity, that courtesy must have some reference to God. Anyone who truly loves his neighbor, loves him as God, as Christ, loves him. He desires God and his gift for him. He wants to see him as God wishes to see him. But loving his neighbor in this way, he loves God, the source of all good. There is no true love without relation to God who is love.

God has therefore given us the Holy Spirit, Love. Through him, he communicates himself to us. Through him we receive the theological gift of charity. He gives himself to us, and with himself He gives us charity, by which we are able to love him. The feast of Pentecost is the feast of this charity and the fulfillment of all the other feasts because they are all an expression of the charity of God: the Incarnation, the Nativity, the Epiphany, the Resurrection, the Ascension. Pentecost is their completion because God in a more direct, simpler way tells us that everything he gives us is love, is himself, *donum Dei Altissimi.* Now, if God gives himself, he necessarily transmits the communion which is the Holy Trinity—*communicatio Sanctus Spiritus est*—we say [in an antiphon at vigils] on the feast of the Trinity. And consequently, 'our communion is with the Father and with his Son Jesus Christ', as St John expresses it in his first epistle (1 Jn 1:3). Now, if we are in communion with the Father and the Son, we are in communion among ourselves (1 Jn 1:7). We necessarily find ourselves there, but not in the ordinary sense of that word, for that communion is charity. His image of that communion among men is the God who gives it to us. If then we are in communion with God, we live it with our brothers.

We could illustrate this reality in many ways, but let us only recall the example of the Mystical Body of Christ.

That is to explain charity in the theological sense. This charity is a virtue, a gift which is given to us by the Lord. 'The love of God has been poured into our hearts by the Holy Spirit who has been given to us' (Rom 5:5). This theological charity is given us in baptism and through the sacraments, and it is increased by grace every time we receive an increase of sanctifying grace. It is evident that this charity urges us to perform acts of charity. It is a talent working in us if we want it. This talent cannot sleep in the bottom of our soul. This charity is a call, a source of inspiration, a force which tends to action.

We understand that charity has a double object: God and our brothers. Now, the love of God and the love of neighbor are interdependent. Consequently, the love of God leads to acts of charity toward our neighbor. These acts, with time, constitute in us an acquired virtue: brotherly charity. It is a daughter of the love of God, a daughter of God. It is expressed in many ways. 'To be in communion with one another' (1 Jn 1:7). To live in community, to live the cenobitic life, this is not a simple living together. To live the cenobitic life is not just not living the eremitic life, which is a life of solitude far from men. But cenobitism is by its very constitution an expression of charity. One might say that the definition of the cenobitic life is charity with all the implications which charity expresses and signifies. This fullness of the cenobitic life, this community life of ours, is, therefore, an image, a reproduction of the community life within the Holy Trinity. It is a revelation of charity, of the divine life upon earth. We understand why Our Lord said that by charity men will know we are his disciples (Jn 13:35).

The cenobitic life is, therefore, an expression of the divine life, a manifestation of God; and we see to what extent it is a witness of God and for God.

Yes, fraternal charity expresses itself in many ways, and with time, we acquire a real ease, a certain facility, in expressing it. As cenobites we live best as cenobites and not as hermits whom circumstances oblige to live in society. We are united in a perfect charity as true brothers or true sisters. This obviously requires a great deal of effort of each of us. We have to leave our individualism and enter fully into this cenobitic life which requires us to hold everything in common, everything that can be had in common, to correct, to overcome, and, in time to suppress, all that separates us, all that inclines us to particularism. This does not mean that we must suppress our personality. On the day of Pentecost, the Holy Spirit came upon each of the apostles with the gift of a different tongue. He does not come to level, to suppress individuality. He comes in each of us with the tongue proper to us, that is to say, he affirms, sanctifies, supernaturalizes the human personality of each person, expressed by the *linguae dispertitae* (Acts 2:3). Consequently, we remain individuals, well-defined beings. Each apostle had his own personality. Let us notice how partners were able to express this reality in their paintings, by giving particular forms to each of them.

Each of us also keeps the personality which is given us by nature and education and which the Holy Spirit has fashioned through his gifts, a personality, therefore, which is sanctified in that way. But there is too much of the natural in us and corrupt nature creates separations and oppositions, and prevents that perfect communion among us, that flowering of fraternal charity which supposes and demands a true compenetration. St Benedict gives us a whole collection of these forms of expression and in his concrete, direct way, as realistic as it is practical, teaches us to recognize the forms of charity. Recall chapter seventy-two, for example.

Before concluding, let us pose yet another question: are there different concepts of fraternal charity? No, we have to answer, because God is unique, and so there is only one charity. But that does not prevent there being numerous means of expressing that charity which vary according to circumstances. Our charity toward one person ought to be expressed in a different way from our charity toward another, because it is always a response to a concrete relationship, it is called forth and determined by concrete persons. Besides, each one of us reacts in his own way and so our effort to be understanding and our charity show themselves in our ability to assimilate and adapt to each circumstance.

If the charity which is in me does not surpass my personal
limits of reaction to people and things, it will not go far, and
may be only selfishness that thinks itself to be charity.
Charity is able to adapt itself to circumstances.

Also, it is obvious that the manifestations of charity are
not the same in a small and in a large monastic community.
Its mode of expression varies according to the number of
cases to which it is applied. A hermit, living far from men, is
not dispensed from charity, but it expresses itself, if I may
say so, by means of the supernatural antennae which are
prayer and sacrifice. The intensity of his charity can be
greater than that of a cenobite. Different life styles often
demand a change of emphasis in our ways of doing things.

May the Holy Spirit who is the source of infinitely vaired
gifts fill our hearts with his love: *Infunde amorem cordibus*,
according to the demands of charity, and may he ever increase
it in us.

# VIVIS EX LAPIDIBUS

There is generally in our monastic communities a very strong
interior cohesiveness—the effective consciousness of belonging
to the group, a phenomenon of adhesion which is able to
overcome even the most individualistic tendencies of each of
the members.

We will not go into the causes of this situation here; they
belong partly to the religious and partly to the natural order.
Let us simply say that in a community group, each person
finds in the vigor of the community the hope for a survival of
what is best in him, beyond his own disappearance. He is part
of a community body which will not die with him. The need
for immortality is deeply rooted in the human soul, and is
not content with the hereafter.

Now, it is probable that one day all that will remain of us
is a name on a baptismal register, or in the solemn profession
record, or the necrology; and if these books disappear, our
very name will be forgotten. The glory of our life is that we

have given it to the Lord, and that we have also died for him. Perhaps in our life we have fulfilled a modest office, the kind that does not get much publicity; we have borne it simply, and then one day we disappeared. At root this is the lot of most people. Only the 'immortals' can dream of a perpetual memory, yet even that glory is fragile and disappears. Their name too is consigned to a necrology. The books they have written moulder in the basement of some library and one day they disappear.

As for us, we know that the value of our life does not come from an extremely relative human fame, but like the apostles', it enters into the *fundamenta ecclesiae.* The Church is founded on the twelve apostles. The ramparts of the city rests upon twelve supports, each bearing the name of one of the twelve apostles of the Lamb (Rev 21:14). Our life can have a similar value, more restricted, but along the same line. Every monastery is a little 'Church'—the monks are its living stones and their names are invisibly inscribed there. Each monastic generation has supplied the building materials for a life more or less rich in the eyes of God and men. The custom exists in certain communities of reading from the necrology every day the names of those who for a time were the living stones and pillars of the community. These are names, and apparently nothing more, but they summon up so many things, the history of a monastery which in the course of the centuries saw both good and evil days, some bright and others dark, victories and failures, periods when conventional life was mediocre and others when it was fervent. This is how history unfolds itself in the Church and in all of humanity.

Today we are writing our name in the history of our community without fanfare. True greatness has no need of publicity. Let us think of the apostles who became the *fundamenta Ecclesiae* and gave their life for the Lord through martyrdom after having worked hard for him. Had they not received the Holy Spirit in a very special way? Almost everything about them has disappeared. We know so little about them, even though St Jerome undertook numerous researches to preserve their history for us, so how can we wonder if we ourselves fall into oblivion after having worked hard and given our lives.

In *The Imitation of Christ* we read these words, which you know: *Ama nesciri et pro nihilo reputari*—love to be unknown and accounted as nothing. We must not try to shine before the world or in history, but strive to have some value before God. It is he who esteems and judges us. It is God whom we must please. St Benedict did not leave us a history of the community for whom he wrote his Rule. This does not mean to say that he did not realize, or that he underestimated, the value and force of tradition—to convince us of this, we need only notice the place he gave to the seniors (63:10, 12, 16; 71:4; 3:12) and to the good tradition of the house generally (7:55). We see how much he appreciated the true values, the spiritual patrimony of the community. It is therefore constructive as well as useful to remember those who have gone before us. In this way we will better appreciate the fact that we are a small link in the chain of men or women who have forged the history of our community. It will encourage us to put forth all our fervor and abilities, to see that it will be solid, keeps its place well, and fulfils its role. In this way we will think more, on the one hand, of this very modest life we lead without any public importance, and, on the other, of the grandeur of this same life in the chain of God's work. We will think also with profound gratitude of our predecessors who through their dedication have left us the heritage of their spirit. We know that they look on us with sympathy and love, and sustain us through their prayer of intercession before the throne of God.

The Rule requires us to immerse ourselves fully in the community, to share the burden of the abbot, who counts on us (21:3), by acting in a way that justifies his confidence. We ought to serve our brothers joyfully and zealously (RB 72). On the day of our entrance into the monastery, then as postulant, novice, professed, an integration, an incorporation, occurred. These steps are not only juridical, ratified by our will, but they have an affective dimension which supports and animates that will. It is through love that we will truly be at home among our brothers, living members of the house of God, *domestici Dei* (cf. Eph 2:19). We will no longer be strangers or guests, but brothers. Let us realize that this incorporation depends much less on the welcome the brothers give than on the love with which we immerse ourselves in the community. It is love alone which makes us real members of our community, living stones of that Church. The word 'community' always implies 'love' because a community does not really exist except in love; this is what binds, what renders common, what establishes the community, communion, union. And to the extent that each of us immerses himself in it with love, he works at building up the Body of Christ which is the Church of his community.

Each of us wants to be a link in the chain, precisely in order to be in his proper place. We will achieve that result to the extent that we are able to blend with the community and especially with the abbot by giving the best of ourselves while yet remaining ourselves. The apostles accomplished a great work because they could accept the Lord's command, because, in shedding their blood, they would efface themselves before that command and before the Lord himself.

We should enter into this spirit, we should imbue ourselves with this attitude of the apostles by mobilizing all the resources of our personality in this effacement. This is not a question of making ourselves a mere number alongside other numbers. Obedience, far from destroying our forces, makes them bear fruit, multiplies them; through it we will win for the kingdom of God a hundredfold reward. It is pride, basically, which prevents us from blending with our brethren, inspiring us instead to follow our own self-will and, in following our own ideas, to tear, to break, in some way that union which is by definition a community. To disappear for the love of the Lord, to blend with our whole will, with all our action, with our prayer, with all the enthusiasm of our most intimate attitude, this is what assures us that immortality which we desire: immortality in Christ, in his Body, his Church.

# COMMUNITY LIFE

Is the community at the service of each of its members, or is each member at the service of the community?

We could, in some sense, answer yes to both alternatives. I entered the community because I saw there an effective means of human and spiritual progress. According to that point of view, the community is at the service of each member. But in entering the community, I may also help it so it better lends its service to the sanctification of all its members.

But the question is badly put and leads to a false problem. The community at the service of each person? This way of looking at things would encourage selfishness and be to the advantage of those who know how to impose themselves and how to put others at their service on every occasion. This formula is not in the monastic spirit. We do not enter a community in order to be served.

The second position: we are all at the service of the community. Is that, then, the aim of all our efforts? This is not true either. We would have there a communist, collectivist rule where the individual disappears into the community, where he no longer counts, but where all his activities, all his honor, is to be able to serve in such a way that humanity may progress, even at his own expense, before he disappears from the scene. Our community has nothing in common with that. Where then is the truth?

The question is therefore badly put, and a mistake is made at the very start. Godless men necessarily question themselves on the problem of their reason for being and see it from the angle of personal profit, or, if they have risen a bit from that selfish position, from the angle of society or humanity. Humanity is the god of the godless.

Our reason for being is God and our happiness is in him. The community itself has no other end than to help us live for God, in God, and according to the will of God. We are no more at its service than it is at ours.

The problem which concerns us does not, therefore, lie there. We are not interested in knowing if the community is useful to us, but whether the community *life* is useful to us, or, in other words, if living in a monastic community helps me and those who live with me. We are going to see a very affirmative answer to this question by following the thought of St Benedict. The point of departure for this problem, we see first of all, is our personal, eternal salvation. How better to assure the good result of our labors than in uniting and joining ourselves in a common effort according to wise and proven rules!

St Benedict addresses himself, first of all, to each of us individually. In the Prologue, the community does not come up. 'Listen, my son', this is the beginning. It is necessary first of all to convince each one to think of his salvation: the Lord invites me and offers me the chance to seek him, to find him, and to serve him. The discourse of the Prologue in its entirety tends to make these simple truths understood and ends with this phrase: 'So we are going to set up a school where one learns the service of the Lord' (Prol. 45). In other words, St Benedict concludes: we are going to set up a school which you can enter; it will let you attain your goal, aided by brothers who have the same concern you do. So the Prologue addresses itself to the individual, to each one of us. Next, the whole Rule treats of the common life, the means of assuring each person's salvation.

St Benedict helps me not only by the letter of a Rule, but also by setting up an ideal community where I am carried along toward the goal. I ought, therefore, to be interested in the workings of the common life, that is, how it profits each for his own good in the sense the Prologue promised.

The common life is, first of all, the co-ordination, the subordination, the integration of each person. To say integration and subordination is to say humility. Humility is a ladder of perfection, St Benedict shows that abundantly. Now, in order to practise humility, we have to live with others in community. A hermit all alone cannot exercise gentleness, meekness, patience, in a word, humility; before whom can he humble himself?

And then, obedience—it is our path leading to God (71:2). It, too, supposes community life, an abbot, brothers. According to the spirit of the Rule, it is not enough to perform an act of obedience from time to time, we must live under the regime of obedience (5:12). Would this be possible without community life?

Monastic prayer is done in common. Of course, it does not exclude free, spontaneous private prayer. But the official prayer is conventual. Let us be honest, if it did not exist, many peoples' prayer would be reduced to a minimum. We would let ourselves be absorbed quickly by a thousand tasks, often very holy ones, relegating prayer to second or third rank. Community life reserves special times for prayer; it leads us to pray, to appreciate prayer, to strive to pray well. Many will say that they pray better alone. Let them do so. Others say that they are not really able to pray unless they feel inspired. Such subjectivism may lead to not praying at all in the end!

Community life helps us pray. It reminds us of the Lord's promise to be in the midst of us when we pray together (Mt 18:19f.): he wants to see us united and joined together before him, gathered in his name. He wants to find us together around the altar to celebrate the Eucharist, that essentially 'community' mystery. To live the liturgy, then, it is necessary to have a community.

Work, individual occupations, could be self-seeking, a means to satisfaction and personal success, a form of self-will. Community life preserves us from these aberrations. In the monastery, common work joins everyone's forces in the same work (48:7, 41:2, 50:3). The work accomplished alone is always done in view of the community's needs (57:1ff., 46:1, 48:24). No doubt the abbot will prudently take into account the talents and preferences of each in distributing work (57:1, 64:17), but each job is centered on the interests of the community and orients the workman toward it. Purely individualistic work is not provided for in the cenobitic life. Working in the community and for the community detaches us from self and reminds us continually of our condition as member of a society, of our duty to work for the common good. The cenobitic life constantly gives us the alternative either of doing what is useful to others (72:7), or of being hatefully selfish—an alternative which helps us continually to get a hold on ourselves and serve our brothers. Anyone who slips away to seek his own convenience is not a cenobite (1:2, 13).

The requirement of mutual service springs from our social condition. Jesus declared that he came in order to serve (Mt 20:28). For St Benedict, the monastery is a school of the Lord's service (Prol. 45), and a school of mutual service. The abbot ought to serve each according to his character (2:31). The principle put forth by St Benedict in chapter thirty-five: 'Let the brothers serve one another', is to be considered universally applicable (38:6). The precept of mutual obedience says basically the same thing (71:1). Community life implies an immense mutual enrichment where each person is conscious of his duty to be for others a source of light, joy, growth, and stimulation, in a word, to be a servant attentive to the good of others. In this way, the monastery receives its entire social reason for being on both the human and the supernatural plane. The community life assures us of their values. In this sense, the Rule is a service manual for everyone, a map of social life of noble inspiration.

The spirit of detachment is the fruit not only of a readiness to serve, but also of the practice of poverty. We are called to renounce ourselves in order to be united to Christ; the Lord proclaimed this in an impressive way: 'If anyone wants to follow me, let him deny himself' (Mk 8:34), 'let him renounce himself, let him detach himself from everything: his father, his mother, his goods' (Mt 19:29) and 'even his own life' (Mt 16:25). The Lord requires us to be free of everything, to be available, to be poor. Community life leads us to this. On the day of his promise and incorporation into the community, the monk renounces everything he has (58:24) and everything he is (58:25, 33:4). From then on, he holds everything in common with his brothers, and he disposes of nothing as his own (33:3, 6). For what is necessary, he depends on the father of the monastery (33:5) who holds the place of the Lord, whom the monk has asked to take charge of him thereafter (58:21). This community of goods, which restricts to a minimum the objects for individual use (55:19; 32), constantly reminds the monk of his dependence, facilitates interior detachment, and establishes him as a poor person. He has renounced his power to make his own arrangements, and he will live out this detachment to the extent that he lives a real community life in all things. Let us note here that a purely juridical poverty in the sense of having nothing of one's own while keeping the right to dispose of everything would hardly produce this detachment.

A life side by side with the brothers is not truly a common life except through charity, the queen of virtues. It is charity which makes a true community of a living together, of cohabitating. But it is no less true that only community life can teach us the whole breadth and depth of charity. A life very close to our brothers offers us numerous occasions to think of their needs, to help them, serve them, substitute ourselves for them when they are tired, advise them, cheer them up, but also at the same time in a hundred ways to make ourselves their debtors by giving them the occasion to use their knowledge and their know-how and prudence, in counting on their generous and charitable help. Without community life, charity often remains an intention and is not sufficiently lived. On the contrary, uninterrupted community life keeps charity continually awake. Only the unfeeling, hard, and self-centred person can shut himself off from the constant appeal which a brother's presence is for someone who understands all the demands of that phrase: 'To be brothers'.

It is fitting to speak of charity being refined and growing by means of the common life. It is its daughter. The good order of the community (47:1), the Rule itself, do not ask a dry obedience, but an obedience for the love of God (7:34) and the brothers (72:2ff.). Living together constantly requires mutual tokens of respect (63:10ff., 72:4), of affection, of collaboration and service. It is easy to imagine how much thoughtfulness the common dormitory (22), even though divided into cells, requires of everyone, for the physical and moral weakness of each (72:5), for their habits, for their rest (48:5). Meals are taken in common and impose just as much renunciation which must be accepted by everyone for the good order of community life and out of respect for the brothers. The good running of the kitchen, we realize, prevents not only fatigue and sickness but also discontent and complaining. The cook ought to be a master of the culinary arts, but still more, of the art of charity and to have compassion on the brothers' weakness (39:1f.). Do the table readers always remember to read so they can be understood and not just for themselves (38:12)? And do the brothers at table remember not to make unnecessary noise (38:5) which disturbs others? We preach to the people of the world about struggling against noise, but do we remember to avoid it ourselves in regard to our brethren? Propriety is also a makr of respect toward others, whereas slovenliness or vulgarity are signs of an unpardonable carelessness. Some young people today confuse sincerity and simplicity with a lack of respect, displaying an offensive boorishness through lack of a real education of the heart. Charity is never ill-mannered (1 Cor 13:5). The common life helps us to compare our own behavior with that of others, to notice what we do wrong, to correct ourselves; it gives us the educational supplement that each of us needs and makes us more sensitive to the respect which living together with our brethren demands of us.

Common prayer, the choral office, is a real school of adaptation to others in charity. Punctuality is already one way of expressing our respect and our knowing how to behave (11:12f., 43). And then, we have to adapt our voice to the group, to pay attention to special services to be performed in order to avoid total confusion and disorder; we also ought to be on guard against mistakes and carelessness (45:1f.). And since common and private prayer are for each of us an entry into very personal contact with God, it is a duty of justice and charity to avoid everything that might disturb our brother (52:3) in his meetings with Him who dwells in light inaccessible and is surrounded by a silence impenetrable to the natural man.

This is where the function of conventual silence

particularly appears. 'My house is a house of prayer' (Mt 21:13) says the Lord; this applies not only to the church of the monastery and to the cloisters—the cloister is the garden enclosed against the noises of the world, but to the dormitories—these cells are little sanctuaries, to the entire monastery. And since silence is less abstaining from talking than it is an act of recollection, silence is therefore a service which each does for the others, a condition of interior peace and withdrawal from everything that is useless in the light of eternity. The common life requires us to speak when it is necessary or when charity demands it; it also teaches us that sensitivity of soul which takes into consideration our brother's deep need for silence and peace. St Benedict wrote a whole chapter to shed light on the social and individual function of the love of silence (RB 6; see also 42:1, 8, 9, 11; 38:5; 48:5; 52:2, 4).

Let us consider cleanliness and the care to be taken of the house again. What a bad impression a dirty monastery gives! Do we not talk a lot about the problem of the increasing pollution of the environment? Charity toward our brethren demands thorough cleanliness in our cell, in regular places, in the monastery. Just as the fight against pollution cannot be effectively waged without a firm will and the joint action of all, so the cleanliness of the monastery is not the exclusive business of those in charge, but rather the effective action of each and every member. Living together is a constant appeal to adopt such attitudes. Utensils, tools, books, furniture, dishes, cutlery, even the linen we use may be used by someone else tomorrow. St Benedict reminds us of this and educates us by requiring that satisfaction be made by those who are negligent (46:1-4). The whole system of the satisfactions (RB 43-46 and elsewhere) aims at training us to be considerate of our brothers. The practical system prescribed by St Benedict for keeping the tools clean and in good working order (RB 32) pursues the same goal. We are struck with the frequency of the word 'negligence' and its derivatives in the Rule. St Benedict sees in this a serious fault against charity toward God (73:7, 50:4, 2:25, 7:22) and toward one's neighbor (36:6, 10), a fault against which his sense of good order, the guardian of peace and charity, rose energetically up.

All these arrangements end at last in a spirit always open to dialogue, that is to say, to the union of hearts and minds through charity. Dialogue, long before it manifests itself through words, is a union of hearts through a profound harmonization of wills in one accord, which is not necessarily a unison, a uniformity, but a harmony on one identical melody with all the richness of its variations. Dialogue is first of all the silence of someone who knows how to enrich himself by listening and reflecting, and then, the statement of his personal thoughts, respecting those of the other. This dialogue, it is true, takes time. The too hasty forming of one's opinion, where patience is demanded, is contrary to the spirit of dialogue, because it lacks respect for different opinions often born of experience and wisdom. Charity alone successfully presides in a dialogue. So the common life, which teaches charity, also teaches dialogue.

After having passed over the whole of community life in a necessarily abbreviated way, we understand better why St Benedict speaks of the 'strongest kind of monks, namely, the cenobites' (1:13). Man is by nature an imperfect being, but perfectible through contact with his fellows by a life in common. Is it not logical to exploit this state of affairs for his spiritual growth, for his journey toward God? Gathered together for the highest goal known to human life, cenobites help each other at the same time in their human growth and their sanctification. The hermit, his admiration for whom St Benedict does not hide—was he thinking of the great hermits of Egypt or of his own younger days as a hermit?—is heavily armored in comparison with the cenobite (Prol. 3), a man deprived of the help of his brethren and exposed to many dangers from which only a special grace, joined to a strong will formed by the experience of the common life, can save him. St Benedict was a realist. Although he was a man of great faith, he did not expect miracles in the monks' ordinary life. We must use the means the Creator has put at our disposal. The common life is one of the most effective of these.

In conclusion, let us be careful not to leave the impression that life in a monastic community is an easy thing. It demands very great sacrifices. It is precisely at the price of these sacrifices that the monastic virtues increase in our hearts. Experience has taught us a long time ago that the common life is far from producing our salvation automatically. The tendency to transform social life into an all encompassing bearhug is as inborn in us as our search for community life. The whole cenobitic life is a struggle against self-will with its atavistic egoism. But only the person who can renounce himself is worthy to be Jesus' disciple (Mt 16:24, 10:37f., Lk 14:26f.).

# RANK IN COMMUNITY
# AND ITS MEANING

The chapter on the rank to be observed in the community is a masterpiece of social legislation. A community needs discipline, a rule, to order fraternal relations and community acts. The cenobitic life cannot exist without legislation, so from its very beginnings we see legislators such as St Pachomius, St Basil, St Augustine, and St Benedict. We find already in St Pachomius, the first legislator of cenobitism, rules which are completely similar to those we find in our Rule of St Benedict; for example, it is the date of entry into the monastery which determines rank and not physical age; the person who entered first walks ahead of the others, is served first at table, goes to communion first, and so on.

Let us inquire, first of all, into the motives which led St Benedict to regulate certain questions concerning relations among the brethren. The seniors call the juniors 'brother'; the juniors call the seniors *nonnus*. We are told that the word *nonnus* probably has an Egyptian etymological origin. The word survives as *nonne* in French, *Nonne* in German, and *nun* in English, meaning a woman religious,

but the word *nonnus* has fallen into disuse. The Order of
Cîteaux still uses it; every Saturday, when the distribution
of weekly offices is read out, we call each monk *nonnus*,
according to the Cistercian ritual, adding his name to it.
*Nonnus* signifies *paterna reverentia*, St Benedict explains
(63:12), 'Father', whereas the juniors are called 'Brother'. It
is true that all are brothers, but for distinguishing between
seniors and juniors, this terminology lends itself naturally. Is
there here an undue discrimination contrary to the spirit of
the Rule, which wants to see us all equal and on the same
footing (2:20)?

Yes, all are truly brothers. But this does not prevent there
being a social order, a hierarchy. A group of persons ought
to be ruled by a law of precedence, however flexible it may
be. A community of human beings cannot be informal. In a
monastery everyone cannot go at the same instant to receive
the kiss of peace or to communion, or intone the same Psalm,
or occupy the same place in choir (63:4). A hierarchical
order is needed.

Now this order is the monk's means of training himself in
respect for others and their rights, a way of discovering the
human and fraternal considerateness with which we should
be surrounded; it trains him also in sensitivity, courtesy, and
charity, and makes him mindful of the needs of others. It is
in this context that we ought, for example, to examine the
question of the advisability in our monastic communities of
addressing one another in familiar terms and disregarding
what is conventionally considered polite. In principle, this is
a matter of convention or custom; mentality and sensibility
enter into play. This is why the solution chosen, in order to
be harmonious, should be integrated into the overall view
of the problem; that is to say, into that profound human
need for mutual respect which is natural among brothers
or sisters.

To these considerations is added the religious, the supernatural, aspect. Pachomius called his community 'the community of saints'. Now, saints treat each other in a holy
manner. Their mutual relations have nothing vulgar about
them. Where a certain vulgarity asserts itself in a community,

there is a lack of an important element of the cenobitic life which is a life of brothers and sisters in Christ and not a life of good fellowship among pals who are happy to see each other again. Nor are we friends joined together to pursue a common commercial, industrial, or social goal, for example, and who, in order to facilitate mutual relationships, treat each other as comrades. The goal of our life is what makes us, and causes us to find ourselves on a higher level. We intend to journey together to the Lord. The tone of our living together ought, therefore, to be marked by this common purpose of the supernatural order. This tone of our relationship, let us repeat, does not necessarily exclude familiarity, but it ought to be adapted to the motivation of our life.*

Here we touch upon the question of the sacred. Our life is sacred; all of our ambiance is sacred because it has a higher, a religious, destination. The common goal for us monks is to tend toward holiness, to praise and to seek the Holy, the Thrice Holy. Consequently, in this sense, our life is sacred, but only in this sense. We cannot deny that before our positivist era, people had a tendency to surround objects, customs, and events with a halo, when actually they arose from the phenomena and forces of nature. Modern men, as we are among them, are not in favor of such extrapolations. The secular way of thinking has the tendency to secularize even when the relation to God is inherent in a person or thing.

Now, as a matter of fact, this kind of weakening of the faith, this spirit of demythologizing the sacred, does not stop at the gate of the monastery, but manifests itself also in our mutual relationships. A tendency to camaraderie affirms itself among the brethren, the spirit of buddies appears. When we abandon the monastic habit, we lose the fraternal respect which is born of the sense of the sacred. Certainly, we must not exaggerate the supernatural character of our mutual relationships. We must not, for example, see in the

---

*In French-speaking communities, the question of members addressing one another as *tu* (familiar) or *vous* (formal) had come up and was being addressed here.

abbot a sort of oracle, or a saint *ex officio.* He is a man like the rest of us. What is sacred in him is not to be confused with the natural man. We must, therefore, know how to distinguish it. Otherwise, a too human experience, according to our point of view, could plunge us into serious perplexities, and even cause a whole world to crumble inside us. Certain crises of vocation are reduced to this: an attitude which over-sacralizes and is not careful enough in distinguishing between the sacred and the profane during one's monastic or clerical youth.

Do we need to demythologize our mutual relationships in our communities today? Nowadays, the struggle is instead to free ourselves from an exaggerated tendency to naturalism. Let us not apply ourselves to making our life a profane one; it is a life of charity based on the law of charity and, for that reason, sacred. Besides, we are persons consecrated by our profession, consecrated by the goal and the nature of our life. Today, the monk is still considered sacred, perhaps in a slightly different sense than formerly, but always in the sense where he is a man who seeks God, in spite of all the weaknesses which hinder that search during the course of his life. The monk is a man of God's praise, of the *Opus Dei.* In the past, he was considered a man of God; he still is today. This idea of being a man of God, is this not what should determine our mutual relationships? Are we not brothers above all because we march shoulder to shoulder toward the Lord in the paths marked out by the Gospel and the Rule? And this profound, humble, and sincere respect which we bear each other, is it not normal, because we are able to discern in the other, whether he is a *senior* or a *junior,* a seeker of God, someone who by sacrificing his life to Him yearns to love with an ardent and generous love? To the extent that the person of our brother is sacred to us, to that same extent will our attitude toward him be imbued with a profound respect, full of faith in the work which the Holy Spirit is accomplishing in him. In this way, we will have no difficulty in *honore invicem praevenientes* (Rm 12:10), showing each other respect by not referring to one another by our simple name in a worldly way (63:11), by rising when a senior comes in (65:16), by asking our seniors' blessing or by recommending ourselves to their prayers (63:15), and finally, by humbly respecting our abbot and loving him with a sincere love (63:13, cf. 72:10). We will also understand the deep meaning of the order by which the brothers are ranked, the visible sign of their calling by God (63:1, 8), and likewise, the hierarchic order of the community will be for us and for everyone a rich source of happy and sanctifying consequences.

# CONCERNING THE BROTHERS' MUTUAL RESPECT

Our Father St Benedict, when speaking of the *zelus bonus*, good zeal, made a sort of enumeration of attitudes required by charity. Referring to the Epistle to the Romans (12:10) he tells us first of all that the brothers should 'honor each other by giving each other precedence' (72:4). It is interesting to notice that St Benedict cites these words from the Epistle to the Romans before the words which precede them in that same Epistle, namely: 'Let them chastely fulfil the duties of fraternal charity', which, although it does not correspond exactly to that text of the Epistle, nevertheless retains its sense.

Why, then, does our Father St Benedict begin with the words 'Let them honor each other by giving one another precedence'? It is obviously not a matter of honoring the brothers according to the rules of worldly propriety, or of offering them a book of etiquette. It concerns the honor we give our brothers by a movement of charity. Here we do not find ourselves on the natural plane where it is easy to pay compliments to our neighbor, compliments which, no doubt, mean to be sincere, but often do not touch the depths of our hearts. The honor which we are invited to extend to our brothers involves us entirely. It is charity which moves us to honor them.

Now, if we reflect a little on the practical meaning of that word, after having looked into its etymology—to honor means to hold in reverence—we will understand our duty of giving our brother the highest place in our considerations. Our words and actions ought to be witnesses to the respect we have for him in our heart, and the honor we extend to him attracts the esteem of his brothers to him. We ought, therefore, to be careful of his interests. We fully grasp, then, that this honor of which the chapter on the good zeal speaks is love. Yet St Benedict does not speak of love, he speaks of honor, citing the words of the Epistle to the Romans; and he speaks less of brotherly love in the Rule than of its concrete manifestations. It is, in fact, more practical to speak of honor than of love. The word 'love' is too rich, too full of meaning, and on the other hand, too complex and too vague, even ambiguous, in its usage, whereas the expression 'to give honor' is more concrete and less subject to platonic and doubtful interpretations. It is as a realist, therefore, that St Benedict chose this expression.

Thus we understand the insistence with which our legislation returns several times in the Rule to this thought of St Paul (Rom 12:10; RB 4; 8, 63:17, 72:4) and why the phrase 'Let them honor each other by giving one another precedence' is placed here at the head of the list which follows. All the good actions which are recommended next are the expression of this precedence of honor which we ought to show toward our brethren. And the commentary begins: 'Let them bear with an unchanging patience the physical and moral weaknesses of their brothers (72:5). It is interesting that Cassian, with a similar expression, says: the perfect man is the one who either can endure 'the horror of solitude' (*Conferences* 19.9), or else, with the same magnanimity, bears the weaknesses of the brethren. Cassian knew perfectly the eremitical life with its advantages and dangers. He therefore advised being practical: Do not think that you can profit by solitude while avoiding the weaknesses of your brethren. You have a choice: either 'the horror of solitude', that is to say, isolation, or else the weaknesses of your brothers. Choose. But above all, do not imagine that you can profit from the advantages which these two ways of life offer, keeping from each the things that seem most pleasant. We would like to live in community and enjoy the advantages of the community, but at the same time, arrange a little life of solitude for ourselves without troubling ourselves about our brother. We have already made the choice; it is no longer to be made. And since it has been made, we have accepted the weaknesses of our brothers. It is therefore time to put into practice these words: 'Let them honor each other by giving one another precedence'.

Now, it is less difficult to honor the abbot, the seniors, the guests, the virtuous, than to honor those who by their weaknesses or faults demand our patience. Yet they are no exception from the general rule, that the brethren should give precedence to one another with marks of respect. When St Paul points out that there are weak members of the Body of the Church, he takes their side by explaining to us that we usually surround with greater honor the less honorable members of our body (cf. 1 Cor 12:23). Therefore, let there be no pretentions among the members. Let all have care for one another without reserve or exception (1 Cor 12:25).

Better still, the weaker members have greater right to our charity, to our help. We are not, therefore, allowed to interpret the word *tolerant* simply in the sense of 'to bear' and to bend our backs, so to speak, under the weight of our brothers' weaknesses. We must go further and honor our brother, respect him even in his weaknesses—not, of course, because of his weaknesses, but in his weaknesses—he is our brother, just as he is. And because he is weak, he has a greater right to his brothers' strength.

To practise that is to live real love. It is not enough therefore to show our brother a sort of indulgent compassion and to let him gently realize that we bear with his weakness and his character faults. We have to add honor, respect; we must be able to discover everything honorable in our brother. To succeed in this, we must realize that every weakness has a good quality as its counterpart, and that by training our eye to see only the side of weakness, we pervert our vision by limiting it to what is negative. If, therefore, every weakness, every infirmity, has a good quality as its counterpart, we should make our eye get used to seeing the positive side of the weakness, the good quality; that will be to honor our brother, to respect him, even in his weakness. 'Does one member suffer? All the members suffer with him. Is one member honored? All the members share his joy' (1 Cor 12:26).

What are the weaknesses which might be involved here? Those of the body are easy to see: illnesses and their many consequences: feebleness, fatigue, old age. But we should also be able to spot the weaknesses of the soul: timidness, discouragement, and all the traumas wrought by the melancholic, the scrupulous, the disillusioned, the unsociable. We should also think of those who are weak in the faith, who have not sufficiently understood the meaning and the value of obedience, who have let themselves be turned away from their brothers, from their superiors, who have allowed themselves to be won over to devious ideas, all those who are poor and miserable because they do not know how to accept the riches of faith, of hope, of the love of God, thinking too much of the shortcomings they find in others as well as in their type of life.

These are all doubly our brothers, these are the ones who really need our love. It is in honoring them that charity is confirmed (27:4) and shows itself to be authentic. With them we have to use all our comprehensive charity, a generous, intelligent, patient will. Only charity knows how to reunite, despite all the obstacles and the resistances which often put those concerned at loggerheads, those brethren who for one reason or another, have placed themselves or have been placed on the fringes of the community.

But let us remember that charity ought above all to express itself through respect. In these cases we need respect for opinions, for experience, respect for character, for closed hearts, respect for a brother's freedom. We must accept the brother in his interior condition; we must lead him back, of course, but with great patience. Any blunder may deepen the wounds instead of curing them.

Especially far from us be any thought of superiority or pride. Let us realize that we ourselves are weak, perhaps not in the same way our brother is, probably in a less spectacular way, but it is certain that we all, each and every one without exception, have our personal weaknesses, and we have need of the understanding, the pardon, and the respect of our brother.

'Let them honor each other by giving one another precedence.' The honor we give to a poor, discouraged brother, more or less left to himself, can work miracles. There is nothing more encouraging, nothing which makes him more conscious of his own value, nothing more effective in restoring confidence in himself and rendering it to others, than the honor of a word of praise spoken by the abbot or a sincere brother.

Did Jesus not come in order to restore our dignity to us? What delicate and patient respect did he not show toward his disciples whom he loved! He made great apostles of these simple and ill-trained men. Has he not bent over our wounds with a boundless goodness? It is told of some saint that he cared for the sick and kissed their wounds. In honoring our brother, we kiss his wounds, we spread balm on the wounds of his soul. And in this way, our own wounds heal little by little.

# A RULE OF
# BROTHERLY CHARITY

St Benedict very modestly calls his Rule 'this rough sketch of a rule' (73:8). He wants it to be a line of conduct for beginners, containing only the first principles necessary for the first stage of the spiritual life. Now, for beginners, simple and concrete principles are needed, rules which strike the imagination and even, in some way, self-love.

Brotherly charity is what maintains community life, even what builds it; it is its foundation. It is through charity that we find God. It is God's way to us and our way to him. It is, therefore, of primary importance to impress this on the monk, and that in a practical and very basic way.

As a matter of fact, we need to be reminded often. Let's be honest with ourselves. It is not always easy for us to have a heart that is generous and warm enough for charity to reign there without shadow. Too easily we are weak in this area. We allow ourselves to be disturbed by daily disagreeable experiences of the common life which repeat themselves and mortify us, by our own deficiencies which repeat themselves no less, by the lack of zeal that we sometimes bring to the fulfilment of our christian duty which is, nevertheless, a gentle yoke. We get irritated over nothing, and too quickly we find ourselves at the limits of our power to love. We need, therefore, to come back to the question of the methodology of St Benedict, principles which strike us in order to impress upon the monk this duty of brotherly charity.

One of these principles is stated in the Rule three times: 'Not to do to another what one would not want to have done to oneself' (4:9, 61:14, 70:7). In the Old Testament, it was said to the Israelites: An eye for an eye and a tooth for a tooth—a principle which does not seem very attractive to us. But the New Testament in some way takes this attitude of the old man for granted in drawing a lesson for the new man when it says: 'All the things that you would have men do to you, do unto them' (Mt 7:12, Lk 6:31). The negative form given by the Rule, taken from the Book of Tobit (4:16), is an appeal to reason and natural reflection, and is easier to grasp. The affirmative form in which Jesus expresses the same basic thought perhaps better underscores the effort of charity, and is in this sense indicative of the spirit of the New Testament.

Although charity does not stop at a two-way bargaining, although it is not conditioned by the expectation or the hope of some recompense more or less guaranteed in advance, there is, nevertheless, a universality to the duty of charity which makes it necessarily mutual. 'Love one another', the Lord Jesus commanded us (Jn 13:34). Surely the idea of conditional reciprocity in charity was not in his mind, or he would have said: Love others if they love you, or so that they will love you in return.

When St Benedict cites this ancient admonition not to do to another what one would not want done to oneself, he also is very far from wanting to establish a sort of new law of retaliation. To convince ourselves, let us read what he says in the fourth degree of humility, or, among the instruments of good works, such advice as 'Not to render evil for evil' (4:29), or 'Not to render cursing for cursing' (4:32), and other similar statements. His intention is probably not to legislate moral principles, but to give advice of an educational nature. This admonition is truly not redundant. If we sincerely reflect on the effect which would be produced on ourselves by some word or action by which we intend to retaliate on our brother if he does something to us, the lack of delicacy, kindness, prudence, and charity which we are in danger of falling into will come to us in a flash.

From this fact let us immediately draw a practical lesson. Charity demands that we be able to bear patiently the physical and moral weaknesses of others (72:5). What does this mean? Is it enough to put up with our brother passively, saying to ourselves: 'That's the way he is, let's accept him'? Let us ask ourselves the question: 'Would I be happy to hear my brother say behind my back, in speaking about me to someone else: "That's the way he is, let us accept him"?' To put up with our brother passively is not enough, and it does not respond to the profound meaning of 'let them bear with the greatest patience'. He must be accepted actively. Why? Because in accepting him as he is, as he came from the hand of God, from the womb of his mother, of his family, I love him truly as I must love a human person, whom I cannot love by halves or discriminately. This does not mean that I ought to love his faults in themselves. We do not love virtues, or good qualities, or faults; we love our brother in his person, just as he is.

And through this understanding, this acceptance, I cause my brother to rise psychologically; I respect him as a human person, as a brother in Christ Jesus. He came from a family community; his father, his mother, his brothers and sisters, his family have made him what he is; they have educated him, trained him. He should now be wholly accepted into the spiritual community, a brother among brothers. Thus it seems that the words 'let them bear with the greatest patience' in no way expresses an attitude of 'let it be', almost a regret, implying a certain depreciation of the brother who is laden with weaknesses or with faults which, in the end, christian charity requires us to bear in spite of everything. Such an attitude would be a caricature of charity, which lays down no limits or conditions, and a parody of patience, which is strong, sincere, and wholehearted.

It is in the light of the axiom, 'What you do not want others to do to you, do not to them', that we understand better what our attitude in regard to the infirmities of others ought to be. We have only to examine ourselves with complete clarity of mind and discover our own poverty and pettiness, and the pretentions we have, to see that our brothers take us just as we are—we who so often, alas, believe our faults are extinct or even see them as good qualities—and we will be humble, and we will arrive this way at a sincere charity which will make us more receptive to our brother, more enlightened about ourselves, and more attentive, finally, to the Lord Jesus who gave himself totally to the sinner we are, loving us even to giving his life.

# OBEDIENCE
# FOR THE GOOD
# OF THE COMMUNITY

In chapter five St Benedict explains the motives for monastic obedience to us (2f.). We need not return to them here. But it is certainly profitable to examine this obedience from the angle of community. We single it out generally in the area of relations with the superior. It is true; we owe obedience to the abbot (3:5f.). But we must look at the problem in all its dimensions.

Let us remind ourselves, first of all, that monastic obedience truly always goes to Christ and, through him, to the Father. We do not obey a man insofar as he is a man, but through the man we obey Christ (2:2, 64:13). There is, however, another very important aspect of obedience, that which relates to life in common with our brothers. In a community, some social order is obviously needed. In a community of citizens, public order is needed, subordination. Without order, there will be wrangling, revolution, and anarchy. Let us pause, therefore, to consider obedience under the aspect of community.

Basically, obedience given to the Father is based on a personal relationship. On the other hand, obedience for the good of the community constitutes primarily a relationship on the horizontal plane, if I may say so, a community relationship. Now, the religious community is the *ecclesia*. So this is not merely a social question, a problem of the purely human order; this obedience has a theological dimension. If we have this faith in the ecclesial character of the community, if we recognize that it is a parcel of the Church, this obedience takes on new horizons. Our community wants to grow in numbers, certainly, but it wants most of all to grow in Christ, or more exactly, Christ wants to grow in it. The Christ who, in the pilgrim Church, journeys toward eternity, toward the final resurrection and ascension, that Christ is the total Christ, in an expression of St Augustine. In him, with him, and through him, we journey toward this ultimate perfection. It is in this sense that Christ grows in the community even to his full stature, his perfect maturity (cf. Eph 4:13). So then, obedience ordered to the good of the community is directed toward Christ in that sense, too.

What does the expression mean: obedience ordered to the good of the community? We know perfectly well that our obedience to the abbot does not have the superior's good as its goal. Besides the motives pointed out above and enumerated in chapter 5 (2f.), we can say that we obey for the good of the community when we obey in order to establish Christ fully and maturely in the community and the souls which go to make it up. It follows also from this reflection that the abbot, when giving orders, ought to keep in view the real good of souls. And since it is not easy to discover this true good, he ought to use all the means at his disposal to discover it. He ought to consult, to study, to pray. It is his duty to work to establish the kingdom of God in souls. When the superior acts in this way, the person who obeys realizes that in obeying him he submits himself to the good of the community, that in this sense, he obeys the good of the community that Christ may grow in it.

But we can also say in all truth that in obeying the superior, we obey the community. Just as the cellarer's job is to prepare material goods for it, the cook's to prepare meals, the novice master's to form true monks, so also the function of the abbot within the community, his social function, therefore, is to direct by giving orders and making decisions, and this always for the common good. He has been chosen for this job.

In obeying the abbot as the person who presides over the good of the community and who is put in office for that reason, we obey the community, and we act wisely in supposing that the superior, insofar as the contrary is not manifest, truly has the intention of ensuring its spiritual and temporal good. It follows from this teaching that each member, in order to assure the smooth running of the organization, ought to remain in his proper place, because no one in a well-regulated society should arrogate to himself the functions of director or impose himself in the area of another's responsibilities. In the monastery, each person has his own post: the prior and the cellarer have theirs, and the abbot has his. On this condition, the community will live in peace. On this condition also, one can obey, because he realizes that in spite of all the shortcomings that may arise, he obeys the community and its welfare when he obeys his competent and legitimate superior.

Let us add, finally, that if the superior has really understood what St Benedict expects of him, he will not decide the interests of the community according to his personal views, but instead obeys him by consulting, regulating, serving, or even imposing, if necessary, what is objectively recognized as being to its true advantage. He is not the author of this wise arrangement; on the contrary, he himself obeys what he believes to be and sees to be the true good of the community. He does not obey by receiving orders by majority vote, but by doing for the community what will truly profit it before God (3:5), in full responsibility towards Christ who is its soul, its hidden life, and its true Good.

As long as the brothers reasonably suppose that their superior is sincerely trying to act in this way, they can and should obey him in complete security. In obeying him, in this sense, they obey the community. The superior, rather than giving orders coming from his own way of seeing things, is basically only the mouthpiece of the salvific will of Christ who, by means of the ecclesial community of which he is the head, carries on his work of redemption. In obeying the superior, we enter this current of grace emanating from Christ, and we submit ourselves to his influence. At the same time, we integrate ourselves more intimately into the community where the work of Christ's salvation is concretely brought about. Our obedience, in the final analysis, then, goes to the community, toward Christ who is in it, and to the Father who thus brings about our salvation.

# PERSONALITY
# AND COMMUNITY

'The eighth degree of humility is that a monk do nothing which is not in conformity with the common rule of the monastery or commended by the example of the seniors' (7:55).

When we read these words, we are tempted to believe that this way of looking at things is no longer valid today. Who would consent to becoming a monk in order to do nothing but what the Rule prescribes and what he sees the seniors do? In our day, a certain concept of personality seems unable to concede an affirmation like the eighth degree of humility. Is the personality not a gift of God? It seems obvious then that each of us ought to act according to his character, without suppressing its characteristics. It seems we cannot require a monk to submit himself to the common rule of the monastery and the seniors' way of doing things. Let us pay close attention to what these words wish to express. The Rule includes ancient monastic traditions, the constitutions, and the particular character of some one community with all its special customs, customs which develop with time and which endure. Let us add that it is not always easy to discern the abuse of reasonable usages and the superfluity of good traditions.

Today we are always being told that we must not let ourselves be leveled out. We are told about human dignity, about everything that can and should accent the personality, how we must affirm it, cultivate it, develop it. This tendency is not basically wrong, individuality being an incomparable nobility in man. From this, we begin to see the clashes that can occur between the rights of the personality and the common rule of the monastery, tradition, the character and customs unique to the community, if one or another of these notions is poorly understood or poorly applied.

Let us begin by considering the rights of the community. There we touch on the problem of charity. Charity is, in fact, the form of the community. The essential form of the community is specifically living, not only in juxtaposition, but in communion. Moved by charity, each person acts, not for himself, but for the good of all. Our monastic profession demands that we enter into the community with all our being and in a supernatural manner, while renouncing ourselves. Now, the community expresses itself by its way of living and of handling common affairs, ways which have been established through a long developed and thought-out cenobitic experience. The common rule of the monastery (7:55) and the example of the seniors constitute, therefore, a true, solidly established right of the community, and charity, not to mention justice, requires that everyone conform to these rules and these good examples, accepted from the very outset by those who become members of that community.

How, then, can this problem of personality be reconciled with the requirements of charity? It would seem at first sight that there is opposition between these two concepts which, taken individually, however, seem to us to be legitimate, and we maintain them. We lay great value on our personality and we intend to preserve and cultivate it; it is a talent with which we must one day present ourselves before God. The personality, thus understood, itself has its rights in respect to charity. The Lord cannot contradict himself and give us one talent which would be in opposition to another. Charity is poured forth into our hearts by the Holy Spirit; it is a gift of God. But is the personality also a gift of God?

Let us first of all make clear what the precise meaning of personality is. If we use the expression *individualitas* as a principle of distinction, it goes without saying that the personality is a gift of nature and, consequently, of the Creator who gives each individual human being his uniqueness. If, on the other hand, we intend to express by that word the original, unique, and irreproducible combination of the properties of a person, then its immediate causality cannot be attributed to God without distinction. Many factors go together to give a man his moral physionomy: nature, physical and psychical heredity, education, environment, the ideas of the times, and especially the personal efforts of the individual, which lead more or less to an harmonious maturation of the talents, gifts, qualities, tendencies, passions, and acquired or infused virtues which form the moral assets with which one must work. In this sense, the personality signifies a person's combination of positive and precious qualities, and often unites qualities which, at first glance, would seem opposed to each other, making of them, however, a more or less coherent moral unity.

It goes without saying that personality taken in this sense could not be legitimately affirmed with no reservation, and that the man entering a community or a society must seek to harmonize his aspirations, his whole personality, with the whole community with its laws, governance, and customs. To wish to make one's personal desires, or one's way of life, prevail at the expense of unity, peace, and charity would be to put the crown on eccentricity, not on personality.

But should we not let the community profit from the values and the riches of our personality? In fact, no one has the right to hide his treasures. What has been given to us, or what we have added by our own efforts, belongs to our brethren as well. For charity shares what it has and does not jealously hold back what it has at its disposal. But, in cases of doubt, who can judge whether a particular talent or a certain ability is really desirable for the community? It is certainly not for each person to decide the objective value and the utility of his own talents or qualities for serving the community. No one is a good judge in his own case. It is for the superiors to decide for him. Which is as much as saying that the common rule of the monastery and the example of the seniors retain their full importance in this case.

A monk may not, on the pretext of offering the community the talents of his personality, heap on it his caprices and his faults, which the community must then accept and assimilate and perhaps even make a part of the common rule of the monastery which everyone must take into account! Quite obviously this would be contrary to good sense and going too far. People of the aggressive type think they are doing good by imposing their own ideas on the community by the force of their energy or their convictions, without sufficiently considering the fickleness of such a course, or even of the very ideas they want to impose, whether this comes from inexperience, or quite simply because they are fashionable. Here too, it is necessary for each person to know how to remain in his proper place and how to feel great respect for the dignity of others and the community itself.

Here we have to make an important distinction, separating the values which truly come from God from those which come from fallen nature. Remember the chapter of *The Imitation of Christ* which deals with the discernment of spirits: 'Of the diverse movements of nature and of grace'. The author teaches us throughout how we should be able to distinguish ever better between what truly comes from God—that natural good which comes from the Creator—and what is a distortion, an exaggeration of that same nature. In diseases of the body, we sometimes find abnormal outgrowths. Likewise in the personality, there are exuberances, exaggerations, which transform true values into deformities and which consequently, while seeming still to be valuable, are not.

In the course of our reading, we sometimes meet with these characters, rich in good qualities, but with exaggerations which destroy the harmony of the personality. We are not arguing that there are not some very positive aspects of these eccentricities. The combination may be very nice, but it is also certainly very uncomfortable. Some natures are extremely interesting and rich, but living with them must be very trying. Some people give an exaggerated reverence to these personality values and take these things for positive talents, which by origin they are, but then exaggerations attach themselves to them which in no way deserve to be honored by being called part of the cult of personality!

We have entered a community, we live there. By experience we have learned the ways in which our charity should be exercised. We ought to bring our talents to the community. They are our riches; and to wish to hide all the virtues we possess on the pretext of wanting to disappear from notice would be to create a false idea of humility. We come to the monastery with these assets, and we owe them to the community entirely. The community, in receiving us, is happy to receive a positive dowry with us. It is not at all that the fear of being a little too much ourselves should destroy in us the true riches of our personality. One may be too much oneself, but one can also have a fear of being oneself which leads to passive conformism and a loss of our true identity.

We have received a talent, and we should not bury it when we enter that garden which is the community; the Lord would then ask us, 'Where is your talent?' He wants us instead to make it bear fruit for the good of the community and our neighbor. We must not hide it within ourselves but turn it to profit—not cultivate it in an exaggerated sense of eccentricity as happens with individualists and may happen with hermits who lack frequent contact with their neighbor. In community life, we should be on guard to estimate what will be of value to others and what will not be. It is charity which allows us to exercise this vigilant control with sensitivity.

To exploit our talents, our personality, is to give ourselves. Now, giving oneself is the formula for charity. Giving oneself entirely, committing oneself totally.

We do not satisfy charity, for example, by doing little services without giving ourselves, without putting our heart into it and involving ourselves in it entirely. That might be an act of courtesy, a momentary feeling of pity, a secondary manifestation, we might say, of charity. Quite different is the mode of action of God who is Charity: 'God so loved the world that he gave his only Son, that every man who believes in him should not perish, but have eternal life' (Jn 3:16). This is what we need to understand: Jesus, through the mouth of St John is describing to us the charity of the Father for the world; its deepest, truest and most substantial expression is having given his Son, and in giving his Son, who is God as he is, he has given himself. The Father has so loved the world that he has given his Son, his *alter ego.* It is in this that charity consists: the gift of self.

The Holy Scriptures tell us many times to imitate the charity which God has had toward us. In giving ourselves to our brothers, we repeat a divine gesture. We have made this gift of ourselves solemnly at our profession. On that day, we went to the Chapter Room or to the Church, and after mature deliberation, we decided to give ourselves entirely. All the rest of our lives, we should live up to that promise—yes, all our lives. And all the effort of our life will be to enter always more completely into the community to give ourselves to it, to our brothers, to God, entirely.

And here we link up with the eighth degree of humility: in giving ourselves entirely to the community, we flee eccentricity as well as false humility, because this eighth degree of humility is nothing but a very concrete form of the charity which caused us to give ourselves to the community.

# THE PEDAGOGICAL VALUE OF COMMUNITY LIFE

For St Benedict, as for the ancients, the eremitical life was the goal of the monastic life. The cenobitic life, community life, was considered a time of formation—the 'long probation of the monastery' (1:3)—for the perfect. In this sense the Rule, written for cenobites, is a Rule for beginners (73:1). This is to say that community life forms monks, or, in a larger sense, the human community forms human persons. A monk cannot risk becoming a hermit before being formed by his brothers *multorum solacio doctus* (1:4).

The community, in its very best sense, is the fruit, the effect, of christian charity; through it alone can we be entirely fulfilled and arrive at our full stature revealed in the God-man, our perfect model; in following him, we truly mature. As the sun causes fruit to ripen, so charity causes human beings to mature. It is, therefore, a privilege to live in and through community. It should not be too small, for then it could not retain for us the same wealth of human values as a larger community. It should not be too large either, for such communities risk suffocating individual values.

St Benedict was perfectly aware of the creative and educational value of the community; although, in his usual way, he developed no theory on this theme, it still leaps off almost every page of the Rule written for the 'strongest kind of monks, the cenobites' (1:13). Why do the cenobites, those living-in-common, in *koinonia*—the name St Pachomius gave his monasteries—form the strongest kind of monks? A look at the three other kinds tells us: they lack the benefit of the community and cannot offer a similar guarantee of success.

Of course, it is not a matter of exalting the collectivity

at the expense of the personality. Quite the contrary: the common life is a success, not of the community as such, but of the persons who make it up and live intensively in it. The individual, and his formation, is the goal of the community. Let us content ourselves here with a few remarks to set this truth in relief.

First of all, the whole system of working out the monk's sanctification is based on the common life. How can a hermit in his desert climb the ladder of humility and practise obedience in order to arrive at charity (7:67), at God (71:2)? It is community life that teaches a monk to be honest with his brothers and with himself. Through it he enters into the common prayer and work, follows the enthusiasm and the spirit of the better monks, is sensitive to the needs and just demands of others, learns to subordinate his interests to the orders legitimately given. It would be easy, but beyond the limits of this work, to show, Rule in hand, how the monk, provided he allows himself to be carried along and knows how to discern spirits, would almost necessarily come under the wholesome influence of all that is best in the community.

And since this community life is integrally and vigorously lived according to the Rule, itself centered upon Christ, the sovereign Model of the ideal man, to whose love nothing should be preferred (4:21), the monk is educated by the community, the mystical body of Christ by participation, not according to the style of some sort of classic or other humanism, but to the image of the Son of God made man. It is to Him that the ecclesial community leads; in him it is fulfilled, to him it leads all those who share its life and who through it are intimately united to him.

Is the abbot's role diminished in the thought of St Benedict, insofar as the formation of the monk is evidently brought about by the community, by the concurrence of the brethren—*multorum solacio doctus?* The contrary is true. For we certainly must not believe that St Benedict's community is an amorphous group obeying a law dictated by the majority and where the governing principles are formed and established by means of a party system—nothing of that sort directs or sets the tone to this community. The more the abbot is a personality formed in the school of the Gospel and the Rule, the more marked is his influence on the community. But he himself, on his part, does not escape various currents and influences—I am thinking here of the force of usages and customs as a weight of wise traditions accumulating in a monastic community. A great politician once said to me: Is it not true that in order to form a good monastic community, you need a good abbot? And, he added, to form a good abbot, you need a good community.

The abbot, therefore, will be both disciple and master at the same time. As a disciple who is supported by the best traditions of his community, he ought to be *multorum solacio doctus*, like the hermit, for his office places him, not outside of, but above, his brothers. His task is to distinguish the good from the bad. He should be faithful to everything good he finds in his community. Most often he does not plant; he waters. St Benedict writes: 'The abbot should act in all things with the fear of God and respect for the Rule' (3:11). This sentence should be his criterion: A good community gives good formation to the member it chooses as abbot. This principle is applicable, *mutatis mutandis*, to every one of the monks: As a general rule, a good community is needed to train good monks. But let us not conclude this consideration without repeating what has been said at the beginning: The community is not primarily the collective members, but rather the charity which unites them. It is charity that makes a true community. Without it, we could speak of living together, but the union of hearts would be absent. There would be a body, but no soul. How could it train souls?

Here we see in a concrete way the utility of a truly common life, its essence, and its fruit: the charity which unites us, that great, generous understanding that dwells in us, the magnanimity of heart. Charity! Oh, how good it is to live together as friends and brothers! *Quam bonum et quam jucundum habitare fratres in unum!* (Ps 132:1)—but as true brothers and true sisters, with all the depth of that expression, that is to say, truly giving ourselves by fraternal charity to our brother and to our sister.

Our Lord himself has placed us in this fraternal life. In honoring our brother, in causing him to progress morally, in helping him, in encouraging him, in surrounding him with our complete respect, we progress, we ourselves grow, because it is only through charity that we can progress and grow, through charity alone. Only through charity can we improve, draw nearer to our Lord, be united to him, be united among ourselves. Charity is the only principle, the only motive, which leads us to him. It is useless to seek other means in books or doctrines; charity alone can make us better. The degree of our charity is also the degree of our holiness. In giving, we enrich ourselves. In refusing, we impoverish ourselves. To withdraw from our brother by lack of attention, rash judgment, narrowness of heart, or sharp words, or to lie in our relations with him, is to withdraw from God. A community life which is sincere and full of active affection will therefore be always and for everyone a living fountain of spiritual progress and fraternal joy.

# BROTHERS WHO LEAVE THE MONASTERY THROUGH THEIR OWN FAULT

A short chapter (29) deals with the case of those who, having left the monastery through their own fault, want to be received back again. St Benedict poses the question and answers it in the affirmative: Yes, they should be received back again, the door should be always kept open for them, but on the condition that they acknowledge their fault. This act of humility will make them understand that they deserve to be corrected. They must, therefore, be given a penance. Consequently, they should be put back in the last place in order to test their sincerity. And if they leave again, they will be taken back up to three times.

Let us note in passing that this chapter has in mind the case of fugitives and apostates, and finally all those who have left of their own accord, and not those who have been expelled, whose re-acceptance is not considered by the Rule.

Now, let's ask ourselves the question: Did our Lord not tell us to pardon seventy times seven times? Should we not therefore receive these brothers back always and without limit? St Benedict answers us: The door will remain closed after the third time. This is not a matter of pardoning or of teaching us the measure by which we should pardon. Of course, St Benedict tells us elsewhere that we must always pardon. But it is one thing to pardon a monk who has left, and another thing to take him back into the monastery. If, therefore, a brother has left three times—let us take this case—it is useless after that to try again, according to the Rule.

St Benedict asks us to test the humility of the monk who desires to re-enter the monastery. Today, nothing to do with humility pleases us very much. It is true, our way of looking at man has evolved considerably, especially since the last war. The experience of the concentration camps, the systematic devaluation of the human person, all moves us to value the human personality to the point of making it a veritable cult. Current philosophy with its anthropocentric tendencies runs in the same direction. The personality is an unquestionable value, but a human value and therefore limited; it is very necessary to know how to define it and to place it correctly within the scale of values; otherwise we risk taking it as an absolute without taking into account the ambiguity which that notion can cover.

Having said this, let us speak again of the problem before us. A brother has left the monastery through his own fault; if he has not understood his vocation well, or if he is not too well-balanced, the door should be kept open for him up to three times. St Benedict does not explicitly describe the sort of person whose intelligence or psychic force is limited. But throughout the pages of the Rule we see characters appear in his monastery whose heads are not exactly in the right place. He treats them as they should be treated; that is to say, as human beings; he accepts them on account of their souls. He has therefore admitted that a person who is not entirely normal could nevertheless have a monastic vocation and his place in a community, provided he is taken as what he is and is led to arrive at the goal. Perhaps today we have views which re a bit narrow concerning the ability of certain temperaments and their aptitude for the monastic life. We close the door to certain people, saying they are sick, sick in the area of physical or psychic formation, character, or temperament. Of course, community life will not support just any human character. But neither must we be too hasty to turn the page and refuse entry to some one on the pretext that he does not measure up to the standards of what we call normal. This is written in heaven rather than in certain ways of judging familiar to people today; this is why we must be careful to keep the door open, as St Benedict teaches us.

Given the public and social context of modern life, however, it is proper to keep from monastic communities those people whose bents or anomalies of character are counter-indicative for the common life, and who for this reason are not called to the cenobitic monastic life. We should see in St Benedict's argument for readmission, therefore, a counsel applicable only to cases which do not spring from pathology. For these, a first attempt which ends in failure is already indication enough not to try a second.

On the other hand, when there are persons who are capable of adapting to the life of the monastery but whose formation leaves something to be desired, then the treatment foreseen by St Benedict should be applied; that is to say, a medicinal humiliation, *ut sanentur* (30:3), to cure them.

# FRIENDSHIP BETWEEN BROTHERS

In the sixty-ninth chapter, 'Let no one in the monastery have the audacity to defend another', St Benedict shows his concern with settling a question in the sociological order. It can happen that a monk, in some circumstance or other, permits himself to defend another, or else plays the role of protector on his behalf. The institution of *tutores* among the Romans, given the social conditions of those times when a great part of the population faced a lot which was hardly equitable, permitted the needy and the common people whose rights had been trampled on the protection of the rich and powerful to whom, in return, they would publicly show their gratitude by making up part of their entourage on certain occasions. In some cases, they accompanied their protector and bore witness to him by grouping themselves around him as his 'clients'.

St Benedict came from a well-to-do social class, and did not want this system practised in the monastery. He had to forbid monks who came from distinguished families to play a role similar to that of *tutor* to their brethren for fear they might think they might count on this sort of support when they needed it. Blood relationship could lend itself to the establishment of similar connections. St Benedict vetoed this tendency of the natural order. Relationships like these do not belong in a monastery, and under no circumstances should the monks permit themselves to act this way. It would cause grave scandals.

How, then, generally speaking, did St Benedict see the relationships of monks among themselves? We observe, first of all, that the monks' relationships are set according to a vertical line. A brother ought to turn to the abbot when he needs something (33:4). The monk can, however, address himself to a senior for the needs of his soul (46:5). St Benedict, therefore, recognized the possibility of other spiritual relationships. The Rule also mentions the deans in their deaneries (21:2); likewise, the cellarer ought to be like a father to the monks (31:2). Finally, he explains the role of the *sympectae*, leading the excommunicated brother, or the brother of faltering virtue, back to the abbot (27:2f.). But what is the position of the Rule on the subject of friendship? Is it possible in a monastery? Can two or three monks bind themselves in closer relationship?

St Benedict, in dealing with fraternal relationships, takes into account the mutual support of one another's weaknesses (72:5). He encourages to mutual zeal (71:1) to courtesy (63:10, 15ff.; 72:4), to willingness to help (35:1, 6; 36), to self-forgetfulness (72:7), to a sincere and generous charity (72:3, 8). No one ought to be allowed to judge his brother (70:2). St Benedict is also careful about the proper rank to be kept (2:19f.; 63), with mutual marks of respect (38:6, 52:3), and with support through prayer (27:4). But, he refuses anyone the right of speaking with someone who has been excommunicated, unless he has permission (RB 26); in other words, he does not want a friendship to be practised in secret.

Yet certain questions remain unanswered in our minds after the above enumeration: Are we not allowed to go and find a good friend when a problem weighs on our heart? What should be our position, in the spirit of the Rule, on the matter of friendship?

We have just glanced at the Holy Rule; its general sense teaches us the extreme importance St Benedict attached to the community: every source of trouble and upset should be removed from it. St Benedict was much more impressed by the objections to particular relationships among the monks than by their possible advantages, as chapters sixty-nine and seventy allow us to see. Let us recall those words of *The Imitation of Christ:* 'Often what seems to be charity impelling us is only a carnal impulse' (Bk 1:15.2); this is in human nature.

In all community life, there is the danger of seeking support in some friend either because we feel a certain hostility toward the others or because we are afraid of them. St Benedict, using a form familiar to the Romans of the time, expresses nothing else; let us simply translate his language into that of today.

An area of tension exists in the relationships of the community and of the individual. A religious can disturb the community by withdrawing himself, by enclosing himself within his ivory tower, by becoming eccentric. He also disturbs it by becoming poorly integrated with it, playing the hermit in the midst of cenobites. Such a monk is no longer, from that point on, a cenobite, but becomes a foreign body. A good friendship may be the most effective remedy against such tendencies.

Groups of two or three Sarabaites, to give them their true name, as St Benedict does (1:8), are a great evil within the cenobitic community. The community suffers. It is shaken by the scandal spoken of above. We think of what are called pressure groups, groups which exercise an influence within the community in order to arrive at their ends. People organize to attain a personal end, to open up the way for their particular desires, often without considering the interests of others. The 'class struggle' often uses weapons of this type.

Our question here is to know whether, in a monastic community, such methods can be allowed, whether someone may affiliate himself with such groups in order to exert pressure either on the superior or on the community. To this question, we have to answer with a clear 'no'. Although it might happen, in exceptional cases, that the brothers with saner judgment may one day, in the fear of the Lord, confer to obviate a particular evil or to avoid an injustice—St Benedict foresees one such example in the case of an unfortunate choice of abbot (64:1)—such an action would be different from that which, according to chapter sixty-nine, we ought to consider prohibited. It can happen in a monastery that a party spirit functions and that groups are formed to realize good designs unjustly, through means which are harmful to the community or fit their particular way of looking at things. St Benedict wants to suppress the temptation to such goings on—from this also come the strict condemnations he pronounces against the complainer who lacks just motives (41:5).

On the other hand, there are horizontal relationships in the monastery, and St Benedict envisages other recourses for the monk besides his abbot, thus enlarging the rigid structure conceived by the [Rule of the] Master. Nevertheless, he conceives of the relations among the brethren not as relationships between two or a small number, but as relationships of all with each individually. He recognizes the right a person has to choose in asking counsel for the good of his soul (46: 5), although this right is not unlimited. On the other hand, the community must not be devaluated, so to speak, by having another developing inside it as a parasite, for if it were to be challenged, if the monk were to seek a substitute community in the very heart of his own, which is thrown aside as not achieving its purpose, then the life of the legitimate community would be seriously weakened. From that point on, it would no longer be able to be the *ecclesia* which is Christ, and it would lose its effectiveness.

But did the Lord not say: 'When two or three are gathered together in My name, I am in the midst of them' (Mt 18:20)? In citing these words of the Lord, we can ask ourselves if a friendship between two monks within a monastic community is possible. When two or three are gathered together in *his* name, united in the Lord by a spiritual friendship, when their union proves constructive for themselves and for the progress of the community, and therefore, when Christ is among them, that undivided Christ who fashions the entire community, then their friendship is that charity by which we recognize his disciples.

St Benedict does not speak of this type of friendship. This does not mean to say that he wanted to exclude a good friendship, but rather that, according to his fashion of writing the Rule—an ample fashion and an extremely vast point of view—he was not able to treat specifically the details of so complex a question, and wanted us to find the solution in this panoramic view. Nevertheless, he shows us, as we see in this sixty-ninth chapter, obviously built on experience, his mistrust of personal relationships among the brethren; they often fall into selfishness.

Naturally, that does not mean to say that we should not, in certain cases, seek advice and support of one of our brothers. It is characteristic of man, of human nature, of our social character, not to be 'an island'. We are geared to others, and seek help from them. One sure way of guaranteeing the authenticity of a true friendship is to leave it entirely under the control of the superiors. This is one of the most beautiful duties the monk has in the course of his purification, to test his human relationships in order to purify them and by doing this to bring them ever closer to the ideal of charity.

Thus, as we advance on the path of friendship, Jesus joins us as third person, and under the influence of his word, our hearts grow to a love which is perfectly disinterested.

# EXCOMMUNICATION

In one of the most beautiful chapters of the Holy Rule (27) St Benedict shows how the abbot is to treat those who behave badly in the community. The Rule's penal code risks giving the shivers to some people, and since these chapters have overtones that are a little disagreeable, we like to say that they were made for a day when people were rougher and hardier than they are today, and that we need pay no attention to them.

Now, what is dealt with in the penal code? It consists of legislation  not for sinful acts, but for faults against the monastic community. We have confirmation of this in the twenty-third chapter, the first of this code: 'If any brother shall be found contumacious or disobedient or proud or a complainer or in any way scorning and contravening the Holy Rule and the orders of his superiors . . . ' (23:1). It is quite obvious that this is a question of faults against the Rule, the community, obedience, and fraternal charity.

But, as there are mortal sins and venial sins, so there are grave and slight faults against the Rule. For a community to be able to prosper, it needs order. Union is disturbed if all are not in unity. It is therefore necessary that there be a rule to which we can refer if anyone wanders off or pursues his own path. This is why we have this code of punishments.

What method should be used? St Benedict tells us that we should start with an admonition. If a monk has behaved badly, he should be reprimanded in private, in secret. If this is not enough, he should be reprimanded in public. And if this reprimand does not cause him to correct himself, we should proceed either to excommunication or to corporal punishment. And if these remedies do not obtain the desired amendment, we must go on to expel the person.

This, then, is the gamut of procedures provided by St Benedict in his Rule. Excommunication, we should immediately say, is most probably not ecclesiastical excommunication, but regular, monastic, community excommunication, because grave exterior faults against divine precepts are not at stake, but rather faults against the precepts of the Rule and the community. Since the abbot of the Rule is not necessarily a priest, as one can deduce from chapter sixty-four, he does not consequently have ecclesiastical jurisdiction and cannot pronounce a sentence of that order. But as abbot, he is the father of the community and can excommunicate.

What is this excommunication, then? To excommunicate is to put someone outside the communion, that is, outside the community. Or rather, it is to declare someone has put himself outside the community. Excommunication, which is a sentence, presupposes the excommunication which someone brings down upon himself when he separates himself, wanders off, and puts himself outside the communion of the brothers by his fault. When the abbot, despite his best efforts, cannot bring him back into that communion, to the place which is his, he finds himself obliged to declare him excommunicated. So excommunication always begins with a personal step of the monk in question.

Now, to abandon the communion of the brethren is to

abandon charity. If someone sins by showing himself stubborn, obstinate, arrogant, a complainer in the community, then he sins against charity, that is, he sets himself outside charity. And charity is specifically union, communion. Therefore, every serious act against charity is an excommunication *ipso facto*. This is the meaning of excommunication.

In the course of the Church's history, the true sense of excommunication has often not been realized and it has been abused, even to the point of declarations of excommunication during political conflicts, In the Middle Ages. and even later, you know, churchmen fulminated this punishment against people who had committed no crime except that of assuring themselves certain political advantages. This was an abuse and an aberration in the use of the excommunication. Such abuses were also to be found in the area of monastic excommunication.

Excommunication, we see, is a problem of all times, today as in past times. We must not believe that the chapters of the Rule which treat this question were made for other times. They are, in the sense that we cannot literally apply some of their prescriptions. What is more, St Benedict foresaw this himself. But here, circumstances, then as now, dictate what we have to do. In the case of the woman taken in adultery, the Lord declared: 'Let him who is without sin among you cast the first stone' (Jn 8:7). They all went away; and he concluded the scene with these words: 'Neither do I condemn you' (Jn 8:11). The adulteress went away without having received a punishment. So we must not believe that a fault against the divine precepts, much less against monastic precepts, ought necessarily to end in excommunication.

The penal code of the Rule was laid down in function of the eventuality of certain cases, in certain circumstances where it would be necessary to apply the means he has provided, since without them we could not arrive at the goal, that is, assuring the salvation of the guilty person and indeed of the community.

Today, unfortunately, things are settled much too quickly and not always to the advantage of souls. We proceed more quickly to dispensation from vows. We no longer have Our Lord's patience. Of course, we can argue from many circumstances to justify our attitude. Today's morals are not those of past times. The life of our communities is much more open in its contemporary expression. Outside monasteries, christian awareness has been lost. Who would understand excommunication? And besides, most monks are priests, and notorious scandal would arise. The means of punishment are more limited. Thus, one is led to settle problems which, because of the possibilities open to those involved, are painful, by secularization or even by the ultimate sentence, expulsion. Could we, in certain cases, go back to the practice of excommunication, especially when its meaning is understood? The question might well be asked.

Excommunication is nothing but a punishment, a medicinal penalty to help and correct the monk and to allow him to return to his rank. He left it to adopt a bad disposition or to place himself in one of those false situations where neither the soul nor the temperament have anything to gain. We must help him come back to the community.

Today, in such cases, we always tend to think of mental diseases, and this is not wrong. Formerly, people saw the problem quite simply in its moral aspect. There is no doubt, however, that illness, whether physical or psychic, looms large in certain anomalies involving sociability or the ability to integrate oneself in a fraternal *milieu*. But these cases, once the psychiatrist has, if necessary, been consulted, should be corrected with great charity, according to the spirit of the Rule, helping the monk to resume his community life and his rank as far as possible. Once again, it is left to the abbot to judge the gravity of the fault and the treatment to be adopted; and consequently, in cases which call for psychiatric help, he must be allowed to use the means suited to the situation.

Although we argue that it is for the abbot, in the last analysis, to take responsibility for judging, this does not mean that the community withdraws from the drama to be spectators. The community is involved, because its own well-being is involved. So it is the community itself which corrects the delinquent and allows him to take his place among them again. Centuries of feudal mentality have isolated the abbot until he finds himself alone in solving a good number of problems. When a brother has taken the wrong road, other members of the community have a tendency to hold themselves aloof to see what the abbot is going to do, whether he succeeds or not in setting the guilty person back on his feet and bringing him back into the community. This is not a good attitude. If we look closely at the Holy Rule we see that the reintegration of a brother is a concern of the whole community. Naturally the abbot should lead, because he directs the whole community. But he should make the community act. In the present chapter, St Benedict speaks to us of the *sympectae*—we need only explain this expression by the paraphrase of the Rule itself, 'wise seniors' (27:2), whom the abbot uses when he needs to approach a stubborn man who is clinging fast to his fault and does not want to submit. Since the abbot cannot act directly, he acts through the intermediary of certain members of the community. Not only does the community furnish the *sympectae*, but it prays (27:4), at the abbot's order, that the excommunicated may understand more quickly and may be brought back to his place in community.

Excommunication is a community affair because by it one of its members is kept outside of the communion of the brothers. It is the community which is wounded through the faults committed, especially through grave faults; and since the whole community is involved, the whole community acts.

Here then are certain points to remember from the disciplinary chapters of the Rule. We must take them into account in order to know, today as in the past, how to treat delinquents, those who step out of line, who do not keep the good rules of monastic behavior designed to keep the spiritual and disciplinary standards, the spirit of the community, forever intact. It is true that human beings easily fall into faults and the superior should not spotlight them; on the contrary, he should try to take no notice of some of them, see them without saying anything about them, and not punish indiscriminately. 'In administering correction let him act with prudent moderation, lest being too zealous in removing the rust he break the vessel. Let him always distrust his own frailty and remember that the bruised reed is not to be broken' (64:12f.). This is psychologically exact. Nevertheless, St Benedict counsels the abbot not to let weeds sprout in the house of God (64:14), those faults which multiply and repeat and which end by making the whole community suffer. To act this way would be against his own interests and contrary to his responsibility as superior, which is specifically to hold the brothers together in a deep communion so that they all act and behave in a way that will keep them truly united by the bond of charity and the common practice of the Rule.

# THE SICK
# AND
# THE OLD

There are two chapters of the Holy Rule dealing with the sick (RB 36) and the old (RB 37). We will study them together since the problems raised by these two states have a great similarity. What is more, old age is sometimes called a sickness.

A new science is developing today, gerontology, the study of ageing. Although there have always been old people, the question now presents itself in a new way. As a result of the evolution of medicine, biology, pharmacology, and related sciences, old age has become a very real social problem. Human longevity is increasing considerably, the mortality of infants is constantly decreasing; consequently, the percentage of people in the non-productive categories of our technocratic society is greatly increasing in proportion to the active class. The time given to production is diminishing. On the one hand, the demands of specialization require more advanced preparatory studies. On the other, people today are often prematurely put into retirement to make room for those younger; left aside, they are considered useless because they are incapable of performing the services expected of a worker. Although sometimes an old person is given credit for the value of his experience, cultural productivity, a certain wisdom, yet this does not go very far. As the number of old people increases, the number of sick people increases accordingly. Clinics and hospitals are full and need to be enlarged and multiplied.

This situation is difficult, we know that, but we immediately see the materialistic principle behind it. Man is considered only under the aspect of material and social productivity and not as a being coming from, and going back to, God. His value is in function of the services he renders to the technocratic and cultural society. This way of judging human worth is unilateral, false, and unworthy of us.

Here we are, then, with a serious sociological problem. The modern world knows how to prolong the life of the elderly, but the elderly often feel in the way and shoved aside. Gerontology seeks and proposes solutions, trys to furnish the elderly who are still healthy with an occupation which corresponds to their resources in order to combat their apparent uselessness and give them value in some way or other. In spite of all the efforts, we can scarcely escape this vicious circle of considering man only as an economic unit.

What is our christian position on this problem? Quite rightly, there are many questions in our modern society about the value of the human personality, of the efforts that should be made to maintain it, of the right of a person to live. Unfortunately, the eternal dimension and value of human life, of a child of God and brother of Jesus Christ, remain in the shadows. Our faith shows us that as sanctifying grace and the theological virtues increase in us, life blossoms and never decays. The soul of the just receives the seed of life; first it is small, then it grows with grace even to the stature of Christ, even to maturity and full spiritual productivity (let us keep that expression 'productivity'), to arrive at last at that age when man diminishes physically but the value of his life increases to the extent that he enters more deeply into the life of Christ in his passion, death, and resurrection. Contrary to those for whom the sting of death (cf. 1 Cor 15:55) is always present and who consider it as the greatest evil, to be cast away as far as possible, we understand it in Christ (cf. Rom 6:8) as the entry, although the door is dark, it is true, to resurrection and eternal life. We might reproach the physician for not considering man in the fullness of his being if he thinks that he has to repel death at all costs as the greatest evil. Is our death not a sharing in Our Lord's redemptive death? Does it not thus become an humanitarian work of inestimable value? If, therefore, science considers it a benefit to prolong life at all costs, this is very relative and may have as its foundation a false and inhumane ideology.

By re-evaluating death, we put sickness, suffering, the cross, and also old age in their true place. All the stages of our life take their meaning from the redemptive death of Christ; by our death, he invites us to take part in his (cf. Rom 6:8). The dying person is not doomed, a rag to be consigned to the earth; he is on the broad highway to life without end. He is potentially risen. His last look plunges into the life beyond. The elderly, the infirm are on their way toward the heights. They bear the redemptive cross of their infirmity, being strong in him who is their strength (cf. Phil 4:13). And that cross borne well is a source of life for others; it bears the promise of life. The sick, the elderly are not useless then. The sick are very specially Christ among us. Has he not willed to be present among us in various ways, as the hungry, the pilgrim, the prisoner? He is also present among us as sick, present as elderly. 'I was sick and you visited me' (Mt 25:36). The sick, the elderly, are the image of Christ; in them Christ is sick and wants to be visited and cared for. 'As often as you did it to one of the least of my brethren, you have done it to me' (Mt 25:40). In a few words St Benedict makes this theology of sickness his

364

own (RB 36:1-3). Let the monks, let the abbot himself, realize that the sick and the elderly are not men who are done for, without importance, brethren whom one cares for well materially, perhaps, but who are not considered of much important value. No, they are men with a great near future. The process of monastic life is explained through its eternal finality; in this context, the elderly and the sick are a powerfully constructive element since they are involved in the work of salvation in a more effective and painful way.

On the other hand, St Benedict is not ignorant of the fact that not all the sick know how to unite themselves to the suffering Christ. Some, perhaps, refuse to enter into this current of energy by conforming themselves interiorly to him. But that makes no difference; we must see and serve the Lord even in the sick who are difficult (36:4f.). And then, let us not forget, a long and painful sickness can weaken the nerves of even the most virtuous and cause them to be difficult and impatient in spite of themselves, 'Let us bear with them patiently' (36:5), let us not despise them. Their weakness reflects that much more the face of Christ, the 'last of men' (Is 53:3). Some older people even change character, becoming capricious and embittered, and do unseemly things without taking account of them. Even in them, Jesus is present among us. We should help them understand the great honor Christ does them in identifying himself with them; it gives them dignity to identify themselves with him and to imitate the patience of the Lamb of God. They should not sadden the brothers who serve them by continual demands or with requests which are out of proportion to the modest means of the community, but they should edify them by their modesty and their gratitude (36:4).

It is important then that the abbot, the infirmarians, and the cellarer (36:10) see in the sick Christ who is served in their person. Let them be imbued with this beautiful theology. This outlook will help them multiply their efforts as love makes them find the useful and fitting means to relieve them. 'Let the abbot, therefore, watch with the greatest solicitude' (36:6, 10) over the sick. Let him be generous and big-hearted for them. 'To be a good abbot, one must not be too healthy!' In an amusing and fresh way, this expresses a deep and beautiful truth: the abbot ought to be very sympathetic toward the sick.

The care given the sick ought, however, to be in proportion to the hoped for results and not ignore the laws of poverty. Although it might be normal in some cases to have recourse to specialists, a sick man should not, under ordinary circumstances, travel far and wide in search of the best physician. He should not forget that in his sufferings and his death he should be conformed to Christ; his sacrifice is pleasing to the Father and salutary for his brothers. On the other hand, to require the sick person, through the spirit of sacrifice, to renounce useful and necessary care would be to show an exaggerated austerity, far from the solicitude demanded by St Benedict. The means at the disposal of people of the sixth century were limited, but St Benedict used them. He allowed the use of baths (36:8), even meat, although on this point he showed himself on principle quite reserved (cf. 36:9; 39:11). It would be contrary to the understanding spirit of St Benedict not to allow the sick and the elderly the diet they need according to the doctor's advice (39:2; 37). Their weakness demands mitigations and this at the proper hours (39:2, 3).

Today sick monks and nuns are often transferred to hospitals or clinics in order to receive proper care, but the monastery still needs a sunny infirmary provided with everything necessary to relieve those suffering chronic illnesses and the elderly. Charity will lead the abbot and those responsible to make the infirmary pleasant, practical, and attractive.

Christ identifies himself with the little, the weak, the sick. If we want to meet him in our brothers, let us not turn toward the strong, the rich, and the prudent, but toward the poor (cf. 53:15), the wounded, those among us who are broken. In them Jesus wills to be honored. They resemble him; did he not wish to be poor and the least of all on earth? Thus he confers on the sick and the elderly an additional personality, his own. They are related to him. Within the community they represent a sort of nobility. Have we understood this well enough?

# Monastic Priesthood

# PRIESTHOOD AND MONASTIC LIFE

'If any abbot wishes to have a priest or a deacon ordained for his monastery, let him choose from among his monks someone who is worthy of exercising the priestly office' (62:1).

Choosing a priest from outside in order to assure priestly service in the monastery could present problems. St Benedict therefore advises the abbot to turn to one of his own monks. But might there not be certain disadvantages in calling on monks to exercise the sacred functions? Actually, St Benedict here envisages an exceptional solution: a priest among his monks. Monks of his day were laymen; that was the general rule. How could so many good people have become monks if someone had required of them the education of clerics or the intellectual aptitude for receiving it in the monastery? In the East even more than in the West, monks were considered laymen. St Paul of Thebes, St Anthony, St Pachomius were laymen, St Benedict probably was too. A maxim venerated among the ancient fathers advised monks to flee women and bishops—the latter, no doubt, so as not to be snatched from monastic life [by ordination].

St Benedict therefore considers it exceptional to call a monk to the priesthood or to the diaconate. What is the deeper reason for this attitude? Among the ancients generally the monastic state was considered the state of humility. The whole Rule of St Benedict bears witness to this. Where does he gives us the outline, the summary of the whole monastic life if not in the chapter entitled 'On Humility'? To promote the practice of humility through sociological measures, St Benedict avoids anything that could give rise to exceptions, dispensations, or privileges. One brother should not be distinguished from another by his social position. Let us recall his insistence in impressing it on the abbot not to make distinctions of person (2:16), for all, bond or free, are one in

369

Christ and do the same service in the army of the same Lord (2:20). The social or economic condition of the young people before their entry ought to have no effect on the order and the life of the community; we find this attitude again in the ordinances of chapter fifty-nine concerning the sons of nobles or of the poor offered to God in the monastery, in chapter sixty-nine (1) prohibiting any brother from arrogating a sort of tutelage over another (69:1), in chapter sixty-three (1) concerning the rank to be observed among monks, established by their seniority in the vocation or by the will of the abbot. One might also cite the regulations of the Rule regarding the personal poverty of each monk.

It is therefore easy to understand why St Benedict did not want to have priests or clerics whose social position would necessarily have elevated them above the others. His repugnance to the installation of a prior is explained by a similar reason: will he not imagine himself to be a second abbot? It is preferable to establish deans among whom a certain equality reigns, for then one can hardly feel himself superior to another. In all his arrangements, we see St Benedict's concern for preserving in the monastic state its character of being a state of humility through equality.

St Benedict was afraid that a monk, having become a priest, might succumb little by little to the temptation of believing himself above certain regulations he considers petty or insignificant, and of dispensing himself from some obligation under the pretext that he is a priest and cannot be held to observances prescribed for a 'simple' monk. In chapter sixty-two, St Benedict set down a whole procedure to prevent such infidelities to the monastic vocation. If a priest ventures to act otherwise, he should be put back in the ranks, and if he does not correct himself, he should be punished and even, if he will not submit, expelled from the monastery (62:8ff.).

The necessity of having a priest and a deacon for sacred functions ran counter to the desire to maintain a reasonable measure of social equality among the monks. Without the Eucharist there is no cenobitic community. This service could be asked from an outside priest. St Benedict seems to eliminate this option. Was this the memory of his sad experiences at Subiaco? In short, the abbot may have a priest ordained and choose him from among his monks. The choice is left, not to the bishop, but to the abbot's judgment. It is clear that this monk, once ordained priest, is not at the disposition or under the jurisdiction of the bishop. The monk-priest remains entirely under the jurisdiction of his abbot, even if the abbot is not a priest. The course of history has shown us that difficulties over this jurisdiction often arose; either the bishop wanted to lay his hand on a monk in order to ordain him priest, or he claimed rights over others already ordained priests. But it is not our purpose here to treat of this subject.

The ancient fervent monks in the East and in the West often therefore refused the priesthood through humility, to avoid the danger of ambition and of a dignity, an authority, which, by placing them 'upon a lampstand' would risk being a drawback to their efforts toward virtue. On their part we must see in this an attitude of prudence dictated by the desire not to let the monastic ideal escape them in order to embrace a priesthood wrongly taken on oneself and therefore contrary to that ideal. It is in this sense that we must understand St Benedict's attitude, and not as a depreciation or a lack of esteem for monastic priesthood.

Monk priests and bishops have always existed, however. Let us think, for example, of St Martin, of that seminary of holy bishops on the island of Lérins; in the East, there were St Basil and St John Chrysostom and many others; the problem, therefore, remains in historical perspective.

To hope to discover in the Rule a sort of monastic anti-clericalism would be a mistake. On the contrary, St Benedict holds the priest in high esteem—in chapter sixty-four he alludes to his possible intervention in a case where an unfortunate abbatial election might disturb the community. On the other hand, this is true: St Benedict forgot nothing of the sad experiences which St Gregory tells us of the priest at Subiaco. But that priest was not a monk.

St Benedict, as chapters sixty and sixty-two demonstrate, therefore, preserved the traditional position of the monk who is not a priest, but did not refuse to make two exceptions. First of all, a cleric or a priest can become a monk. What is more, he consented to having a monk ordained priest or deacon for the service of the altar and of the monastery.

At present, most educated monks are priests. In the West, being a monk was synonymous for centuries with being a priest; and up until the Second Vatican Council, or shortly before, the young man who became a monk had to have, at the same time, the aptitudes necessary for the priesthood and be prepared for ordination; this was practically an established rule.

How did this evolution come about in the Latin Church? We notice, first of all, an historical development in the direction of the arrangements made by St Benedict in chapter sixty-two. It is interesting to note—Dom Delatte recounts the fact in his commentary on the Rule (p. 484)—that at the Abbey of St Denis around 838, there were a certain number of priests, deacons, sub-deacons, and acolytes for the service of the altar. But what is most interesting is that among these monks, there was even a bishop for conferring Holy Orders so that they had no need to resort to an outside bishop. The case of St Denis does not seem to have been alone. The monastery wanted to be self-sufficient even in the sacraments. The development of this idea led to having a bishop right in the monastery so it could be totally independent. Thus splendid liturgical celebrations, like those of Cluny, became possible. For the same reason, cathedral monasteries had to include among their members all the clerical ranks.

Another historical reason which influenced this evolution toward the priesthood was the Rule of St Augustine used by the institutes of canons regular. St Augustine, in fact, lived the common life with his clergy while still having them perform the occupations of ministry. In the Middle Ages, this institution had a great development and led to the foundation of Orders of Augustinians, Norbertines, and others. Without doubt, their expansion influenced the clericalization of the monastic state in the West.

Finally, the custom of founding chapels for celebrating Masses in perpetuity for the repose of the souls of the founders, the benefactors of the monastery and their families, contributed in the West to the general practice of advancing monks to the priesthood. In Cistercian churches, although this custom predated Cîteaux, four lateral chapels constructed on either side of the high altar show us that from the beginning of the Order, monks adopted the custom of being ordained priests. Foundation Masses for the departed were numerous. The abbatial churches and these lateral chapels in particular often served as burial places for noble families. Mass had to be celebrated in their respective chapels on certain days, or daily in certain cases. Sometimes one certain monk was entrusted with such a Mass foundation. In addition, in the Order of Citeaux there was from the beginning, or nearly so, a daily Mass for the dead and another of the Virgin Mary. They had to have enough priests, therefore, to meet all these different obligations.

The reason the priesthood became generalized is not to be found therefore in the duties of ministry. The ministry came later. It is true that certain missionary monks, like St Boniface or St Ansgar, and especially the Irish and English monks, were priests and brought groups of monk-priests with them. They exercised a ministry in contemporary terms, that is to say, they preached the Gospel. But this way of doing things was not common; far from it. It remains no less true that little by little the custom of ordaining monks prevailed in the entire monastic order, at least in the West.

The Council of Vienna in 1311 marked a further step in this evolution; the decision of Pope Clement V gave greater impetus to the development of divine worship: 'We set down that monks, whoever they may be, should, if their abbot commands them, become ordained to sacred Orders unless there be legitimate reason against it'. Thus, as early as 1311, the monk had to be ordained if his abbot so decided, and he could not oppose that decision as, for example, did St Pachomius, who hid himself in order to avoid ordination to the priesthood.

Three centuries later, in 1603, Clement VIII took another big step in this discipline by forbidding the acceptance as choir religious of candidates who had not the required intellectual formation for receiving the priesthood or who were incapable of it. This way of doing things remained in force in the Latin Church until the Second Vatican Council. The situation had completely reversed itself. Formerly a young man could not think of the priesthood if he wanted to be a monk; in more recent times, in order to be a monk he had to fulfil the conditions required for becoming a priest.

The Second Vatican Council, after consultation within the monastic order, has taken account of the position of the Rule of St Benedict. From now on, it will again be possible to be a monk in the full sense of the word without going on to Holy Orders. (*Decret. Perf. Carit.* no. 15). Some people, it is true, would like to go still further and go so far as to say, 'To be a real monk, one is better off not being a priest'. Paul VI, our sovereign pontiff, is not of that opinion. In an allocation pronounced in 1966 before the major superiors of Italy, he expressed himself in this manner:

> The canonical possibility of a monasticism in itself, without priesthood, has been sanctioned by the Council (*Perf. Carit.* 15). But this form of monasticism without the priesthood should absolutely not lead us to consider as a deviation the fact that, for many centuries in the West, the greater part of monks were ordained priests. Nor should one take as a general rule now that monks ought to be called to the priesthood only according to the needs of the pastoral ministry within or outside the monastery.

Paul VI, supported by an age-old tradition, does not, therefore, want us to go back to the discipline suggested by the first sentence of the sixty-second chapter of the Rule where the abbot has a monk ordained to the priesthood or to the diaconate only when the service of the monastery requires it. But neither does the Holy Father accept the position of those who hold out for an exclusively ministerial priesthood, whether within or without the monastery. Indirectly, then, the Holy Father poses a question: that of harmonizing the priesthood and the monastic state.

We cannot deny that wherever monks who are priests and those who are not priests live together, there is a certain difficulty. The Order of Cîteaux from its inception, and according to the ideas current in those days, accepted the practice that monks should be ordained priests; but to ease the situation this created, the founders of Cîteaux, according to the social ideas of those days of feudal class spirit, established the institution of lay brothers; they were neither priests nor monks. You know abour the change which has come about in our own day and the deeper recognition of human dignity and liberty, of personality, as well as the keener sense of the state of inequality which can sometimes show itself in the distinction between monk-priests and non-priest brothers in the same community.

The nuns do not have this problem. This is an advantage, because it is often a false problem, and in this form the question of equality or inequality does not come up in a community of nuns. This does not mean to say that other reasons cannot exist for creating unjustified inequalities by gifts of nature or grace. Let us remember, then, that ideal whose defense St Benedict carries all through the Rule, especially in chapter sixty-two, that in the monastery we are brothers and that this brotherhood is one of the foundations of gospel teaching (cf. Mt 23:8).

# THE MONK-PRIEST

It bothers many people today, when so many parishes are without pastors because of the lack of priestly vocations, to see, sometimes in the immediate neighborhood of churchless villages, a monastery numbering some fifty priests who seem to be indifferent to the lack of ministers to announce the Good News. The monks often hear this argument: 'Get out of your cloisters, show yourselves, and make yourselves useful to souls'. 'The salvation of souls is the highest law' they add. At first sight, we have to agree, it seems irrefutable.

Another argument favors the involvement of monk-priests in the pastoral life; it is a moral reason. The monks in their monasteries are in danger, it is said, of becoming self-centered. With the years, their horizons shrink to the community and its interests to such an extent that they have no time to occupy themselves with the concerns of the kingdom of God. Still worse, this deformation can go so far as a selfishness occupied only with self. On the other hand, what could help the monks more than a ministry opening them to others in the service of the Church and of souls? Their fervor would grow with the exercise of priestly charity. This argument also seems very persuasive.

History shows us that there has always been a ministry exercised by some monks. In fact, there is no lack of opportunity. We need only recall the geographical situation of most monasteries, built near a city or a village, and the custom the faithful have of going there. In the Order of Cîteaux, as among the Carthusians, the chapel at the porter's lodge is meant for people from outside; a *plebanus*, or more simply, a monk, celebrates Mass there for outsiders. The celebration of the Eucharist, of course, involves also the sacrament of penance. Therefore, it is also necessary to hear confessions, in short, to exercise some kind of ministry. Today preaching is added so that the faithful do not miss the proclamation of the divine word. And so we arrive at a ministry. In abbatial churches which are open to the public some ministry is required, and one priest alone cannot do everything: several discharge this office. Soon someone is led to leave the monastery in order to exercise a ministry in the neighborhood.

This has been the evolution. Need we add that at the time of the Reformation, in areas where it had penetrated, there was a shortage of priests, and that monasteries everywhere incorporated parishes, which in certain regions were numerous, and drew their resources from them. This is why the abbeys became obliged to provide for the needs of these parishes and sent their monk-priests outside in order to serve souls.

Let us also add doctrinal considerations to get a clearer

view. Luther and the other reformers, in preaching the Gospel, attacked the Eucharist and hence the priesthood. For some of them, the Eucharist was a simple memorial of the Lord's death. According to them, therefore, the task of the priest consisted, in celebrating that memorial. It was no longer a matter of his consecrating the Eucharist. Stripped of his principal office, he no longer offered the sacrifice of the New Covenant. He was the minister of the people, ordained to celebrate the memorial of Our Lord. Luther rose up against what he called the *Winkel Messen*, Masses celebrated in a corner—a reference, in poor taste, to the little chapels of our abbatial churches and those of the Carthusians, chapels scattered throughout the monastery where the monks might withdraw to celebrate the Holy Mysteries privately. For Luther, the Eucharist is for the people, and therefore cannot be celebrated without a congregation.

We must admit that the concept of the priest ordained principally for the public celebration of the Eucharist is a way of looking at things popular today among a clergy seeking an authentic image of itself. For those who hold this thesis, the Eucharist is more often a memorial supper than a sacrifice. In this doctrinal situation, which calls for a practical involvement, some monks say, 'If things are that way, it is better not to be priests', and to avoid being put in the position of becoming ministers of the people, they prefer simply to renounce the priesthood.

To combat such an attitude, which is not without a certain resignation, the Holy Father, Paul VI, wrote to the prior of the Grande Chartreuse on the 18th of April 1971: 'Today some people think it undesirable for cenobites or hermits who will never have to exercise the sacred ministry to receive the priesthood. As we have already had the occasion to say, this opinion certainly lacks sure and solid foundation'. We find the same logic in a declaration made by the Sacred Congregation of Religious a few years ago to the Cistercians of the Strict Observance. It emphasizes that to deprive a monk of the priesthood and to believe he should not be a priest, would be to return to an antiquated position.

What should our doctrinal position be? Is the priest

ordained only for the ministry, or can priests be ordained simply for the priesthood? More concretely, is it right for monks living in the cloister of their monastery without exercising the ministry to be ordained priests simply in order to be monk-priests? Let us listen first to St Thomas (*Sent. Dist.* 24, q.1, a. 3): 'The priest has two functions: the principal one has for its object the real body of Christ; the other, the secondary one, his mystical body. The second does no go without the first, but the opposite is not true. That is why some are ordained priests to whom is confided only the first function, such as religious who do not receive responsibility for souls.'

The priesthood, then, implies two functions: one concerns the real body of Christ, that is to say, the Eucharist; the other concerns his mystical body, that is, the Church. Now, St Thomas tells us that the principal function is the one directed to the real body of Christ, the Eucharist. The second, which concerns the Church, the mystical body, flows from the first. The first can exist without the second; the second cannot exist without the first. Consequently, there are religious, monks, who are ordained priests without being destined for the ministry. This is very clear.

Has the Vatican Council declared itself on this subject? During the Council, there were certain disputes, but the decree *Presbyterorum Ordinis* (1 c. a. 13) concludes that the principal function of the priest is exercised in the sacrifice of the Mass. The doctrine of St Thomas was, therefore, adopted in substance.

In studying the Gospels, we might believe at first glance that the apostles were destined above all to announce the Good News and went among the nations of the whole world to instruct people, to baptize them, to teach them to observe the commandments of Jesus (cf. Mt 28:19). If we ask the theologians at what moment the apostles were ordained priests, they will answer: at the Last Supper, at the moment Our Lord said to them, 'Do this in memory of me' (Lk 22: 19). He gave them the mandate to offer the Holy Sacrifice, that is to say, to celebrate the Eucharist. He ordained them first to the Eucharist, later he ordered them to baptize and preach. So there are two different functions, and the eucharistic function is clearly distinguished from the apostolic function.

Besides these considerations of a dogmatic character, there is an appropriateness which, added to the above-mentioned reasons, justifies a monastic priesthood. The priest belongs to God in a very special way. This requires of him a consecration of his whole life to a sacred service so he will be able to be a worthy minister of the sacrifice of God. There is, then, in his very function a moral requirement. In his life, he ought to conform himself to what he does, to what he is. In the rite of ordination, the bishop says to him, 'Imitate what you do', *Imitamini quod tractatis.* The priest is not only the one who sacrifices, therefore, but with the Lord he will be the sacrifice, the victim. He ought to make Him present not only on the altar, but also through the example of his life. That is why he must be a *segregatus* (cf. Acts 13:2, Rom 1:1), one set apart.

This is one view of the priest from the theological viewpoint with its moral consequences. Let us now compare the condition of the monk with that of the priest. The monk's vocation is also a life of sacrifice. He is someone consecrated to God, and he lives this personal gift out through his monastic profession. He offers himself to God in a particular way. This religious consecration is not, of course, the same as priestly ordination which is constitutive. The monastic consecration has a moral implication. It is the offering of one's life to God with the intention of directing it entirely to his service and consequently to the service of the Church. The monk is, because of his vows, a *segregatus*, someone set apart for the love of God, and through the intrinsic logic of that divine love, for his brothers' salvation.

Can anyone fail to see the spiritual relationship between these two vocations, the connection between the monastic vocation, the vocation of one who is sacrificed, and the vocation of the priest, the vocation of one who sacrifices and is sacrificed? The two vocations complement each other and can quite naturally be joined. In addition, monastic formation prepares the monk to enter fully into the spirituality of the priesthood. The Church has always, and for these reasons, judged that the two vocations, far from being incompatible, harmonize very well in one person. Thus bishops have always sought out monks in order to ordain them to the priesthood, and bishops have also been sought among the monks.

One may ask if St Benedict saw some incompatibility in the union of the two vocations. Did he perceive this intimate and spiritual harmony between the priesthood and the monastic life? Certainly, he saw it clearly. For him, the priesthood ought to be the occasion of advancing more and more toward God: *Magis ac magis in Deum proficiat* (62:4). The priesthood, he says, far from causing him to forget obedience to the Rule and discipline, should stimulate him to grow more and more in the Lord. For St Benedict, therefore, there is no basic difficulty of a theological character with a monk becoming a priest. His hesitations are rooted in a strong desire to safeguard the purity of the monastic vocation for which he wrote his Rule. There is, then, a real harmony between the two vocations. This is why Paul VI was able to declare to the major superiors of Italy:

> If, in fact, the priesthood has been associated with monasticism, it is because people have perceived the harmony which exists between the priestly consecration and the religious consecration. The union in the same person of the priestly character and the religious consecration through which he is offered entirely to God configures him in a special way to Christ who is at the same time priest and victim.

So the priesthood is considered a dignity grafted on that of the monk. It corresponds well to the monastic vocation, enriches it, and raises it to a privileged spiritual condition through the grace of the Holy Spirit, helping the monk-priest to progress more and more in the Lord: *Magis ac magis in Deum proficiat.*

Monks may, therefore, and this is our conclusion, go on to the priesthood, even if they do not exercise a pastoral function. Once ordained priests, they cannot be obliged to leave their cloister if their vocation is to live a life of prayer, self-effacement, and silence far from the world. In their own way, they serve mankind and their brothers by imitating Jesus on the mountain (*Lumen Gentium*), praying for the people and effacing Himself in the silence of the passion and the cross.

# Following Christ

# FOLLOWING CHRIST
# IN HUMILITY

The monastic tradition and the benedictine Rule testify that humility is the epitome of all perfection. The seventh chapter by itself is a complete code of holiness, and there it is interesting to see St Benedict, following in this *The Rule of the Master*, use the image of the rungs of Jacob's ladder which we must descend to the extent of how far we want to ascend. The image is there to make us notice that the descent is exactly the same length as the ascent. The more we descend, the more we ascend. It is, if you wish, a sort of ascetical geometry. This ladder to be climbed, let us note, has often served ecclesiastical writers as a model to describe the degrees leading to holiness. St Benedict seems to have found this idea in St Jerome, in a translation made by him of a letter of the bishop Theophilus of Alexandria. Before the 'Master' and St Benedict, Cassian had already developed the criteria of humility in enumerating the exercises we find completed in chapter seven.

To construct a tall building, the Gospel (cf. Lk 6:48) advises us to dig its foundations first; the higher the building, the deeper these should be. There, too, we notice a proportionate relationship between the height of the project and its foundations. Likewise, in building the edifice of holiness, we must set it on the foundation of humility in the mathematical proportion indicated to us.

St Benedict refers to this law of humility every time he speaks of the superiors; for example, when he deals with the cellarer: 'above all, let him be humble' (31:13), because he occupies a vital position in the monastery. The community depends on him. The same story with the prior (65:18); with what insistence St Benedict demands that he not be proud! For the deans, the same principle (21:5). As for the abbot, although he does not make a direct remark such as 'Let him be humble', it is obvious that he provide him with motives for humility, that he owes it to himself to be humble. In the spirit of St Benedict, the abbot ought to be the humblest in the community because he is placed the highest.

This doctrine is the very one Our Lord practised during his lifetime: 'He humbled himself still more, obeying even unto death, . . . Thus God has exalted him' (Phil 2:8f.). We find here the same proportionate relationship: the humiliation of Our Lord—the Son of God becomes *servus*, a man—and the exaltation humiliation leads to. 'He who has descended is the same as he who has also ascended above all the heavens' (Eph 4:10). Who, if not he, could conceive a greater humiliation? 'He humbled himself' (Phil 2:7), that is to say, he stripped himself of the privileges of divinity to become man, to become like us, except in sin. This humiliation is an infinite humiliation, and in order to accomplish it, the Son of God covered an infinite distance. Consequently, the exaltation which he derives from it is also infinite. After having descended this ladder of Jacob, he ascended its rungs. Or rather, by descending he ascends, but this ladder loses itself in the infinitude of the divinity.

The Lord Jesus is our great example: 'He humbled himself' (Phil 2:8). Why did he will to descend even to the point of deserving that at his name every knee should bow in the highest heaven, on earth, and in the depths, as the text of the Epistle to the Philippians (2:10) tells us? Why did he humble himself? Because not only did he become man, but still more, God 'made him sin for our sake' (2 Cor 5:21), He was crucified, so that the body of sin might be destroyed (Rom 6:6). He let himself be identified with sin for us, therefore. He descended, humbled himself, truly to the lowest point—*humus*—down to the ground, so to speak. He truly took upon himself the sin of the world in order to dispose of it, that sin of the world which is our sin. 'He bore our sins in his body' (1 Peter 2:24). He is the man of whom Isaiah speaks, the lowest of all: *novissimus virorum* (Is 53:3). Let us think here of all the criminals whom we regard as the last among men, as only half human. But Scripture tells us he is *novissimus,* the last of men, because he laid upon himself all the sins of the world, without being a sinner himself. Truly, he humbled himself as low as it was possible. *Humiliavit semetipsum.* These words of Scripture are so filled with meaning that it is hard to realize fully all the dimensions, all the depths, they express, that the Son of God humbled himself to our level, and not only to our level, but even to the bottom place of our humanity. We understand the *exaltatio* that follows on this.

For us, the same rule exists, and we ought to succeed in understanding it better and better, to make it our own, to realize it in our lives. May humility truly direct our sanctification, our perfection. Let's not deceive ourselves: it is not fasting or vigils or even prayers which will exalt us even to heaven, but humility, in exactly that mathematical proportion, to repeat once more, whereby we ascend in relation to how far we descend.

Humility is truly our road and our rule of life. Let us think about sin. We are sinners, not like Our Lord who was burdened with sin, not because we somehow bear the sin of Adam, but we ourselves are really sinners, and in that sense, we find ourselves even lower than Christ. We do not have all the sin of the world on our shoulders; we could not bear it. But we have enough with our own sins to feel ourselves overwhelmed, without needing to bear the sins of others as well. And when we repeat these words, 'He was bruised for our offenses' (Is 53:5), for our own sins, let us realize that we are personally concerned that we really are sinners. In the monastic life, we can imagine that we have nothing to say in confession, we can believe that what the evil one does is insignificant. This is true in one sense. But if we make a comparison, even a quick one, with Jesus, who is the last of men because of the sin he bears without being a sinner, then our own place, what we really are, even if in little things, is the humble acknowledgment of ourselves, it is humility. And let us not forget in this connection that the sin of the person who lives in the light is more serious than the sin of the person who little knows the lovable person of Jesus who is deeply hurt by our lack of love and sensitivity. Let us beware

here of every kind of Pharisaeism which, supporting itself
upon a formalistic and purely material division of mortal or
venial sins—a division which is correct in itself but which
stops at appearances—accuses the Publican and believes itself
pure because it totally lacks the humble knowledge of the
depths of the soul.

Nor should we fall into the snare of a guilt complex. Certainly, reasons for feeling guilty are never wanting. But that
complex is founded more on a refusal to accept our guilt
than on the humble and frank acceptance of our state of sin
which would free us and let us taste the treasures of the
divine mercy.

So let us follow the Lord on the path of his humiliation,
of his abasement. Let us consider him condemned to death,
scourged, bearing his cross, crushed under its weight, crucified, and mocked by the scribes, the high priests, and the
Pharisees who now dare to raise their heads. Let us go over
each of the humiliations which he had to accept and notice
that these abasements of Our Lord demand his final ascension and glorification. Let us follow him on that path; it is
ours in a special way. It is our monastic road *par excellence*.
For although it is true that it is the path of every Christian, it
is ours by special vocation and by choice.

We have numerous occasions in our consecrated life really
to humble ourselves. Obedience, first of all, puts us in a state
of dependence and submits us to the orders of others. If
St Benedict sets before us, in the text of the Epistle to the
Philippians cited above, precisely the words relating to
obedience, he does so because that virtue, practised frankly,
is the most concrete and authentic manifestation of humility: 'He humbled himself, obeying even unto death' (7:34).
In the fourth degree, St Benedict expresses this in a moving
way. Community life can have hard knocks for us; to take
them with a profound conviction of being a sinner is worth
more than renouncing some little pleasure, a sacrifice at
table, for example.

And then let the practice of humility not be a cause
of pride for us, or of complacent reflection on ourselves and
our actions. In fact, the truly humble person does not take

the time to be occupied with himself, completely devoted as he is to others and to God. It is for this reason that the humble person does not seek humiliations, but accepts with a simple heart those which come along and which the Lord decides to send him. In this way the humiliations truly lead to holiness.

May humility, therefore, never turn into pride for us. May the Lord grant us this great grace of seeing ourselves as very small, very humble, very sinful, and thus arriving at our true dignity. Let us ask him to grant us this great grace; for us it is one of the greatest, if not the greatest, because humility alone introduces us to charity (7:67) which leads us to union with the Lord (7:70).

# OBEDIENCE IN THE IMAGE OF JESUS CHRIST

To understand the sixty-eighth chapter of the Rule, 'If a Brother is Commanded to do Impossible Things', it is necessary to grasp the entire theology of obedience. This is not based on a mutual contract between the superior and the inferior, between the abbot and the brother, his son. Nor is it based on a human relationship, but it has its roots in the godhead itself. Obedience is founded on the relationship of the Father to the Son, of the Son to the Father. In the Most Holy Trinity, it is the Father who orders, who sends. It is to him that the work of creation is attributed, whereas the Son is the envoy. He executes. He is the instrument-author of creation: *Omnia per ipsum facta sunt* everything was made through him (Jn 1:3). God created the universe through the Word. Here we catch a glimpse of the whole mystery of the relationship of the Father to the Son and of the Son to the

Father; it is not a relation of subordination in the way we conceive of it, but it is nevertheless a relationship of order. The notions of Father and Son are not interchangeable, even in God where through the equal possession of divinity, the Father and Son are equal. It is in the very notion of paternity and filiation that the Father is the origin, the first, he who sends, who orders, and the Son is the envoy, the one who obeys. Thus the whole relation of paternity and filiation is expressed.

The relationship wherein the Father and the Son meet and speak is a deep mystery for us. As God, the Son is equal to the Father. There is no subordination in the Most Holy Trinity; in the paternity-filiation relation, there is a difference between the Father and the Son. The words of the Son can be interpreted in this sense: 'The Father is greater than I' (Jn 14:23). Let us recognize that for our intelligence this is an abyss of mystery.

Now, we are called to enter into this relationship. We are called by the Father, through the Son, to enter into this relation of filiation with the Father as adopted sons. We have been chosen for the completely extraordinary dignity of being admitted through the Son, the First-born, into this relation of filiation with the Father. We are called, therefore, to obey the Father, to be submissive to him, and this in a much more demanding way than the Son, because there is no relation of equality between us and the Father. It is for us an unspeakable blessing, an infinite honor to be called the children of God; likewise it is our blessing and honor to obey, to be respectful, obedient sons, totally disposed to receive the Father's will. As it flows from the nature of the Son to obey the Father without contradiction, since there is between the Father and the Son perfect conformity of will, one sole divine will, so in principle there cannot be a divergence of will between the will of the Father and that of his creatures, his adopted children.

The Son, therefore, agreed to be sent to become man. With great insistence he declares to us that he came down from heaven not to do his will, but the will of the One who sent him (Jn 6:38); his food is to do the will of the One who sent him (Jn 4:34); he can do nothing of himself (Jn 5:30); and does always what the Father commands him (Jn 14:30). In other words, the Son desires always to express his obedience toward the Father in some new way; to be Son for him is to be obedient. He wants to do only what pleases the Father (Jn 8:29), because he loves him, because he is the Son of the Father, entirely Son.

The whole dignity of being the Son, Jesus leads us to understand this relationship of filiation, consists in obeying the Father as a good Son. And this, we have seen, *usque ad mortem*, even unto death, that is to say, without any limit. Nothing is impossible or too painful for the Son. If there were an impossible act, would it not be going to one's death through obedience? Is this not the most painful, the most impossible reality, to be sent to one's death? For the Son, nothing is impossible. He agreed to deliver himself to death through obedience.

The obedience of the Son is total, radical, knowing no bounds. It is the obedience of the Son: the whole mystery of the relationship of the Son to the Father lies there. Once again, we are invited to enter into this relationship. Already as Christians, as baptized, we have been adopted as sons, we have been incorporated in the Son in order to follow him, to imitate him entirely. To be his disciples, he gives us to understand, we have to enter with our whole being into this relationship of obedience to the Father. No relationship or valid consideration, neither father nor mother nor brother nor sister nor anything whatsoever may keep us from obeying God the Father with an unlimited obedience while following the footsteps of the Son, our eldest Brother.

It is into this context that we must place the sixty-eighth chapter of the Rule: 'If a Brother be Commanded to do Impossible Things'. There were no impossible things for the Son, because the Father cannot be mistaken in what he imposes. St Benedict knew perfectly well that the abbot is not infallible, and although his word ought in principle to be accepted as the word of Christ, he can be mistaken and command something impossible, unreasonable, or harmful. Obviously, a sincere act of obedience cannot morally harm the person who obeys, but the content of the act can more or less seriously infringe upon certain interests. Although in chapter five the act of obedience is presented to us theoretically, in the sixty-eighth chapter, St Benedict places it in its concrete situation. In the latter, we must take into account the possible case where the abbot would give an order that either cannot be carried out by the one who is to do it, or should not because of the end to be achieved.

We enter into monastic life in order to have a sure means of pleasing the Father by imitating the obedience of his Son. In it we find structures designed to permit us to do the will of the Father always and in everything. There we find an abbot vested with the power of commanding us in the name of the Lord; for it is He whom the monk obeys in obeying his superior (5:5f.). There we find a community into which we can integrate ourselves through obedience (7:55) and brothers whom we can obey through a generous willingness to help (RB 71). So it is relatively easy for us always to remain obedient. In due proportion, then, we find ourselves in a special situation similar to that of Jesus: 'I speak that which I have seen with my Father' (Jn 8:38).

There remains, however, that considerable difficulty dealt with by St Benedict in chapter sixty-eight. How can we remain in union with the Son's obedient will toward his Father if we are commanded to do impossible or difficult things (68:1)? How can we harmonize our firm will to obey in union with the Son when the commandment we receive seems to us not to be given in union with the Father?

Everything depends, of course, on the sincerity and the firmness of our obedience. If that virtue is weak in us, if it lacks maturity or perseverance, our first reaction to an order will be: That seems impossible to me, is beyond my strength, is against my nature, my character, my conscience, my dignity, finally, against the interests of my office. Or again, I find that the order is not prudent, is scarcely practical, is contradictory and solves nothing. In other words, my first reaction does not proceed from obedience but from a pre-set attitude opposed to, or at least little disposed to receive, the order. Does this negative attitude correspond to

Jesus' way of acting and St Benedict's way of thinking? The Rule gives us a clear answer: 'If it happens that something hard or impossible is laid on any brother, let him receive the command of his superior with all docility and obedience' (68:1). The first reaction, the first response, of the obedient monk will quite naturally be to want sincerely to obey. Did Jesus not react this same way? Did he not ask his Father, not that his own will be done, but that the Father's be (Lk 22:42)?

The obedient monk's first step will be followed by an effort to assess the command, to understand its implications and the degree of difficulty. In seeing the chalice of the passion with its immense pain before him, Jesus turned with a touching filial confidence toward his Father: 'Father, if you will, take this chalice from me'. So what does the monk do if he sees himself incapable of carrying out the order he received? He will explain the reasons for its impossibility patiently, *patienter*, and in a timely way, *oportune suggerat*, to the person who gave the order (68:2). He will do it without pride, without resistance, and without argument (68:3). Since his basic attitude in this case, as in others, is to obey as far as he can, he will know how to explain his point of view with humility and a spirit of submission.

Finally, we arrive at the third act of this dialogue: If, after this explanation, the prior believes he should insist on his order, the moment has then come for the junior to persuade himself that the matter is to his advantage (68:4). Notice that the junior is not asked to believe that the order given is objectively the best. St Benedict asks him simply to obey; that is the best attitude. The order could be based on an error; St Benedict implicitly admits it. But in obeying the monk will perform a salutary act. He will learn to obey through love and with confidence in God's help (68:5). Jesus, after having spoken with the Father, rose to go to his death in order to say at the last moment: *Consummatum est* (Jn 19:30), I have accomplished the work that you gave me to do (Jn 17:4). And the Virgin Mary, after having explained to the angel of the annunciation her humble objections, accepted simply: *Ecce ancilla Domini. Fiat mihi secundum verbum tuum* (Lk 1:38). Is the clear example of Jesus and Mary not the best commentary on chapter sixty-eight?

Let us notice that St Benedict does not speak of the abbot in this chapter but simply of the person who presides or commands (68:2). Who is this? Might it be quite simply a brother older than myself, who, according to the chapter 'That the Brothers be Obedient to one Another', has the right to command me (71:1,4)? Or any one of the officers? The word *prior* (68:4) can mean the abbot. But here the expression seems to be in contrast to *junior*, so it refers to a senior. Although the importance of the chapter and its implications make us think of the abbot, the expressions chosen by St Benedict permit a broader interpretation.

St Benedict deals here with the obedience of a monk receiving an order. Nevertheless, the chapter lets us also think of the duty of circumspection and prudence to which the person giving the order is held. St Benedict warns the abbot against any sort of thoughtlessness in this matter (64:17). And as a matter of fact, if a monk is asked to obey promptly and perhaps even heroically, then the abbot ought to be at least as prudent as the order is difficult to carry out.

Likewise, if a brother receives an order which, according to his knowledge, is harmful to the interests of the community or its members, he is obliged in conscience to mention it to the abbot or to the person in charge, in order to prevent the evil he fears. This chapter of the Rule, without seeming to, lays responsibility on all those who find themselves involved in actions of some importance. So obedience itself, in the surely rare cases envisaged here, can require that a monk given an order which he recognizes harmful make his hesitations known to his superiors with humble frankness; if he does not, he is guilty of the harmful action he performs.

One more word on authority. If monastic obedience has as its goal uniting us to the will of the Father through his Son, then we likewise understand that all authority is instrumental: that of the abbot and that of anyone who orders us. This authority has a character of service. Its purpose is to give, in the sight and fear of God, useful orders whose execution places the obedient monk within the will of the Father. But how can the abbot, who in principle does not enjoy the power of inspiration, issue an order whose execution unites the monk to the will of God? If the abbot himself does not know what the express will of God is in some circumstance, how can he oblige the monk, who wants nothing more than to do the will of the Father, to carry out that order in the name of obedience, that is to say, to the will of God? The answer is important. Aside from cases which concern a commandment of God or a truth of Holy Scripture, the orders given by a superior do not compel us because of their content, or, in other words, because they express the will of God; but because the monk has made a promise of obedience before God, it corresponds to that will of God which wants us to submit to the orders given by a superior. Although the abbot represents Christ, this does not mean that Christ, so to speak, ratifies the judgments and orders given by the abbot. It is we who receive the orders of our abbot 'as if God himself had given the order' (5:4), knowing perfectly well that it is not God himself who commands, but the superior, whom we obey 'for the love of God' (7:34).

We understand, too, that the relationship between the monk who obeys and the superior who commands is not a purely human relationship. Our act of obedience is always obedience to the heavenly Father. When the abbot teaches or commands, he represents Christ. We accept his command in order in this way to imitate the Son obedient to his Father. Whereas the abbot holds the place of Christ, the master and shepherd of our souls (2:31), the monk is united to Christ as the obedient Son of the Father.

Finally, let us realize that Our Lord redeemed the world through obedience. *Obediens usque ad mortem* (Phil 2:8): this is the formula of redemption. He died through obedience, and in this way he has redeemed us. Certainly in God's omnipotence, there could have been other ways of bringing about the liberation of the human race from the slavery of death. God the Father chose redemption through the death and resurrection of his Son, or more precisely, through the submission of the Son to that plan of redemption.

Now, in entering into the relationship of obedience between the Son and the Father, we enter into his work. Through our obedience *usque ad mortem* we enter fully into the work of redemption. We become, in a certain sense, co-redeemers, in order to complete what is lacking on our part in the sufferings of the whole Christ (Col 1:24). Certainly, our contribution is far different from that of the Virgin Mary, the Mother of Christ. But we enter into the work of redemption through an obedience *usque ad mortem.* It is, indeed, not through our physical death that we share in the work of the redemption, but through the death of our will which should, however, be ready to accept even physical death as the ultimate act of obedience, as a burnt offering.

This obedience, we have understood, is the most authentic and most profound expression of the Son's love for the Father. The Son loves the Father, and because he loves him, he obeys. Obedience is the true, full, authentic expression of his love for the Father, and his love for us. We inherit and learn this love from the Son in obeying his commandments. Besides, we have promised monastic obedience for the love of the Father (7:34). How, then, could we speak of our love for him if we did not obey our superiors, those who represent God to us? How could we speak of our love for the Father if we did not enter fully into this mystery of obedience in following Our Lord Jesus Christ?

# WE SHARE BY PATIENCE IN THE SUFFERINGS OF CHRIST

The Divine Office is a mirror for us. When we listen to the readings and sing the psalms, of necessity—for all the Scriptures serve our salvation—we take a look at ourselves. Yet, although the Office makes us conscious of what we are, before all else it places us in God's presence and sets us continually back on the right road, on the path of Christ.

Now the way of Christ is the way of the cross. It is therefore ours as well. Even on the natural plane, our life is no bed of roses, and if we do find roses, we also run into thorns. The circumstances of life, everyday reality, the problems we meet, all inevitably bring pain, and adversities are never far away. We often have to make painful efforts, we suffer disappointments, renunciations, and privations which we should not or cannot avoid, and our acceptance of them is often painful.

All right. It is important and consoling for us to realize that we are in Christ's company. He came on the earth in order to walk in front of us, bearing his cross and to teach us to carry ours by showing us the way. Thus we learn ever better to associate the difficulties of the human condition with the lot of God's Son. We realize that we can unite our life, which naturally involves preoccupations, cares, humiliations, sufferings, to the Lord carrying his cross, and that in this way our life becomes the road along which he advances.

St Benedict expresses this teaching in a classical fashion always profoundly true, in the last words of the Prologue: 'By persevering in the monastery in the practice of the divine teaching, we share by patience in the sufferings of Christ and we deserve to share in his kingdom' (Prol. 50).

The secret of the christian life lies there. Holy Scripture
confirms that life on earth is a life of suffering (Sir. 40:1ff.).
Suffering is our lot, an effect of sin (Gen 3:16ff.). Yet we can
choose to carry our burden alone or carry it in union with the
suffering Christ. To do this is to follow Christ. It is the way
the Lord points out to us: 'Follow Me, carry your cross, be
my disciples, suffer in union with me'.

How can we not listen to this call! With our full devotion
we unite ourselves to the Lord, not only in order to be consoled—of course it is a great consolation to be able to carry
the cross with him—but because we are sure that our cross
has a meaning, that it is the promise of a future, a purpose,
that it is united to his. Thus the cross of our pains becomes
luminous. Without losing its burdensome character, it becomes as a sweet yoke and a light burden (Mt 11:30). To
follow Jesus' path becomes a consolation. Let us imagine
that we are on the road to calvary; Our Lord is carrying his
cross and we are following him. We can follow him at a distance and consequently be cut off from him by the crowd
through our slowness, through our lack of courage and zeal.
Then we carry our cross more or less alone and are stooped
under its weight because we do not see him well enough. He
is too far away. There are too many things hiding him from
us. But if we follow him more closely, we feel him near, we
do not lose sight of him. The way he carries the cross encourages us. From time to time he does for us what he did
for St Peter when he denied him: he turned toward him and
looked at him, and Simon, completely overcome, was converted and became Peter (Lk 22:61f.).

This happens to us, too, as we travel along and carry our
cross; we lose sight of the fact that we are carrying it after
Jesus. It weighs us down excessively because we forget that it
is our share in his sufferings. Then he turns to us for a moment and pierces us with the sweetness of his gaze. His grace
touches us, and we understand. We remember then that he
is going before us. That encourages and comforts us. We
continue our journey in his love because he invites us to
carry our cross behind him (Lk 9:23), and he makes us
realize that we must not forsake this path but be faithful in

accompanying him all the way to the way to the end. This is how, through our constancy, our perseverance, we share in the sufferings of Christ.

In this way, as our blessed Father says (Prol. 50), we deserve to share as well in the glory of his kingdom. Is this glory only that of eternity, or is it promised to us also for the present time? If the christian life and the religious life in particular have an eschatological sense, it is to show us that to the extent we live the sufferings of Christ, we share beginning now in his glory. This glory is still veiled in faith and hope; we do not yet possess it. But as we are not only dead with Christ but also risen with him, so with the cross is mixed the joy of the cross whose sweetness we grasp along with the suffering.

Then we begin to run the course with a true and profound joy, *inenarrabili dulcedine* (Prol. 49). St Benedict expresses himself soberly and even laconically and rarely makes mystical digressions; this is why the phrase *inenarrabili dulcedine* opens extraordinary horizons of his soul to us. In it we see the profound experience of a man who followed the Lord, laden with his own cross and who knew what he was talking about; and his admonitions encourage us to share in the sufferings of Christ with a firm patience.

Let us add another consideration. If we are faithful in the Lord as he carries his cross, then we will all have an unforgettable experience behind that cross. It is not only Christ's glance that encourages us. We see at our side our brothers, our sisters, who are also carrying their cross in one way or another, more or less closely, but always in his train. What an encouragement. How can we help but have a heart bursting with brotherly charity? We find ourselves in the same circumstances, we discover the same love for the cross, for Christ suffering beneath his cross; and journeying side by side like this lets us find ourselves. If small displeasures and misunderstandings arise—and there are some; it's only human—they fall away in this blessed company and crumble in a moment. The only thing to hold our attention is this friendship in the imitation and the following of Jesus. This is true brotherhood: to be brothers in Christ, brothers in his cross and in his joy. Members of the same community, we are truly united among ourselves through this love of Christ whom we desire to follow 'wherever he goes' (Rev 14:4) because he is our most precious good and we hold nothing dearer (5:2).

# THE PHILOSOPHY OF THE CROSS

What could be the philosophy of us monks? Do we have a philosophy unique to our state? To be a philosopher is to love wisdom. Is the monk a true philosopher, a lover of wisdom? Can he say, 'In my youth I have sought wisdom . . . I decided to put it into practice . . . My soul has fought to possess it . . . I directed my soul toward it, and in purity I found it' (Sir 51:13-20). What then is this wisdom we have sought? What is our philosophy?

In the early days of the Church pagan philosophers opposed Christianity as a doctrine shocking to reason. They derided and mocked St Paul at the Areapagus when he wanted to speak to them about the resurrection. Now, of all the Lord's disciples, no one knew better than St Paul how to develop our philosophy, how to teach us the true doctrine, to show us the path to the eternal wisdom, opposing it to the proud philosophy of men, to their inflated knowledge. To the Corinthians, enamoured of their philosophy, he preached his philosophy, the wisdom of Christ: 'For Jews demand signs and Greeks seek wisdom, but we preach Christ crucified, a stumbling block to the Jews and folly to Gentiles, but for those who are called, both Jews and Greeks, the power of God and the wisdom of God' (1 Cor 1:22-24). Folly is opposed to philosophy, to wisdom. Therefore, our wisdom, our philosophy is folly—*stultitia crucis.*

So let us open our monastic Rule to check whether we find there this same philosophy and whether St Benedict preaches the folly of the cross to us. As a matter of fact, at the end of the Prologue he sums up monastic teaching as the Master had done before him, telling us in very few words: Let us never withdraw ourselves from the teaching of God our master; let us persevere faithfully in the monastery and let us share in the sufferings of Christ (Prol. 50). God is our master and St Benedict, the servant of God, is the professor of our philosophy. We intend to persevere even to death in the wisdom of the cross of Christ. Our philosophy is to share in his passion through patience, that is to say, through the *passio*, through our own passion.

This philosophy of the cross is therefore ours. The philosophy of the world, on the contrary, is to know how to escape the cross. Ours consists in accepting the cross. Of course the cross is not something pleasant for us. But with time, 'with an unspeakable sweetness of love we hasten in the way of God's commandments' (Prol. 49). With time, love lets us carry the cross ever more easily and even find a special joy in it. True happiness in this world, time helps us feel, is to be found there, because it leads us directly to God, the great and only happiness.

This is our doctrine, our philosophy. In entering the monastery, we may at first have confused ideas on this point, but obscurely we know that we will encounter the cross. We even seek it. What does it consist of? All his life Our Lord climbed the way of the cross; his life was a continual passion. Not only did he persevere in it, but he was borne along, sustained by the fire which finally consumed him, the fire which he came to bring on earth and which he willed to see ablaze (cf. Lk 12:49), the ardent fire of doing the will of his Father in order to save us. That is why he left aside everything that had to be abandoned, in order to be entirely free, and he entered wholly upon his mission by accepting the lot to which he was destined even to mounting the cross to die there.

And we want to follow Him. Is it possible? How can we imagine following Jesus along the royal road of the cross? How can we imagine dying with him to rise with him? Is it pretentious? Yet he calls us, offers us the cross. 'Anyone who does not take up his cross and follow me is not worthy of me' (Mt 10:38). In order to follow Him, therefore, we must take up the cross. We must share in his passion in order to be able to follow him to glory (Prol. 50). Let us be precise, however: he does not ask us to take up *his* cross. Each one of us ought to take up his own special cross. 'Anyone who does not take up his cross is not worthy of me'. Is it enough, then, to seek a cross at our convenience, custom-built for us according to our personal estimation of our forces? Is this sharing in the sufferings of Christ (cf. 1 Peter 4:13)? Am I crucified with him—*Christo confixus cruci* (Gal 2:19)—if I am content to carry a cross designed to my liking? I will be carrying one, of course, but I will not be following the Lord who did not will to choose his. It is here that the idea of participation, of sharing in the sufferings of Christ, becomes clear. Sharing in the suffering of Christ is done *perpatientiam* (Prol. 50), through our personal suffering which is not the size of the Lord's, of course, but is in the image of his. To the extent that we come sincerely and generously to embrace everything that is part of our own cross for the love of Jesus and in union with him, we enter into intimate and life-giving contact with his passion. The whole burden we carry more and more for him and in him receives the mysterious imprint of his burden, his cross, becomes as it were a part of his cross. We share in his passion through our own passion. In this way we understand better the meaning of that expression in the Rule: *Per patientiam participemur* (Prol. 50), borrowed from St Peter who, like his brother Andrew, in an exceptional and special way deserved to share by his death in his Master's cross.

*Patientia* is not only endurance, longsuffering, forbearance; patience is suffering, the passion. *Patientia* comes from *pati*, to enter into the passion. This patience, then, is not a patience centered upon ourselves; it is sharing in the passion of Christ.

This is our philosophy: the folly of the cross. But that folly blossoms into glory, 'so as to deserve to share also in the glory of his kingdom so that through the resurrection, we may share in his eternal reign'.

This patience, what is it exactly? The answer is astonishingly simple: Patience is our whole life, everywhere and always. The texture of our daily life is patience; for even if we work with joy, our life carries with it a burden of incertitude. In everything we do or undergo, in what we accept in good spirit or against our will, there is always an aspect of renunciation, of death, if only by the fact that everything passes away. By its very nature, our life diminishes at the same time it grows. We go on in life and by that very fact, we leave what has been, we abandon the past. Our whole life then is a sharing in that journey of the Lord toward Calvary, provided we live it in the union of love with him. As long as we walk separated from Christ, our suffering basically has no meaning. Human wisdom tells us to avoid, to flee from, suffering. It is nothing but an accident, a disgrace, an infringement on our rights, hindrance to enjoying life, and, in the final analysis, an obstacle to the development of our personality. That is how the *homo animalis*, the 'natural man' (1 Cor 2:14), the pagan, the Greek (1 Cor 1:22), for whom suffering in union with the cross of the Lord is a folly, reasons.

Our philosophy, on the contrary, and our progress toward life is specifically to bind ourselves to the cross. Our happiness comes from understanding the lesson of the cross, from knowing how to integrate it into our lives with serenity and love. Nothing can unite us better than this to Our Lord. Accepted in this way, it becomes light, intimate joy, consolation. Then we discover the meaning of our cross; Our Lord's cross gives its full meaning. Thus we live with his life. This is our wisdom: the wisdom of the cross.

But our wisdom is fragile, let us realize; we are tempted to discouragement, to see nothing but folly in the cross. Why choose a life which exalts it, recommends patience and preaches renunciation? Almost without our knowing it, we are beset by the temptation to elude what displeases nature, to circumvent the cross, and to organize our life according to our own pleasure. But with time, as we enter further into the true christian ideology, we understand that union with Our Lord's cross is our happiness and our hope, our victory and our resurrection, our life. The monastic life helps us enter fully upon the royal road of the cross by placing the humble events of our day, through prayer and meditation, in continual relationship with the life of Jesus.

# TO PREFER NOTHING
# TO THE LOVE OF CHRIST

The personality of Jesus perplexed the Jews. This was obviously a man, but an extraordinary man. Some were scandalized to hear Him speak as well or better than a rabbi without having studied; others were scandalized to see him work miracles. How can a man work signs? Others, finally, opted for possession: 'You have a devil' (Jn 7:20). To everyone, he was an enigma, a question touching the deepest fiber of life and arousing existential anguish: who is he? They could not simply see him and pass by after having discussed it superficially among themselves. He demanded an answer from them. So Christ was a question mark for the Jews. In reading the Gospel, we can see the anguish of many. 'In the crowd, many believed in him' (Jn 7:31). Others did not know what to think.

Who is this man? This same question poses itself to our consciences. For us, Christ is the central mystery, that Being in our lives who demands a response, a commitment from which we cannot withdraw ourselves. Even the intellectual of today cannot ignore him; sooner or later he meets Jesus and questions arise. Anxiety takes hold of him, and he realizes that this man demands a response coming from the depths of his being. Even for those who are content with the 'death of God', a question remains: who is Jesus?

This question we monks find in the Rule. This is certainly no theological treatise, and we cannot speak of a christology of the Rule. But we realize none the less that we meet him present everywhere in its pages.

Let us consider first of all the general principle which St Benedict lays down from the beginning, and then the final words of the Rule: 'To prefer nothing to the love of Christ' (4:21, 72:11), absolutely nothing. We meet Our Lord everywhere: in the abbot (63:13), in our brothers and sisters (36:1), in the guests (53:1, 7), in the poor (53:15), in the sick (36:1). Christ is present everywhere. St Benedict tells us that our whole life should be a search for God (58:7), a search for Christ in whom God manifests himself to us. For us Christ is the model of obedience (7:34, 5:13), of humility (7:34), of the love of brethren and enemies, of renunciation (7:38, 42; 4:10). Carrying our cross we follow him (2:20), sharing his passion (Prol. 50), in order one day to be glorified with him (72:12). In the Holy Rule Christ is the center of our life. If we read it superficially, it seems to us to be a disciplinary rule offering a certain number of precepts and monastic regulations. St Benedict did not want to theologize. But, he based his Rule so much on the love of Christ that we cannot practise it without meeting him at every step.

We recognize that Christ is the center of our life. Yet, like the Jews, we raise a number of questions about him. We have met him, we know we must believe in him and follow Him. Do we follow him through constraint? Is he for us a source of anxiety? One day he will be our judge. Are we concerned only with the historical side of the Gospels, with a man whose acts, miracles, and teaching we study? Is he for us the Teacher of a wonderful doctrine, never surpassed in the course of the centuries? Or the healer who never ceases to astonish us? Do we accord him only limited interest, or do we allow him to enter more deeply into our being? Is he the friend of the soul? Is he the intimate joy of our days? Do we venerate him with great respect, or do we bear a tender love for him? Is our relationship with him a person-to-person relationship, an 'I and Thou'? Is Christ actually present now in our life? Do we see him living in the Church, in the community, in our brother, in our superior, in every person we perceive through him in the light of theology, of eschatology, of Christology? Is Christ truly the center of our life? Do we

think of him really present in the Eucharist, in the tabernacle where we can meet him, talk to him, tell him of our
confidence, our joy, our love?

To love, we realize well enough, is to be captivated by the
one we love. To prefer nothing to the love of Christ is this:
to be truly captivated by him, to be his, to center everything
on him.

All these questions arise for us in a very practical way. Our
whole being is a search for Christ. We must meet him in as
personal and as intimate a way as possible, that he may truly
be the great truth, the great mystery, the great love of our
life. This is our vocation. We call our vocation 'contemplative'. So first of all we must contemplate Christ. When we
say 'to contemplate', this is not a matter of a purely intellectual contemplation, but of a contemplation which leads
to love. It is a simple glance which, by its very simplicity,
necessarily encounters Christ in the depths of ourselves
because he is our life. Through an existential, intimate, vital
bond we are united to him. With what love we adore him
present in us with all his mysteries, all his transparence. He
is there as infant, man, teacher, our master. He is raised up
crucified. St Paul preaches nothing but Christ, and him
crucified, and our father St Bernard tells us, 'I find no savor
where the name of Jesus is not'.

To have Christ in our life: this is the teaching of the Rule,
its substance and its marrow. We must find him in our work.
The Rule lays the labors of the monastic discipline on us so
we may be able to find him more easily. It is through
humility, through faithful obedience, patience, even scorn,
that we find Christ (7:42). It is not an intellectual contemplation which opens our eyes to him, but the carrying of the
cross which lets us receive him whom we follow.

We need a formation of this caliber to make us know
Christ, love him, and imprint on our soul his face so
ardently desired. It is in this way that he reigns over the
whole person and that we strip ourselves of what in us
cannot be assimilated by him. Only love can bring about this
mystery, for this alone, by a painful childbirth, can form
in us the new man made to the image of Christ. Slowly,

in a gradual, progressive way, we penetrate into the mystery of the face of Christ in which shines the majesty of God who lives and reigns forever.

# That in All Things
# God May Be Glorified

# THAT IN ALL THINGS GOD MAY BE GLORIFIED

The most beautiful emphases of our liturgical prayer are those which, borne by our joy, exalt the glory of the Lord. The soul has a deep need to repeat constantly: 'Glory be to the Father and to the Son and to the Holy Spirit'. This rhythm, this continual refrain, develops in us an ever more acute consciousness of the aim of our prayer, of the Divine Office, and still more, of our whole life: the glory of God. To him be all honor and glory (Canon of the Mass).

Our life, then, has a character of consecration to God. It is a sacrifice of praise to his love, a burnt offering entirely dedicated to the divine Majesty. Basically, no life, no creature is exempt from this destination. The very existence of life is a declaration of the grandeur, the power, and the love of God. Even the devils have to recognize divine mercy and justice.

The religious life has a sense and a goal of worship, that is to say, it is a sacrifice offered to God to express his sovereign rule over all creatures. To be a religious means specifically to be a worshipper of God, wholly given to his service. So it is that, after having pronounced our promise (58:17) before him (58:18), we are received into the monastic community as someone consecrated to the service of the divine Majesty, 'to the praise of his glory' (Eph 1:14). From that moment, before the whole Church, our life officially takes a decisive turn. In following Jesus, the great Religious of the Father, and in deep and loving union with him, we are offered in perpetual sacrifice to the honor of God. The Holy Eucharist, the Mass, thus very truly becomes the holy sign of our own life and its supreme fulfilment. Our

411

whole life, with its best intentions and desires, its good thoughts and actions, its sincere love, takes the form of a liturgy. The thousand expressions of divine praise borrowed from the 'Work of God' become the underlying theme of all our human activity. They are no longer foreign words on which we model our attitude, but they unite themselves to our being and become its existential manifestation. Morning Lauds especially sum up a way of being which basically stretches over the entire day.

How does our Holy Rule express this thoroughly monastic religious behavior? Here again we realize St Benedict's practical mind; he could have put on the title page of his Rule a sentence in the form of an outline to tell us that glorifying God is the aim of the monastic life, or that it ought to be such that people recognize in it a worthy manifestation of God's greatness; but no, there is nothing like that. On the contrary, St Benedict defines this attitude of soul in a place where it might go unnoticed, so hidden is it within a context which seems very down to earth. Yet tradition has recognized it as a key phrase introducing us, like a flash of light, to the understanding of the Rule: *Ut in omnibus glorificetur Deus* (57:9). What St Ignatius formulated with the words: *Ad majorem Dei gloriam*, St Benedict expresses in this famous phrase: 'That in all things God may be glorified'.

Does the Rule, so named because it rules our actions and gives a firm, clear orientation to our life, lead us by its spirit, its counsels, and its precepts to a constant preoccupa- with being entirely ordained to the glory of God? St Benedict, we know, did not construct learned theoretical arguments to convince us of some doctrine, and gives less a teaching than a spirit which is formed in us little by little through constant contact with the Rule. If, then, this phrase, 'That in all things God may be glorified', expresses a basic attitude of the Rule, closer analysis ought to make this more apparent. As a matter of fact, St Benedict is imbued with this spirit, and makes it clearly visible. Let us limit ourselves here to a brief sketch.

Let us begin with the Prologue. This whole introduction is an eloquent expression of the transcendence, the glory, and the goodness of God. Since his grace goes before us, even our good actions are the work of the Lord who works in us (Prol. 30), and therefore we can say with the prophet: 'Not to us, O Lord, not to us, but to your name give the glory' (Ps 113B:1). What we are, we are by his grace (Prol. 31). We may think we have a reason for glorifying ourselves, but that glory redounds to the Lord (Prol. 32, cf. 4:42).

For people today, conscious of their creative powers, this attitude of naïve faith is not so easy to achieve. Yet nevertheless, the spirit of the Gospel and of the Rule imbues us with this faith. It is in itself a form of praise to God. Is it not the recognition of the greatness of our Creator and the mercy of our Redeemer which has given us the liberty of the children of God? To recognize this is our humble participation in the manifestation of his glory. The Rule is wholly imbued by this faith. It is the soul of the Rule.

The monastic vocation to glorify God in a very special way appears particularly in the obligation of the *Opus Dei.* From the viewpoint of material productivity, it makes no sense. Its value lies in its transcendence, above what is calculable and measurable. A beautiful Office, it is true, may also edify on-lookers and listeners, but its real beauty, we should never forget, lies in its capacity for expressing an authentic search, for letting the glory of God show through; it is a gratuitous act, with a certain independence of external expression when this is balanced by a true interiorness. According to the concept of the Rule, such is the purpose of the Divine Office; all the things later attributed to the monks' Office—intercession for the founders and the edification of christian people—although they are not excluded, do not appear in the Rule and are secondary. The Divine Office is celebrated 'for the honor and reverence of the Blessed Trinity' (9:7). This is its goal, its meaning, its reason for being.

Let us add that reverence is the fundamental attitude for every kind of prayer. If we present a request to a person of rank, we implicitly do honor to his generosity and his power. Now when, with deep humility (20:2), our prayer is addressed to the Lord of the universe, our attitude of reverence is total and becomes a recognition of his glory and his greatness, he who in his merciful goodness goes so far as to inspire us to pray to him (20:4).

This is, moreover, implied throughout the Rule, where the overriding conviction of the omnipotence of the glorious divine Majesty in his unspeakable greatness manifests itself through an attitude of 'fear of the Lord'. Once again, we see this fear of the Lord which is so often a dread or an anguish at the beginning of the conversion, rapidly change in the religious soul into a filial fear wholly penetrated with love— St Benedict teaches this masterfully in his formula, 'Let them have a fear for God which is inspired by love' (72:9). This is basically the only attitude possible for a created being before God, the 'wholly Other', Love in his Justice and Justice in his Love without limit. Thus the fear of God is the expression of an authentic human attitude in the presence of His glory, the truest recognition of his powerful and loving Majesty. And since this fear is, as it were, the clue to the spirituality of the Rule (7:10), it tends to train the monk in a constant awareness of zeal for his glory (for the expression, see 64:6). This is, we understand here, necessarily nuanced in the soul of each person according to his personal relationship to God. It is one thing in the soul of the penitent sinner and another in the soul of the innocent, but it always remains fear of God, of the ineffable absolute Being, the 'wholly Other'.

The life of the monk is therefore profoundly marked by this basic concern with being a witness to the glory of God manifested in the work of salvation. This is why the monk consecrates himself solemnly and entirely to him through the promise of his personal sanctification (58:18); the conversion of manners is a homage offered to the Most High; obedience to one's superiors, since it is addressed to God, is an act of worship, that is to say, a sacrifice of adoration (5:15).

The whole life of the monk is orientated by his profession to the Lord's service; it would therefore be a nearsighted view to accuse him of selfishness, and a behavior preoccupied only with self would be a caricature of holiness. The effort of sanctification, and especially the glorification of God, has nothing in common with self-centeredness or a concentration of our energies on him at the expense of excluding our neighbor. The teaching of the Rule is very clear on this. As a matter of fact, it presents the services rendered to our neighbor as expressions of the Lord's glorification. In the consecrated life, the ultimate motive of the many daily acts which we perform for our brethren is not some brother, but God himself, who gives us the strength and the grace. We call the abbot 'lord and abbot for the honor and love of Christ' (64:13). We serve the sick 'to honor God' (36:4), we honor the guests (53:2) by receiving Christ in them (53:1). Finally, in seeing him in the person of others (2:3, 36:1, 53:1, 53:15), we serve him and honor him in them. The monastery is the school where we learn gradually to serve the Lord in proportion to our spiritual maturity (Prol. 49). Is there a greater glory for the sanctifying God than to see the image of his own glory being formed in man by the work of his grace?

These considerations allow us to perceive the reason why St Benedict slips the remark, 'That in all things God may be glorified', into an apparently insignificant point in the course of the monastic day, that of the sale of the monastery's products where the monks charge a lower price. Our life ought to aim at the glory of God in all things and without any exception, even when it comes, for example, to giving up a little material profit (cf. 1 Cor 6:20).

Let us not think, therefore, 'But God possesses all his glory in himself! How can he be glorified by created beings?' Everything that is good bears witness to the Creator and shares in his goodness. Endowed with intelligence and free will, the human person joins to them his conscious testimony by honoring him as the source of all good, in offering him his whole life and all its events in a gesture of free and profound gratitude to the fullness of the glory. Yes, what we give God is very little, barely the renunciation of a small advantage, and St Benedict makes us to understand this. But for us, it is everything, absolutely everything.

Let us end this conference by opening our eyes to the greatness to which we have been raised by being called consciously to give glory to the divine Majesty. All our acts are elevated far above all their minute natural ends (cf. 1 Cor 10:31). Our very weakness can become a witness to the strength and the grace of God (cf. 2 Cor 12:9).

Lord Jesus, you have entered into our human life in order to reveal to us the glory of your Father (cf. Jn 17:6) and to carry us along with the zeal which animates you. That same zeal can and should fill our whole life and give it its fundamental orientation; make us understand this. Your greatest concern was to glorify your Father on earth (Jn 17:4) that he might be glorified in you (cf. Jn 14:13); open, then, the eyes of our heart, enlarge it to receive the divine greatness of that Father. Your vocation and your mission on the earth was to be the 'religious' of the Father; deign to teach us this and to associate us in it so that 'in all things God may be glorified'.

UT IN OMNIBUS GLORIFICETUR DEUS

# CISTERCIAN PUBLICATIONS INC.
## Kalamazoo, Michigan

## Texts and Studies in the Monastic Tradition

## TITLES LISTING

### THE CISTERCIAN FATHERS SERIES

*Temporarily out of print*　　　　　　　　　　† *Forthcoming*